JOURNEY WITH "JUSTICE"

OUR FAMILY'S EXPERIENCE WITH "SHAKEN BABY" ALLEGATIONS

BY

DAN SCHROCK

www.bookstandpublishing.com

Published by
Bookstand Publishing
Morgan Hill, CA 95037
3587_5

ISBN 978-1-61863-171-8

Printed in the United States of America

JOURNEY WITH "JUSTICE"

OUR FAMILY'S EXPERIENCE WITH "SHAKEN BABY" ALLEGATIONS

PREFACE

Over the past five to six years, numerous people have said to Elaine and me that a book should be written about our experience with shaken baby syndrome and the judicial system. Most of the time I simply shrugged those suggestions off, since I had more interest in forgetting that experience than in writing about it. But within the last year we learned of another event that threatened to potentially bring us back into the workings of the judicial system once again. Prior to that event, I was satisfied to let an awful experience just fade into the past. But now, this possible new threat (which is mentioned only briefly in the final few pages), became the stimulus that convinced me to make our story known.

I have written this book in an effort to raise some fairly serious questions about (1) how our judicial system operates [particularly the very peripheral position that "truth" often occupies within that system], (2) how the medical community [in partnership with the judicial system] attempts to elicit black and white "scientific answers" from some very ambiguous medical situations, and (3) how the unnatural merging of that "tandem" [judicial and medical] can wreak unintended "collateral damage" on the families involved. My book shares more personally how our own family has been negatively impacted through this process. At the same time I have written to describe the abundance of personal support we have received throughout this tragedy, and to express our deep thankfulness for friends, extended family, and a faith community that did everything possible to bear this burden along with us. Without them we would not have survived the onslaught.

Truth is an important commodity for me. I have tried to be as truthful concerning the situation described in this book as I know how. Consequently there are a significant number of direct quotes from police interviews, trial transcripts, and other official documents to keep me from putting my own words into other people's mouths. Even so, the "truth" in a shaken baby case like ours is as elusive as mercury. While I do refer to many quotes, I have used them mostly to highlight some of the judicial system's "techniques" (modus operandi) in such a case. Because they are direct quotes, however, you may notice some grammatical anomalies within them.

This is not a book to be quickly and easily skimmed. The logic (or lack thereof) of this shaken baby case builds throughout. There may be times when you need to go back to a previous passage to "connect the dots." What passes for "fact" in a courtroom trial may astound you. Since there are multiple times and situations which involve the same topics, I'm hoping the repetition of those topics, quotes, and comments will be <u>reinforcing</u> to your understanding rather than simply redundant. I have put <u>quotation marks</u> around all direct quotes. Other narrative is without quotation marks. Underlining has been used to bring attention to certain words or phrases. And two other devices have been used, hopefully to clarify: (1) <u>parentheses,</u> or sometimes brackets, are used to enclose additional information; and (2) *italics* for my own personal comments and reflections. Occasionally these last two items may overlap. In relation to my <u>personal comments,</u> some readers may feel at times that I am treating the tragedy described in this book too lightly. I assure you that I personally feel the heaviness surrounding our situation deeply and fully. One would have to be totally callous to do otherwise. It has left a permanent scar on my psyche. But sometimes I <u>do</u> try to lighten the mood a bit so that I don't end up tearing out my remaining hair and weeping uncontrollably. It's a way of coping. And I also have no interest in the message of this book being interpreted as the rantings and ravings of a disgruntled old man.

It has also <u>not</u> been my intent to put anybody down in this book. It <u>is</u> difficult, of course, to raise questions and point out shortcomings in the system without having those inevitably reflect poorly on someone. So I will apologize in advance for any hurt feelings I may have caused. I get no particular pleasure from hurting anyone. As Mennonites, we grew up in a community that values the <u>means</u> to an end every bit as important as the <u>end</u> itself. The journey is as important as the destination. We continue to spend our time primarily in such a community. It was, therefore, somewhat of a shock to our family to experience people who not only felt they "knew" immediately what the right <u>end</u> should be, but also were sometimes willing to employ devious means and questionable ethics to reach that end. That was one of our learnings.

Included in the forward of this book are two reference pages with the names of doctors, judicial system members, family members, and acronyms used. If a name is listed, it has been part of the public record. In those cases where doctors were not part of the public record, and I did not specifically get permission to use their names, I simply described them in more general terms. Although there are undoubtedly more questions than answers raised by this book, I do not apologize for that. The starting point for any meaningful improvement always has to be the asking of the right questions.

While most books include a section thanking everybody for their help in arriving at a final product, this book is almost entirely my own. I did have a number of people read the manuscript to determine if it was coherent, and I am deeply thankful to them for that. Although Elaine (I'm her spouse) and Barb (I'm her father) are deeply involved in the heart of the content of this book, it is written from my perspective. If Elaine were to write this book it would likely focus a bit more on the intense sadness, multiple family tragedies, and the spiritual questioning and growth which she has experienced through this ordeal. Barb and Elaine have been very supportive of my writing, and Elaine has read the manuscript multiple times to help improve it. She also made certain that I broke up my desk time by scheduling 30-minute walks with her every two to three hours, since I have a tendency to develop blood clots in my leg if I sit too long. Elaine liked to refer to these times as "walking the dog." In spite of that terminology, she actually <u>was</u> helpful.

Dan Schrock

TABLE OF CONTENTS

DOCTORS, ATTORNEYS, POLICE, JUDGE, FAMILY, and ACRONYMS

Testifying For the State:

Dr. Simpson-O'Reggio: Family pediatrician for Natalia and Isabella.

Dr. Okanlami: Pediatrician in the Pediatric Intensive Care Unit (PICU), South Bend Memorial Hospital.

Dr. Emenim: Pediatrician in the Pediatric Intensive Care Unit (PICU),
South Bend Memorial Hospital.

Dr. Cory: Pediatric radiologist consulted as expert for bone injuries and timing.

Dr. Cockerill: Neurosurgeon serving as expert to assess the type and timing of the brain injury.

For the Defense:

Dr. Rutt: Senior Psychiatrist certified in adult psychiatry and depression, served 21 years as Medical Director of Oaklawn (Mental Health Center and Hospital with staff of 700). Called in to assess whether Barbara had postpartum depression.

Other Doctors:

Dr. Gerber: Ophthalmologist (eye specialist) who checked Natalia (medical report).

Dr. Boll: Radiologist called in to interpret bone scans (medical report).

Dr. Fischbach: Radiologist called in to interpret brain scan (medical report).

Dr. Barnes: Chief Pediatric Neuroradiologist at Stanford Medical School, formerly at Harvard Medical School in similar position (reviewed Natalia's brain scan).

Attorneys:

    Mr. Ken Cotter: Prosecutor
    Mr. James (Jim) Korpal: Defense Attorney:
    Mr. Jeffrey (Jeff) Sanford: Defense Attorney
    Mr. Charles (Chuck) Lahey: Defense Attorney

Police Officers:

    Sergeant Randy Kaps: Investigator
    Lieutenant Steve Richmond: Investigator

The Court (Judge):

    The Honorable Roland Chamblee, Jr.

Family Members:

Natalia Benson:	Three-month-old daughter of Barbara Schrock and Brant Benson
Isabella Benson:	Two-year-old daughter of Barbara Schrock and Brant Benson
Brant Benson:	Father of Natalia and Isabella
Barbara Schrock:	Mother of Natalia and Isabella
Elaine Schrock:	Maternal Grandmother, Mother of Barbara
Dan Schrock:	Maternal Grandfather, Father of Barbara
Charlene Mullins:	Paternal Grandmother, Mother of Brant
Gary Mullins:	Paternal Grandfather, Step-Father of Brant
Donna Schau:	Married to Brant's cousin
Michelle Schau:	Married to Brant's cousin
Sara Siewert:	Cousin to Brant

Acronyms:

CMC:	College Mennonite Church
MYF:	CMC Youth Group (high school age)
NICU:	Neonatal Intensive Care Unit (at birth)
PICU:	Pediatric Intensive Care Unit (children)
DCS:	Department of Children's Services

CHAPTER ONE

It was Wednesday morning, July 27, 2005. Our two-year-old granddaughter, Isabella, had stayed with us in our Goshen, Indiana home overnight and we were planning to go with her to the Warren Dunes on Lake Michigan (about two hours away) for some fun in the sun and sand and water. She always enjoyed the small parks around our home, and we knew she would really like "The Dunes."

Some time between 8:00 to 9:00 am, our daughter Barb, who lived about an hour away in South Bend, called. She said that Natalia, our three-month-old granddaughter (and Isabella's sister), was having difficulty breathing earlier that morning and they had taken her to the Emergency Room at South Bend Memorial Hospital. We were concerned, but not overly alarmed, since this was not the first time Natalia had demonstrated breathing problems.

About four weeks earlier we had kept Natalia overnight, and Elaine, my wife, became concerned over Natalia's labored breathing. Elaine called for Barb, but Brant (Barb's fiance) answered the phone. Elaine described Natalia's breathing problem to Brant. He suggested that since it was Saturday and their family pediatrician, Dr. Simpson, would not likely be in her office, maybe it could wait until Natalia's regularly scheduled appointment two days later on Monday. But Elaine, a school nurse, said she thought Natalia needed to be checked out before Monday. So Barb called Dr. Simpson's office and found that another pediatrician was "on call" and would see Natalia. We loaded Isabella into our car and headed for South Bend to pick up Barb and Brant on our way to the doctor's office. The pediatrician on call examined her and concluded that she was only suffering from a sinus infection. Elaine felt a little embarrassed that perhaps she had experienced a grandmother's overreaction to Natalia's condition. Anyway, we stopped by a pharmacy on the way home to pick up and begin administering the ten-day antibiotic prescription that the pediatrician had prescribed.

Now, four weeks later, while Barb was still on the phone concerning Natalia's trip to the ER, Elaine suggested that before we headed to the South Bend Memorial Hospital, we needed to have some arrangement for Isabella's care. Barb said she would try to work out something and call us back later in the morning. We then woke up Isabella, told her that "The Dunes" trip was off, and packed her things in preparation for heading to the hospital. As we waited, Barb and Brant attempted to find someone who could keep Isabella while we visited Natalia in the hospital. Some time later we received a call indicating that Brant's cousin would meet us in the hospital parking lot to pick up Isabella. So we strapped Isabella in her car seat, loaded her things, and headed toward South Bend, about an hour away. At the hospital parking lot we met Brant's cousin. Isabella recognized her and was okay with going to her home to stay with her.

We parked and headed to the Pediatric Intensive Care Unit (PICU) where we found some of Brant's family in the waiting room. It was around 11:00 to 11:30 am now, and Brant and Barb were back in the area by Natalia's bedside. Everyone in the waiting room was in a somber mood. Only a few people could be at Natalia's bedside at a time. After a short while, Elaine and I were permitted to see Natalia. Barb was still there, too. By this time various scans had been taken and the description of Natalia's problem was well beyond the original breathing concern. She <u>was</u> on a ventilator. But the doctors were also saying that Natalia had broken ribs, a fractured skull, her brain was bleeding, and she had retinal hemorrhages. Their prognosis was that <u>she would not likely live</u>. *Whoa! Had we <u>underreacted, rather than overreacted</u> to the breathing issue this time? Perhaps. But Elaine had observed Natalia for several hours just yesterday at Barb's house when she picked up Isabella. There were some concerns about her eyes, cool body temperature, and not acting normal (whatever normal is for a preemie). But that had been the case for weeks, and Natalia was eating and had good vital signs. Still, they had called Dr. Simpson yesterday for an appointment and were told to set one up today.*

Now here was poor little six-pound Natalia, lying in a bed and all hooked up to various tubes and monitors. For those of us who reveal our emotions easily, tears of grief and overwhelming sadness poured out. For others less likely to express emotion outwardly in public, the reaction was just an intense numbness and inner turmoil. We had about 60 seconds to mourn Natalia's dire condition before the doctors dropped another bomb. They informed us that these injuries were "non-accidental." In other words, somebody <u>did this</u> to Natalia. The term "shaken baby" was mentioned. And the doctors said it had happened in the last <u>12-24 hours</u>. *Whoa again! There's nobody from either family that would ever hurt Natalia. This is unbelievable!*

By early afternoon we noticed that several police detectives were roaming the area around the waiting room. They were inquiring about who had been around Natalia during the last <u>12-24 hours</u>. That was simple enough. Barb, Brant, and Elaine. After a while these detectives took all three to the Homicide Division in downtown South Bend. *Homicide? Has someone been murdered?* Barb and Elaine each were questioned seperately by the two detectives. Barb's interview was about two hours long, while Elaine's was closer to an hour. Brant then was questioned later for an hour, after Elaine was finished. By late afternoon we all had regathered at the hospital and both families had a meal at the Ronald McDonald House there. Then Elaine and I drove back to Goshen, while Barb and Brant stayed overnight at the Ronald McDonald House to be nearer to Natalia. On Friday, I wrote the following email and sent it out to some of our closest friends, our family, and our church office:

Poor Natalia! Our preemie granddaughter is three months old this week. Early Wednesday morning she began very labored breathing, had dilated eyes, and wasn't responsive. Barb called 911 at about 5:00 am and Natalia was taken by ambulance to South Bend Memorial Hospital. In intensive care at the hospital their testing found seizures had occurred and very extensive brain swelling and damage. In addition, she had a skull fracture, fractures in both legs, a detached retina, and previously fractured ribs. If she survives, her functioning will be minimal. The neurosurgeon says the injuries are obviously intentional. Please pray for Natalia.

Poor Barb! She is devastated by Natalia's condition, yet cannot adequately mourn since the police are building a potential case against her. Her friends, her extended family, and Elaine and I have watched Barb love and care for her girls and have marveled at her natural instincts for mothering. Her self-image has increased and a certain sense of pride has developed in her as others have witnessed her gifts in this area. Now all of this is being attacked and she may face a possible five years to life in prison. Barb just sits by Natalia's side in the intensive care unit, in and out of tears, as she tries to grieve while thinking of possible answers to Natalia's injuries. Her only break in that routine has been for police questioning and court appearances. Today Natalia was assigned as a ward of the court, at least until the investigation is over. We have found no one who knows Barb that thinks she intentionally caused Natalia's injuries. Please pray for Barb.

Poor Isabella! She is nearing three years old now and is one of the sweetest, happiest, talkative, and polite little girls we know. (Just an unbiased description by her grandparents.) She doesn't really understand what's going on in this situation. but isn't allowed to stay with her parents, or with either set of grandparents until the investigation is over, since all are potential suspects (anyone who took care of Natalia in the two days before her hospitalization). Fortunately, Isabella is able to stay with one of Brant's cousins, whom she knows quite well. But it's a hardship for them, since they both work. Please pray for Isabella.

Poor Brant! His dad died in May. This was quite traumatic for Brant, not only because of the family relationship, but because the two of them worked as a business team for the past number of years. Now Brant has been working nearly twice as long daily to get the work done. He loves his daughters dearly, but doesn't get as much time with them as he would like. He is a gentle person, and if anything, Brant and Barb both are at times overprotective of their girls (they seldom let them play out in the yard for fear a tree limb will fall on them). Brant is also at the hospital day and night, and is trying to hold the family together. But too many things are out of control right now. And he is not working (or earning). Please pray for Brant.

Brant and Barb have retained a criminal attorney. Since the ongoing investigation is designed to find evidence of negative childcare, they felt it necessary to have someone lead the gathering of evidence on the other side of things. I guess I should say that Elaine is also a suspect and was interviewed by homicide police, since she was caring for both Isabella and Natalia in their home the day before Natalia was hospitalized.

Well, there's more that could be said, but this "note" also has gotten out of control. Elaine and I are OK, but find ourselves sobbing at some inopportune times (like just writing this "note.") Please pray for us, too.

Dan and Elaine

Thursday and Friday we again headed back to South Bend Memorial Hospital. The extent of Natalia's injuries were becoming more clear now. In addition to the brain, skull, ribs, and retinal hemorrhages, doctors now spoke of broken legs and arms. *What in the world happened here? How could we miss noticing all of this?* One of the two pediatricians in charge at the PICU, Dr. Okanlami, a female, was relieved by the other pediatrician, Dr. Emenim, a male, after the first day. Dr. E seemed much more certain and vivid in his description of what had happened to Natalia. He dramatically described how it would take a fall from a five-story building onto concrete to cause a skull fracture and brain damage like this. Someone would have had to have grabbed Natalia by the legs, swung her around, and smashed her head into the wall (he demonstrated). These graphic descriptions were mind-numbing. It wasn't until much later that we understood all of these descriptions are part of the "shaken baby" theory that was being alleged.

Natalia's injuries, with the exception of the retinal hemorrhages, were all discovered on brain and bone (CT) scans. Dr. O acknowledged that these scans also showed that Natalia was born with brain damage (her "corpus callosum" --- the part of the brain that allows communication between the

4

two hemispheres of the brain---- was missing). This was previously undetected because no scans were taken at birth other than one chest x-ray, and <u>symptoms</u> of damage to this part of the brain do not show up at Natalia's age. When Dr. E was asked about this brain anomaly he said he didn't know anything about a missing corpus callosum. *Did he actually look at the CT scans? Did he read the radiology report? Why does Dr. O know about this and her partner claims he doesn't?* I asked if Natalia had any neck injuries, and Dr. E responded, "Why do you ask that?" I said I would think if six-pound Natalia were swung by the legs and her head smashed into a wall, that her neck would show some serious damage. Dr. E answered that he had never heard of any case where damage to the neck was present. "Was there any bruising or swelling on her head" I asked? "No." Police indicated that there was no suspicious wall damage in the home. They had checked that out. In fact, they said the home was very orderly and well kept. But the doctors still <u>knew</u> what had happened and that it had happened in the last 24 hours. As time went on, it became increasingly obvious to us that if anything didn't fit with their diagnosis, it would be ignored.

Elaine and I were clear from the outset with Barb and Brant that we did not believe either of them had done anything to harm Natalia. There was absolutely nothing that we knew about either of them that would allow us to think of them causing harm to their own daughter. We told them <u>that</u> on several different occasions. Yet the doctors were loud and clear that someone had done this to Natalia. Elaine and I reasoned and prayed during the next 24 hours. We felt that we had to ask Barb directly, as difficult as that might be, and as risky to the trust level in a parent/child relationship, whether she had done something to Natalia. Brant's parents could decide for themselves if they would ask him directly.

During one of those first days we were able to be alone with Barb in her Ronald McDonald House bedroom. Elaine and I had prepared a little speech, and I asked Barb not to say anything until I was done. Then I proceeded to let her know once again that we have been pleased with the way she has been raising her girls. (Elaine verbalized some similar thoughts.) We told her that we have no reason to suspect her of <u>anything</u>. "But <u>you</u> know, and <u>we</u> know, that the doctors are saying <u>someone</u> has hurt Natalia. So if you did do anything to Natalia---if you got angry, or stepped out of character in any way and hurt her---you need to admit it now. Elaine and I will forgive you. God will forgive you. And the police will likely go easier on you." Barb waited until I was done and then responded rather vehemently, "Dad, I did <u>not</u> hurt Natalia, and I will not admit to something I didn't do." She briefly acknowledged to us her understanding of why we needed to ask that question, but then said, "I need to get back up to PICU to be with Natalia."

Brant hired Tony Zirkle, the brother of one of their family friends, as an attorney for Barb and himself. Tony immediately started interviewing doctors and began making grandiose plans to sue the hospital. He also told us all to keep quiet, since they don't have any evidence of who did it. *Come on, Tony. We* <u>*want*</u> *to know who, if anybody, did this to Natalia.* Maybe it was the counselor in me. Or maybe I was just naïve. But I trusted the doctors, police, and the judicial system. I felt pretty strongly we could sit down, talk this out, and get to the bottom of what had happened. Besides, we still strongly suspected that something other than "shaken baby" had caused Natalia's problems.

By Friday, just over 48 hours into this tragedy, things took an abrupt change. Until then our two families had been together mourning both Natalia's condition and questioning the diagnosis of "shaken baby" given by the doctors. We supported each other through the fog. But late Friday afternoon, Brant's mother, Char, came beside Natalia's bed where Brant, Barb, Elaine, and I were standing. She immediately started yelling at Barb loudly and saying, "<u>You</u> did this to Natalia!" Barb responded, "I did not!" And it continued, "Yes you did!" "No, I didn't!" Visitors around the PICU, doctors, and nurses, all looked up in wonder. Then Char's wrath shifted to Elaine. "And <u>you know</u> Barb did it, too!" Elaine replied in a more normal tone of voice, "I do not." This continued for about 30-60 seconds, but seemed like an eternity. *Where in the world is this coming from?* Finally, Brant addressed his mom. "<u>They didn't do anything</u> to Natalia." "Yes, they did. <u>Barb did it, and Elaine knows it,</u>" said Char, again loudly. Brant purposefully stepped in and ushered Char to the waiting room. Our family remained around Natalia's bed with mouths hanging open.

With Char and Gary (Brant's stepfather) living several hours away in Michigan, we hadn't seen much of them except on occasions like the shower given before Isabella's birth, at the hospital for Isabella's birth, an open house at our place celebrating Isabella's birth, Isabella's first and second birthdays, Natalia's birth, and a random meeting or two at Barb and Brant's house in South Bend. Our relationship, though not deep, was quite cordial. It wouldn't be until several months after this bedside incident that we would understand just what caused such an abrupt change in behavior by Brant's family on that Friday afternoon.

Also, earlier on that same Friday, in a hurried family court appearance, Natalia became a temporary ward of the state. We were in and out of the courtroom before we actually understood what had just happened. Things were moving quickly and we didn't always grasp the potential longterm devastation each decision, in which we were merely spectators, would have on our family. Natalia no longer officially belonged to Brant and Barb. Or to her grandparents.

Saturday morning we arrived at the hospital to find that Natalia had been taken off of the ventilator. She was breathing on her own. Now one doesn't always know <u>how</u> or <u>what</u> to pray for in circumstances like those. It appeared that Natalia would not have a chance to experience much meaning or joy in life if she lived. The doctors said she had brain stem functioning only. The brain scan showed that the cerebrum was dying, and the cerebellum was drastically altered. That meant no thinking, feeling, or reasoning, and severely diminished motor skills, balance, etc. Only breathing, heartbeat, and other essentials were keeping her alive. But as grandparents we gave thanks for her breathing, and asked that God's will be done in what the future held for her.

On Saturday Barb informed us of another change. She and Brant had decided it would be better if our family visited Natalia during the morning until early afternoon each day, and Brant's family visit during late afternoon and evening. Brant was also moving to his brother's house, while Barb would continue to stay at the Ronald McDonald House at the hospital. We didn't particularly like what this arrangement signified, but it <u>was</u> a decision that was Barb and Brant's to make.

CHAPTER TWO

The decision for Brant and Barb to go separate directions was one that was quite foreign to our own family history. Elaine (Gerig) grew up in a Mennonite family that lived in Iowa. Her dad farmed, but also was a Mennonite minister. Later he became a bishop for the Iowa and Nebraska Mennonite churches. Elaine's mom had attended Goshen College in Indiana and taught in a one-room school for a number of years before staying at home to raise her three girls, of which Elaine was the youngest. As you might imagine, church activities were a priority in this family. They were a very close and loving family. Today, however, Elaine is the only family member still living.

Elaine loved animals and people, had an interest in healing them, and decided very early in life that she wanted to be a nurse. She attended Iowa Mennonite School during her high school years and was not only a strong student, but also an athlete and talented singer. Following graduation Elaine was selected by the International Christian Youth Exchange program to spend a year in Germany studying in school there and living with a local German family. That experience opened her eyes and interests to the larger world and the varied people who live within it.

After returning to the U.S., Elaine took one year of pre-nursing courses at Hesston College in Kansas, and then transferred to Goshen College where she graduated with honors and a B.S. in Nursing degree. Immediately following graduation she was hired as the Goshen College campus nurse.

I (Dan) was born in Ohio and also was raised on a farm. In addition to farming, my dad became a real estate broker. Dad liked everybody he ever met, talked to everybody he ever met, had a strong sense of humor and a heavy dose of personal integrity. My mom had earned a teaching license from Kent State University, and taught in Canton, Ohio schools for six years during the depression. That ended, however, when the scarcity of jobs meant many females needed to relinquish them to male wage earners. Mom was well-read, limited only by time and money, and had a very practical understanding of psychology for child-rearing.

Church was central for our family, too. If the doors of the Oak Grove Mennonite Church were open, we were likely there. And what you learned in church on Sundays or Wednesday evenings was to be practiced throughout the week, or it was wasted learning. I have one older brother, and one younger sister, although three other brothers died at birth or shortly thereafter. We traveled and camped as a family, played ball as family, baled hay as a family, and went to church as a family. In high school my only Saturday night curfew regulation was that I needed to be ready for church on Sunday morning, and alert enough to worship and learn.

Following high school I attended Goshen College for four years, graduating with a B.S. in Education with a natural science major, and a health and safety minor. Along the way, however, I seriously considered majors in math, physical education, pre-medicine, journalism, and music. After graduation, I enrolled in a two-year Master's Degree program in social work at the University of Illinois. When that was completed I took some additional courses at the U. of Illinois in counseling.

Elaine and I met as a blind date while she was an undergraduate student at Goshen College and I was a graduate student at the U. of Illinois. Although many would consider that chance meeting coincidental, we would call it providential. Our interest in each other grew rapidly and it seemed prudent to move closer together geographically. Consequently, my search for employment resulted in my being hired as high school counselor at Bethany Christian High School in Goshen, Indiana. After the first year there I was offered and accepted the position of Coordinator of Counseling Services at Goshen College.

Elaine and I were married in 1966, and in 1968 as I said previously, she also began working at Goshen College as College Nurse. Both of us, however, were interested in serving abroad in some role. While we looked into various avenues of church service, we eventually decided to work at the American School of Kuwait. She was employed as school nurse and I as high school counselor during the four years that we lived there. Kuwait was just developing then, and was a very interesting place to be. Opportunities for travel and intercultural connections were abundant during those years. Our school had 43 nationalities in the student body, and we had the opportunity to travel to 56 countries during the summer months. The English language Protestant church we attended had members from many different denominations, and included many of our closest friends in Kuwait. Our experience in Kuwait further shaped us as world citizens.

Both Elaine and I were in our late twenties, and were talking seriously about having a family of our own. We felt, in our own modest way, that we might have some fairly decent genes between us. But we had also traveled enough to become aware of the many children around the world that

10

didn't have a family, or much of a chance at life in general. After much thought and prayer, we decided to adopt a child from one of the orphanages in Iran. Just prior to this decision, however, in a rather lengthy process, I had managed to get tickets in Kuwait for the 1972 Munich Olympic Games nearly 18 months before they started. Unfortunately, the dates turned out to coincide with the dates that we later arranged to be in Tehran for the adoption venture. So during our summer camping in Europe in 1972 we stopped in Munich to return our Olympic tickets, and then made our way to Iran.

Tehran at that time was a city of approximately three million people, with few multi-level residential buildings. What this meant was that while it had roughly the same number of people as Chicago did, it was more spread out. Elaine and I walked that city through the maze of residential and governmental buildings for over a week trying to get various papers and seals, while not knowing a word of Farsi. It was hard work from early morning to evening. For the <u>following</u> two weeks we decided to hire a driver to help us get around the city and out to the orphanage. Empress Farah, the Shah's wife, was very instrumental in the development and workings of the orphanages in Iran. It was a pleasant surprise to observe both the quality of care, and the condition of the buildings at the orphanage with which we connected. Finally, after three physically, mentally, and emotionally exhausting weeks of wondering whether we had understood adequately all of the forms we signed that were printed in Farsi, the conversations with the social workers at the orphanage, the judge's comments in the courtroom, the myriad of stamps and wax seals that adorned all the paperwork, and the application necessary for her visa to enter Kuwait, we walked out of the orphanage triumphantly with one-month-old Barbara in our arms. We had adopted her, and she was legally a part of our family now. *Yes! And we both had a chance to experience the labor pains involved.*

But the red tape didn't end with getting Barbara. We were then told, almost as an aside, that she could not leave Iran unless she was a Christian. *What? She's a month old. Did we hear that right? So must we all live here the rest of our lives to be with her?* The answer we were given to our question was that we needed to <u>baptize</u> her. That seemed straightforward enough to the ones giving us this advice. But for Elaine and me, it raised some fairly significant theological concerns. We believe that baptism should be upon the confession of one's faith. Infants seem a bit young for that. So we went to the minister of The Community Church in Tehran, Reverend Pryor, and told him of our dilemma. His sage comment was, "Well, I believe God has a sense of humor about such things." Together we worked out a combination child dedication service and baptism for Barbara that ended up with his issuing a baptismal certificate. If she wanted to get re-baptized in the future, that would be up to her. Now we could leave the country. With Barbara. *Well... almost.*

Now all we needed to do was to head back to Kuwait. So we said our goodbyes as we checked out of our modest, but adequate hotel where we had lived for the last three weeks. It was Friday afternoon and we needed to stop by the Kuwait Embassy for Barbara's visa before we headed out by taxi to the airport. We had arranged for someone from our school to meet us at the Kuwait airport.

As we arrived at the outer room of the Embassy where we were to pick up Barbara's visa, we were invited into an inner office where the official had Barbara's visa in hand. He smilingly informed us it was not signed. So we asked him to please sign it. His reply was, "My hand is tired." I looked at Elaine, knowing full well what that meant. He wanted extra money to sign it. Probably a lot of extra money. For whatever reason, we decided not to play that game. So we asked, "When will you sign it?" He replied that it would be signed and ready on Monday. Determined not to give in, we left the Embassy, headed back to the hotel where we had just checked out, and arranged to stay for three more nights. Then we called the airlines and canceled our flights to Kuwait. We were able to purchase tickets back to Kuwait for Monday. (None of those arrangements were particularly easy.) So we spent another weekend in Tehran. When Monday came, we went to the Kuwait Embassy, met with the same official, and he gave us the signed visa. *Did we ever show him!............... Didn't we?*

We spent one more year in Kuwait. Barbara garnered the attention of all of the other teachers, since most were even younger than us and did not have children. Coming back to the U.S. from Kuwait in 1973, I again was hired by Bethany Christian as counselor for four more years. Elaine worked part-time, while caring for Barbara. I requested a four day/week contract so I could share in the child rearing duties, and was grateful when the school agreed to that. Barbara became known as "Barbi." And Elaine and I became members of College Mennonite Church, located on the campus of Goshen College.

By 1976 Barbi had lived in the U.S. for three years and was eligible to become a citizen. We completed the necessary paperwork, and drove about 70 miles to northwestern Indiana for Barbi to be interviewed by the federal judge for our district. Barbi had just turned four years old. We found his office and waited until he was ready to meet with us. He was a large man with a booming voice. As he tried to connect with Barbi and make small talk with her, it was apparent that he was too close, too loud, and too intimidating for her. She ended up calling him a "dummy," and Elaine and I were certain at that point that we would be living with a non-citizen in our family for the foreseeable future. Fortunately, this judge must have understood the ways of four-year-olds, and recommended her for citizenship.

Elaine, Barbi, and Dan

A few weeks later we again made a trip to northwestern Indiana to the courthouse where all new citizens were to take their oath of citizenship. As we got close to our destination, Barbi exclaimed, "Oh, no. We forgot our tennis racquets." At first we were caught off guard. What is she talking about? Then it became clear that whenever we had talked about courts before, it was related to playing tennis. And she thought that's where we were heading now. Apparently we needed to do a bit more orientation on this citizenship thing. When we got to the courthouse, we walked up the steps and into the building. There we were guided to a seat on one of the benches. Twenty or thirty other international persons were there to become citizens also. When it became time to take the oath, Barbi stood up on the bench, raised her right hand, and swore never to overthrow the government of the United States of America. Then we went to McDonalds to celebrate.

Barb ready for school

After four years back in the U.S., we headed for another overseas working adventure, this time in Cairo, Egypt. My position at Cairo American College (K-12) was high school counselor, and Elaine was again school nurse for all grades. This time there were 56 nationalities in the school. Barbi attended kindergarten through third grade during our four years there. Once again our family attended an English language congregation with numerous denominations represented. This church community became a very meaningful group for us. As in Kuwait, we still have connections with some of those people today.

After the Shah of Iran died, three of his children enrolled in our school in Cairo. We felt pleased to be able to care for Laila, Ali Reza, and Farahnaz, and to partially return our gratitude for the indirect way Empress Farah had cared for Barbi through her help with the Iranian orphanages.

During our fourth year in Cairo we received word that our house back in Goshen had been flooded when the hot water heating pipes burst during a winter storm. Our renters had moved out without notifying anyone. Inside the empty house the electricity had apparently gone out for some extended period of time, and the pipes froze and cracked. When the electricity came back on, steamy hot water continued to spray everything for nearly ten days. Hardwood floors had buckled up, glue melted and furniture collapsed, walls and ceilings were heavily covered with large mildew and mold spots, and books and photographic slides were soaked. Our Sunday School class at College Mennonite (from nearly four years earlier) didn't miss a beat. They spent many, many hours drycleaning drapes, carting salvageable furniture to a neighbor's warehouse, wiping down books page by page, and drying several thousand slides. It was impossible to express just how grateful we were from nearly 8,000 miles away. But even with all of their help, there were shelf brackets (like one sees on the side of trees) growing on our walls when we arrived home five months later. The contractor that we hired first suggested that we bulldoze the house down. Fortunately, however, he was able to salvage the house and we had a celebration with those who had helped us through this disaster. What a wonderful group of people!

During our first year back in the U.S. (1981-82) Elaine and I took a variety of courses at the Mennonite Biblical Seminary in nearby Elkhart. This was a good opportunity to grow in our faith, and to gain perspective on what we wanted to do next. When we were not at the seminary, we were completing a workbook on our "options" for the future. Elaine and I would fill out each chapter separately, then discuss them together at Burger King. After a year of growth and reflection, I took a position in the Personnel

Department at the Mennonite Board of Missions in Elkhart. This was a good match for me, and I stayed for the next 13 years, again on a four days/week contract. Following that I took some coursework in San Francisco and became a massage therapist for nine years. I found that I enjoyed working with my hands, running my own business, and interacting with massage clients.

Barb as a freshman in high school

Elaine took several part-time positions over the next few years before once again becoming a school nurse, this time in the Westview Schools (working with fifth and sixth grade students) for 17 years until she retired. Meanwhile, Barbi was becoming "Barb." During her middle school and high school years she was an average student, but not very serious about it. Barb was much more concerned with social relationships. To this day, she finds it easy to make friends. After graduating from Goshen High School, Barb worked in various job settings over the next 12 years.

Barb met Brant Benson in 1998 and was engaged within a year or so. Elaine and I were silly enough to think that meant they would be getting married soon. *Not!* We gave them what we considered to be a significant sum of money that they could use on their wedding, or as a down payment on a house. They chose to make a down payment on a house. All in all, not a bad decision. We're not much for expensive weddings, anyway. But an inexpensive one would have been nice. Barb and Brant closed on a house in South Bend on September 11, 2001, which perhaps was an omen of another disaster yet to come a few years later. Isabella was born on September 20, 2002. And Natalia was born April 23, 2005. Brant worked with his father putting trim in new houses, and together they decided that Barb should stay home to be with the children.

Barb turned out to be an excellent mother. She read parenting magazines and had a sense of pride in her success with Isabella. Brant normally brought home an adequate income, although work was sometimes spotty. From our perspective, neither Barb nor Brant was particularly good with handling money. The fact that they chose Barb (as the one gifted in money management) to monitor their finances spoke volumes to us about Brant's apparent ability in this area. Earlier we had hoped that she might find a strong money manager as a life partner. But overall we were pleased with Brant. He loved Barb and seemed like a good father when he was around home.

Barb had a difficult pregnancy with Natalia. Already at the first six-weeks checkup, Barb was experiencing nausea, anemia, and headaches. These continued throughout the pregnancy, and by the seventh month she was vomiting frequently. This was a concern not only for the discomfort, but also because she was unable to keep much of her food and vitamins down. During one of her regularly scheduled appointments with her doctor (week 33 of her pregnancy) her blood pressure was extremely high. The doctor had her hospitalized with <u>preeclampsia</u> (soaring blood pressure, swelling of hands and feet, the leading cause of premature delivery, and also the leading cause of maternal and fetal illness and death worldwide).

After a day in the hospital she was sent home, but told to be alert to this situation. The following week she was back in the hospital again. Doctors were becoming increasingly concerned about the potential risk of death for both mother and child. She was now in week 34, and they decided to wait no longer. The doctors gave Barb medication to induce labor on Thursday, and again on Friday--- but to no avail. On Saturday they gave her pitocin, also to induce labor. As monitors were showing Barb's blood pressure to be dangerously high, the delivering doctor decided a C-section would need to be done if the delivery didn't happen very soon.

Barb, Brant, Elaine, and I were all in the delivery room through this ordeal. The doctor told Barb to push really hard, and we all were giving her our encouragement. After some long and heavy pushing, the doctor attached a suction device to Natalia's head and pulled her out. *Whew! My first delivery had exhausted me, ...and I was just a spectator. Well, okay, I was a grandfather, too.*

Natalia seemed so tiny (3 lbs, 11oz). And blue. I was standing by the small receiving table that served as a temporary parking place for Natalia when Barb's voice came from across the room. "Is she okay? Will she live?" No answer. Once again Barb repeated the questions. Again no answer. Perhaps the medical staff were too busy giving Natalia the help she needed. The APGAR score for "color" was zero (on a scale of 0-2). I had thought Natalia's color to be blue, but the nurse recorded it as "dusky." Oxygen was administered. After five minutes her color improved to "one" on the APGAR scale. After weighing, measuring, and taking footprints, the nurse gave Natalia briefly to Barb to hold for some photos. Then Natalia was rushed off to the Neonatal Intensive Care Unit (NICU) where she remained for the next 19 days. Being grandparents for a second time was something to celebrate, but we also had an accompanying uneasiness about Natalia's health.

Barb stayed in the hospital for the next few days. She, Brant, and the doctor had a conversation about about the dangers of another pregnancy. They all agreed that Barb should have her tubes tied to eliminate that concern. So that brief surgery was done while she was still a patient.

Barb and Brant had only one vehicle that was working while Natalia was in NICU. Brant needed that vehicle on a daily basis to use for his work. So Barb was home without transportation. She used a breast pump to have milk available for Natalia in the NICU. As it had with Isabella, Barb's breast milk dried up early, and formula was used from there on. After work when Brant came home, one or both of them would drive to the NICU to be with

Natalia. Since grandparents were also allowed to visit, Elaine and I would occasionally make the drive from Goshen to see how Natalia was doing.

The nurses at the NICU talked to Brant and Barb about the fact that with Natalia being five to six weeks premature, they should not be expecting her to do the same things as Isabella did at a similar age. Natalia will develop at a very different pace. Don't compare the two, or have the same expectations. This is not a full-term baby. And not only was Natalia premature, but also she was small for her gestational age. In other words, she was smaller than other 34 week preemies.

Towards the end of Natalia's 19 days of NICU, Barb began to recognize that she was not bonding with Natalia the same way as she had with Isabella. Whether she brought it up with the nurses there, or whether they brought up the subject while alerting Barb to the possibility of postpartum depression (PPD), is not clear. Anyway, they apparently talked and said Barb should contact them if her feelings about "lack of bonding" even turned to "wanting to harm Natalia." Barb being who she is--- never one to keep her thoughts or feelings secret from anyone--- spoke openly about her detachment and lack of bonding with Natalia to those close around her. Sometimes she referred to it as PPD, sometimes not. But she never described those feelings as wanting to harm Natalia, and responded when asked about 'wanting to hurt Natalia' with "No, it's not like that."

When Natalia came home from the NICU in mid-May, Barb and Brant were more than somewhat uneasy about caring for a preemie. Barb had been very confident with Isabella, but this was quite different. (Or so they felt). Within a week of Natalia's coming home from the NICU, Brant's biological father, Wilbur, died. Brant and his father had done finishing work together in new homes for several years, and Brant was with him on a daily basis. So this was a very stressful time for Brant with a preemie at home, his father's death, and his work in question.

During the time of Brant's father's funeral, Elaine and I kept Natalia for two days so that Barb could be free to attend the service and connect with Brant's family. Natalia was not supposed to be exposed to groups of people yet for fear of her underdeveloped immune system being unable to ward off germs. Brant's parents, Char and Gary, were fearful of keeping Natalia overnight. As Char would later tell the police, "Right from the beginning it seemed like there was something wrong with that baby. Something just didn't seem right." None of us, including Elaine and me, felt comfortable being responsible for a preemie. Elaine, although a nurse, had spent her working years as a school nurse, and had never taken care of a preemie before. But we <u>were</u> grandparents, and we managed all right for the two nights that we kept her at that time.

There were, however, things about Natalia that seemed to be different during the several times that we kept her. Whenever we would feed her, much of the formula would run down the sides of her mouth and soak her neck and whatever she was wearing. Later, by the weekend of July 4, Char and Gary finally decided they were ready to keep her overnight. Char shared in her police interview in response to a question about whether she had any problems feeding Natalia, "Well, a little. It came out of the side of her mouth." Natalia also would make snorting sounds (it sounded like little pigs from my earlier farm days), indicating to us that she was having some difficulty breathing. Char told police, "on Friday (July 1) it seemed like she wasn't doing that snorting..like snuh, snuh..so much."

When you held Natalia she would occasionally arch her back and get very stiff, almost hurling herself out of your arms. Barb, Brant, Elaine, and I all felt she had problem with gas, and assumed that was responsible for these actions. At other times she would wink one eye at whoever was feeding her. We thought that was cute. Doctors at the hospital later described these actions as seizures. Brant then told police, "I truly believe that ever since Natalia came home (from NICU) that she was having seizures." We believe that, too.

Natalia never smiled or made direct eye contact that we could tell. Later, her eyes were often to one side or the other, so it seemed at times like she was looking at us, simply because her eyes had to be pointed in some direction. Hearing, too, was hard to determine. None of these observations alarmed us at the time because we had been warned not to expect the same type of development as in a full-term baby. But near the end of June Elaine and I kept Natalia overnight again. We enjoyed being grandparents for all of the obvious reasons. But I particularly connected with Natalia. I don't know if it was because of her "snorting" breathing problems. Or her size. Or her vulnerability. I've had breathing problems much of my own life, so maybe that was it. Anyway, it was good to have her at our home again. But Elaine was up with Natalia much of the night observing her. She felt Natalia was having <u>significant</u> breathing problems this time. That resulted in the quick trip to South Bend and to the pediatrician's office mentioned earlier. The doctor said not to be alarmed. Just a sinus infection. So Natalia was put on an antibiotic for ten days. Two days later, at her regularly scheduled appointment, Natalia was given a full round of immunizations. She was now about two months old, but really only one month or less gestationally. Doctors had said her full term would have come around May 30.

20

We have not been anti-vaccination zealots. Elaine, as a school nurse, has given many immunizations. We made certain that Barb had them when she was young. But looking back to this time in Natalia's life, it is clear that things became much worse for her about a week after her vaccinations and continued that way until she was taken to the ER. One evening I listened as the spokesperson for the Center For Disease Control in Atlanta answered a question on TV about the safety of vaccinations. "They are safe. And we are working every day to make them safer." *Whoa. Did I hear that right? How can you make something that is safe.....safer? That's like saying someone is dead, and in a few weeks they'll be more dead.* Now I do know what the Center For Disease Control (CDC) was trying to say. It is safer for all of us if everyone has their vaccinations. We can't just stop doing vaccinations and still be safe from certain illnesses as a country. And I agree with that. But please don't deny that individuals have had reactions of varying degrees of severity to vaccinations. That is well documented. Why else would federal law require providers to give you information regarding the risks and benefits of vaccinations before taking them, and encourage you to report adverse reactions to the CDC?

As I said earlier, the weekend of July 4 Char and Gary decided for the first time to keep Natalia for several days. She was taken to an all-day party with well over 20 relatives present. That was her first time with a large group of people. Following that weekend, according to Brant and Barb, Natalia's previous symptoms worsened and vomiting became more of a problem. (This was also 5-7 days after her vaccinations.) July 16-18 Elaine and I kept Natalia again. I recall sitting in a chair feeding Natalia her formula. I no longer stood with her very often, due to her occasional strong stiffening and my fear that she would lurch out of my arms. She took most of the bottle rather easily, with the exception of some of it running down the corners of her mouth, and as I looked at her face, she seemed to be looking out of the corner of her eyes and winking at me. I was feeling pretty good about myself when all of a sudden the entire contents of the formula she had drunk came pouring out of her mouth all over her and all over me. Elaine hurried to the rescue, and after a while she had both of us cleaned up fairly well. I gave Natalia another bottle of formula, turned her the other way in my arms, and this time she took it all and kept it down. But her eyes appeared to be looking out the window instead of at me.

The following week Elaine and Barb were on the phone several times trying to decide if Natalia should see the pediatrician. Her symptoms seemed to be worsening at times, but then they would subside. They finally decided to wait until Elaine observed her again. Barb had set up an appointment to get her hair cut on Tuesday, July 26, and Elaine agreed that she would drive to South Bend to babysit the girls and observe Natalia more closely. Before that day came, however, Barb took Natalia along with her to Michigan on Sunday, July 24 to visit Brant's grandmother who was severely ill with cancer. Char was there with some other relatives.

Monday evening, July 25, Brant was home alone with Natalia while Isabella and Barb were at Long John Silvers. Char phoned Brant to tell him that she was concerned about Natalia. She felt Natalia was "not moving her arms and legs as much as a normal baby. Her eyes go off to the right." (She apparently hadn't seen Natalia for a while.) Char said she had held "the baby" for 2-3 hours. Something seemed wrong to her. Char was thinking, "Is it because she's a preemie?" Brant went into the bedroom to look at Natalia and told his mom on the phone that "she's been eating...she looks okay...her eyes are okay....she seems okay to me." Brant asked if Char felt they should take Natalia to the ER. Char said she didn't know if it was that serious, but that she needs to get in to see the doctor.

When Barb got home Brant told her of the phone call from Char. Barb responded that Elaine would be coming over in the morning to babysit, and that she could check Natalia out to know what to report to the doctor. Tuesday morning Elaine came at around 9:00 am. Brant had gone to work. Barb's haircut appointment was called off because of water problems at the salon. Elaine suggested that since she was already there, Barb could take this opportunity to be with her friends for a while. So Barb left and Elaine spent roughly the next three hours babysitting the girls and observing Natalia.

During those three hours of babysitting Elaine observed several things that were of concern to her. Natalia's problem areas had increased since Elaine had seen her nine days before. Elaine's comments to the police later were: "Natalia didn't seem very good." "Was not very responsive." "There was no eye contact that I could tell." "Her temperature was low (91+ degrees, 93+ degrees, and 92+ degrees the three times she took it)." "She didn't cry at all." "Natalia did not suck with the gusto she often did." "And her body was not active."

But on the positive side of things, Natalia's other vital signs were okay. "She was breathing normal." "Pulse rate was normal." "She did take her bottle." "She did not spit it up." "Natalia urinated in the diaper." "There was no bluing of her lips." "Her fingernail refill was good [circulation]." (The above temperatures were axillary [armpit] and taken with a digital drugstore thermometer. Elaine had used this type of thermometer at school and assumed that when a temperature readout like this occurred, and the other vital signs were okay, that the reading was <u>inaccurate</u>. Three years later

22

Elaine requested the Lead Nurse in her school corporation to go back through Elaine's records to see how often a temperature in this range had occurred, and what the followup was. That nurse determined that during Elaine's final two years prior to retirement, she had seen 39 students with recorded temperatures in the range of Natalia's. All had other vital signs that were okay, and all were sent back to class. The lead nurse, herself, indicated that she had similar experiences with that type of thermometer. [Elaine took approximately 500 temperatures during a normal school year].)

So Elaine was concerned, but not alarmed at the overall picture. When Barb returned around 12:30 pm, Elaine talked with her about what to report to the pediatrician. Elaine stayed to listen as Barb made the call. Barb described Natalia's condition, including Natalia's specific temperature, to the person who answered the phone, asking her to have Dr. Simpson, the family pediatrician, call her. That person made a note of the conversation and said she would have Dr. Simpson call back. Elaine then left for Goshen with Isabella who was planning to go with us to the Warren Dunes the next day. Barb fed Natalia another bottle at about 5:30 pm that afternoon, and she kept the full four ounces down.

Dr. Simpson called Barb back (after office hours) at about 6:00 pm that evening. She had the phone note in front of her, including comments about Natalia's not acting normal and the temperature reading of 93 degrees, as she asked Barb other questions about Natalia's condition. At the end of the conversation, Dr. Simpson asked Barb to make an appointment in the morning. Barb then called Elaine in Goshen to report what the doctor had said. (Dr. Simpson would later say in court that she felt the temperature was inaccurate since it didn't match the level of consciousness. She added that "often temperatures are not accurate.")

Later that evening (Tuesday, July 26) Brant returned home from work about 7:00 pm. He later told police, "she (Natalia) was fine. Her eyes were normal. She was focusing. She was squeezing my pinky. Her breathing was normal. I was playing with her in bed." Then around 9:00 pm Natalia would not take her bottle. The prior week, when Elaine and Barb were trying to figure out whether to take Natalia to the doctor, Elaine had borrowed a pediatric health book from her school nurse's office. Tuesday morning Elaine had brought this book along and left it for Barb. Following Natalia's refusal to take her bottle around 9:00 pm, Barb became more concerned. She felt her eyes looked worse. Natalia fell asleep around 11:00 pm, but Barb skimmed the book to see if she could find anything helpful, and watched Natalia to check her breathing. Around 1:00 or 2:00 am Barb must have fallen asleep.   She was awakened by Natalia's high pitched scream at about 4:30 am. The 911 call followed.

CHAPTER THREE

Following the weekend when Brant's family shifted their support away from Barb... *way away...* Brant released the attorney who was representing both Barb and him. It had <u>somehow</u> become clear to Brant that <u>he</u> would no longer need a criminal attorney. That left Barb without one, too. Since we had become aware of the "shaken baby theory" and its "last person to be with the child" dogma, we figured that Barb would be the prime suspect. I inquired around the Goshen area with my few attorney acquaintances about next steps. They all seemed to agree that it was important to get a criminal attorney that was familiar with South Bend (St. Joseph County) court procedures. That meant finding a South Bend attorney.

How do I find a South Bend criminal attorney? I looked through the yellow pages and on the internet. Elaine had mentored a girl from our church from grades seven through high school graduation and had continued that relationship beyond those years. She was now a young woman who had become an immigration attorney at the University of Notre Dame and had married another attorney. With their help, we finally settled on Jim Korpal, whom I had also found on the internet. Jim was experienced and honest, two of our primary requirements. Since Barb had no money, we knew she would need a public defender. Jim explained that there was no difference in quality between a public defender and a private attorney in South Bend, since private attorneys there also serve part-time as public defenders. He could serve as either. The only difference was <u>cost</u> and the <u>amount of time</u> an attorney could give to a case.

I worked for twenty years in agencies and schools of the Mennonite Church, plus I was employed for eight years in overseas schools. The final nine years of my working career I was self-employed as a massage therapist. In none of those years was my salary higher than $28,000. (I chose to work on an 80 percent-time basis many of those years, which partially explains the salary level.) The highest years of income were with the Mennonite Board of Missions when I served as Director of Personnel. The lowest were the nine years in massage therapy when I never cleared $10,000 in a single year. Elaine's income was lower than mine, with the exception of her final few years as school nurse at Westview. I include this information here not as a complaint, but as background information. In fact, neither of us has <u>any</u> regrets about where we worked. We made our own choices and would likely make similar choices if we were to do it all over. The opportunity to work four days a week to spend more time with Barb, and with each other, was extremely important us. We are grateful that our employers allowed us to do this. And money was never that important to us, anyway. We spent rather frugally, yet were able to travel, live comfortably, and have many friends. By saving and investing we had accumulated a nest egg for retirement.

But should we enlist Jim as a public defender, or as a paid private attorney? Natalia's situation seemed so thoroughly complicated (although not to the doctors, police, and prosecutor) that we decided it would require more time than a public defender could give. So we drew from our retirement money. This was not a time to scrimp. Our daughter's freedom and future life might be at stake.

Will Barb be charged? Can they build a case against her? Days drag on. We hear early in the week that charges may be coming against Barb. Waiting. Later in the week, we hear through the judicial grapevine that charges were presented to a judge for a "probable cause" signature, but he would not sign them because of inadequate evidence. (Another rumor that we have no way of evaluating.) Natalia is moved to St. Vincent's Hospital in Indianapolis for special therapy and rehabilitation. Can we visit her there? A week goes by. Barb visits Natalia in Indianapolis. Elaine and I inquire about our visiting Natalia. Jim sees no reason why we cannot. But we want to be sure. Calls and messages left at the Division of Children's Services (DCS) in South Bend are not answered for three consecutive days. Another week passes. It's been over a month now that this tragedy emerged. Sunday we had a large potluck dinner at church for the incoming college students. People continued to express their concern for us. Finally on Monday, August 29, Jim hears that charges will be brought against Barb <u>and</u> Elaine that day. *Both of them?* Barb and Elaine will need to go with Jim on Tuesday morning to the St. Joseph's County Jail to turn themselves in. I will go along to post bond. Monday night's TV news hypes up the arrest warrants that have been issued, and indicates that Barb and Elaine are still "at large." *This is getting crazier all the time.*

Tuesday, while I'm standing at the front desk of the jail waiting to issue my check for the bond, Barb and Elaine are taken through three locked doors to a desk to complete the arresting process. They remove all jewelry and watches, shoes are taken off and checked, and patting down takes place. Information is gathered and forms completed by officers at another desk. Then finger printing. And finally mug shots. They are checked into the jail. This all takes about 45 minutes. Then the officers call the front desk, and I am told to post bond now. Once the bank check has gone through the appropriate channels, Barb and Elaine get their jewelry and watches back, and are ushered out to the front desk. We all are free to go now. As we look out into the parking lot, we see that a TV cameraman and reporter with microphone have arrived and are trying to figure out which car we will be driving so they may get the best closeup shot and possibly a comment for their channel. I leave through a side door and walk purposefully (jog) to our minivan, start it, and pull it up to the front door of the jail. By now the reporters are running at us. Barb and Elaine jump in the vehicle and we pull out of the parking lot and are on our way back to Goshen. (It feels like we are riding away from a posse.) That evening there was plenty of footage of the family that "abused Natalia" all over the early and late news. Newspapers had their headline stories and mug shots, too.

What does being out on bond mean? We don't know, but continue our normal routine (almost). We still haven't heard anything from the DCS. And the multiple calls to the social worker at St. Vincent's in Indianapolis have not been returned either. Elaine and I haven't seen Natalia for nearly two weeks. Barb has made a second trip to visit her. On Wednesday Barb and Elaine appear in court to plead "not guilty." More TV cameras, reporters, and newspapers writers. Wednesday evening Elaine and I go to Amish Acres to see "Aida" in their Round Barn Theatre. Very well done. Thursday <u>Elaine returns to school</u> and her school nurse position (she had to miss Tuesday and Wednesday because of court appearances.) Once Natalia had been transferred to Indianapolis, Barb moved from Ronald McDonald House back to her own home. Brant was living with his brother. (The house mortgage and title are in Barb's name because she had a better credit rating than Brant.) That same Thursday, however, Brant gave her until 2:00 pm to be out of the house or "he'd throw all of her things out in the front yard." <u>Barb quickly arranged to move down the street</u> to stay with their friends. <u>I attended a cross country match</u> which involved one of the youth from our church.

On Friday late afternoon we met with our pastors at church. We requested the meeting because these church people (over a thousand members) are the people who have known us closely over the past forty years. It is these people to whom we have pledged to "give and receive counsel" as part of our membership vows. It is to these people that we feel a responsibility to inform them honestly and openly about what is happening in our lives. I have written a statement from Elaine and me to the congregation and have asked that it be read by the lead minister on Sunday morning. He now reads through the statement in his office, feels this is a good idea, and agrees to do it. Someone asks if we want the radio broadcast of the Sunday service cut when the statement is read. They could just play music during that time. We respond that we don't care, but our attorney might feel better if that were done. Then the conversation shifts to our needs. We are asked over and over if there is anything the church can do for us. We don't really know what would be helpful at this point. They ask if we need financial assistance. We respond that we do not need financial help now, but may need help in the future depending on how things develop. They assure us of the congregation's readiness to help. The meeting ended with a prayer--- perhaps the one thing that is most helpful right now. Elaine and I leave pledging to keep the congregation updated as we learn more. Friday night I attend a local football game at which we have several band members and a cheerleader from our youth group participating.

By Saturday morning we still have not heard from anyone whether or not we are allowed to visit Natalia in Indianapolis. We had decided earlier that if we have not heard by this date from the people in a position to give us an answer either way, we would simply drive to Indianapolis, tell the people at the hospital who we are, and ask if there were any restrictions put on our visitation of Natalia. So Elaine and I headed out on the six hour round trip to St. Vincent's in Indianapolis, not knowing what situation we would find when we arrived there. We parked, walked up to the front desk, said who we were, and asked if we could visit Natalia. The nurse on duty of Natalia's section said we should wait there in the large room several feet from Natalia while she checked on the official status of our visiting privileges. It was so good to see Natalia, even from a short distance. *Grandma and Grandpa Schrock were filled with joy again.* In a few minutes the nurse came back and stated that Elaine had been put on a restricted list, would not be able to visit Natalia, and would need to wait in the lounge area. *Huge disappointment! Bigger than huge!* Elaine walked quietly and dejectedly with the nurse to the lounge. I, however, was allowed to visit. For the next 45 minutes I held our granddaughter. What a blessing! Tears welled in my eyes as I savored this moment, while at the same time knowing how low Elaine was feeling in the lounge. Tears of joy and tears of sorrow. What we did not know was that this would be the last time that either one of us would ever touch Natalia again.

The next day, Sunday, we were back in Goshen again. Elaine and I sat near the front of our circular sanctuary at church, as we normally did. A few weeks prior to this service we had informed the congregation of Natalia's serious condition and her entrance and continuing status in PICU. But now there were charges and more information to report to the congregation. Following the sermon was a time for announcements. Our lead minister read the following statement that we had prepared earlier in the week:

AN UPDATE FROM DAN AND ELAINE SCHROCK

Many of you have heard, or will hear, information in the public media, some accurate and some inaccurate, concerning our legal situation. We feel the need to share this matter with the congregation since many of the people who mean the most to us gather here weekly, and we feel accountable to all our brothers and sisters in this place. Our own receiving of accurate information throughout this crisis has been a significant challenge, and gives us some pause that we may be communicating inaccuracies ourselves. However, we believe the following information is truthful and accurate.

The morning of July 27 our daughter, Barb, called 911, since our three month-old premature granddaughter, Natalia, had begun breathing abnormally. Hospital staff found broken bones and significant bleeding in the brain, and indicated to us that Natalia, barring a miracle, would likely die or have permanent, severe brain damage. The grief aroused by that pronouncement was almost unbearable. Our whole family was in a state of shock. Our pain grew more intense when the medical staff said that since these were injuries consistent with child abuse, they had called in investigators. The investigators questioned persons that were alone with Natalia over the preceding days. That included parents, Barb and Brant, and grandmother, Elaine.

Natalia made good progress fairly quickly, coming off the ventilator and gradually being unhooked from all monitors. A feeding tube was put in and she no longer needed intensive care. Improvements, however, were mostly in brain stem functioning. Natalia was moved to St. Vincents Hospital Rehab Center in Indianapolis. There she seemed to improve at first, again in mostly brain stem activity. Lately, however, improvement has slowed and further rehabilitation is being questioned.

This week, charges were entered against Barb and Elaine, and both were arrested. They both are currently free on bond. We are very concerned about these charges, not because they are accurate, but because they are very serious. Elaine faces the possibility of up to 20 years in prison, and Barb up to 40 years. We do have a criminal attorney hired and are thankful for his experience with the judicial system in South Bend. But this is a very, very difficult time for us.

There is much we **do not know** about what is happening. It often feels that things are out of control. What we **do know** to be true is:

That Elaine has never knowingly done anything harmful to Natalia; and that Elaine does not have more information about the situation that she is withholding from investigators.

What we **believe** to be true is:

That neither Barb nor Brant has intentionally harmed Natalia. We have only seen them as caring, loving parents of both children.

Yet Natalia's injuries (or condition) is still there. And we have no explanation for it. The medical staff and investigative staff believe firmly that it could have been caused by nothing other than abuse. Nothing else has even been explored as far as we know. (One of our ongoing problems has been our inability to see any of the hospital medical records at this point.)

Many of you have asked what you might do to be helpful in this situation. We struggle with the same question. Certainly the strongest positive in this whole nightmare has been the overwhelming support we have felt from you through your prayers, cards, e-mails, phone and personal contacts, and other expressions of love, care, and concern. In the midst of our deep pain and ongoing grief, you have lifted us. We feel truly blessed and are grateful to be a part of a community like this. Some have asked if we could use material or financial support. That is not a need right now, but could become a need. We will try to honestly weigh that need with the ministerial staff if/when it occurs. If other needs arise for which we think you may be helpful, we will try to make that known, too. Thank you so much for your willingness to help in many different ways.

We are hoping to remain faithful in the midst of a judicial system that often functions on a different set of values than ours. Part of that difference for us includes letting our "yes be yes" and our "no be no" at all times, not just when we are under the oath of the court.

Unfortunately, these matters move through the courts at a snail's pace. We have been told to expect from four to six months more of the same. Right now that seems like an eternity.

We value your continued prayers on our behalf.

Dan and Elaine Schrock

The outpouring of love from the congregation was overwhelming. They hugged us, wept with us, assured us of their support, and encouraged us. We knew right then that we had made the right decision in being as totally open as we could with them. This was essentially the beginning of a long, long walk for the congregation and for us. We were in it together. The church was being the church. And I don't know how we would have survived otherwise.

Meanwhile, Barb had only lived with the friends down the street for several days when Brant again issued an ultimatum. These were friends of both Barb and Brant, and in his mind their allowing Barb to stay with them indicated a choosing of sides. She must leave. At that point Barb had no where to go. Outside of us, her closest friends were mostly Brant's extended family and friends. Barb did not consciously make that choice. It had more to do with geography. Our extended family lived throughout the U.S. Brant's was nearby. So when Brant's family, and gradually Brant, turned against Barb, she was very much alone. We invited Barb to stay with us in Goshen for "several weeks" while things got sorted out. Little did we know that "several weeks" would stretch into three and a half years.

We made a place for Barb to sleep in our basement. It was a comfortable space. But living together again after nearly 15 years meant some major adjustments both for Barb, and for Elaine and me. We shared a bathroom and kitchen. With some mutual sacrifices, however, things went reasonably well. And it was good for us to get to know Barb better as an adult. She had developed some strengths we had not known about.

Family Court was held in another building in a different part of South Bend from the Criminal Court. This is where the (DCS) is also located. Since Natalia was now a temporary ward of the state, Barb needed to pay child support to the state for Natalia's care. And Brant had successfully received temporary parental custody of Isabella. So Barb needed to pay child support to Brant for her, too. The magistrate sitting on the bench for this case somehow was confused from the very beginning concerning where the children were. He somehow got it into his head that both children were living with Brant. The DCS attorney tried to correct his understanding on this, but this confusion was never really resolved. Consequently, Brant paid nothing towards Natalia's support.

Barb was ordered to pay $73.24 per week in child support, to be divided equally between Isabella and Natalia, when she got a job. Barb, however, had no income at this point. She had stayed at home to take of the children. Now, all of a sudden, she had to pay her own way in life, including child support. All of this she was willing to do. But hunting for a job in a new community while having felony charges is a formidable task. Yet Barb managed to find a job in housekeeping at the Goshen General Hospital within six weeks. They hired her knowing of her charges, and for that we will always be grateful. She earned $9.85 an hour, plus benefits. This allowed her to help support her girls financially.

Barb requested visitation with Natalia numerous times through the DCS. But always she was turned down. That was very difficult for Barb, even though she had only known Natalia for about ten weeks. Isabella, on the other hand, and Barb were very close. They had spent nearly three years together daily, and both bloomed in that relationship. Now she was requesting from the Family Court a weekly visit with Isabella. Brant fought this with all of the strength he could muster. Somehow in Brant's mind, Barb apparently posed a serious physical threat to Isabella. Or he simply wanted to retaliate for what he thought she had done to Natalia. The magistrate felt that having Isabella visit her mother was extremely important. He suggested that it happen in a neutral setting. But Brant did not want this. Finally the magistrate ordered visitation of Isabella and Barb for four to six hours a week at Families First in South Bend, an organization that arranges for supervised visits at their facility. And Brant would need to pay half of the cost for that visitation.

From the outset of this arrangement Brant resisted. Either Isabella was sick, or she had to attend the county fair with the family, or she didn't feel like seeing her mother, or they were out of town. Many times Barb would drive over to South Bend only to discover that Isabella was not there. Families First tried to get Brant to let them know in advance when Isabella wasn't going to be there, but it was not their responsibility to make Brant bring her. Other times he would show up late, or pick up Isabella early before the end of a visit. Barb's only recourse was to go back to court and have him found in contempt. But that would take another $1000 or more of attorney fees ($200 per hour) for a court appearance, which she couldn't afford. It was already costing $40 an hour just for the Families First fees. And things might change with a contempt citation, or they might not. But one thing would certainly change if Barb were to go to court over this. Brant would become even more recalcitrant.

So the visitations limped along. Notes taken by Families First indicated that Barb and Isabella enjoyed their contacts immensely. That part of the process was working. But after several months of Brant's not paying his half of the visitation, Families First met with Barb and said visits could not continue without his payments. Barb needed to decide whether to go to court to get Brant to comply with the court order, or pay the full amount herself. Barb was bringing home an average of $275 a week from her hospital work. But now with $73 a week in child support payments, and $160 a week for four hours of Families First visits with Isabella, plus another $30 a week in transportation costs to get to South Bend and back, Barb had $12 a week left for food, housing, clothing, transportation, medical expenses, etc. Although the criminal trial that was originally set for February 2006 had now been postponed until May, Elaine and I still felt we could assist her through those months. Little did we know that the trial would not take place for years.

After another month or so Barb got a letter in the mail indicating that Brant had somehow decided Barb was making more money than she had declared to the court and was asking for another hearing. *Brant! How are you and Barb going to pay the $200 per hour that family court attorneys charge?* I went to Jim, our criminal attorney, and showed him all of Barb's payroll stubs and asked if he could help. This was not Jim's area of expertise or interest. He said I could present this to the family court magistrate and it would likely have more impact than if he did it. That sounded okay to me, but I still wondered if I would be allowed to do that. Just to be sure, I went to the DCS finance officer who determines what is reasonable support in these matters. She was very kind and helpful, and also offered that the magistrate was often an understanding person. I should just show him the payment stubs.

Our court date came, and Brant and his attorney, and Barb and I went up before the magistrate. Brant's attorney introduced himself as Spence Walton, and said he would be representing Brant. I introduced myself, and said that I would be representing Barb. The magistrate looked at me and asked if I was a licensed attorney. I said that I was not, but that I was there to provide necessary information for her. The magistrate's response was, "You may not speak." *Thanks, Jim and DCS financial officer. You got me into this. I guess I have just been humbled.* Mr. Walton presented Brant's contention that Barb was earning more than she had reported to the court. Since I was not allowed to speak, I shook my head rather briefly and reflexively to his comment. *Mistake number two.* Now the magistrate barked out to me, "You go back there" (pointing to an area of the courtroom) "and sit down." I headed to the area he had suggested with my tail between my legs and sat down. Mr. Walton continued and received court permission to get copies of Barb's pay stubs from the hospital. I had them right there in my folder, but no one seemed to care about that.

A week or so later Barb received a letter in the mail from Mr. Walton requesting the mailing address of the Goshen General Hospital. She sent a letter back to Mr. Walton giving him the address information. He then wrote to the hospital and requested Barb's pay stub information. Six weeks later the pay Barb originally reported to the courts was determined to be accurate. (Some time later I was looking around the halls of the Criminal Court building downtown South Bend and found that Mr. Walton, Brant's attorney, previously had been a judge there for quite a few years.) *I wonder if the family court magistrate might have been aware of that?* Well, at least my brief attorney resume will indicate that I went up against the best.

Our trips to the family court were frequent. Since that is where DCS was located, there were numerous meetings with them in conference rooms. Courtroom #1 was where Barb went when issues concerning Natalia needed resolution. This courtroom was presided over by a judge that had previously been the mayor of South Bend. Courtroom #2 dealt with issues concerning Isabella and was the jurisdiction of the magistrate referred to earlier. This separation of jurisdiction never was clear to us for the first year or two. The confusion of the magistrate's believing that both Natalia and Isabella were living with Brant contributed to this lack of clarity for everyone.

The court appointed a CASA worker to represent Natalia. Court Appointed Special Advocates (CASA) can be very helpful in speaking up for a child's needs when the child is unable to do so. CASA workers are volunteers from whom no particular professional expertise is required. They just care about the welfare of children. So far so good. But the CASA worker assigned to Natalia---Paula---, took her involvement to an aggressive leadership role. That type of role seemed well beyond her arena of competence or her assignment. I remember attending DCS meetings where Natalia's caseworker would start out leading the case conference, only to be overruled by Paula who would end up leading the meeting. That happened more than once, and I'm sure was frustrating to the caseworker. Within the first week Paula apparently became convinced of Barb's guilt. From that point onward, she dropped her early declaration of neutrality and began sitting at all DCS meetings with Brant, his family, and Natalia's foster mother. In the court lobby she was always part of Brant's family group. And later she would attend Barb's trial and sit with the prosecution team. *I wonder whatever happened to the American judicial maxim of "innocent until proven guilty." Must have just been a cliché.* Actually, one of our defense attorneys shed some light on this. He said that in the eyes of most of society you are "innocent until <u>charged</u>."

After the judge in Courtroom #1 had declared Natalia a temporary ward of the state, DCS asked Barb to get counseling and do psychological testing. If Barb neglected to do this, Natalia could become a permanent ward of the state. DCS indicated they would pay for it if Barb went to Holy Cross for counseling. Barb set up an appointment with Holy Cross and went. The therapist asked her what she would like help with, and Barb responded that she was seriously missing her children. They worked at that for 4-6 weeks and then decided that there was no more help that could be given. It later showed up in the CASA worker's report that the sessions were terminated because they were "unproductive." As a former counselor, I asked at one of the meetings what outcome they (DCS) were looking for that would have made the sessions "productive." There was no answer given to that question. One wonders if their idea of "counseling" was for Barb to work on the areas they felt made her "smash Natalia's head against the wall," or were even hoping for a confession. Anyway, the sessions were "unproductive."

DCS had offered to pay for counseling for Isabella, also at Holy Cross. We felt good about that because she was undoubtedly feeling deeply troubled at being separated from her mom in this way. And Barb, when visiting at Families First, was not allowed to say anything to Isabella about why she could no longer live with her. One week, however, an emergency court hearing was asked for by Brant in Courtroom #2. Allegations were presented that Isabella had indicated to the counselor that she had seen Barb hurt Natalia, and Brant was requesting immediate stoppage of Barb's visiting of Isabella at Families First.

When we read the document containing the allegations, it seemed like Paula's figurative fingerprints were all over it. DCS was also asking for visitation termination. Barb was to report to Courtroom #2 in a few days. With my experience as a counselor, and Elaine's as a school nurse, we recognized immediately the problem of taking what a two-year-old might or might not have indicated verbally or through play therapy at face value. Or what she might have heard at home while living with Brant. We crafted what we believed to be a thoughtful, non-threatening email to the CASA office stating our concerns, with hopes they might reconsider their action.

When we arrived at Courtroom #2, Barb went up front, and Elaine and I sat on the benches at the back. The magistrate entered, we all rose, and then sat down when he gave us permission. He began his remarks by saying he saw that Natalia's grandparents were in the courtroom and that it was his understanding that we had written an email to the CASA office. While he indicated that he had not read the email, he warned us sternly that he would charge us with harassment if we were to speak with the CASA again. *He*

35

hasn't read our email, and yet he threatens us with harassment? Paula must have gotten to him behind closed doors. How else would he even know that there <u>was</u> an email?

Barb and Isabella

The hearing proceeded. A young caseworker from Holy Cross took the stand and basically said that Isabella had indicated to her Barb had hurt Natalia. The magistrate listened carefully. After a few questions, she was dismissed. Fortunately, we had asked a child psychiatrist to be present at this hearing to review the research and to give his own understanding of comments made by a two-year-old. He shared in a helpful way that two-year-olds have a moveable boundary between reality and fantasy, and that it is not possible to know for certain when they are in which realm. Reality and fantasy tend to merge together for them, and it all seems real. That's why you get some really strange stories out the mouths of two-year-olds. Research literature was cited to back up his point. The magistrate again listened carefully. He issued a decision that Barb's visits with Isabella should continue. *Hallelujah!*

More that a year later another case conference was held at the DCS. Barb had been requesting visits with Natalia for nearly two years. Always she was turned down, but never with a solid reason. Most often Paula would just say the foster mother, Cynthia, did not want Barb in her house. This time, however, there was a new caseworker. She insisted that Indiana state law requires that Barb have the right to visit her child. If the foster mother, Cynthia, did not want Barb in her home, then supervised visits could take place in a social service agency within a few miles of her home. Apparently things got rather heated as the new caseworker, who was sitting beside Barb, stated that visitation would happen, while Cynthia, Brant, and Paula seemed unable to dissuade her. Brant and his family had always been welcomed into Cynthia's home to visit Natalia. But not Barb. Now, (according to Barb), Brant made some loud, colorful comments and stormed out of the room. A first visitation time for Barb and Natalia was to be set up, and a schedule of visits to occur over the coming months was also to be arranged. Barb came home elated, not only because she would get to visit Natalia, but also that someone from among all of the people in Brant's family, the foster mother, the CASA worker, and DCS caseworkers had actually supported her. She eagerly anticipated her coming visits with Natalia.

When the day came for her first visit, Barb and Elaine drove the nearly 90 miles to the social service agency where it was to be held. Elaine had no permission to visit Natalia, but went along because she knew it would be an emotional experience for Barb on the way home. Barb had a very good visit, and it <u>was</u> very emotional. Elaine stayed in the car during the visit, but caught a glimpse of someone in the distance that she thought to be Natalia. There was much to talk about on the way back to Goshen.

At the next periodic status hearing on Natalia in Courtroom #1, all of the important players were there. Documents sent out ahead of the meeting indicated the routine nature of this meeting. Any requested changes were to be in writing ahead of the status hearing. None were listed. But in the middle of this hearing, the foster mother, Cynthia, requested that the judge stop all future visits by Barb. She had concerns that Natalia might vomit when she traveled. (And that <u>was</u> possible). But is was only a few miles, not like trips to Indianapolis or other places Cynthia took Natalia. Her second reason for wanting the visits stopped was that <u>Natalia gets no benefit</u> from the visits. *Would that not be true for Brant's visits, and his parents visits? And could a third reason be that she wanted to adopt Natalia as she had with other needy children she had kept as a foster mother? Barb would only get in the way of that.* Anyway, the Judge appeared to rather arbitrarily grant Cynthia's request, and stopped all future visits. Barb was devastated. "Can he do that?" she asked the caseworker after the hearing. "He did it" replied the caseworker. It certainly seemed to us that this foster mother was given much more authority than any I had ever dealt with when I was serving as a case worker.

At the next scheduled DCS meeting, the caseworker who had supported Barb, was no longer there. We hoped she chose to leave on her own, but fear her support of Barb might have cost her the job. She seemed more genuinely interested in the needs of the child and family, and less interested in predetermining guilt or innocence, than some from DCS that we encountered. Our appreciation for her remains high, and perhaps someday we'll be able to thank her.

Barb and Natalia

CHAPTER FOUR

Looking back at that first week after Natalia was taken to the ER, we wondered how the prosecutor could bring charges against <u>anyone</u> without having facts (1) to establish firmly that a crime was committed, and (2) to point out clearly who did it. Charges <u>were</u> filed against Barb and Elaine, however, and our attorney, Jim, confidently informed us that this case will be decided <u>on perception</u>, <u>not on fact</u>. After thinking about that for a while, Elaine and I nervously agreed with him. There was no other way.

If one looks at the status of the "shaken baby" theory today, it is far from a settled matter. Well, many doctors, particularly pediatricians, would disagree with my statement. It <u>is</u> settled for them. They are so firm in their belief of this theory that there is simply no room for any questions concerning it. They can be nowhere near the setting in which something happened, yet somehow divine the history of that situation. <u>What</u> happened, <u>how</u> it happened, and <u>when</u> it happened are stated unambiguously in court, without any doubt at all. But why such extreme clarity on this one area? *I need to find such a doctor for all the misdiagnoses I have received in my lifetime.* (I will state here that I have quite a number of friends who are medical doctors. At one point I considered medicine myself, since I wanted to help others, too. Doctors are largely people who care... and care deeply. Many are humble, and know the limits of what medicine can, and cannot, answer.) But because the courtroom requires certainty--- on this particular subject--- medical certainty is delivered. Strong caring for children turns opinion into unchallengeable fact. One of the members of the International Advisory Board of the National Center on Shaken Baby serves as an example of this total certainty when she says she would convict a member of her own family based on it (shaken baby theory). *Can't get any more certain than that. Or is this a response intended to slow down the increasing questions and challenges to this diagnosis?*

Was there definitely a crime committed here? Many well respected doctors and scientists have challenged the believers within the medical community to approach this shaken baby theory a little less rabidly. Work very hard at prevention. Make certain all possible diagnoses are considered. But don't say things as a certainty that are not scientifically demonstrable. When many doctors <u>inside</u> the medical community do not agree with each other, and many scientists <u>outside</u> disagree with convinced doctors, it's not because one side is lying and the other side is telling the truth. These professionals <u>all</u> believe they are correct and telling the truth. So why is a lay jury, normally with absolutely no medical expertise, asked to determine who is telling the truth? No one is intentionally lying.

Elaine, I, and our attorney assumed that the strategy for the prosecutor likely would be to use a team of doctors who were willing to make strong statements in court, and have Brant's family throw up as much circumstantial stuff as they could, hoping that the jury might convict. And we were correct. There were no witnesses to a shaking. We don't even know what happened for certain, or if there was a crime. Many people in society, including Elaine and me, have very strong feelings when children are hurt intentionally. And we do believe that babies are abused, sometimes in a manner threatening to their life and health. We strongly support preventive programs. We know putting a child back into a knowingly abusive home is risky. But we've also become painfully aware of the damage done to families where abuse is alleged, and then prosecuted using a theory that keeps changing as new research is done. It is our feeling that it is time to halt the prosecution of these cases, with the exception of those having non-coerced confessions or witnesses to the shaking, until medicine, science, and law can come together to quell the controversy and set some acceptable, safeguarded standards.

Given the current highly politicized and emotional scenario over shaken baby theory, Barb, Elaine, and I decided to ask for a "bench trial" for our case. This would allow a judge to decide innocence or guilt without a jury present. We felt this type of trial would eliminate a large part of the emotion any jury would bring to it, and concentrate more on the facts. Defense attorneys, however, rarely, if ever, want a bench trial. They have confidence in their ability to convince at least some members of a jury that their client is innocent. That was no different with our attorney. But the more we talked with Jim, the more he began so see that the community hype in this type of case would be a strong factor, perhaps the strongest factor, in any decision made. He gradually agreed with us that a bench trial would be best, and requested it. We were thankful and felt somewhat relieved that he took that position. The judge assigned to the case also agreed to conduct a bench trial. Great. That left the prosecutor yet to decide. He agreed at first, but in a few days reversed his decision and indicated that he did not want a bench trial after all. At that point we were assured what the prosecution's strategy would be. And it didn't feel right, or fair. Justice should be about fact, not emotion.

Putting any case in a "shaken baby" context appears to give it that black and white clarity that we all desire. According to the "shaken baby" theory, it is all very simple. The "answers" just emerge from the pre-set

40

formula. "Guilt" is a matter of being present, not necessarily of evidence presented. If a baby shows up at the ER with bleeding in the brain, retinal hemorrhages (bleeding in the eyes), brain swelling, and possibly broken bones and bruises, with no logical explanation of how these symptoms came about, the person who was with the baby last is the party guilty of causing these injuries. In a sad, sad way it is very much like playing "musical chairs" within the justice system. The last person left standing without a chair when the music stops is guilty.

This theory was first defined by radiologist Dr. John Caffey in 1972, based upon "research" done in the 1950's and 1960's. Today most pediatricians have been taught this theory and many accept it. Some even rather fanatically promote it. (If it were scientifically clear and replicable, it seems you wouldn't need to promote it.) In essence, we have a political "scientific" theory that has its own set of lobbyists. There are even people who go around the country to influence judges, prosecutors, and police of their particular viewpoint, so that viewpoint might have a better chance of "winning" in the courtroom, with ever diminishing amounts of actual evidence needed.

Nevertheless, a backlash has been happening in more recent years. An increasing number of pediatricians, doctors from other medical specialties, even more members of the scientific community, and those working within the justice system who strongly challenge this theory and the research behind it. One only needs to check out this "shaken baby" controversy on the internet to see that some judges are not allowing this theory into the courtroom, that conferences are being called to discuss it, that "innocence projects" are growing throughout the U.S. that focus solely on "shaken baby" convictions, and that leading law professors are suggesting that courts stop prosecuting "shaken baby" cases until the scientific community is able to do more helpful research. The province of Ontario is reviewing all shaken baby cases over the last 20 years, and England has reviewed numerous cases also.

In our daughter Barb's case, this controversy among doctors was barely mentioned. That was largely a shortcoming of our own making. Later in this book I will say more about that. The prosecution took the traditional "shaken baby" concepts and ran with them. The doctors "diagnosed" that a crime had taken place, and the police took a look at the last 12-24 hours to see who did it. Within the first few hours it became clear to police that Barb, the stay-at-home-mother would be the easiest to build a case against. She, admittedly, had more time with Natalia than anyone else.

We had seen, on one of the first nights after Natalia went to the ER, television news showing pictures of Barb and Brant's home with yellow tape around the perimeter. A "crime" had been committed. Next were statements that Natalia's injuries were "non-accidental." Other comments by police were attributed to Barb that were totally untruthful, and gave the impression of a mother with no credibility or feelings. Then the community was left to reflect on this horrible crime for several weeks. And it worked. The community grew into a frenzy over this despicable act, and a note was put on Barb's car at home that said, "We know who you are and we know where you live. And we don't like child abusers." (No trial needed!)

Once charges were brought against Barb and Elaine, the television and newspapers were filled with more images and stories designed to give the impression of guilt. Mug shots were another part of the technique. Included among the pictures in this book are Barb's and Elaine's mug shots, along with more normal photos of them. Each day that these mug shots were put before the public was one more day in which the community could more and more easily believe that these people were guilty. Even I was scared of the people in these mug shots. *Wow! They look like they could tear little babies apart with their bare teeth.* This whole scenario of mug shots, inaccurate information given to the press, yellow tape around the house shouted one verdict. GUILTY. We needed reassurance that "innocent until proven guilty" was still in effect. Elaine was unable to renew her teaching license (she held both a nursing license and a teaching license as a school nurse). She was assumed to be guilty. And that's certainly how it felt whenever we were in South Bend.

The heaviness of having two out of the three of us in our home facing trial for felony charges was palpable. Not being able to see Natalia, and having only limited contact with Isabella, was equally hard to bear. But we were blessed with many, many friends and a church that cared about us. Most days we were able to sense God's presence either directly, or through God's people. And that made all the difference. We were not alone.

Many of those closest to us were shocked as much as we were at what was happening right before our eyes. Knowing what to do to stop this runaway train was as difficult for them as it was for us. While they weren't able to stop the train, they certainly came up with many varied ways to show their support for us. And we tried our best to keep them updated on the situation.

Home > News > Story

Mother and grandmother plea not guilty for injury of baby

Print   Email   RSS

Posted: 08/31/2005 04:27 pm
Last Updated: 08/31/2005 05:05 pm

St. Joseph County, IN - A mother and grandmother accused in the injury of a baby appeared in a St. Joseph County courtroom Wednesday.

Thirty-three-year-old Barbara Schrock and 60-year-old Elaine Schrock entered an automatic plea of not guilty Wednesday. Both woman face charges stemming from injuries to Schrock's three-month old.

The baby was taken to the hospital in July with a fractured skull, detached retina, broken ribs and broken forearms.

The women will appear in court for their initial hearing on September 27th.

Barbara Schrock   Elaine Schrock

More news from St. Joseph County, IN

Back to news | Archives | News in your town | News in Pictures

Looking for a job? Visit JobsMichiana.com

Free Classifieds
Autos, Houses, Rentals and Merchandise.
Find or sell them in our free classifieds.

Barbara and Elaine mug shots

College Mennonite Church is gifted with many professional, business, and educational leaders. One of the first things we did was ask the church to set up what we called a "Reference Group" of members who would meet periodically to give us counsel and direction. In this group were medical doctors, nurses, therapists, ministers, and educators. They offered valuable guidance to us throughout the entire ordeal. We continue to be thankful for each one of them.

Elaine and I had grown up with the idea that police were people whom you could trust. We believed in that concept, and our experience, although limited, had largely born that out. We even argued to that effect with our attorney. I still believe in that general idea, but now in a more limited way. Several months after this all started, we received from the prosecutor's office "discovery" materials that included audio and videotaped interviews of all the persons talked to by police. Once I listened to those tapes, I couldn't believe what I was hearing. The police were taking what was said to them and either distorting it, or making up things that were never even said at all. It was at this point that I lost some of my naivete. These people weren't after the truth, they were after a conviction. It was also at this point that I began to understand what we heard our attorneys say throughout. "Don't talk to them." This was difficult for me, personally, as a counselor. But now I could see why it wouldn't help to talk to them. Somehow, all of this was not surprising to Jim, our attorney. And that, too, was a concern for us. This must be the norm.

Right then I decided we had to do something to expose in court what was on these tapes. There must be people in whatever jury is selected who would be as repulsed by these distortions as I am. But Jim said we would have to play the whole interview tape to a jury and could not stop to point out anything specific to them. Then, well before the tapes would be finished playing, the jury would be asleep. So, unfortunately, we never played them. That didn't stop one or two jurors at the actual trial from nodding off anyway.

The more I listened to those tapes, though, the more I became incensed at what the police were doing. The doctors made the diagnosis of a crime based totally on the shaken baby theory, but the police controlled the conversation and "evidence." Several times the police investigators said, "the doctors hear what we tell them." (One can suppose that the doctors also didn't hear what the police didn't tell them.) And most of what was said in those interviews never became public. To me, the term "witness tampering" was always associated with someone trying to coerce a witness into testifying dishonestly in a court case. But I was beginning to see another side to that term. Is it not also "witness tampering" for police to make dishonest and character eroding statements about one suspect to other possible suspects (who may also be <u>potential</u> witnesses), in an attempt to get those persons angry enough to <u>become</u> witnesses? Anyway, that is what happened. And one of the doctors gathered potential witnesses in a room to tell them about Natalia's medical conditions and medical history, and how it all happened and when it happened---- all things that should have been safeguarded by the HIPAA laws. Much of this same medical information and police information was then later fed back in the courtroom as "testimony" by those very family members who now had become witnesses.

As time passed by, I had increasing difficulty remembering everything that was said in those police interviews. They included approximately 11 hours of verbatim conversation. Trying to find a small item you wanted from a videotape was time consuming and frustrating. Trying to find things on multiple videotapes was totally mindboggling. I finally decided I needed to transcribe those tapes into print. That turned out to be no small task, particularly since I'm not much of a typist. And I had no transcribing equipment--- just a video playback machine, an audio playback, and a computer. It took hundreds and hundreds of hours running the videotape one phrase at a time, then stopping it, and typing what was said. The end result was 158 single spaced pages of quoting every word that was said in the police interviews. But even then it was a bit unwieldy. Reading through all 158 pages every time you wanted to find a particular item was also tedious. Consequently, I picked out 73 topics that seemed relevant to the case, and made an <u>index</u> showing multiple page numbers for each item. That meant reading through all transcribed interviews a minimum of eight to ten times to find where each item was mentioned. By the time I had completed this project, I pretty well had in my mind everything that was said in those police interviews, who said it, and where to locate it. I made an extra copy for Jim, who found the transcriptions to be extremely helpful, and used them extensively.

The interviews revealed clearly that the doctors and police were focused on the last 2-24 hours. Later, as I learned more about shaken baby theory, I understood why. But for now, my main observation was that there was <u>never any hesitancy</u> by the doctors that this was a "crime." Both Dr. O and Dr. E had said so with their <u>diagnoses</u>. Police parroted it back to all of us. "No doubt" was a favorite phrase. I had never heard doctors talk with this level of certainty before regarding <u>anything</u>. Dr. E was the most forceful and certain in his language. He would state the following later at trial:

"It was very clear my very first day......<u>without any doubt</u>, this child suffered a non-accidental injury."

"...once you know what it is, it's not hard to pick out at all." (shaken baby characteristics)

"There is no doubt, not one iota." (Dr. E used 'no doubt' at least six times during testimony)

Meanwhile, Sgt. Kaps and Lt. Richmond, the police investigators, were honing in on the last 24 hours with the three people they interviewed on day one: (Barb, Elaine, and Brant). Examples:

Sgt K: "As far as the head injuries, those are recent...within the last day."

Sgt K: "..could be immediate, or within 2 to 24 hours."

Sgt K: "the doctor is saying it happened within the last 24 hours."

Barb, in her interview, seemed confused over this timing as it related to symptoms she had seen in Natalia.

Barb: "My mother and I both saw her ...that's why I'm really confused when she (Dr. O) says the last 24 hours."

Sgt K: "That puts the baby with you and your mother."

Barb: "Yes. Let's see. Monday..."

Sgt K: "That's more than 24 hours." *Don't talk about Monday. This happened Tuesday or later.*

Barb: ...Monday I took Bella to Long John Silvers. And Brant was home with her..."

Sgt K: "We're just going to Tuesday morning. It was you or your mother." *This case is now four hours old, and Sgt. K is making statements like this.*

Brant was also confused by this shaken baby timeline of the last 24 hours in his interview with Lt. R, as he described how Natalia's ongoing symptoms dramatically increased around the July 4 weekend.

Brant: "We were concerned about her eyes. That's the first thing we noticed. That was the July 2 party....that weekend. And I don't know if one of the kids got a hold of her and somehow shook her.."

Lt R: "With all the technology that the doctors have, July 2, I think, is totally out of the ballpark." (This was three to four weeks earlier than their 2-24 hours timeline. Yet, two years later in the courtroom, the state's own expert doctor would say three to four weeks was the likely timing of the major massive brain injury. But police picked their suspects from the 2-24 hour time frame.)

Brant: "You think so?"

Lt R: "They're saying from what they can see from their scans, that this thing happened within, like they told you, the last 24-48 hours...they're thinking that the bleeding to the brain occurred." (Lt. R uses 24-48 hours for the first time here).

Brant: "But we noticed her eyes looked the way they did on Sunday, July 3. So I just don't understand...I just don't understand none of this, really." *None of us do, Brant.*

Lt R: "I know the doctors are going to be looking really hard at the last 48 hours."

This timing reflects the "shaken baby" doctrine that there is no lucid interval, meaning that symptoms happen almost immediately. There is no period of time between the injury and the emerging symptoms. So find the person who was there most recently. As Sgt. K later responded to the question at trial, "On July 27 (day one) you were pretty confident you had your person (Barb)?" "Yes, I was very confident." (And yet, Barb, Elaine, and Brant were all there within the last 24 hours. And as the police would find out later, Natalia's massive brain injury was already three to four weeks old by then.)

The problem for police in building a case, however circumstantial, against Barb was how to get Brant and his family, who were supporting Barb, to turn against her. The police needed witnesses who would say something against her---anything--- and Brant wasn't helping their case.

Brant: (Comments made to the police)

"After I found out today the injuries Natalia sustained, I asked Barb, 'Did you do anything to our kid?' She said, 'Absolutely not.' I 100% believe her. Barb has never lied to me."

"I honestly believe she would tell you (if she did something to Natalia)."

"Barb's real good with kids."

"She's done a great job. I've never seen any kind of abuse. The house is always clean. The dishes were always done. The kids always had a bath. They were always in decent clothes."

Lt R: "You guys kept Natalia in your bedroom most of the time...that's where she slept?"

Brant: "Oh yeah."   (Barb's having Natalia right beside her in the bedroom hurt police attempts to characterize Barb as a non-caring, non-loving mother who didn't want Natalia around her).

Lt R: "Did Natalia sleep a lot? Was she fussy?"

Brant: "I don't think out of the ordinary." ("Shaken baby" dogma alleges a fussy baby, and a parent who shakes the baby out of frustration. Actually none of us who kept Natalia would say she was a fussy baby.)

So Brant was not particularly helpful to the police. Maybe Brant's parents could help turn him. (Char and Gary were interviewed on Friday, two days after Brant, Barb, and Elaine. They were not considered suspects because they were not around Natalia in the last 24 hours.) But they, too, had a difficult time seeing Barb as someone who would hurt Natalia.

Sgt K: "The baby is suffering from <u>shaken baby syndrome</u>."

Char: "I can't imagine that."

Sgt K: "I know. It's hard for everybody to believe. But there's <u>no doubt</u> about it."

Char: "Why would she do that, and didn't to Isabella?" (She has already been told that Barb is the suspect).

Sgt K: "According to her and everybody we've talked to so far, <u>she was suffering from postpartum depression</u> (PPD)."

Char: "This can't be anything wrong with the baby without her doing anything?"

Sgt K: "No."

Char: "Wouldn't she (Natalia) have cried if she had a broken rib?"

Sgt K: "Not necessarily."

Char: "If she was shaking the baby, wouldn't she (Natalia) have a broken neck, as little as her neck is... or anything?"

Sgt K: "I've never had a case of shaken baby syndrome where the neck has even been damaged." (This follows shaken baby theory, but is changing somewhat more recently.)

Char: "If she had broken bones, wouldn't she have had black and blue marks?"

Sgt K: "No." (Actually, he's right this time. These aren't broken bones like you and I know about. These are tiny bone splinters, or chips at the end of a long bone that are hardly noticeable. Some radiologists see them, others do not.)

Char: "I didn't see anything. Otherwise I would have got her (Natalia) out of there."

As I wrote in an earlier chapter, Char and Gary, didn't know Elaine and me all that well, but they knew Barb. They couldn't imagine her doing this. Yet, as they are confronted by doctors and police who over and over again say it was either Barb or your son, Brant, that hurt Natalia, it gradually got easier for them to believe that Barb was the one. They trusted the police, too.

> Gary: "As God is my witness, I know Brant wouldn't touch those babies."
>
> Char: "If there was something going on, I know for sure that it wasn't my son."
>
> Gary: "He's proud of his kids. He loves his kids."
>
> Char: "I mean, if we know it's between Brant and Barb, and we <u>know</u> Brant didn't do it. He wouldn't be capable of that."

Here's where the police begin to make it easier for everyone to believe that Barb did this to Natalia. They consciously feed future potential witnesses inaccurate "facts" that would undermine Barb's (and later Elaine's) credibility. As a counselor I have learned not to call statements "lies" unless I have undeniable proof. So I'll let you decide for yourself. At the very start of Char and Gary's police interview Char pulled out recently developed photos of Natalia to show Sgt. K.

> Sgt K: "She's crying in that picture.... Can we have reprints of any of these?.....I'll tell you the reason why..... Barbara has told us that the baby never cried at all....I mean she said the baby didn't cry, period......<u>Never cried</u>."
>
> (Barb's actual comments from five or six places throughout her police interview: "she cried a little bit," "she was kinda crying a lot," "she just cried a little bit this morning," "but she started crying," "she made a little crying sound.")

But Char and Gary are being told something far different from what Barb actually said. What was their reaction? Later in their interview Sgt. K left the room for a while and Char and Gary talked to each other alone:

> Gary: "I wonder why Barb would have told them that the baby never cries. She cries."
>
> Char: "I don't know. Everybody knows babies cry."
>
> Gary: "But what he was saying was that Barb told the detective that Natalia <u>never</u> cries.
> We have a picture of her crying. They all do."
>
> Char: "You would have to be an <u>idiot</u> to think that a baby never cries."

The degradation of Barb's believability, and even her rationality, had begun. And Char and Gary are beginning to turn. Following are more of Sgt. K's comments to Char and Gary:

> Sgt K: "From some people we talked to, she didn't want this baby. It was an unplanned pregnancy. <u>She didn't want this baby</u>." (The police had only interviewed Brant, Barb, and Elaine at this point. These people <u>did</u> say the pregnancy was unplanned. But not one of them said anything even remotely close to "she didn't want the baby.")

So what does Char say two years later in trial? She (Barb) told me she "wasn't very happy with this pregnancy" and "would be glad to get it (Natalia) out of her." *The police get what they wanted. Feed potential witnesses information, get them mad, and listen to them feed that same information to the jury later.*

> Sgt K (continuing): "She said she stayed up until 2 am, cause she wanted to make sure the child was still breathing. If I am worried about my child breathing, the first thing I am going to do is go to the hospital" (Another comment intended to raise uncertainty and to inflame.)
>
> Char: "She has a thing on the baby's crib, a monitor, that if she quits breathing, the thing goes off."

Barb had <u>actually</u> said to Sgt. K: "I had put my head here to listen to her breathe....so obviously it wasn't erratic, or I would have been able to hear it." (Now, admittedly, parents do vary on how quickly they head to the ER with their children. But Natalia was rushed to the pediatrician four weeks earlier, again with a breathing problem, that was diagnosed as just a sinus infection. And now this time [Tuesday evening] Barb had called her pediatrician just hours earlier that same evening about Natalia's condition, and the pediatrician did not seem overly concerned. She told Barb to set up an appointment in the morning.) Sgt. K again comments to Char and Gary:

> Sgt K: (concerning <u>postpartum depression</u>, a term Barb had used as a <u>label</u> for her feeling of distance from Natalia for a period of time): "In severe cases, she'll (Barb) need some help. But it takes me back to that Andrea Gates in Texas... <u>killed her five kids</u>. She was suffering from PPD <u>with a psychosis</u>." (No one who saw Barb in the last three months observed any psychotic behavior. Neither did the psychiatrist at trial. In fact, most were unaware that Barb was even feeling "detachment" and "lack of bonding" with Natalia from the

50

NICU time. Sgt. K just threw in the PPD "with a psychosis" connection to bring Andrea Gates into the picture to make Char and Gary's hair stand on end, and to further erode their perception of Barb's sanity.)

Later Sgt. K followed up with this comment:

> Sgt K: "I don't even know how they determine PPD. I don't have a clue. The thing that would worry us and the DCS (*and should worry you, too*), is if for some reason this isn't prosecuted, even though 'she loves Isabella to death' (a comment made by Gary), if she gets back in that house, <u>we don't know how far this will go</u>." *Translation: Save Isabella. We don't know when Barb will snap next.*

Other comments by Sgt. K to Char and Gary:

> Sgt K: " I haven't seen anyone who says she (Barb) showed any emotion yet." (Only Brant, Barb, and Elaine were interviewed at this point. Brant and Elaine said nothing about Barb's emotions at the hospital. Barb said she and Brant were crying.)
>
> Char: "She did (cry) yesterday a little bit. But that's another thing. I didn't know if she was in so much shock."
>
> Gary: "I would be hysterical."
>
> Sgt K: "Well, you saw the way your son reacted. <u>We've</u> seen your son's reacting." *He cried.*
>
> Char: "He was devastated." (Brant had told investigators earlier that "I still bawled like a baby when she (Isabella) was born. I'm a very emotional person.")

The difference between Brant's expression of emotion, and Barb's more stoic holding it in much of the time, <u>became a huge issue</u> for police and the prosecutor. The psychiatrist and the prosecution's own pediatricians, however, testified at trial that because people <u>express</u> emotion differently, it doesn't mean they don't <u>feel</u> emotion." Nevertheless, the prosecutor hammered on this throughout the trial. (They needed to absolve Brant, and this was one of the few things police and prosecutor could point to as "facts". Brant cried....Barb, not as much.)

Another attempt to get Char and Gary to question how well they really knew Barb didn't get as far:

Sgt K: "Did you notice there was an absence of any photos of the baby (in the house)?"

Char: "They don't even have a camera. I just got these back."

Gary: "Wasn't Natalia's picture up by the TV? Didn't you guys see that?"

Sgt K: "We didn't see any of Natalia. We didn't see anything out there. There may have been a baby picture up there from when she was first born, but I couldn't tell if that was Natalia or Isabella. Uh..." *I just thought I'd mention it anyway.*

Char: "But that's why. I always supply all the pictures."

Undeterred, he pressed on, sharing "information" intended to help Char and Gary continue to shift from Barb.

Sgt K: "I know we don't want to believe it was Barbara, but it isn't like some stranger was breaking into their house every day. Who was the primary caretaker? Who had the baby the most? Who had the most access to the baby? Who's the one who first started noticing the symptoms and the differences? So far, everything is pointing at Barbara."

Not a very promising outlook for stay-at-home moms. "And we understand that Brant wasn't home a lot. He worked a lot, generally, seven days a week...long hours." (The police begin to make the case for Brant to be written out of the picture.)

Char: "Is JT here today?"

Sgt K: "He's here. But he's not in the office. He's working some other cases." (JT is Lt. R's partner, and a good friend of Brant's family).

Char: "I wanted to see what he looked like after he lost all that weight."

Sgt K: "Gosh he is looking good. Haven't you seen him for a while?"

Char: "Not since his surgery."

Back to business.

Gary: "It's been a concern of her and I...how long this investigation could last."

Sgt K: "I really can't (tell you). Generally we get confessions. Generally the perpetrator of shaken baby is a <u>male</u> figure. Probably 80 percent of the cases. Usually a boyfriend or the natural father. Those are the two top ones. Then you got the babysitter or caretaker. The <u>mothers</u> actually fall into the lower range as far as shaken baby."

Char: "But if you can't talk with her (without attorney permission), how are you going to get her to confess?"

Sgt K: "<u>We don't need her to confess.</u>" *That's the beauty of this theory.*

Char: "How can they say it's her, and not Brant, or Barb's mother (Elaine)?"

Sgt K: "It's gonna be a <u>circumstantial</u> thing, unless we can get Brant or her mother......<u>her</u> <u>mother knows, too</u>." (Absolutely no basis for this statement. Totally made up. But Char and Gary don't know this.)

Gary: "Really?"

Sgt K: "Absolutely! Absolutely!"

Char: "Her mom (Elaine) was up there (PICU) and said 'I can't believe that Barb or Brant, either one, would hurt that baby'."

Investigators tell Char and Gary that they talked with Isabella with DCS workers present.

Sgt K: "We don't expect to find anything wrong with Isabella. Obviously the family was happy with Isabella. It was just the detachment that she (Barb) described that she had to Natalia. She said 'the only thing I really wanted to do with her was just get her changed, give her a bottle, and put her back in bed.'" (This is a fairly accurate quote of what Barb said to Sgt. K --- the same thing she had said to Brant and to Elaine earlier. She wasn't withholding anything from the police. She shared this with them voluntarily, not in response to a question. That <u>is</u> all she <u>wanted</u> to do with Natalia for a few weeks during an uncertain time period. And this is what she referred to as PPD. There really isn't much more you can do with a preemie. But Barb was concerned because she didn't have the depth of attachment to Natalia that she wanted to have.)

Sgt K (continuing): "Well, I can say it....this depression thing. It happens in good families. It happens to people that..."

Gary: "Maybe there's something wrong with her. I don't know."

Char: "It seems like they could give her some test or something."

Sgt K: "That's way out of my field." (Actually, he's correct again. It <u>is</u> way out of his field. He had earlier said to Barb in her interview, "When you hear the word 'depression'....<u>you</u>

53

automatically think that someone wants to hurt themselves or....." *Not a very enlightened understanding of "depression."* But it did give him a reason to bring up Andrea Gates to Char and Gary.)

More comments to raise further doubt about what Char and Gary really know about Barb.

> Sgt K: "You know your son better than I do. You know Barb better than I do....or at least you probably thought you did at one point." *Now maybe I know her better than you do.*
>
> Char: "I told her... there's only two people...you and Brant. And I know my son didn't to it. So who does that leave?"
>
> Gary: "She (Barb) says, 'I know I didn't do nothing.'"
>
> Sgt K: "She's trying to find ways out that are accidental ways out." (These are potential suspects he is talking with.)
>
> Char: "Well, she said, 'I could have told them I accidentally dropped her. But I'm not going to lie about it."
>
> Gary: "She (Barb) said just her (Char) and I went against her. Everybody thinks that...Brant's side of the family thinks that." *Unfortunately for Barb, that is everybody.*

Other comments that indicate that Char and Gary have now been drastically turned against Barb:

> Gary: "Well, if they say she did it, she's gonna have to pay the price" and "if she did this...you know, fry her."
>
> Char: "If you guys find our she did it, I want her to pay for it," and "if she did something, I want her to fry."

The conversation continues:

> Char: ".....cause if she did do this, I want you guys to nail her."
>
> Sgt K: "I can't see anybody else that was capable...I shouldn't say capable....had the opportunity, other than any people in the last 48 hours before she was brought in....who had access." (The time frame with Sgt. K is now the last 48 hours). "We can rule out Brant for sure. I feel comfortable, and my partner feels comfortable, that Brant didn't do this." (The police are now 48 hours into this case, and have ruled out Brant.)
>
> Gary: "I know Brant didn't do this."
>
> Char: "Oh, I know Brant didn't."

Sgt K: "We just need to clear Brant's name out of this. That's what we need to do."

Sgt K: "We've talked to the doctors. The first thing you do is...What's the reaction? Is it a reaction you would normally expect to see? (But these same doctors testified later in trial that you cannot make judgments about the way people respond differently to the same circumstance.") *Someone is not telling the truth here.*

Char: " I know in my heart that Brant didn't do it."
Sgt K: "We don't feel he did it either. We've got to eliminate him however we can. I don't think her mother did it, but her mother....we've got to eliminate her, also."
Char: "I'm sure you figured out she didn't do it."
Sgt K: "I've got a good feeling she didn't do it. But then, again, we've gotta look towards the future....and possible defenses. Is it possible they did it?" *What does this mean? Will the charges be based upon what they think the defense approach will be? I guess winning is much more important than the truth.*

Char and Gary are being encouraged to find more information that could clear Brant and implicate Barb. And they need to work on getting Brant to quit supporting Barb. The threat that Brant is still not out of this is offered as incentive:

Sgt K: "If her mom (Elaine) or somebody happens to say something...like you think where did this come from...if you give us a call and let us know...it may raise a lot of red flags with us."
Gary: "If we hear something, I guarantee it, we'll be the first to call you. Like I say, if she did this...you know, fry her."
Sgt K: "The Prosecutor's Office is not convinced that Brant didn't know what was going on. If he had suspicion something was going on, he's just as guilty."
Char: "I don't think he ever saw anything. I think he just believes everything she says about it. I think he really believes her. I don't know if it is because he loves her, or what. I think he just really believes her."
Sgt K: "Like I said, we still haven't proven that he didn't do it. We believe he didn't do it. But believing....and actually showing

that he didn't have anything to do with this....". *When* *did* *they ever prove this?*

Char: "Okay. We'll talk to him."

Gary: "If we come up with anything else..."

Sgt K: "Yeah....if you hear anything, or believe anything..."

Gary: "We'll do what we can do talk to him."

Char: "Are you done with us?"

Sgt K: "Yes."

Char: "They said JT was here. I'd just like to say 'Hi' to him.....and see how much weight he has lost."

Sgt K: "I really don't know, but he has lost quite a bit."

The above police interview was Friday afternoon, July 29, two days after Natalia entered the ER. An hour later or so, Char came into the PICU and began ranting loudly about how Barb had hurt Natalia, and how Elaine knew about it. At the time we were baffled. Now, having read this transcript of Char and Gary's police interview, we understood where that all came from. Then over that same weekend Char rounded up three members of her family (Donna, Sara, and Michelle) that were at the Fourth of July weekend party and had seen Barb for a few hours there.....the only hours they had seen her since Natalia was born....and Char had Lt. R arrange to interview them. Sgt. K went on vacation for two weeks, and was no longer a part of the interview process. But he had done the crucial work of feeding bogus statements and convincing Char and Gary of Barb's guilt, and thus setting into motion their own convincing of Brant.

CHAPTER FIVE

Dr. Simpson was the pediatrician for Isabella and Natalia. She and Barb had developed a good relationship over the years. They trusted each other in the mutual exchange of information. Barb had taken Natalia in for all of her scheduled baby visits. Tuesday afternoon (July 26) Barb had called Dr. Simpson's office and had talked with the receptionist that answered. She told the receptionist (as Elaine listened) what Elaine had observed during her three hours of babysitting that morning and asked Dr. Simpson to call her back. The receptionist wrote a note about the call that included (1) the temperature that Barb reported (93 degrees); (2) Natalia was eating; (3) she was not acting normal; and (4) please call. Later that evening after office hours Dr. Simpson returned Barb's call. They talked about Natalia's condition, and according to Barb, she told Dr. Simpson of her earlier feelings of detachment from Natalia, wondering if that could have caused Natalia to be slow in developing. After a few minutes on the phone Dr. Simpson told Barb to call in to the office in the morning and set up an appointment. Later that evening Natalia's symptoms increased, and they took her early the next morning by ambulance to the ER.

When Dr. Simpson was informed that Natalia had entered PICU, she came to the hospital to see Barb and Natalia. As they talked, Barb shared that the police were looking at her as the person who had hurt Natalia. Dr. Simpson told Barb not to worry, that she would tell the police she is a good mother. That affirmation was reassuring to Barb, but the police hadn't interviewed Dr. Simpson yet. How would they get around Dr. Simpson's support of Barb? They talked to Dr. Simpson late in the afternoon on Friday, after they had finished interviewing Char and Gary. Since they had been successful in turning Char and Gary away from Barb, they used a similar technique on Dr. Simpson.

According to their own police notes, and apparently before Dr. Simpson said anything, the police explained to Dr. Simpson "the details of our interviews with Brant Benson, Barbara Schrock, and Elaine Schrock. Dr. Simpson denied that she instructed or suggested that Barbara toss Natalia Benson into the air to check reflexes." *Of course she denied it. That's because Barb never said that. I've listened to Barb's interview, I've typed it out word by word, and I've read it multiple times since. IT WAS NEVER SAID!* (A few times during the ten-week period that Natalia was at home Barb hoisted Natalia in her hands up in the air to check her reflexes. Elaine saw that once and told Barb she was afraid that might scare Natalia. Barb told the police that. But <u>never</u> did Barb say that Dr. Simpson <u>told</u> her to do that.) "Dr. Simpson <u>denied</u> that <u>she instructed or suggested that Barbara</u> raise the legs of Natalia Benson in any fashion for the purpose of relieving abdominal and/or stomach gas, or for the purpose of assisting Natalie [Natalia] Benson in having a bowel movement." *Where are you getting this stuff? Once again, it's not anywhere in the things Barb said to police. I just reread her entire police interview to be absolutely certain. Barb did not say that. It was just* <u>*made up*</u>.

But by this time it is not hard to imagine that Dr. Simpson is seriously questioning why Barb would be saying this stuff to police. Is she trying to make <u>me</u> (Dr. Simpson) look bad? Maybe I'm going to have a liability problem here. Of course, that's exactly what the police wanted Dr. Simpson to believe. Make her back away from Barb, whatever it takes.

The police continued with Dr. Simpson. "Dr. Simpson <u>denied</u> that she had any knowledge or information to indicate that Barbara Schrock has postpartum depression. Dr. Simpson said it was possible that she may have had a <u>passing discussion</u> with Barbara Schrock concerning postpartum depression, but she normally makes a record on an infant's medical record concerning such conversations. Dr. Simpson told us that the conversation was not noted in the medical record of Natalia Benson." (For a change, Barb actually <u>did</u> say she had talked to Dr. Simpson about her feelings of detachment from Natalia.)

> <u>Sgt K</u>: "Did anybody suggest that you go talk to anybody about that depression? You said you called Dr. Simpson."
>
> <u>Barb</u>: "Well, I told her about it yesterday (Tuesday evening on the phone). I said I thought Natalia was withdrawing because I wasn't paying attention to her, because I went through PPD." (Barb's terminology for her feelings of not bonding with Natalia.)

Dr. Simpson is also correct about the conversation not being noted in her records. She does, however, allow for the conversation possibly happening in passing. When the discovery materials were given to our attorney, the only record of the evening phone call when Barb said she mentioned her detachment feelings to Dr. Simpson, were words written by Dr. Simpson on the original call note to the receptionist --- "told mom to make appointment A.M." Dr. Simpson also acknowledged to police that "she called Barbara Schrock <u>after regular office hours</u> on Tuesday," confirming Barb's statement regarding the timing of that call. Dr. Simpson then said Barb's "descriptions of the medical problem were 'non-alarming, so she

58

suggested Barbara call her office <u>the next morning</u> to schedule an appointment for Wednesday, 07-27-05." (Actually in Barb's <u>and</u> Elaine's minds, Natalia's symptoms <u>were</u> cause for concern, but non-alarming. Both Elaine and Dr. Simpson believed the temperature reading to be inaccurate because of the other positive vital signs.)

The police and prosecutor also used much of this same totally false "information" when giving press releases and interviews. So not only were these statements made to Dr. Simpson, but also they were played endless times on television news reports. Each time over the next few years when a trial date was set and then "continued" to a later date, these clips were pulled out of the file and played once again. Even in the actual charges brought against Barb later, the <u>supplemental support for "probable cause"</u> contained four items in support of charges against Barb:

(1) Natalia "had been in her care and custody;" *True.*
(2) and (3) "Barbara stated that she was <u>told by doctors</u> to do this" (the same <u>two</u> untruths detailed above that were denied by Dr. Simpson;) *Blatantly false!* And
(4) according to Dr. Simpson "the injuries were 'downplayed' to the doctor by the mother." *As if you could downplay a 93 degree temperature.*

("Probable cause" is a document submitted for a judge's signature indicating the reasons why the prosecutor believes that more likely than not (1) a crime has been committed, (2) the suspect named has committed it, and (3) an arrest warrant should be issued.)

The police used this technique--- making outrageous statements and passing them off as true--- throughout their development of this case. The prosecution would then later repeat these statements as <u>facts</u>. And in response to this particular instance above, Dr. Simpson at the trial would back away even further from Barb. The police had made her aware of her own vulnerability and put her on the defensive against Barb. What had worked so well on Char and Gary had now also worked on Dr. Simpson. Barb was increasingly being isolated, as one by one the police turned her supporters first into deserters, and later into antagonists.

That same weekend, according to police notes, Char Mullins contacted the investigators to let them know that "Barbara Schrock had been sitting at Natalie's [Natalia's] bedside reading books to her through the weekend of July 30 and 31, 2005." *This is significant enough to call police?* Char also told investigators "of two young women who were present at a July 2 party and observed Barbara Schrock's behavior and treatment of Natalie

[Natalia] Benson. Charlene Mullins said she would contact these women and have them contact investigators." Who were these women? (Sara: a cousin of Brant's; "Brant was kinda like a brother to me. Brant lived with us for a couple years growing up" [when there were problems in Brant's own home.] And Donna: married to Brant's cousin.)

On Monday evening (August 1) Lt. Richmond interviewed Sara, again on tape:

> Lt R: "I was called by Char, Brant Benson's mother, and she said you might have information to provide us."
>
> Sara: "I don't know how my information will really help. I don't have a whole lot." *Perhaps she didn't come here totally voluntarily.*
>
> Lt R: "How about the baby?" (Have you seen Barb interact with her kids?)
>
> Sara: "Just the one time. At the July 4 [weekend] party...I think it was the July 4 (actually July 2) ...it was the family get-together."
>
> Lt R: "Brant has indicated he didn't know any of this, that he was unaware that the baby had suffered injuries. He was shocked. Barb's mother was there the day before. We're kinda surprised that from what she saw...and described the baby to us that day...that something wasn't done 24 hours earlier. Especially with her being a nurse." *Brant's in the clear. He was "shocked." Elaine...she's pretty suspicious. Watch out for her.*
>
> Sara: "That kinda took me by surprise, too." *The word must be out on Elaine. Sara already knows.*

Sara told police that Barb used off color language towards Natalia, handled her more roughly than she would have, and was frustrated that Brant was not helping her with the kids.

> Sara: (telling Lt. R in her own words what she alleges Barb said)): "Here they told me to bring the baby...they wanted me to bring him (Natalia) so every body could see him. And they promised me they would take care of him when he was here." And later, "Brant started helping out a little bit and she (Barb) calmed down. And eventually I got to hold him (Natalia). And other people held him. He actually liked being held. He calmed right down. My opinion is that he was just being

held too roughly." *One has to wonder how good her memory really is about this day? And this baby?*

Lt R: "Was there anyone else at the party that you were at.....we heard there was another...."

Sara: "Donna? Donna Schau was sitting...Barb was sitting here and I was sitting here and Donna was sitting across from me."

Lt R: "Was there a lady that works in Niles for the Child Protective Services?"

Sara: "Yeah, that's my sister-in-law, Michelle. But she says....I was talking to her last night...and she says she didn't see anything at the party."

Lt R: "Char had indicated to me...I think she said something to Michelle. Michelle's a friend of Char's (actually a part of the family)...that she felt bad that she hadn't.....Apparently she observed something. She felt maybe she should have intervened." *Or maybe Char was just interested in getting Brant out of the picture, and Barb into it.*

Lt R: "...we heard the story late last week (from Char) that she (Barb) is telling family and friends that the baby is going to survive...reading books to her..." *Wow. How awful!*

Sara: "She told me that. That the baby is getting better...there was fungus in the blood"...(lab reports did indicate streptococci in the blood and Dr. O acknowledged that it could cause bleeding)..."that the doctor also says that the baby was born with brain damage." (Dr. O also did say brain scans showed a brain deformity that was unknown at birth.)

Lt R: "All those stories....she's told you this?

Sara: "Yes." (All three of the above things Barb told Sara proved to be true.)

Lt. Richmond never did bring Michelle into his office for an interview. But he did call her. Police notes of that call indicate that Michelle "witnessed Barb's agitated behavior (verbally and physically) at the pool that day, but didn't observe any abusive behavior directed towards Natalie [Natalia]." "Michelle said she has seen Natalie [Natalia] twice since her birth (July 2 party and July 27 in the PICU.)" *Doesn't sound like she has much to add as a witness.* (Nevertheless, the prosecution brought Michelle to the trial, since it never hurts to have someone who works with infants to help influence a jury's perceptions.)

Lt. Richmond interviewed Donna Tuesday morning (August 2). She confirmed that Barb had chewed Brant out for not helping with Natalia. And she, too, said that Barb has used nasty language with Natalia.   Donna continued:

Donna: "And when she went to get something to eat, the baby started crying.   So I took <u>it</u> out of the carrier and just put the binky back in <u>it's</u> mouth.   <u>It</u> opened <u>it's</u> eyes for a second, then <u>it</u> just fell back to sleep when I was holding <u>it</u>....   Another person, to the side of me said, you look great for just having a newborn.   I said, '<u>It's</u> not mine!   I'm just watching <u>it</u> until Mom gets back.'   Then I kinda just rocked <u>it</u> a little bit...and <u>it</u> went right back to sleep..and I put <u>it</u> back, and Barb came back and just sat down out by the pool."   *Poor Natalia. Nobody seems to know your gender.   Just that your mother was cussing at Brant for not helping.*

Lt R: "What did Barb do at that point?"

Donna: "She went into the pool with her other daughter (Isabella) and was like a great mother. he was very observant to make sure that she was swimming where she should be, and that the kids were playing with her right.   She was being a great mother from what I could tell............   I've seen her with kids. <u>And I would trust her with my kids</u>."   *This is definitely not going where Lt. R wants it to.*

Donna (continues): "She (Barb) said, 'Look guys.   I got my tubes tied. I'm never gonna have kids again.'"

Lt R: "Did that surprise you?"

Donna: "I was just kinda surprised that she got her tubes tied.   I had no idea she was going to do that."   *Lt. R has his opening.*

Lt R: "But we have heard her refer to the baby as a <u>thing</u>.   I can't wait to get this thing out of me."   *Once again, Barb absolutely never said this, or anything remotely resembling this.   But Donna does not know it, and it undoubtedly marginalizes Barb even further.*   "Did she ever indicate to you...we've heard it was kind of of a one-sided decision, that ...we've heard stories, I think even from Brant...that said they were hoping for a boy...or at least he was."   *Once again, a totally made-up statement.   Brant even denies this later in his second interview, and tells Lt. R that the decision to tie tubes was a medical one by the doctor, Brant, and Barb.*

Lt R: "In your conversations with her, did she ever indicate that <u>she</u> was abused?   *This might have been a more appropriate question concerning Brant than Barb."*

Donna: "No."

62

Lt R: "That can sometimes be something that turns over." [If you hear that] "she's a victim of whatever...abuse, we would like to hear that."

And now Lt. R makes degrading comments to Donna about Elaine:

Lt R: "She (Elaine) sits her in the same chair and tells me she sees low body temperature and lethargic behavior" (with temperature accuracy seriously in question)... "disconnected behavior" (she never said that...what is it in a three-month-old?)... "the eyes are two different directions" (never said, but Lt. R uses this on both Donna and Brant). "I'm thinking, you're a registered nurse, and all these red flags, and she packs her grips...and heads back to Goshen...and leaves the baby there in the house for another 24 hours" (after listening to Barb's call to Dr. Simpson's Office).

Back to conversation about Barb:

Donna: "But for a new mother, she never really opened up or had the excitement about having a new baby. I never saw the same connection with this one (as with Isabella)." *Sadly, this comment is likely true. At least for some period of time.*

Lt R: "And then yesterday, I'm told yesterday afternoon, I guess, Char finally confronted Barbara up in the hospital....and there was kind of a scene." *I wonder who could have precipitated that? The "finally" sounds like this is what Lt. R wanted to happen.* "And Brant continued to maintain that there is still a possibility that this is sort of a disease that was contracted in NICU when the baby was left there after her delivery. And I'm like... what's wrong with you? Wake up and smell the coffee here. How many times can you be told.....this is not an accident....not a disease." *Lt. R sounds a bit frustrated with Brant as he talks to Donna. But when the facts that Brant has seen with his own eyes conflict with the other "facts" that doctors claim have happened according to their theory, stating them over and over, or yelling them more and more loudly, doesn't always change a person's mind. Then, again--- sometimes it does.* Nevertheless, Char now had her three witnesses to help the police "clear Brant's name out of this."

But how can you bring charges against Barb, when Elaine, Natalia's grandmother and a school nurse, observed the same things in Natalia that Barb and Brant did? <u>The police had to figure out a way</u> to deal with Elaine.

<u>Elaine</u> has always been one of the kindest, friendliest, competent, caring people you will ever meet. She does not have an enemy in the world among those who know her. Much of her life has been spent giving her time, her energy, and her love to those around her. Elaine thinks of what is best for others, sometimes to the detriment of herself. She is a wife, a mother, a grandmother, a Christian, a Mennonite, a strong advocate of non-violence, a person of integrity, and a believer in living out your faith and values.

To give the reader a better feel of the above, I have decided to mention a few of the groups and ways in which Elaine has spent her time over the last 30-40 years. It's one method of opening a window into her character.

OVERSEAS SCHOOLS:
Elaine was a school nurse in Kuwait for four years, and in Cairo, Egypt also for four years. Kids in grades K-12 from all over the world experienced her gentle care for them. And in those settings, she also became the de facto nurse for the whole teaching and administrative staff. Whether singing in the church choirs, at school musicals, or at the Kuwait Hilton, Elaine shared her beautiful soprano voice through solos, and as part of groups. She also, while waiting for an ambulance that never came, doggedly gave mouth-to-mouth CPR for nearly an hour to a senior boy who was gravely injured after school on the athletic field, as the contents of his previous meal kept emerging. Elaine and I formed friendships internationally that continue to this day, partly because of Elaine's nurturing of those relationships over the years through written communications.

SPIRITUAL DIRECTOR:
Elaine decided about 20 years ago that she wanted to have someone help focus and give direction to her Christian life outside of the church. She has met with this director once a month for 19 years and finds this a very meaningful part of her life. During the last six years (coinciding with issues related to Natalia) Elaine increased the meeting frequency to twice a month. She feels this keeps her grounded in the faith.

MOTHERING:
Elaine spent much quality time with Barb during her formative years. She was always there to guide and nurture her, and to listen to her concerns. In order to do this, however, she decided for many years to take only part-

64

time work outside the home. That's a decision she has never regretted. And Barb has been thankful, too.

SCHOOL:
At Westview Elementary School (Grades 5 and 6 only) Elaine served as the School Nurse for 17 years. She was dearly loved there by both the kids and the staff. With nearly half of the school being Amish, this assignment offered Elaine a chance to draw from her experience in earlier multicultural settings and gave her much joy. When Elaine retired, the administration and staff put a permanent plaque outside the door of the nursing office with Elaine's name on it.

WOMEN'S GROUP:
For the past 12 years Elaine has been part of a group of four women, some from CMC and some not, who meet weekly to reflect on the lectionary scriptures for that week, pray together, and discuss personal life issues. This group of four (one taught preaching at the Mennonite Seminary, two are Spiritual Directors, and Elaine) have become very close and support each other in a variety of ways.

[The following groups have involved both Elaine and me:]

COLLEGE MENNONITE CHURCH (CMC):
Elaine both served on and chaired the Caring Commission, a group which helps meet the needs of both members and non-members, for six years. Her combination of a compassionate heart and leadership skills helped her function well in that role.

The Church Elders' role is to give overall spiritual direction of our congregation, including the paid ministerial staff. Elaine was one of those nominated and then called to be an Elder. She served in that way for six years, and led the congregational business meetings for several years as Congregational Moderator.

At other times Elaine has taught Sunday School and led Grief Support groups.

SMALL GROUP:
Because of the size of College Mennonite Church, members are encouraged to form small groups to work at the issues of the church and to challenge each other to live more faithfully. Elaine and I have been part of a small group that met every Wednesday evening for 17 years. We would sing together, share our joys and sorrows together, pray together, and usually have

a discussion on some topic. Being able to share our deepest personal and spiritual concerns in a loving, confidential group like this was a valuable gift for all of us. After 17 years Elaine and I, after much deliberation, decided our needs and schedules had changed, and we told the group we would be leaving it. Some others, too, left around that time, and the remaining group decided to meet monthly. After a two to three year absence Natalia's situation came into our lives, and we once again began meeting with that group. They have been very helpful and faithful in supporting us.

FRIENDSHIP GROUP:

We meet weekly, sometimes more and sometimes less, with two other couples that have a faith and values similar to ours. While we get into good discussions, the undeclared purpose of getting together is for fun, support, joy, humor, friendship, food, caring, and more fun. We enjoy each other and bless each other. And we can count on each other.

PATHFINDERS:

We joined this Sunday School class at CMC in 1973. It has been a meaningful source of growth, a place to discuss questions of faith, a service group, a supportive group, and a social/relational group.

The above groups and roles are representative of how Elaine has spent her time during the past years. It does not reflect the many gifts she has that apply to the less formal, non-scheduled areas of her everyday life. But I know that Barb and I have benefited from her cooking, her love, her relational warmth, and her playfulness. And Barb and I learned anew of her calming influence as we would drive that long one-hour trip to the South Bend Courthouse so many, many times with so much at stake. She would pull out the Rejoice devotional magazine and read the passage and commentary for that day as we drove along. Often it seemed totally appropriate to our needs, such as Isaiah 43:2; "When you pass through the waters I will be with you; and through the rivers, they shall not overwhelm you; when you walk through fire you shall not be burned, and the flame shall not consume you."

When the charges were handed down, and Barb and Elaine were arrested, our church and our friends reacted in disbelief with a variety of emotions, from extreme sadness all the way to anger. Most had known Barb through age 18, but had not seen her much in the 15 years that followed. From what they knew of her, these charges seemed highly unlikely and inaccurate. They were "shocked." As were we. There were very strong reasons that we felt Barb did not hurt Natalia:

66

(1) We knew Barb as a person who talked loudly at times, but was "soft" with children and animals.

(2) We had seen Barb's mothering skills and admired them.

(3) We had asked Barb directly, and let her know that _if she had_ done something to Natalia, authorities would go easier on her if she admitted it.

(4) We had lived closely with Barb for several years following Natalia's condition, and knew that she would have said something during that time. Barb always tells everything to everybody. She couldn't hold a secret for five minutes.

(5) We knew that her two little girls were the only known living "blood relatives" that she had in the world, and she valued that connection above all else. And finally,

(6) We understood that if the prosecutor could so erroneously bring charges against Elaine, who we _knew_ was innocent, then it was also quite likely that he had come to the same faulty conclusion with Barb. Something was _very wrong_ here.

As we said in our initial statement to the church, we saw Barb _and_ Brant as loving, caring parents. We continue to believe that today. We definitely believe neither of them hurt Natalia. But we were not there, which means it is theoretically possible that one of them stepped _way_ out of character and injured Natalia. Because of that, Elaine responded to Lt. R's possible scenario of Barb hurting Natalia:

Elaine: "I can't imagine it. I've never seen her like that. And I can't imagine her doing that."

Lt R: "Do you think she would be honest with herself....with you....or with the doctors to say....okay, look... "

Elaine: "_I don't know. I hope so._"

In the judicial world of black and white, Elaine's last response is taken as "waffling," rather than the "honesty" it is intended to reflect. We have seen too many nuances and exceptions in our lifetime to move solidly into the black and white world, even though the faux certainty of that world would be welcome at times. Perhaps Elaine should have responded adamantly as Char and Gary did when speaking of Brant's innocence, but that is not who we are. Anyway, the police took Elaine's response as evidence that Barb's own mother doesn't trust her. Later, in his second interview with Brant, Lt. R _dramatically changed Elaine's response_ to "probably not," in a successful attempt to finally turn Brant against Barb. The implication was--- her own mother doesn't trust her---why should you?

While our church and friends were "shocked" at the charges brought against Barb, they were --- to use the words the police used in the same document to eliminate Brant as a suspect --- "totally stunned" at Elaine's charges. You don't share your most candid thoughts with someone, pray with them, work with them, play with them, ask them to be guardian of your children if something were to happen to you, be cared for by them over the course of 30-40 years, and then sit idly by while they are being attacked at the very core of their being (integrity, love, and caring for others). But this was what the felony charge against Elaine was alleging....that not only was Elaine lying, but she lied to keep her granddaughter from getting medical help. Our friends, and we, saw that as an outrageous accusation.

Dozens of people wrote character references for Elaine. I've included two of those letters here.

To Whom it May Concern:

I am writing on behalf of Elaine Schrock and to reiterate what I am sure has been written by others who know her well and who are concerned about the allegations raised against her.

I have known Elaine for thirty years. I have attended church and Sunday School with her. I have been part of a small group with her, and a Bible study group as well. My husband and I have traveled with Elaine and her husband and have socialized with them through the years. We share professions. Never   have I had a friend who has been more ethical, trustworthy, and respected than Elaine. Her sensitivity to others, her compassion, her Christian faith, her loving kindness to all around her, her high moral standards are evident in all areas of her life---her home, her family, her friends, her colleagues. I have been enriched and blessed as her friend.

It seems ludicrous to me that a judicial system that wants to pride itself on searching for the truth and upholding the law can entertain for even a moment the notion that Elaine might be guilty of a wrongdoing---let alone one that is so horrific as the one brought against her. It is egregious to think that our judicial system could be so wrong.

I support the laws of our land and am thankful for the work of our judicial system and the protection that is awarded to us citizens. I cannot, however, be supportive of (nor can I understand) the work

68

of a system that so miserably fails by even considering that someone of Elaine's stature could be guilty of a crime.

Elaine is a person worthy of being emulated. I am appalled that you haven't discovered that about her and that proceedings against her are continuing.

Another Letter:

To Whom It May Concern:

The purpose of this letter is both to express my support for my colleague, Elaine Schrock, and to state my disapproval and disbelief of the charges that have been made against her.

I teach in the building where Ms. Schrock is the school nurse. The school, Westview Elementary, was opened in the 89-90 school year. Therefore, as a fifth and sixth grade instructor, I have worked side by side with her since that time. The church she currently attends, College Mennonite Church, was also my church for many years before my family moved to LaGrange County.

These charges and this case are as baffling to me as any I have ever encountered in my 32 years of teaching. I have known the molested, the abused, and the abusers. I have talked with social workers, counselors, therapists, attorneys, detectives, and judges. There is something wrong here: there is something that just is not right. The potential for a terrible injustice is frightening.

Ms. Schrock works tirelessly and selflessly on behalf of the children of Westview. Her work ethic and her compassion are second to none. She is a counselor and a friend and constant source of support for any child in whom she sees a need.

The idea (or conceptualization) that she would permit harm to her own grandchild, and then try to conceal that harm with intentional neglect, is absolutely outside the realm of possibility. My judgment as a professional, as a church worker, as the son of two career educators, as a constant observer of humans interacting, tells me that she has not done what prosecutors say she has.

It is not my place to argue the facts (or lack of them) with the prosecution. I feel that much of their evidence is circumstantial or speculative. Elaine can't talk with me about that, so I must simply say that I believe that she is incapable of the charges brought against her. Her Christian faith and her dedication to her profession, her love for her family, her service overseas to the poor and the oppressed, make these charges a cruel joke, and the darkest of humor.

If there is anything I can do to convince anyone of Ms. Schrock's innocence, do not hesitate to contact me. For all of us at Westview Elementary, this is a heart-breaking situation. This is not about "saving face" or "stonewalling" or "circling the wagons." It is about injustice.

BASIS FOR CHARGES AGAINST ELAINE

The police had successfully turned Char and Gary, and later Dr. Simpson, from being supporters of Barb into witnesses against her. Now they would issue a felony charge against Elaine, the grandmother and school nurse, who was babysitting with Natalia less than 24 hours before she was taken to the ER. Remember that Barb had asked Elaine, who was planning to come over to Barb's home so Barb could get her hair done, to check out Natalia that Tuesday morning to allow Barb to report more accurately to Dr. Simpson what was going on with Natalia. When Barb returned home around noon, Elaine informed her concerning what she had observed (listed in a previous chapter). Barb then called Dr. Simpson's office and reported Natalia's symptoms while Elaine listened. Once the call to the doctor's office was made, Elaine left with Isabella for Goshen.

Twenty-four hours later, Dr. O and later Dr. E would look back at Elaine's time with Natalia and say with absolute certainty and assurance to the police that with these symptoms (not very responsive, no eye contact, 93 degree temperature) Natalia should have been brought to the ER at that time. Of course, neither of these two doctors had seen Natalia over the past month when all of these symptoms were present to a lesser degree. And why is there no mention of the fact that Natalia was breathing normally, did take her bottle, urinated in her diaper, had no bluing of her lips, and had good fingernail refill (circulation)? *If you've bought into a theory, you have to make things fit.* It was obvious to them. Elaine was lying about these positive symptoms. She evidently told the truth about the temperature and other concerns, but lied about Natalia taking her bottle and other positive observations.

So Elaine would be removed as an obstacle to proving Barb's guilt, simply by bringing charges against her, too. Now we have charges against two of the three who were with Natalia in the last 24 hours. I indicated previously the reasons to support probable cause that the prosecution used in charging Barb. In this same supporting document, the prosecution states that

70

Elaine told officers that on July 16 -18 (when Elaine and Dan kept Natalia a little over a week earlier) Natalia was in her [Elaine's] care and "did not have any problems or health issues at that time. She stated that the child was alert, ate properly, and was returned to her mother." *All through the police interviews are comments by Char, Brant, Barb, and Elaine about problems seen in Natalia throughout her time at home. These problems seemed to increase in intensity over time. I wasn't interviewed, but saw the same problems.* On the specific week referred to (July 16-18) Elaine had the following to say:

> Lt R: "Was spitting up a problem?"
> Elaine: "It was in the last three weeks." (including July 16-18)
> Lt R: "Did she spit most of her meal back up?"
> Elaine: "It was sporadic. Sometimes it looked like the whole bottle came up, and then she would take some right after that and keep it down, and sometimes she wouldn't at all. That puzzled me."

And later in the interview:

> Lt. R: "We're looking at how she would have been....the weekend before last (July 16-18)."
> Elaine: "Well, I mean...the developmental rate is different. I mean she isn't going to be like a three month old baby at this point."
> Lt R: "No, at three months, she's still behind the times."
> Elaine: "Yeah..half that, or less, since she was in intensive care. What was I saying...?"
> Lt. R: "Her behavior...it was not typical."
> Elaine: "Yeah. I never did know exactly...I was always questioning...what should I expect? At three months, obviously I would have expected more response, and that kind of thing, than I ever had with her (Natalia). And you know, Barb said that ....in a part of the discussion about PPD...that she did not hold her, cuddle her, and nurture her as much as she did the other baby (Isabella)...and so I thought that was probably part of why she was slower developing. I think she talked to Dr. Simpson about that, too...because those babies are sometimes later in smiling and reacting and so forth."
> Lt. R: "Do you know if she is still on the antibiotic?"
> Elaine: "No, this was later (after the July 4 weekend.) And then she seemed to be progressing after that, although again, not like

a full term baby. I don't know if I knew exactly what to expect."

Lt R: (Was there a difference between what you saw eight days ago and yesterday?)

Elaine: "There was quite a difference in that time.....and in between there Barb would talk to me (phone) about different things...she was concerned...and then we talked about whether she'd call Dr. Simpson or not, and she decided to wait another day, because is seemed like things were better."

Lt R: "Do you know what these things were....these last eight days?"

Elaine: "Well, we were talking about this spitting up thing. Then she also said she was cold...her body temperature was real cold. She told me to bring my thermometer (yesterday) because hers broke. So we did that and reported that to Dr. Simpson."

Lt R: "Do you remember the temperature?

Elaine: "Yeah. We took it three times...this was axillary. It was 91 something first, then 93 something, then 92 something. I forget the tenths."

Lt R: "Armpit?"

Elaine: "Right."

Lt R: "So that's.....I don't know how unusual that is. Some adults run low."

Elaine: "She (Barb) reported that to Dr. Simpson. She didn't seem real concerned about that."

Later in the interview:

Lt R: "(Tuesday, July 26.) It gave you the feeling that she had no eyesight, or something."

Elaine: "Yeah,..I questioned that."

Lt R: "And she had that before, you think?"

Elaine: "I don't know."

Lt R: "When you cared for her that weekend before (July 16-18), did she seem to follow, or turn and look?"

Elaine: "Not as much as I expected."

Lt R: "But she did?"

Elaine: "Yeah.....I think so......I really shouldn't say that for sure. I know I did think of it that there wasn't the kind of...again because of a preemie....that she didn't have the kind of eye contact that a baby should have at this point."

So "she did not have any problems or health issues at the time" is a very large stretch, as is "the child was alert and ate properly." To put that in the

72

support of probable cause document seems disingenuous. What is true is that Natalia's symptoms had intensified between the July 16-18 weekend and Tuesday morning, July 26.

More from the "probable cause" document:

"On Sunday, July 25, (another error: actually July 24 is correct) numerous family members and friends all told the officers that the child (Natalia) was lethargic and limp." (Actually, the only family members who saw Natalia that day and were interviewed by police were Char and Barb. Neither used the word "limp" to describe Natalia).

The document continues:

"According to Elaine Schrock, Natalia had no night vision." *I'm not kidding! That's what they said. Where do they come up with this stuff? Isn't this an official document?* (Of course, Elaine never said anything close to that in her police interview). "Elaine Schrock is a registered nurse with the Goshen School System." (Actually a School Nurse with the Westview School Corporation of LaGrange County.) "She stated that not only was the child lethargic and limp...." (Again, Elaine had never used the word limp, but actually use the words "not very responsive" to describe Natalia. And that describes Natalia, in varying degrees, pretty much since she came home from the NICU---not very responsive.) "She took the child's temperature of 91, 92, and 93 degrees on three separate occasions that morning. However, as a registered nurse," (and grandmother), "she just told the child's mother, Barbara Schrock, to call the doctor, but did not call the doctor herself." (Barb was the mother of Natalia, 33 years old at that time, had the relationship with Dr. Simpson, and Elaine had told her what to report, standing by as she made the call. Nothing would have changed if Elaine had made the call. Dr. Simpson received the information correctly.) *These people are looking for anything possible.*

Continuing in the document of charges, "According to the doctors who examined Natalia, if those symptoms were discovered by Elaine Schrock who is a registered nurse, they were warning signs that the child needed to be taken to the emergency room immediately." (There is no mention of the reported normal breathing, eating, urinating, or circulation in this document. One can only assume that either (1) the doctors never heard these factors from police; (2) that they heard them and discarded them because they didn't fit their theory; or (3) they chose to believe that Barb and Elaine were telling the truth about the temperature, but lying about these positive factors.) Barb and Elaine saw Natalia and described her behavior

73

that day. <u>Brant</u> came home that evening and was with Natalia, too. He told police "She was fine. Her eyes were normal. She was focusing. She was squeezing my pinky. Her breathing was normal. I was playing with her in bed." Yet the pediatricians somehow determined that was not possible. (Apparently <u>everybody</u> was lying).

> <u>Barb</u>, in layman's terms, was charged with <u>two</u> counts;
>> Count I, <u>Neglect</u>.
>> Count II, <u>Battery</u>.
>> (Each count carries a possible 6-20 year prison term.)

> <u>Elaine</u> was charged with <u>one</u> count; <u>Neglect</u>.
>> (Possible 6-20 year prison term.) That <u>charge</u> removed the effectiveness of any support Elaine might have been able to offer Barb in court.

Now, the only person that was left to be turned against Barb (and Elaine) was Brant. The police and prosecutor were undoubtedly aware that to charge all three of them with a conspiracy against Natalia likely would not fly. Yet all three were giving similar accounts of what they had seen. Brant's family was now actively trying to get him to believe something other than what he saw and knew to be true. Later we'll look at how police worked at turning Brant. They needed him badly. *By the way....what <u>did</u> happen to Brant, the third person who was with Natalia in the last 24 hours?* The supplemental information for the charging documents refer to him with only two brief sentences: (1) "Officers spoke with the father of Natalia, a Brant Benson, who was <u>totally stunned</u> when told of the injuries to his child," and (2) "He told the doctors and the officers that the child was in the care of her mother, Barbara Schrock almost the entire time and during nearly all hours of the day." *I guess that was the "iron clad alibi" needed to eliminate him. You can't get more rigorous proof than that.*

It is amazing to me that <u>any</u> judge would sign a "probable cause" document like this one. The supporting evidence is pitiful. Most of it is totally incorrect. It's almost as if the police and prosecutor knew ahead of time that they really wouldn't need anything <u>except a diagnosis</u> from doctors to bring charges. And they were right. The judge signed it.

74

CHAPTER SIX

Brant continued his support of Barb's and Elaine's accounts of Natalia for a few more days (after July 27). But as Sgt. K had said on July 29 to Char and Gary, "We've got to eliminate him however we can." And his agreeing with Barb and Elaine was not going to eliminate him. Brant's family was primed to get him to "wake up and smell the coffee." *Doesn't he understand that if he continues to say what he's been saying, "he'll go down with Barb" and Elaine?* As his family began to go at him more strongly, he began to waver in what he saw, and question his trust in Barb. The police had decided the first day that they must have Brant as a prosecution witness before going to trial. That explains Lt. R's frustration with Brant when he (Lt. R) expressed to Donna, "And I'm like...what's wrong with you? How many times can you be told?" They needed Brant in order to get a conviction of Barb and Elaine. Brant was shifting, but not fast enough. Lt. R decided to call Brant in for a second interview on Saturday, August 6, 2005. Later this second interview of Brant would be referred to by prosecutor as proof that the police actually <u>did</u> pursue Brant as a suspect. But it was definitely not an interview of a <u>suspect</u>. From beginning to end the police were force feeding Brant fabrications, designed to break his support for Barb and Elaine.

Lt. Richmond wrote the following in his police notes: "On Friday, August 5, 2005, (the day <u>before</u> Brant's second interview) a meeting was held at the St. Joseph County Prosecutors Office. Information gathered to date in this investigation was provided to St. Joseph County Prosecutor Michael Dvorak, Chief Deputy Prosecutors Frank Schaffer and Ken Cotter. I (Lt. R) shared with the Prosecutors the information necessary to provide them with Probable Cause to support the arrest of Barbara and Elaine Schrock on the charge of Neglect of a Dependent, a Class "B" Felony. (Notice that a charge of "battery" is not mentioned. Even the police must have assumed that there was not enough evidence for a charge of "battery." But let's not miss the larger point here. The police had already given their evidence against Barb and Elaine to the Prosecutor <u>before</u> they interviewed Brant the second time.)

Continuing on with Lt R's notes: "On Saturday morning, August 6, 2005, I conducted a five hour interview with Brant Benson at the Metropolitan Homicide Unit (MHU)." (On the surface it might sound like this is investigative work. But note again that the interview occurs the day <u>after</u> information for probable cause is given to the Prosecutor for charges against Barb and Elaine.) *Are we to seriously believe that Brant was a suspect at this point?* Lt. R begins the interview with Brant:

Lt R: "We talked at the hospital yesterday. You're here voluntarily at my request. We want to talk in a little more detail about Natalia....your relationship with Barb...and see if we can't get down to <u>figuring out what happened to Natalia.</u>" *WHAT HAPPENED TO NATALIA? You mean you don't know?! You've already turned over information to the prosecutor to support the arrest of Barb and Elaine, and now you are going to talk to Brant "to see if we can't get down to figuring out what happened to Natalia." Maybe you aren't really trying to find out what happened to Natalia at all. Maybe you would like to turn Brant into a prosecution witness.*

Lt R (continues): "Was the second pregnancy something that was planned...or something that just occurred?"

Brant: "Something that just occurred."

Lt R: "You felt how about the second pregnancy? Were you happy?"

Brant: "Yeah. Absolutely."

Lt R: "How about Barb?"

Brant: "As far as I know she was fine with it, too."

Lt R: "Did she ever indicate to you that she didn't want to be pregnant?"

Brant: "No."

Lt. R: "We've talked to people that said that Barbara mentioned to them that <u>she didn't want this baby</u>. *The same line he used with Char and Gary.* She didn't like being pregnant with Natalia....that you wanted the child, but she didn't really want....you know...Isabella was fine... but she really didn't want to be pregnant the second time." *Ask him who, Brant. Who said that?* Once again, there is absolutely no record of this being said in any of the police interviews. And if somebody had said it, you can be certain the prosecutor would have had them at the trial to testify to that fact. But he didn't.) "Did she voice any of those concerns to you?"

Brant: "No."

Lt R: "She made mention that <u>you wanted a boy</u>....that you were hoping for a boy." *It's getting more and more difficult for me not use use the word "lie" when describing what this man is saying. But, again, Barb simply did not say this. Nowhere!*

Brant: " Well, I guess we <u>had</u> a daughter. And a boy would have been okay. But, again, I didn't care."

Lt R: "Again...before delivery...we would have gals come in here and say they talked to Barbara, and she would make comments....that <u>she wanted 'it' out of her.</u>..and some of the women that talked to us found that kind of comment a bit odd...that she would refer to the baby as 'it.'" *Brant, ask him to tell you who these women are. I know you trust this guy, but can't you see what he's doing?* "Did you ever hear her make any of those type of comments?"

Brant: "No. Never"

Lt R: "Some would say that before Barb became pregnant, she was kind of a <u>party girl.</u>...she liked to go out and have a good time. Did she ever make comments that being pregnant kinda infringed on her lifestyle? Did she ever give you that opinion?" *What's next?.....Some would say that Barb wanted to throw Natalia off the Eiffel Tower...Did she ever give you reason to believe that? This kind of degrading is despicable.*

Brant: "No." (Even though Brant is answering honestly, he must be seriously questioning at this point <u>how well</u> he really knows Barb. This same approach was used with Char and Gary, and with Dr. Simpson. It's a sad commentary that Brant finally chose to believe Lt. R rather than Barb. But most of us do tend to operate on the assumption that police are honest.)

Lt R: "We've heard the story where on the weekends...she (Barb) set here and I think she told Randy (Sgt. K)...<u>Barbara told Randy</u> the day she was here that <u>she feels like she is a Monday-Friday Mom</u>.....that on the weekends she likes to get rid of the kids. Is that your recollection?" (Once again, Barb did not say this. It's totally made up. But Brant doesn't know that. And Lt. R knows that Brant doesn't know that. So he feels safe.)

Brant: "No. Huh-uh."

Lt R: "She said she dropped the kids off...mostly would take Bella...to your Mom and Dad's house...to get rid of her for the weekend so she could go out and have her weekend and do whatever she wanted to do." (Here Lt. R uses a piece of information he learned from Char and Gary.....that they keep Isabella often on the weekends....to try to convince Brant that Barb's a party girl. As if Brant wouldn't know Barb that well. Gary's actual comment to police was: "We ask for Isabella every weekend if we can get her.")

Brant: "See..I don't think that's true either. I think it's more...my mom and Gary...that was their time to have Isabella. My mom has always wanted a grandchild. It never seemed to me....on my part it was never...let's get rid of the kids. It was my mom and Gary wanted to spend that time with Bella." (Brant is correct. But Brant says "on my part" because he believes Lt. R is telling the truth, and now is uncertain of Barb's motivation. What else can he say? We expect police to tell the truth.)

Lt R: "And she (Barb) was to bring milk back to the hospital (for Natalia). But at some point she stopped. Do you know what happened? Her Mom didn't know. I've heard stories that she just chose to stop." *More stories. He must stay awake at night thinking up stories.*

Brant: "I believe that was the reason why... the milk dried up. She breast fed Isabella and the same thing happened then." (Another honest answer).

Brant (continuing): "And now that this has all come out, and we learn of her injuries, I truly believe that ever since Natalia came home that she was having seizures. We would think that it was...I would think that it was cute that Natalia would act like she was winking at me. And it wasn't both eyes, it was one eye that would wink. We noticed that she would posture sometimes, and we thought it was just her trying to have a bowel movement. And now that we know what a seizure looks like in a newborn, I believe ever since she's been home that she's been having seizures." (A hugely important and accurate observation. Brant saw what we all did. I wonder if this observation made by several family members ever made it to the doctors. Of course it doesn't fit into the Shaken Baby theory, so probably not.)

But even though Brant retains some of his own observations like the one above, the relentless line of questioning by Lt. R has shaken him. He now begins to doubt Barb more and more.

Brant: "Now my entire life that I've lived with Barb.....I have to question everything. Was she (Natalia) eating? I know that when she was in my care she was eating....she had a good suck....she wasn't vomiting." *I thought Brant was never anywhere near Natalia. The prosecution claimed he was working 16 hours a day, seven days a week. Now he talks of Natalia being in his care.* (But Lt. R is glad to hear about his questioning of everything Barb has said or done now. He smells victory.)

Lt R: "That's what I need to hear from you. These are the things I need to hear from you."
Have a lump of sugar.

Later in the interview:

Brant: "No, Dan is retired. He was a social worker for 13 years. I think he was a high school counselor. They (Elaine and Dan) have always been ...that I know of...real good people. Now you say yesterday (in the hospital) that Elaine looked at Natalia (Tuesday, July 26) and her eyes wouldn't track..and one eye's going one way and the other eye's going another way...and she seemed lethargic." (Elaine never said one of Natalia's eyes was going one way and the other one another way. That would be totally ridiculous. It is nowhere in her interview. Just another concoction by Lt. R.)

Brant continues. "For Elaine to not call an ambulance, or to put her in the car and take her down to the hospital, is unbelievable."
Lt R: "I can play the tape for you."
Brant: " Un-be-lieve-a-ble!"
Lt R: "I can show you the videotape. You can sit here and watch it for yourself." *Say you want to see it, Brant. I've seen it. The eye statement is not there.* (And "lethargic" is Lt. R's word. Elaine said "not very responsive." Brant later says to Lt. R, "I don't even know what lethargic means.") *But he's certainly heated about it.*
Brant: "I believe it. Why didn't she call 911? Why didn't somebody take Natalia to the doctor right then? (gasps, sighs.) (Brant at this point sounds overwrought.)
Lt R: "I know. That's what the doctors are asking us. That's why we wanted to talk with you all this while....to clear up some of this." *Now that everything we told you is clear....????*

Brant calms down a bit and returns closer to rationality:

Lt R: "We've got a report (from the July 2 party)...She's (Barb) cussing you...and she is mad. And apparently she calls you

over from horseshoes and just <u>lit you up</u>...<u>read you the riot</u>
<u>act</u>...<u>cussed you out</u>..."

Brant: "Well, I wouldn't say she cussed me out. I mean she was
upset because...Gary and I were playing horseshoes...and
Barb was a little irritated...there wasn't anybody helping her
with Natalia.... It's just saying okay, this is the July 4
weekend...and as long as everybody helps out...I wanna be
able to have a half-decent time." *Watch out, Brant. You're
not playing his game. Be aware of what's ahead!*

Lt R: "Well, at this party <u>they</u> have these conversations with Barb
where she says that you were still wanting to have yet a third
child...to try to get a son...and she didn't want any part of it."
(Again, no names.) *Absolutely made up. No third child
conversations.*

Brant: "That was apparent that wasn't gonna happen, when Barb had
the complications with Natalia. She had a tubal done the
very next day."

Lt R: "Was that done with your knowledge and consent?

Brant: "Oh, yeah. Oh, yeah."

Lt R: "Well, she sorta made it sound...the other women would say
they felt...it was done without <u>your</u> knowledge and <u>your</u>
consent."

Brant: "Now what? <u>What</u> women?" *Yes, Brant. Push him.*

Lt R: "These other women were saying to us"....(Lt. R continues to
tries again to convince Brant that he   wasn't part of the
tube-tying decision. As for the other women.....no names.)

Brant: "Well, no, that doesn't even make sense that she would even
say that. We discussed it after Natalia was born with her
complications...her preeclampsia..."

Lt R: " So you <u>did</u> discuss it with her?"

Brant: "Oh, yeah. And we discussed it with Dr. McGregor."

Lt R: "Both of you did?"

Brant: "Yes." *Can he be any more clear?*

Lt R: "We...I heard the "we"".

Brant: "...with the tubal."

Lt R: "I'm just saying to you..." *This guy is tenacious.....or has a
short-term memory loss. He must be desperate for Brant as
a prosecution witness!*

Lt. Richmond continues to try to tell Brant that he <u>didn't really agree</u> to the
tubal procedure as the conversation continues a good while longer. Then,
mercifully, it ends:

80

Brant: "Right. Which after the complications and her age, Barb's age, we agreed to have the tubal"....... "and we both agreed."

Lt R: "...that's why we wanted to hear your side of the story." *Thanks for listening so well.*

Lt R (continues): "We hear this story that Natalia's not doing well... And we're trying to narrow down....."

Brant: "Who is saying she is not doing well?" *Excellent question.*

Lt R: "Well, Elaine says she's told that Natalia's not doing well when she get's there...or she's called to come over there... we're not really able to straighten it out, (*another understatement*) again, because of the attorney thing...with her. I can't get her back down here to clarify exactly what...kinda fine tune." *That's OK. Just make it up. No one will know.* (Actually, Elaine was planning since the prior week to come to Barb's house to babysit while Barb got her hair done. There was nothing new with Natalia's condition that day, other than her symptoms had increased during the previous eight days.)

Brant: "Natalia was starting to eat better."

Lt R: "Tuesday morning?"

Brant: "No, actually on Monday. Eating better. But she is a little cool...as far as to the touch...she felt a little cool."

Lt R: "Well, Elaine says that when she gets there, there is some concern about Natalia's well-being...(Elaine only ever talked of an ongoing concern. Tuesday morning was not special in this regard.)...that causes her to begin checking her temperature. She says that Barb had said that she (Natalia) felt cool...and she (Barb) couldn't take Natalia's temperature because the thermometer that you have in the house was broken."

Brant: "Right."

Lt R: "Do you remember anything about a thermometer being broken?"

Brant: "Yeah...there was a thermometer that was broken....I told Barb I would go buy a thermometer."

Lt K: "When did you tell her that?

Brant: "I think it would have been on Saturday. Yeah, Saturday morning. That's when Barb said, 'Well, I turned the A/C down'...(because Natalia was feeling cold)...she set the thermostat so it wasn't so cold."

Lt R: "Well, Tuesday morning Elaine arrives and there's this debate about whether or Barb should leave the house to go to the hairdressers....Natalia's not feeling well." (This is a debate that never took place. Lt. R either needs to check his tapes, or take better notes).

Brant: "Actually that wouldn't have been true. Because Jenny called Barb that morning and told her that Tonya's water had been shut off. (Brant is correct. The haircut was canceled.)

Lt R: "This is the story we're being told." *Not!*

Barb told Sgt. K in her police interview that her hair appointment had been canceled.

Barb: "Tuesday I had a scheduled haircut. My girlfriend that I was going with called and said Tonya just called. They're doing construction out in front of her (hair stylist) house and they shut off the water."

Sgt K: "You canceled your haircut?"

Barb: " Yeah, we had to cancel our haircut." (Lt. R apparently didn't get the memo....or he chose to ignore it.) *What's the point in talking to these guys?*

This is the type of thing that is so maddening. One is forced to decide whether the investigators are <u>incompetent</u> or <u>dishonest</u>. Either way, Brant gets worked up because he now thinks Barb has lied to him. And earlier he said she had <u>never</u> lied to him. Whether Lt. R did this intentionally, or because of sloppiness, the effect is the same. This kind of stuff rips families apart. *Then, again, perhaps that's what he's been trying to do.*

Lt R: "<u>We're being told</u> that she (Elaine) knows the baby is sick." (This was never said. Just made up. Remember that Brant looked Natalia over carefully Monday evening and said she was fine.' But there <u>were</u> on again/off again increasing symptoms.) "There is this debate about whether or not Barb should leave to go to this hairdresser appointment ....because of the sick baby. Should I stay home and call the doctor, or should I go and get my hair done? Back and forth....should I go...should I stay...should I go...should I stay?" (There was <u>no debate</u>. This little alleged monologue is fiction. Elaine and Barb <u>both</u> knew the hair appointment was canceled. So did Sgt. K. But Lt. R continues to make up stuff to pull Brant's chain.) "She says her eyes are in different directions." (Elaine <u>never</u> said anything about Natalia's eyes going in different directions. Char had told Sgt. K that Natalia's eyes would go off to one side, and then the other side. And Brant said several times that her eyes looked off to one side. We all had observed that.)

Brant: "Her eyes are opposite of each other?" (Brant's voice is rising).

Lt R: "She (Elaine) says...yeah...they're like in different directions." (Not said.) "She doesn't suckle right" ('not with the gusto she had before'.) "She's lethargic" (yes). She's non-responsive ('not very responsive,' 'not very active'.) "Her eyes are all messed up" (Lt. R's words). "Her body temperature is really low." (Elaine didn't say 'really low', but gave the actual temperatures, which she considered to be inaccurate because of the positive vital signs she observed.) "Okay. What is it you do? NOTHING! What does Barb do? She leaves to go get her hair done." (Speaking very loudly.)

Brant: "That's just <u>unbelievable</u>." *Yeah, Brant, you're right. It's not believable.*

Lt R: "She (Elaine) says, 'We were waiting for the doctor. I told Barb that she should go get her hair done.' The doctor's office wasn't open at the time she got there....and she would call right away when the Doctor's office did open, like at 8:30 or 9:00 am." (This is totally bizarre. Elaine said none of this. It's totally untrue. But it leads to even crazier stuff.)

Brant: "Now say what again. Can you repeat that?"

Lt R: "Elaine says they're gonna stay there....go get your hair done...there's nothing you can do about it right now. I'll call the Doctor's Office when it opens."

Brant: "That's what Elaine said?"

Lt R: "Yeah. She's there before the Doctor's Office is apparently open. 'Go get your hair done and come back here.'....cause Barb is saying she hasn't had her hair done for a while."

Brant: "Yeah. But what I'm not understanding is if she <u>knows</u> all these things..."

Lt R: "I understand what you're saying. We've had those same questions. But I'm just telling you what she's saying happened here ...is that Barb takes off with her friend, Jenny, and they go and they find out that the water's shut off..." *Again, Lt. R is not telling the truth.*

Brant: "Well, actually they didn't find that out. They didn't go anywhere to find that out. Jenny called Barb."

Lt. R: "She already <u>knew</u> this?" *Everybody knew this except Lt. R. And just maybe he did, too. I'm not repeating myself. He actually goes through all of this again.*

Brant: "Barb already knew it. Jenny called.....now this is what Barb told me. I come home Tuesday night....and Barb says, 'Tell Daddy how well you ate today.' Well, I walk in the bedroom and ask Barb, 'Did you get your hair done today?' It looked the same to me."

Lt R: " Let me stop you there. Is it not an <u>odd</u> thing to say? I mean it's like asking your dog, 'Tell your Daddy what you did today.' <u>Natalia has no better communication skills at this stage of her life than the dog does</u>." *Is this a total lack of understanding of mothers, or a diversionary tactic to get away from Brant's exposing his whole line of questioning as fraudulent?* (Unfortunately, Brant doesn't even recognize that by explaining Barb knew before she ever left home about the water being shut off that he's caught Lt. R making things up. Instead, he now feels Barb has lied to him).

And Lt. R starts all over again:

Lt R: "<u>But I'm telling you</u> that Elaine shows up...cause Barb leaves and goes with Jenny to get her hair done. And they went to breakfast and whatever else they did. She didn't get home until like 12:30, in the middle of the day. Now this is after, we're being told....I don't know... <u>I understand you don't know this</u>...but we're being told by Elaine and by Barb...that there's this <u>big debate</u>..." (On and on and on with the same stories over and over again. And they aren't any more truthful the sixth time than the first.)

Brant: "Well, that right there...that's not what I know to be true."

Lt R: "Okay. That's what we're dealing with here in this office"....(Brant tries to speak, but is overridden)... "to get there. We know we leave. We got a sick baby at home. We go get our hair done, cause we we haven't had it done in a while. So I'm gonna go up here and get it...whack...whack...cut, and get it whipped back into shape...to get back home to a sick baby at home. But, when we go, we find that where we're supposed to go to get our hair cut...is out of service. So instead of saying, 'Well, shoot...I've got a sick baby at home....I've gotta get right back home, she goes out to breakfast...and does <u>whatever she does</u>"...*He's going so fast now, he can't even make things up fast enough to keep pace...* "until 12:00 pm. And she comes home and she calls Dr. Simpson's office at 1:00 pm in the afternoon."

Brant: "Well, I thought Elaine was supposed to call Dr. Simpson's office at 9:00 am."

Lt K: "Well, that didn't happen. We know. Dr. Simpson showed us the record. At 1:00 pm Barb called." *Good detective work. But you could have checked what Barb said and found out the same information.*

Brant: "But Elaine told you...or Barb told you...Elaine was supposed to call at 9:00 am." *Actually, neither one told him that.* (Brant is frantically trying to keep up with the story he's being told.)

Lt R: "Somebody was going to call when the Doctor's office opened." *Maybe the dog.* "But it didn't happen." (Barb had told Sgt. K "I called in to Navarre Pediatric....about <u>12:30 pm</u>......and Dr. Simpson finally got back with me at 6:00 pm last night." There was never any plan to call at 9:00 am. Elaine had barely gotten to her house by that time.)

Lt. R continues on:

Lt R: "We found out cause we were looking for the record...when did this call get placed? Was it early, the first thing? Standing there waiting...like you at the bank? Was somebody standing there at the door...somebody on speed dial.....waiting to hit that last button at 8:30 am... or 8:00 am, or whenever that office opened up..to say look, I've got this sick kid...I got all these issues. What do you want me to do? And the call isn't coming in until 1:00 pm. We're being told Barb 'sugar-coated' the symptoms to Dr. Simpson." *This sounds like a hallucination. I no longer know what he's talking about.*

Brant (having talked with Dr. Simpson a couple days ago): "Dr. Simpson told me then that there was a 93 degree temperature that she noticed... that Barb left a message for her...and she.." (tape ends here). (Later) ...and she also told me she didn't sense the urgency. So I don't understand. <u>You can't sugar-coat a temperature.</u> There's no way you're gonna be able to sugar-coat a temperature of 93 degrees." *Exactly!*

Lt R: (Tuesday night late): "She (Barb) is reading the family medical book, trying to figure out what's wrong with Natalia."

Brant: "<u>That's the book that her mother brought over.</u>"

Lt R: " And she's looking up terms like 'lethargic'. And 'lethargic'...like on page six...in the front of the book...under Medical Emergencies it says if you feel that the symptoms are like this...and it describes 'lethargic'...you should be in one of two places....either the ER, or at your doctor's office..." (Later this same passage was read at trial by the prosecutor).

The police took this medical book mentioned above as "evidence." We no longer had access to it. Consequently, they could say whatever they wanted about it now. That didn't seem right to us. So we bought the identical book for our own reference. What is being passed off as "lethargy" by the police and prosecutor, is actually under the heading of "severe lethargy" in the book. Also, in quoting what to do in case of "severe lethargy" (a term that no one used with police), the police omitted this description preceding the listing of various conditions, including "severe lethargy": "The following emergency symptoms, however, are highlighted because they are either difficult to recognize or not considered serious by some parents. If your child has any of these symptoms, contact your child's physician immediately." (Nothing is said about the ER. And Barb had just talked with her pediatrician a few hours prior to reading this passage late Tuesday night and was told to make an appointment the following morning.) But this is now being used to work Brant into a fever pitch against Barb and Elaine. And later it was used at trial against Barb to show that she just didn't care about Natalia.

> Brant: "See, that's not true...."
>
> Lt R: (not stopping for Brant)..."but we're not responding to anything. The doctors and us...we're hearing these stories like this. Flags are flying up everywhere. Christ, we got a registered nurse early in the morning that's got all this...you know. The doctors hear the story we tell them...that Elaine has provided for us.... That's why I said to you yesterday, they (doctors) looked at us like this.... What kind of nurse is this?" (According to shaken baby theory, Elaine, Barb, and Brant should have been seeing a comatose baby.)
>
> Brant: "Well, yeah. You're telling me that she's (Elaine) there on Tuesday, and she tracks the eyes....the eyes are going in opposite directions...she's lethargic.......Why wasn't an ambulance called?"
>
> Lt R: "Right. Why weren't we in a car on the way to the hospital?"
>
> Brant: "You know, to heck with the hair appointment. To heck with the breakfast. All that just does not make any sense to me whatsoever." *Me neither, Brant. Maybe it's because it's NOT TRUE.*
>
> Lt R: "But Brant....that's what we're told (by Elaine.) I have no reason to set here in this chair and lie to you." *WOW! DOUBLE WOW! This guy is callous.*

86

Brant: "I got home Tuesday. Barb told me Natalia ate real good today. Close to four ounces at every feeding." (And Elaine said the same.)

Lt R: "She's told us that."

Brant: "Now <u>Tuesday night</u> when I got home at 7:15, she was fine. Her eyes were normal...she was focusing...she was squeezing my pinky...her breathing was normal. Barb was sitting Indian style on the bed. Barb kinda picked her up to see if Natalia could support a little weight."

Lt R: "The baby was fine?"

Brant: "She was fine except about 9:30 pm …..Barb said she wasn't eating.......I was up playing with her (Natalia) in bed. Her eyes looked okay" (Tuesday evening.) She (Barb) also told me that Jenny called at 8:00 am in the morning, and told her that Tonya's water was shut off...and they weren't going to be able to get their hair done."

Lt R: "I'm listening."

Brant: "On Monday (the previous day) I went golfing, and I stayed home the entire day (after golfing.) Natalia seemed fine. As far as her not being normal when Elaine got there (Tuesday morning), <u>that's the first I heard of this</u>." *There's a reason for that, Brant.*

Lt R: "Baby was normal when you came home?"

Brant: "On Tuesday. The baby was normal...other than having maybe a slight coolness....Barb told me that Dr. Simpson called around 6:00 pm....and said to make an appointment in the morning."

Later Brant continues:

Brant: "I talked to Dr. Simpson and she said the two statements....eating close to four ounces, and body temperature of 93 degrees... those two things don't go together." (She and Elaine both believed the same thing...that the temperature was inaccurate.) "Dr. Simpson told me 93 degrees in on the verge of organ shutdown." (This could be, although Cynthia Lorentzen, the foster mother said at trial, "So maybe three or four days out of the week she [Natalia] will drop below 90 degrees, and we have to warm her up.")

Lt R: "When you talked to Dr. Simpson, did she ever indicate to you that Barb had told her the exact temperature? Or did Barb..."

Brant: "93 degrees"

Lt R: "That's what she said Barb told her?"
Brant: "And that's what Dr. Simpson said."
Lt R: "That's what Dr. Simpson told you."
Brant: "...told me that."

The police investigators have always tried to get everyone to believe that Barb "played down" Natalia's symptoms to Dr. Simpson. But Brant mentions above the note regarding Barb's phone call to Dr. Simpson's office. The police earlier were somewhat pleased with their detective work that "discovered" Barb's call was at 1:00 pm (even though she had told them that in her interview.) Dr. Simpson showed them the record of the 1:00 pm call. Now you would think it would be unlikely for police to say Dr. Simpson didn't know the exact temperature, because the exact temperature was written on that same note...93 degrees. *But Lt. R still tries to insinuate that anyway.*

Lt R: "So as we've focused...and primarily...to tell you some things, too....is the reason we've dropped back 10 days to two weeks before Natalia comes to the hospital...to look at things...based on the medical evidence doctors have provided us." *TEN DAYS TO TWO WEEKS BEFORE!* (How many times did they say doctors are telling us to focus on the last 24 hours. Once or twice they expanded it to 48 hours. Now it's 10 days to two weeks. Later at trial it will become 3-4 weeks. And the supporting evidence for charges against Barb and Elaine has already been given to the prosecutor. This is some investigation).

Lt. R continues:

Lt R: "The very first day....even we come into these cases, you know...it's just like....Barb. Let's not jump the gun...and start throwing handcuffs on everybody here because..." *He doesn't need all of these injury timings. 24 hours. Two weeks. Whatever. It's Barb.*
Brant: "...you wanted to find out what happened..... and if Barb is giving you a different story...that she went to get her hair done, and they found out the place was closed, then....that's a lie. That's a lie. Cause that's not what she told me." *That's not what she told investigators either, Brant. You should be focusing your wrath elsewhere.*

Brant continues:

88

Brant: " Let's put it this way. If I woulda seen those things. If she woulda seemed...uh...'still'... is that what you're calling lethargic?"

Lt R: "Yeah. It's kinda....not with it."

Brant: "If I was seeing that.....the eyes were going in opposite directions....a low temperature in a newborn. But I definitely...I'm not a nurse. I'm not a doctor. That would raise a question in me right then. Why wasn't something done?" (Brant forgets that he <u>has</u> seen Natalia--- <u>after</u> Elaine did.)

Lt R: "That's what <u>we're</u> asking."

Lt. R continues:

Lt R: "Someone is responsible for this. <u>Basically, you find the people who have charge of the child....and you got the people who did this.</u>" *It's just that simple.* "Okay? So, it is kinda like the three of you (Barb, Elaine, Brant) or four, if we consider Dan...are the people that we are being told....you find the people in charge of the baby....you're gonna find the persons responsible for this." *Shaken baby theory.* (So are they seriously thinking of charging all four of us, in a huge conspiracy, of injuring Natalia, our daughter and granddaughter? Remember the police have already given the supporting material to the Prosecutor's Office for charging Barb and Elaine. Or is Brant really here for some other purpose? And what about me? I was never even interviewed.)

Lt. R then starts in on another one of his "stories" for Brant. But this one tops them all.

Lt R: "<u>But we also have a report</u> of a waitress who apparently knows...or waited on a customer....at a restaurant here in South Bend....who overheard a conversation....who apparently knows your family...and knows Barb. The waitress said she overheard the conversation about....how...the baby's been hospitalized. And there's this conversation about how Barb drank alcohol during the day...while you were gone at work. The conversation from this waitress was....that the people who know your family say that you work a heck of a lot...and are hardly ever home....and that the kids are left in her charge...Barb's charge...taking care of them....and during the day while

you're gone...she drinks. <u>Do you know that to be true?</u>" *Wow!*
Each whopper gets wilder.

Brant: "No. <u>No way!</u>"

Lt R: "<u>Is it possible</u>....that it could happen? Are you seeing evidence
    in your trash?"

Brant: "No. Because that's exactly what I would find."

But Lt. R has a dogged determination to convince Brant of things both of
them know are not true. He <u>must</u> have him as a witness. So he continues to
say things that might turn Brant against Barb.

Lt R: "You've heard the stories. <u>I have alcoholics in my own family</u>.
    I've had people who've injected alcohol in grapefruits, for
    example...and taken them to work...so they could drink
    during the day." *Do you really know that Barb's not a lush?*

Brant: "No. There's really...I mean...well...I guess there's a
    <u>possibility</u>.... But if she did <u>that</u>, I think I would smell
    alcohol on her breath."

Lt R: "You know her well enough to know that? *Planting doubt,*
    and more doubt.

Brant: "I know her well enough to know...to say that she doesn't
    drink while the kids are there....She doesn't even smoke in
    the house." (But even if Brant is not convinced by these
    "stories," the seeds of doubt have been planted in his mind
    about who this "Barb" person really is, and he begins to
    entertain the thought that maybe he doesn't know her. And
    that appears to be Lt. R's incredibly devious purpose.)
    Destroy the family, and then maybe we'll find something out.

Lt. R shifts the conversation to postpartum depression (PPD).

Lt R: "When we talked earlier you told me that there was some
    conversation that you've had with Barb right after birth about
    PPD. What prompted those conversations. Did she come up
    and suddenly tell you, 'Brant, I think I'm suffering from
    depression?'"

Brant: "She told me it was more like...she used the term 'separation
    anxiety.' I said, 'What do you mean by that?' She said, 'Well,
    I don't feel the bond between Natalia and myself.'"

Lt R: "Just out of the blue she asks you that?"

Brant: "Yeah, right. That's when I asked her, 'Do you have any
    thoughts of hurting her?'... I've never had any other reason to
    think...of her even smacking one of our children..... Up <u>until</u>

that point, and even <u>after</u>..... I didn't have <u>any</u> reason to think otherwise. And I asked her the question, and she said, 'No, it's not like that.' She said, 'I just don't feel the closeness.' <u>So she's telling me the opposite of wanting to hurt her.</u> It's telling me that 'I don't feel as close to Natalia as I should'.... She didn't tell just me. She told the nurses at the hospital..."

Lt K: " Before...or after?"

Brant: "I would say right around the same time. The nurses...while Natalia was in the NICU."

Lt R: "Were you there for the conversation?" *Maybe she's lying to you.*

Brant: "Yeah, I was. I know she told me, she told my mom, and Elaine, and Dr. Simpson."

Lt R: "Well, when we interviewed Dr. Simpson, she said she's never had a conversation with Barbara concerning <u>PPD</u>. It has been her habit that when she's had mothers that have brought that issue up, that she's made a note of it in the record of the baby."

Brant: "Dr. Simpson told me a couple days ago that she knew Barb was a little depressed."

Lt. R: "Well, that's not what she indicated to us at all. She said she had no......"

Brant: "See, and Barb never indicated any <u>depression</u> to me. She did state that <u>she didn't feel the bond</u>. She's never been treated for PPD."

Lt R: "Well, that's a very different story than we've heard, to be honest with you. The doctor said 'Absolutely not.'" *So Dr. Simpson's saying she might have had a passing discussion about it with Barb has turned into "Absolutely not" for Lt. Richmond.* "If there were any conversation...or any inclination... it would have been noted in the reports." *Not if it were on the phone.*

Brant: "I thought they always documented phone calls. I asked Dr. Simpson about that. She goes, 'I don't remember if I talked with her (Barb) or not.' She said, 'Sometimes everything's not documented. That's what Dr. Simpson told me." [Heavy sigh]. (Remember that in the police notes Dr. Simpson said she might have talked to Barb about PPD <u>in passing</u>. But Barb didn't usually refer to her "lack of bonding" as PPD. It is the police that keep using that term. As for documentation, Barb and Elaine went to Dr. Simpson's office the day after the Natalia went to the ER, to get a copy of all records. They were told, too, that phone calls are not always documented.

And you will recall that there was only a brief phone slip of the Tuesday evening phone call that Dr. Simpson made to Barb at 6:00 pm, even though Dr. Simpson, the police, and Barb all agreed it <u>was</u> made. So in the midst of all of Brant's angst, he is correct about this.)

<u>Brant</u> (continues): "Why wasn't an ambulance called? Why didn't Barb and Elaine put Natalia in the car and go to the hospital?" (Brant's emotions have been totally abused during this interview. He expresses deep sorrow, disbelief, support, anger, and questioning in cycles during Lt. R's nearly four hour good cop/bad cop solo interview. Occasionally Brant even seems to become disoriented.)

<u>Lt R</u>: "Well, we've got it narrowed down to the three of you." (But now it's moved beyond the original 24 hours to <u>up to two weeks</u>. And <u>I</u> continue to be left out of the picture.) "I've told you that before. <u>Jim Taylor</u>..." (and here it seems Lt. R remembers he's on tape,) "another officer you may have talked to...he may have told you...I don't know what he talked to you about. He's not on this case." (So why did he bring up Jim Taylor? He's Lt. R's partner, and a friend of Brant's family.) "Our <u>focus</u> is down to the three of you." *What focus? You've already given the prosecutor probable cause information to charge Barb and Elaine. Why pretend it's still three?*

<u>Lt R</u> (continues): "We tell the story about....when you were down here before...Tuesday night everything was fine. You wake up Wednesday morning, and everything's gone downhill. We asked <u>Dr. Emenim</u> yesterday afternoon, after I spoke with you. And I asked him again about …. both the bleeding in the brain, and a few other things. He says, 'Something could have happened <u>an hour before</u>' (right before going to the ER, which is classic shaken baby theory of no lucid interval ...symptoms happen immediately). 'I don't know. There's no way to tell. Something could have happened to her at <u>9:30 at night</u>, Tuesday night. Okay.'" *YOU DON'T KNOW? I thought research made it clear. And why is Elaine being charged when she left over 16 hours before this speculation? This just isn't making any sense at all.*
<u>Brant</u>: "All I'm saying is, on Tuesday she seemed fine."
<u>Lr R</u>: "You go to bed and everything seems fine."

Brant: "Other than Barb saying that she's (Natalia) not feeding......
Now I raise the question, now...whether she ate at all on
Tuesday. That's a good question to ask Elaine....cause Elaine
was there." *Brant's mind is being ripped all over the place.*

Lt R: "Elaine said she wouldn't eat in the morning." *Come on! Say
something truthful for a change.* (Elaine's actual comment:
"She did take her bottle. And she has had some spitting up,
but she didn't do any of that.")

Brant: "On Tuesday?"

Lt R: "Yeah. But everything your mother-in-law tells us...it was not
good. But nothing happens." (Elaine does nothing).

Brant: "That's what I don't understand."

Lt R: "And we're so taken back by...when your girlfriend...or
fiance...turns home from the morning gallivanting off to the
hairdresser...or whatever the hell else she did that morning,
okay." (Deep breath, sigh, and chair creaking.) "And [when]
you get home, she says she's eaten more in that last seven
hour time frame than any other day in her life." (Actually
Barb had said that Elaine fed Natalia (4 oz.) twice in the
morning, and Barb had fed her (4 oz.) at about 5:30 pm.) *Lt.
R is not only getting Brant worked up, he's getting worked up,
too.* "Then at 9:00 pm she's not eating anymore...... None of
this is making any sense." *Now it doesn't even make sense to
Lt. R.* (This is the same comment both Brant and Barb have
made individually at least 4-6 times during their interviews--
-it doesn't make sense. And it's the same thought the rest of
us have been harboring during this whole episode.) "You've
come down here... you've probably told the story a thousand
times. There's probably not going to be any inconsistencies
in your story...because it is what it is. But we got phone calls
being placed to doctors that there's no record of." *Consistent
Brant has told you that he was told they didn't record all
calls. It is what it is.* "We've got the story about the
projectile vomiting. There's no record of any projectile
vomiting." *Consistent Brant told you "And she (Barb) didn't
even know the word." Brant said "projectile", and Barb
said, "She's not shooting it across the room...but it's not just
dribbling out.'"* (Barb never once mentioned "projectile
vomiting" in her interview. Brant mentioned it numerous
times.)

Lt. R continues on:

93

Lt R: "Elaine saw something Tuesday. And whether she just....why she didn't do anything.."

Brant: "that's just....that's just strange." *Brant can't believe Elaine would do nothing to help.*

Lt R: "It's probably gonna cause her some problems."

Brant: "...(Whew!) That's just strange. I can't believe that." *Me neither.*

Lt R: "...to pack her grips.....and go back home to Goshen."

Brant: "That's just absurd!"

Lt R: "..leaving Natalia to lay there in the house...in the condition she saw her. To me...that's unspeakable. We have all these problems. Barb says this. Barb says that. We got phone calls (that don't appear in the records). We got....you know..."

Brant: "Obviously she's trying to hide something. She's lying. She's lying to me. (Loudly).

Lt R: "She's lying to all of us....including herself, if she is totally responsible for this. You're not responsible for this. That's why you're here today."

Brant: "I just can't believe....well, I can't believe Barb's capable of this...or her mother....either one of them. Now I know [*because you said so*] that it was either her mother or Barb that did this. If Elaine seen these things on Tuesday, why wasn't somebody called?...... I find it real strange that this was never brought up to my attention. And I find it real strange that...."

Lt R: "I'm the first person to tell you this?"

Brant: "Yeah." *Think about it, Brant. There's a reason you're hearing it first from Lt. R... IT'S NOT TRUE!*

Lt R: "Elaine's never talked to you and go, Brant, I was there Tuesday morning, and I saw all this stuff happening, and I didn't..."

Brant: "No. That's why...I wasn't trying to call you a liar...But why I raised the question that Elaine told you this. Why wasn't this brought to my attention. About Barb talking nasty to Natalia...or putting her into the carseat fast...or people saying they seen her slam her into the carseat." (After talking to Sgt. K, Char and Gary came up with things like Brant's above references that were never mentioned to Sgt. K during the police interview.)

Lt R: "Has your mother told you in the days since...the story about the carseat? You use the same words your Mom does... "slamming her into the carseat." *I wonder why.*

Brant: "Yeah. Mom and I have been talking through this entire ordeal." *Heaven help us.*

Lt R: "Gosh, it's been three and a half hours we've set here and talked. We've had to take the time and try to fine tune the life of Natalia....from birth, up until this incident on the July 27, when she was brought in to the hospital. And we needed to try to figure out what's going on. And I think, more so, you needed to hear from us, again, some of these stories." *My mom used to tell me as a youngster when she thought I was not being truthful, "You're telling stories." Lt. R certainly was "telling stories." Whoppers.*

Lt R: "I asked her own mother (Elaine), 'If your daughter is responsible for hurting her child... because of whatever reason...is she gonna tell us? Would she tell us?' And her mother said 'Probably not.'"

Brant: "Probably not...that Barb would admit?" *That's not the Barb that Brant knows.*

Lt R: "Would admit to doing anything wrong, even if she had. That's her mother's statement. I asked Elaine flat out, 'If Barbara is responsible'.....this is the very first day, okay. You were setting right outside the interview when I asked her Mother that question...cause I heard you guys come in. And I asked her in that interview, that very first day, 'If your daughter were responsible for hurting her....or doing something to Natalia to cause these injuries...would she tell us?' She said, 'Probably not.'" (Elaine's actual words to answer this question: "I don't know. I hope so.") *Probably not? Not even close. I find it increasingly difficult to respect this man.*

Brant: "Shew! ….... Well...I never...I haven't really got into Barb's childhood and that kind of stuff. But there was never any sign to me. Never....ever. (He knew Barb as truthful.)

Lt R: "Would you do me a favor? Give me two minutes. There has been a prosecutor here in the office all the time. I just wanna make sure that he doesn't have any questions to ask you before you leave." *So they do this stuff right in front of prosecutors? That's not good news for any trial that may be ahead.*

Brant: "Whew!" (Pause). Lt. R comes back. "I had questions before I found out what you told me about Elaine doing these checks on Natalia." (Elaine did nothing that Brant didn't already know about, but he thinks she gave some test that showed Natalia's eyes going in opposite directions. And why would he think that?... That's what Lt. R told him.) "That's the first I ever heard of it."

Lt R: "Okay. Like I said......I have no.....<u>I can play the tape for you...</u>" (But Brant doesn't ask.)

Brant: "No....<u>there's no reason for you to tell me that she said that, if she didn't.</u>" *Brant still trusts this guy. He's even more naïve than I was.* "I was just wondering why Dr. Simpson didn't tell Barb, when she found out the <u>temperature</u>.... 'Take her.'" (And to this day Brant is likely unaware that other strong vital signs override a questionable temperature. As are the police. And the prosecutor.)

Lt R: "She didn't recollect that there was a temperature." *Here we go again. Lt. R continues to claim Dr. Simpson didn't know the temperature.*

Brant: "Yeah. It's on the medical record. It was 93 degrees."

Lt R: "Okay. Then I don't know. That would be something we would have to ask." *I can be more agreeable now since you've come over to our side.*

Brant: "I was just wondering if they did a CAT scan...or if they did x-rays before she went to NICU?"

Lt R: "I don't know. Those are questions that....will be something that I will look at." *He undoubtedly knows the answer to Brant's questions. NO.*

Brant: "It's hard for me to even ask this question now, after what I've learned."

Lt R: "No, we know... and in some cases baby's bones do get broken during deliveries, for whatever reason. And that would be a legitimate question for us to ask--- If there were complete body scans done?" (None ever showed up in discovery materials, or at trial).

Brant: "Now that you and I have talked, and I find out what you are saying on Tuesday, that was never brought to my attention .....<u>other that the body temperature being low.</u>"

Lt R: "[Your earlier attorney] had indicated to my partner and I, Jim Taylor....that he was going to file a law suit. But [the bone "fractures" didn't happen at the NICU] because the fractures of her skull, and of her legs, are.... the doctors are saying ...between an hour and 10 days old." (At trial it became 2-3 weeks old for legs, and 3-4 weeks for the skull.)

Brant: "I was just, I just....well, I mean...<u>I just can't believe what you told me about Elaine.</u>"

(Brant has literally been "brainwashed" over the last 3-4 hours and is likely experiencing "cognitive dissonance"--- the psychological conflict resulting from simultaneously held incongruous beliefs. I use the term "brainwashed" since Brant was fed disinformation and whipped into a frenzy. And according to police notes: "At the completion of the interview, Brant Benson began experiencing chest pains. Paramedics and First Responders from the South Bend Fire Department were called to the Metropolitan Homicide Unit Office and transported Brant Benson to Memorial Hospital for treatment. It was later learned that Brant Benson suffered an 'Anxiety Attack' and recovered following treatment." *He never even knew what hit him.*

CHAPTER SEVEN

The support coming from our church, our family, and our friends, once charges were brought against Barb and Elaine, was overwhelming. Almost immediately scores of people offered to serve as character witnesses for us if we needed them. E-mails and letters poured in from 18 states and Canada, Germany, Cyprus, Thailand, Laos, Spain, Philippines, and Japan. More locally we were receiving food, flowers, phone calls, tickets to various concerts, and many, many requests for how people could help us. In the grocery store an older woman, whom I knew only distantly, came up to me and asked how we were holding up. And then with tears in her eyes, she assured me she was praying for us daily. She was not the only one. In that same grocery store at least 15-20 other people over the weeks, many from church, saw me and expressed their concern and support. At church it became difficult to know how to respond to the many personal verbal inquiries about our health and well-being. People cared! And we knew it--- and felt it. What a blessing! But the medical, judicial situation was so complex that we couldn't begin to update each of them on a particular week's activity in less than thirty minutes. That wasn't the kind of response people wanted or expected. So we tried before heading to church each week to have a 30-second response that captured some of the week's happenings and feelings. We also tried to keep people informed by group e-mails that included more content. Many of these people were hurting for us nearly as much as we were, ourselves. And that felt not only overwhelmingly supportive and humbling, but also increased our need to get this all resolved soon to allow them a reprieve, too.

Speed, however, is not a word that is resonates within the walls of justice. Court dockets are full to overflowing, as are attorneys' schedules. More and more charges are being brought by prosecutors. Society demands it. We soon learned a new use of the word "continuance." Approximately three weeks before each scheduled trial date is a "record date," the time when attorney and prosecutor declare whether they are actually ready or not to go to trial. While we were physically present at each of these record dates, we really were there more as a part of the courtroom furniture than as actual people. If one of the parties was not ready, a continuance would be granted and a new trial date set for later on down the road. And when they told us what that date was, we adjusted our schedules accordingly. This happened eight different times for Barb's trial, and eight times for Elaine's trial.

Supposedly in Indiana a trial must occur within six months of charges if the defendant is being held in jail during that time. If you are out on bond, your trial must begin within a year. The prosecutor is not supposed to ask for continuances beyond those times. The defense attorney, however, may ask for continuances beyond those times. What happens in actual practice is that there are various ways for the prosecutor to almost force a defense attorney to ask for a delay. For instance, the central (and <u>only</u>) real piece of hard evidence in our case was the brain and bone scan CD that was taken the day Natalia entered the ER and PICU. This was what doctors looked at to make their <u>diagnosis of shaken baby</u>. How one read that CD was critical to whether there was even a crime. And this was also the scan that was used to give estimates of the timing of her injuries. This main piece of evidence was <u>not</u> among the "discovery" materials that were given to us by the prosecution. Repeated attempts to get the scan were only met with responses that it would be coming. As time dragged on, the message was changed to "it must be lost." *THEY COULDN'T FIND IT!*

This went on for months. Consequently, Jim, our defense attorney, had to request a continuance of the February 2006 trial date. Since it was requested by the defense attorney, it did not count against the one year time limit set for the prosecutor. This lost CD game continued for over 12 months until it was mysteriously found in a police file. But since it was now getting close to the new September 2006 trial date, Jim once again had to ask for a continuance. The prosecutor's one year time clock has not even started ticking yet. And so it went.... on and on. Dragging out for years.

In the midst of all these delays, the family continued to be ripped apart. And Barb continued to pay $40 an hour to visit Isabella four hours each week. The church, our friends, and our families kept faithfully looking for new ways to show their support during these seemingly endless delays.

The women's group that Elaine met with weekly planned a service at College Mennonite Church (CMC) that was entitled "Walking The Journey." It was a service filled with scripture, songs, and prayer. Those present were invited to bring their walking shoes and to walk around the outside of our circular sanctuary, leaving and reentering the sanctuary at will, symbolically walking and praying with our family on this journey. Shoes of many different types were displayed at the front of the sanctuary. This was a very moving experience (no pun intended), and the walking continued for <u>several years</u> each Wednesday at the church. Many, many times people would apologize to us for not actually being at CMC each Wednesday to walk, but would then assure us they <u>were</u> praying for us wherever and whenever they did walk. Week after week......for years.

Walking the Journey

The staff at Westview Elementary, the small fifth and sixth grade school where Elaine worked as School Nurse, in addition to giving many words of encouragement, took up an offering of well over $800 to help with our expenses. During the week of the trial, Westview staff members voluntarily gathered for prayer for our family before each school day. Their principal was one of the first to agree to be a witness at Elaine's trial. And other staff wrote strong supportive character reference letters.

The Pathfinders Sunday School class, the class Elaine and I had joined in 1973, held an evening gathering of class members in one of their homes. There was food, fellowship, support, and a time for asking questions about details that would have been impossible to discuss in the short time we normally had available at church on Sundays. It really felt good to be able to talk about the many facets of what had happened and was happening, as best we knew it, with people that we trusted would not twist our responses to their advantage. We also had a similar conversation with another adult Sunday School class at CMC during its regular meeting time. That, too, was helpful for allowing us to share our story in more detail with those who cared.

One of my high school (class of 1960) classmates from Ohio, a single mother of strong faith who has had her own share of difficult experiences in life, became aware of our situation and made the effort to connect with Elaine and me whenever she came near Goshen. She was a former teacher, and certainly not a person with much extra money. Reminding us of how important it was for Elaine and me to keep a strong bond with each other during these turbulent circumstances that had the potential for tearing apart a marriage, she would give us money and tell us to "go out on a date." This happened more than once. We were usually able to get numerous dates out of that money. Others gave us financial gifts to allow for Barb to visit Isabella more. It was somewhat difficult to accept gifts like these, since it required acknowledging that we were not the independent, self-sufficient people we always thought we were. Now we had to admit to being vulnerable and needy. It took a surprising amount of adjustment to begin receiving, rather than giving, support.

We were the objects of more prayers than we will ever know. Many days Elaine, Barb, and I would just shake our heads in wonderment at the number of people praying for us, not only locally, but around the country and world. One woman from CMC made a commitment to send us a weekly quote from the Bible or elsewhere, often in different hand crafted formats. Another woman representing CMC brought us a hand made comforter that she wrapped around us as she prayed for us, symbolic of God and the church wrapping arms around our family. One of Elaine's colleagues would pray for us daily (with her eyes open) during the same two-mile stretch of road while driving to school.

A surprising number of our overseas friends responded to our situation. "Surprising" in that we knew them from 30-40 years ago. A former teacher from Kuwait and a self-proclaimed agnostic, wrote that he is badgering God on a daily basis on our behalf. Another former Cairo colleague who was currently teaching first and second graders in a New England Catholic school said she "asked 125 children to pray for you. You are in my prayers and the prayers of a Bible group and a Sunday School class." Another former overseas teacher asked her students at the Christian College where she teaches in Canada to pray for us. "I reminded them of this case which I originally spoke to them about last year. My husband and I also pray for you regularly." One more teacher from our Kuwait days wrote, "Believe it that I will be praying for you. Please know that at a very young and vulnerable age, I was touched profoundly by Dan and you, Elaine. Whether you realize it or not, you gave me strength to do the right thing in my life. And when you brought Barbi into your family, I was so touched. Throughout the years I've prayed for Barbi, thanking God that he gave her a Christian home and that she would not have to suffer in a culture at odds with her best interests as a girl." (The irony in this latter remembrance is obvious, since being a stay-at-home young mother meant Barb was the one around Natalia the most, and therefore, the culprit according to our own culture's shaken baby theory.)

The Wednesday evening CMC Prayer Choir included us and our situation each week for years. A retired Goshen College professor shared that he prays for us every day. People at Goshen General Hospital where Barb worked while living with us told her of their ongoing prayers for her and her children. And we also had very close friends locally who called daily to check on our psychological and judicial status, and supported us in numerous ways.

Each of our (Elaine and Dan) siblings, although living in Ohio, Michigan, and New Mexico, gave varying amounts of financial, emotional, and prayer support throughout this ordeal. Others in the younger generation of our extended family also contributed support of various kinds. Elaine's cousins prayed, sent e-mails, monetary gifts, and visited during this time, too. Dan's sister and husband from Michigan attended each day of trial as did their daughter who lives in Washington, D.C.

I probably should not have started down this road. There were/are way too many instances and types of support to include here. I don't remember all of them, and I know I was never even aware of many of them. The point is that we recognize and cherish the outpouring of love and support that came from so many people and in so many forms. We, as a family, have truly been blessed. Both God, and God's people, have cared for us and continue to care for us. And we are the richer for it.

But while we were being personally uplifted in such a miraculous way, that did little to help us understand what was going on. We knew almost nothing about shaken baby theory prior to Natalia's arrival at the ER. So we decided early in our situation that we had better learn something about it. After reading hundreds of articles and studies on the subject, it became clear that we would need medical doctors on our side to rebut the claims of the prosecution's doctors. It was also clear that the doctors for the prosecution would be uncompromisingly certain of their diagnosis. It turned out to be no easy task, however, to find doctors willing to challenge the prevailing theory.

We had read many stories of families that were accused of shaken baby or other child abuse in which the child later was discovered to have had another disease causing these symptoms. Also, people kept coming up to us with stories of families they had known, or heard about, who had a similar experience. Many instances concerned incidents that were originally diagnosed as shaken baby, but later turned out to be something else. Very rarely were the original diagnosing doctors the ones that discovered the real causes. They were too heavily vested in their own theory. Some other doctor would take a more skeptical look at the symptoms and begin to see things that had been overlooked, or didn't fit the diagnosis. These doctors would enter the scene and offer a diagnosis that fit <u>all</u> of the symptoms, or at other times highlight observations that <u>didn't fit</u> the original diagnosis.

It was very difficult in our case to get second opinions. The DCS had taken Natalia and placed her in a foster home about 90 miles from where we lived. We had no legal access to Natalia. We <u>were</u> able, however, through a subpoena, to request that Natalia be genetically tested for brittle bone disease. I had made arrangements through the appropriate clinic at the Indiana University Medical School in Indianapolis to have Natalia tested there. The subpoena, however, like most other things, was weeks and then months in coming.

Somewhere during this process Natalia's foster mother had taken Natalia to the IU Medical Center in Indianapolis for treatment of another of Natalia's serious maladies. Apparently the DCS attorney had known about the subpoena and made the foster mother aware of our request for testing. Anyway, I was at home when I received an unexpected phone call from Paula, the CASA worker. You will recall that the magistrate warned us that if we ever talked with the CASA worker again, we would be risking harassment charges. And here she was calling me. *What to do?*

I reminded Paula of this threat and she replied, "Oh, that was nothing. Don't worry about that." *Don't worry about it! I personally don't need harassment charges.* We had taken the magistrate's threat quite seriously, and my trust in Paula had diminished significantly over the months. What was she up to this time? She said she wanted the doctor's phone number who was planning to do the genetic testing on Natalia so she could call him to request the testing be done while Natalia was there in Indianapolis. This would save both Natalia and the foster mother another trip, which was difficult for both of them. That sounded reasonable, so I gave her the number. *How soon would we be getting a letter from the magistrate's office charging us with harassment?*

At least the testing would be done, and we would know one way or the other if brittle bone disease was a factor in Natalia's situation. We waited a few more weeks. No word about anything. Finally I called the doctor's office and reached him after several tries. He informed me that he had gone to the hospital to see Natalia, but that another physician had charge over her, and he was unable to test her. *Nuts! It's been over a year an we don't have the first basic test done on Natalia yet.* He did offer that he would be holding clinic in South Bend in November (it was currently August) and would look at Natalia there. More time. And we had just received the mysteriously "found" CD of Natalia's brain and bone scans. Obviously the September 2006 trial was out of the question.

Whenever we would complain to our attorney, Jim, about how long all of this was taking, he would respond with one of the pithy little maxims that attorneys keep in their briefcases for such times. This time it was "I've never had a client yet that was hurt by having the trial continued to a later date." *What?* We knew he was trying to reassure us psychologically. But it didn't work. Perhaps if you were guilty, and had no family destruction going on during the waiting time, it might have been true. But in our circumstances, waiting was a slow death. Yet, we did wait. There was no other choice. And the trial was "continued" to December 2006.

In November the Indianapolis doctor saw Natalia in South Bend. He took genetic samples and sent them to a lab in Seattle. As it turned out, the Indianapolis doctor held his clinic at South Bend Memorial Hospital, and the information he got from the Memorial doctors there showed up later in his report. In fact, full sections of his report were taken from the Memorial records. We had hoped to get an outside view which would be more questioning of Natalia's situation and serve as a second opinion, but that didn't happen. The lab reports from Seattle did not arrive in time for the December trial. And the trial was "continued" to April, 2007.

When the lab results from Seattle came in January, they were negative for 90 percent of the known types of brittle bone disease. The Indianapolis doctor mentioned other possibilities we could test for, but he wasn't particularly encouraging us to do that. We felt the odds were likely slim, and the time was too short to do further testing of this type. And we were trying our best to make the April 2007 trial date this time. So we told the Indianapolis doctor that we would not pursue any more testing.

Although in our abnormal lives we were moving towards trial, our normal lives continued as well. Elaine and I celebrated our 40th wedding anniversary in December, and Elaine wrote an annual letter out to our friends.

Tuesday, January 02, 2007

Dear Friends,

We recognize that we sent some of you a communal letter last year about this time, and have not followed up since. Yet some of you have heard lots. And all of you seem to care! For that we are deeply grateful. Actually, we are dependent on the care and love from both you and God during this journey in our lives.

The problem of updating you regarding our situation is that so much happens to stir the emotions every month. Yet, when we sum it up, we are at about the same place as a year ago. Very little has changed. I know that doesn't seem possible. For example, I have two scheduled court hearings in January; Barb has three. But, though we will experience lots of anxiety, it is likely that we will be about where we are now when these are completed. That sounds cynical, but it comes out of our experience, so far. In a sense, Barb and I are living in a time of "ongoing captivity."

Barb's criminal trial has been delayed until April 16. Mine will likely be delayed until after that. Of course we still hope and pray there will be no trial---a dismissal of charges. So far that hasn't happened. Dan (who has no charges against him) nor I may see either grandchild. Barb may not see Natalia, who is in a foster home, at all. From what we've been told, Natalia has not progressed developmentally during the past year. With supervision, Barb may visit four-year-old Isabella, usually twice a week for a total of four hours. Isabella lives with Brant. The separation of relationships and the consequences of that are the saddest and most difficult parts at present. It could get worse (20 years in prison)---or better (freedom and restoration of family relationships)---or somewhere in-between. We wait. (To get a feel of our experiences with Child Protective Services and the judicial system, you may want to read "A Parent's Worst Nightmare" in the January 2007 Reader's Digest.)

Dan continues to support the cause however he can. (Actually, depending on the outcome, he stands to "lose" three generations of his immediate family.) It has been helpful that he is retired and has less structure in his life. At the same time, it is also good that Barb and I are employed through this time. It is the only time that we can take our minds off this circumstance in which we find ourselves. Our work is a place "away", among people who care for us and discuss mostly other things, and where we are in control of something and are contributing somehow to others. Barb continues to live with us in our finished basement area. It is working OK, but of course is not the way she or we want life to be.

106

We all three are trying to take care of ourselves physically, spiritually, and emotionally. We are so thankful for good sleep and health, our home, and our safety. (Looking at the world picture, many do not come close to having those gifts.) I believe it is also true that not many people have known and felt the support from church, friends from all over, relatives, and work colleagues as we have. How would we ever live through this journey without that?

Dan continues to enjoy his fourth year of attending events (soccer, ice hockey, orchestra concerts, academic super bowls, piano recitals, dramas, etc.) in which the high school age youth of our church (MYF) are involved during the week. He averages about 150 events a year plus attending MYF classes on Sunday mornings. Dan is energized by these kids (about 40 of them at seven different high schools), and they really seem to appreciate him and his support of them.

Though our unfortunate circumstances seem to dominate our minds and lives, and seem to put life "on hold" much of the time, we did decide to gather a group of friends for our 40th wedding anniversary in December. The evening included attendance at a performance by a comedy trio named Ted, Lee, and Ingrid, doing a version of the Christmas story called "DoveTale". We really appreciate the emotion and humor that they have found in that story, and have made attendance at "DoveTale" an annual part of our Christmas season over the past number of years. So to have our group of friends there to enjoy this event with us was special. After the performance we all gathered at the nearby home of one of our friends for snacks and hanging-out. Ted, Lee, and Ingrid were there, too (they have become friends over the years). We all had a great time, as it became one of the few evenings of carefree laughter this year.

We all three (Barb, Dan, and I) have grown deeper in our faith and trust and love for God. Not every day could I write that, but overall, I can. Some Scriptures and hymns and prayers have become very meaningful in a new way. I believe we keep changing and growing all our lives. Sometimes I would rather not be given this much change and opportunity for "growth"!

We trust that this past year has been a good one for you, and hope the coming one will be even better.

Elaine Schrock

Some friends knew of a neonatologist (medical doctor specialist focused on infants for the first few weeks after birth) who worked at the IU Medical School. He agreed to listen to our story and help in any way he could. So Elaine and I went down to Indianapolis (three hours each way) to meet with him. We took all of the medical discovery materials that we had been given, which now included the CD scan of Natalia's brain and bones. After we shared our story with him for about 30 minutes, and said that the police were looking for the last person who cared for Natalia, (a la shaken baby theory) he asked to look at the CD scans. As he viewed the various scans of her brain he would ask us questions. Then there was silence for a short while. When he broke his silence, he spoke in a manner exhibiting a certain level of shock. <u>"This is an old injury."</u>

Elaine and I looked at each other. "How old? More than 24 hours?" we asked. "Yes," he answered. "Several days?" we asked again. He responded, "several weeks." "How many weeks? Could it go all the way back to birth (which would have been 12-13 weeks)?" "Well, possibly, but I doubt if it goes back that far. I'm not a specialist in dating brain injuries," he said. "But it's an old injury. It didn't happen in the last several weeks." He also was of the opinion that the injury was likely the result of abuse. *Not so good. But half a loaf is better than none.* We asked if he would be willing to state in court what he had said to us, and he said he would. But he also said, "You don't need me. The radiologist at South Bend Memorial is saying this is an old injury, too." (Among all of the reports that we had shown him was one from Dr. Fischbach, the Memorial radiologist suggesting that Natalia's brain condition might have been a sequela [due to] of 'birth trauma.' And this radiologist characterized the injuries as "subacute to chronic [not new].) This IU Medical School neonatologist graciously spent about an hour of his time with us, and more importantly, took us seriously. We thanked him for that, and he responded "yes" when asked if Jim, our attorney, could be in touch with him.

We headed back the three hours to Goshen with much to talk about. Within the next day or two we scheduled a time to talk with Jim in South Bend. Following that meeting Jim called the neonatologist in Indianapolis. It is not totally clear to us what all happened during that phone call, but the outcome was that Jim decided not to use the neonatologist. Apparently Jim felt it would do more harm than good for our case to have our own doctor state that he felt Natalia's situation was likely caused by abuse, in addition to all of the prosecution's doctors saying that, too. And that turned out to be our ongoing dilemma. Do we challenge the diagnosis (which we really <u>believed</u> was inaccurate)? Or do we challenge the prosecution's choice of Barb and Elaine as the guilty persons? Or both? Our family clearly wanted to

108

challenge both, but you can't challenge a diagnosis without doctors. So we prepared for trial with what we had. And the April 2007 trial was "continued" to May 2007.

We were almost desperate to meet the deadline for this May trial. But when we met with the prosecutor several weeks prior to this date, he indicated that they were still waiting on the results of the further testing being done in Seattle. He believed that we had requested another test and were trying to hide the results. We hadn't requested anything. But the May trial date was "continued" to September 2007. *Unbelievable!* Later we found out that the extra test was requested by the foster mother. But again, the "continuance" was charged to the defense, not the prosecution.

Elaine had many points of contact that I mentioned earlier which kept her grounded in her faith. And Barb had work at the hospital that kept her mind on other things. That was a blessing for her. My own sanity and hope for the future was dramatically heightened by a decision I had made in 2003, over a year before this all started. Actually it wasn't just a decision. I knew I would be retiring in May of 2004 and was looking for how I would like to invest my time and energy following retirement. Having been a member of CMC since 1973, I was aware that the church usually finds some assignment it would like you to fulfill once you retire. And I had an appreciation for that. But I knew, too, that sometimes the assignment and the retired person did not match very well. I also knew that I have a hard time saying "no" to the church. So I could see myself being asked to do something that I had little passion for, yet saying "yes" and feeling somewhat trapped. And I would have only myself to blame for that situation.

Consequently, I began praying and searching about a year before retirement, asking God for direction in what I should do within the church in retirement. After some time, the answer came through to me strongly. Not clearly, but strongly. "Go and be with the MYF" (our church youth group--- high school age). I say strongly, not because it was a loud voice, but because it was a very solid, growing conviction that God was calling me to that task. There have been only a few times in my life that I have gotten what I would name a "call" from God. And while this call was definitely intense, I would have preferred a bit more clarity. "Go and be with the MYF." *What in the world does that mean?* I'm somewhat ashamed to admit that I had never even been in the room where the MYF meets on Sundays and Wednesdays. And in many ways I'm not much of a risk-taker. Following ill-defined directions in life is not one of my personal characteristics. But neither was I ready to ignore a call that strong. So I wrote out a one page proposal of what I might do with the MYF.

Since I believe firmly that any call from God should be accompanied by a corresponding affirmation from those responsible for the area to which one feels called, I presented this proposal to Kristen, who was our youth pastor at that time. In the proposal I volunteered to be present at the various events in which our youth were participating during the week, mostly at their schools. Kristen liked the idea very much, so I asked her to share it with the MYF Executive Council (youth). They, too, were open to the idea, even though only one or two had any idea who I was.

I went to the MYF room on the first Sunday of the new Sunday School year and tried to explain to this group of 35-40 teenagers why I was there. I'm certain my call to "go and be with the MYF" wasn't any clearer to them than it was to me. But they were gracious (well, at least they didn't chase me out of the room) and allowed me to continue to be with them. And so I began attending their events, and normally having a brief contact with them following each event.

There were a wide range of events that included basketball games, choir concerts, tennis matches, academic super bowls, piano and organ recitals, soccer matches, orchestra concerts, faith statements, baseball games, dramas and musicals, hockey games, awards nights, graduations, volleyball matches, and many more. With seven different high schools represented in our MYF within an hour of Goshen, these visits gave me a good feel of where and how the youth were spending their weekdays and nights. I loved it! And I still do. By the time Wednesday evening and Sunday morning rolled around, I had at least some information with which to initiate a conversation. With over 150 weekday events, and roughly 50 Sundays and 30 Wednesday evenings, I was able to be in contact with them nearly two thirds of the days in the year.

I started out thinking I could maybe be helpful to them in some way. And they have expressed strong appreciation for what I do. It turned out, however, that I was the one who gained from these contacts. They helped me and lifted me up during the most difficult years of my life. And now, eight years later, I feel totally at home with each one of them. In fact, more positively, I look forward to being with them. I have been incredibly blessed by them as persons, and enjoy walking with them as they grow in their faith, personality, and skills. Thank you God.

But now, as we continued to prepare with Jim to go to trial in September, it began to look like it might finally happen. There was no "continuance" in sight. Although working at the hospital was a pleasant distraction, Barb was missing her children badly after two years. Visiting

Isabella in a controlled environment, and paying $160 for four hours each week, was better than nothing, but was expensive and wearing thin. She wanted to move ahead with things. Even with the fact that the rate of conviction in shaken baby trials is extremely high, Barb felt she couldn't stay in this limbo situation much longer.

Jim, from his depositions of Brant and Dr. Simpson was finding that both of them had "forgotten" certain things they had each told police. We could only imagine what Char and Gary would "forget" at trial. Yet, we hoped that somehow that the truth would prevail.

At CMC we were having a series for several weeks about "Following God in the Wilderness." The ministerial staff had asked Elaine and me to share our experience in the "wilderness" following the sermon on July 29, 2007 as we headed toward the September trial date. Elaine began her sharing with the following:

From Psalm 31:

In you, O Lord, I seek refuge: do not let me ever be put to shame: in your righteousness deliver me....

Be gracious to me, O Lord, for I am in distress....

But I trust in you, O Lord: I say, "You are my God." Deliver me from the hand of my enemies and persecutors....

Be strong, and let your heart take courage, all you who wait for the Lord.

This Scripture, and so many others, have become my own words--my own prayer. Sometimes it is a hymn that becomes my inner message. Last week it was "Rain Down .... rain down your love on your people ... "

Today, as we continue our "Following God in the Wilderness" theme at CMC, Dan and I are sharing from our wilderness experience. Like the Israelites in Exodus, I complain, become angry and confused, and ask for help to save me when hope diminishes. Yet at other times I am filled with gratitude, trust, and readiness to worship God.

It is very hard in this wilderness:
-not knowing what's coming next (bad surprises).

-not being in control of my life.
-having someone in authority separate me from someone I love so dearly.
-being accused unjustly.

So I Cry out to God.
-Where are you?
-Don't you care? Don't you know what is happening? How long?
-Why did you lead me here to suffer, to rot?
-And maybe me, suffer, but why our daughter and small grandchildren?
-What about your promises of "Ask and it shall be given. Seek and you will find. Knock and the door will be opened."... "Call to me and I will answer" .. and many others.
-And even--Who are you God? This isn't how I knew you.

The answers to these intense questions were not exactly what I wanted to hear.
-"Wait." "Watch." "Trust Me."
-"Trust me more than your rational reasoning."
-"Trust me more than the attorney."
-"You don't need to know, to understand."
-"You don't need to be in control."

Firman, Klaudia, and John Hershberger all three at some time in a sermon about the wilderness, talked about not fighting the wilderness place...to accept reality. That is certainly not my natural response. I didn't like it. It was no fun. It took me over 1 1/2 years of fighting the wilderness before I could accept living in the reality of---this is where I am now, whether it makes sense to me or not. Whether I want to be here or not. I thought the "Promised Land" was closer.
-Accepting the wilderness, if I were going to survive, meant finding and gathering the manna and allowing myself to be fed; drinking the "sweet" water; following the pillar of fire.
-I had to recognize my neediness.
-I was in a position to receive, not give. I didn't know how.
-It was (and is) humbling.

Many of you have been our manna--our nourishment.

I have deep gratitude:

-for so very many at CMC who love me, walk the journey with me, pray for our family and all those involved, and contribute to the fund that helps with visitation fees for Barb to be with her daughter. Even such simple statements like "I trust you" (when I was feeling accusations of being untrustworthy); "You are still the same good person" (when I was wondering who I was becoming); or "We believe you" (when others didn't) were life-saving.

-for safety...a home... food that so many in the world do not have.

-for the sharing of hope and spiritual blessings/understandings at home with Barb and Dan.

-for a drawing of me from Isabella, my granddaughter.

-for Dan fighting vigorously for our cause.

-for notes, e-mails, prayers, and calls from friends all over the world.

The wilderness is definitely a place of learning: (an uncomfortable, unending process).

-what it means to turn it ALL over to God. ALL.

-that I really can't plan my future.

-what it means to be loved by a community, to be ministered to, to receive, to be accompanied as I walk the journey.

-that the Scriptures and our hymnal are true and right and timeless and unbelievably personal.

-that prayer is NOT a last resort.

I'm still in the wilderness:

-but I know as I go into the courtroom with great anxiety, God is already there before me.

-I know I am not alone. When I can't pray, someone is praying for me.

-I know I can be angry with God, prosecutors, social workers, family members, attorneys, --and God is big enough to take it, still love me, and still hold me tenderly.

-When more and more things seem to go wrong and out of control, I know God is over me, protecting the rocks and debris from hitting me on the head.

> -When I feel so very sad, I know this is where I
> am for now, and I hope and pray for God's gift of
> a "new thing".

Dan then shared the following:

> The last two years have been the most difficult of my 65-year life.
>
> 1. While I don't personally have any felony charges against me, or
> have the threat of prison time hanging over me ....I still feel very
> much in the middle of all of this.
>
> 2. We have a very small family.... just <u>five</u> of us.
> > A. I haven't seen our two grandchildren, Natalia and
> > Isabella, for nearly two years.
> > B. I have watched as my wife, daughter, and
> > granddaughters have suffered through these same two
> > years.
> > C. And the possibility is very real that I might lose <u>all</u>
> > <u>three generations</u> of our family in the coming months...
> > and end up alone.
> > D. It's also clear that my normal ways and methods of
> > working with major problems .... don't work in this
> > situation.
> > E. My attempts to prepare myself, exert influence, search
> > for options, break it down into smaller parts, keep the
> > process moving, and bring some   sort of rationality and
> > control to problems we face... have had little-to-no impact
> > at all.
> > F. In fact.. I'm not certain anyone on this planet has any
> > control over this situation.
> > G. So I try to find the humor in what is happening. There
> > is some .... but not much. I try to help others... that
> > improves my perspective and my attitude. I try to remain
> > faithful to my calling... and that gives me hope.
>
> 3. But I do struggle at times with certain problems.
> > A. Perhaps the most difficult thing for me is to find that
> > line between where my responsibility to work at this
> > situation ends .... and where I simply turn it over to God.
> > That line seems to keep moving back and forth from day
> > to day. Where do I work diligently... and where do I let
> > go?
> > B. I feel that I can accept a good bit pain and grief ..... and
> > remain solid and steadfast in my faith...IF I know what
> > 'purpose' is being advanced by my doing that. At this
> > point, however, I'm uncertain what that 'purpose' is. Who

is being helped by all of this? .. And that makes it more difficult.

C. Since we're in the middle of this awful mess .... and the conclusion is still unknown .... I might see this situation differently a year from now. But right now I have serious doubts that we will ever know the truth of <u>what</u> happened to Natalia, and <u>when</u> it happened.

4. What I do know, and will affirm to you, is that:

A. We are currently in the wilderness. And...

B. God is there walking with us.

C. Sometimes God makes that clear to me in a direct way ..... But more often I see God's presence in God's people. You all ..... and many others ..... are a very significant part of being the face of God for me in this situation.

D. I know how difficult it's been for you to know how to help us ..... and for us to know what to tell you would be helpful for us.

E. But I would like to let you know that we have felt a tremendous amount of support from you. Your prayers, personal inquiries, notes, walking the journey with us----- have been more helpful to us than you could ever know.

5. And I would especially like to thank the MYF for their support of me in so many ways.

A. They have listened to my story .... and I have felt the presence of God.

B. They have laid hands on me ..... and I have felt the presence of God.

C. They have prayed for me ..... and I have felt the presence of God.

D. When Stephanie asks "How are you <u>really</u> doing?"... I see the face of God.

E. When Martin chooses to walk out of his way to sit with me in the bleachers at a soccer match .... I see the face of God.

F. When at Choir Contest in Indianapolis, Laura invites me to sit with her at lunch and introduces me to her non-CMC friends...I see the face of God.

G. When Zach put his hand on my shoulder and says nothing... I see the face of God.

H. When Meredith prays aloud for me after our MYF Sunday School sharing time ....I see the face of God.

I. When Clayton stretches out his arm to shake hands with me and says "How's it going, man?".... I see the face of God.

6. And I could go on and on and on. The point is this:

    A. When you don't know what to say ..... or what to ask. .... or what to write ....

    B. Or you sense that your question must have been poorly worded ..... because our response was vague ....

    C. Know that the 'words' are often not the most important thing. Your reaching out indicates to us that you care .... whether verbally ... through your touch .. or through prayer. We have felt your loving care ..... and know that God cares for us through you. And that is HUGE! That is AWESOME!

You people are our manna and water in the wilderness.

And now we're ready for trial.

CHAPTER EIGHT

It was now September 2007, and Barb's trial was scheduled to begin Monday, September 24. We felt reasonably confident during this time. Elaine was experiencing her first fall of retirement, and not heading into a new school year. Barb was continuing her work at Goshen General Hospital. And I was starting a new school year of MYF events. We were trying to keep life as normal as possible. Elaine sent the following email to our friends:

Now that we are in September, I want to give you a short update of where we are now in our journey.

First, Barb, with her attorney, has decided to go for a bench trial (no jury). We have discussed the pros and   cons with some of you. In short, on the "pro" side, a judge is more likely to understand the medical facts and not be influenced by the emotions of the stories.   Also, he will be clearer on the meaning of "reasonable doubt." On the "con" side, our attorney will not have a jury of 12 to "manipulate." There is only one judge. Whatever he decides is it.

For some reason as times goes by, we are feeling more positive about the outcome of all this. I don't know all the reasons for that subtle inner change, but we give God and the prayers of friends some of the credit!

We did have a downer this week. The family court again sent Barb a summons to appear in court next week for a hearing regarding a permanent termination of her parental rights of Natalia. We don't know if Brant got one or not. When this happened once before and we agonized for weeks, the day came and Barb appeared, there was no judge, no court time, and they said sending that summons was a "mistake". Wow. A painful and costly mistake for us. We thought we could assume the same this time, but a phone call revealed they are going ahead this time. Do they not know Barb's criminal trial is later this month? It just doesn't make sense. We are hoping that once again the left hand doesn't know what the right hand is doing. It is two different courts, two different judges, a whole other system. Please remember us. That date for Barb is Wednesday, September 5. We're asking both our attorneys to be there, but haven't heard a response from them.

Barb's "record date" for the criminal trial is Tuesday, September 4. That is the time you go to court before the judge with the attorney to confirm readiness for the trial date (September 24 week). So far, we have always received a delay of the set trial date. We are expecting that his time there will not be a delay. We'll let you know later in the week.

My "record date" is 9/25 with trial date 10/15 week. It is all getting more real, again.

We love and need and covet and are grateful for your prayers.

Elaine

Between the first week and the third week of September Elaine was our communicator and prayer. We found out that we would not be able to have a bench trial. (That was a huge disappointment.) In the meantime, I was able to attend 16 MYF events. And Barb kept working. Elaine sent out one final email before the trial for both of us:

Dear Loving and Supportive Friends,

One more week and we will be in the courtroom. Actually, September 24 starts Barb's trial, but in essence it impacts my (Elaine) trial, scheduled for the week of October 15. In most ways we feel more hopeful than we have for the past two years. Maybe this is what happens when you wait? Maybe we are numb? Maybe it is the power of prayer.

That's not to say that we are totally relaxed and are having fun. No. The cloud is still hanging heavy over our heads. But it is lighter most of the time. We want to move on. Barb and her children need each other. Dan and I need grandchildren again. And we all need to resume a more normal life.

Barb requested a bench trial (no jury, just a judge only) due to the nature of the charges and medical   evidence. In spite of the fact that our attorney and the judge agreed, the prosecutor denied us that.   So Barb and our attorney will start with jury selection Monday afternoon, September 24, with the actual trial likely starting the next morning about 9:00 am, possibly lasting the entire week. Dan and I are witnesses for the defense, so cannot be in the courtroom for any of it.

Several of you have asked about being present. We welcome your presence, but know that this Superior Court in South Bend, 101 S.

Main Street (northeast corner, 2nd floor, Judge Chamblee), has only 18-20 seats for observers. There is a large open area outside the courtrooms.

We also welcome your prayers wherever you are, both now and during the trial. Thank you for your help and care in so many ways.

Elaine & Dan

Thursday, September 20 was Isabella's birthday. The prior year on Isabella's birthday, Barb and Elaine had gone to Families First in South Bend with gifts in hand to meet with Isabella. Brant never brought Isabella for the visitation time, so after waiting for about an hour, Elaine and Barb decided to head back to Goshen. Then they saw water underneath their car in the Families First parking lot. Fortunately, they were able to borrow a hose and fill the radiator, but that lasted only a few miles before it overheated again, this time near a car dealership. It was dark and I was at a soccer match in Goshen. *I'm not certain what I would have suggested if they could have reached me, but I know I was supposed to have had some wise advice to offer.*

The car dealer gave them a gallon of water to take with them, with instructions to keep the heater on, stop when the gauge reached a certain point, wait 20 minutes with the engine off, and then put the water in the radiator. So Elaine and Barb headed toward Goshen, waited beside the highway for 20 minutes when it overheated again, poured in the water, and started up again. This time they were able to reach Goshen safely, and we got a new water pump put into the car the next day. But their birthday visit to Isabella was both an enormous disappointment and a scary nightmare.

This year (2007) Barb was able to visit with Isabella at Families First for her birthday. It was a time of joy and celebration. On her return to Goshen and less than a mile from our home, she was hit by a car and trailer that hadn't noticed the stop sign. She braked and was fortunate that he only took off her front bumper. The man stopped and apologized, and Barb was gracious with him. She was thankful that the situation was not worse. (In her younger years Barb might have been less generous in her response, but her perspective on what is really important was changing. It was just four days before her trial date, yet she actually was able to laugh a bit when describing the accident.)

Our normal routine of life continued. Barb went to work at the hospital. Friday evening Elaine spent four hours at CMC hosting homeless people. Saturday I was at a volleyball tournament. Sunday we went to church. And Monday afternoon jury selection began. Once I had read exactly what was said to police two years earlier by Barb, Brant, and Elaine, I was amazed at the congruity of their stories. For three people with little sleep, and in initial stages of shock, their recollection of events was quite consistent. And they certainly didn't have time to rehearse. They had each arrived at Memorial Hospital at different times in different vehicles and almost immediately the questioning began.

There were some normal glitches in memory like Brant giving his wrong age and wrong date for purchasing their house, and Barb's inability to come up with a specific time in which she experienced her period of detachment with Natalia. I didn't find any gaps in Elaine's memory. But the three of them certainly gave much more similar accounts of what and when they observed things than Matthew, Mark, Luke, and John did in their gospels. We knew, however, that the prosecutor would do <u>anything</u> he could to expose even the smallest inconsistency in stories. And that is particularly nerve-wracking when you are on the witness stand trying to remember exactly what you saw, and when you saw it, more than two years after the fact.

Barb and Jim spent Monday afternoon in the courtroom selecting a jury. Here, again, one has to question to what extent anyone is actually interested in the <u>truth</u> of what really happened in a given case. The prosecution tries to eliminate all jurors they believe might be inclined <u>against</u> conviction for the case they are presenting, and the defense wants to eliminate jurors that might vote <u>for</u> conviction. There are even <u>jury consultants</u> that will give you statistical data for the different characteristics of jurors who voted for or against conviction during similar trials in the past, so that you may choose accordingly. Nevertheless, a jury <u>was</u> selected. Barb felt fairly positive about the selection process. (In fact, she cited one juror who said he could not remain unbiased in this case. When asked why, he responded that he had known Barb from somewhere and had always liked her. He didn't feel she could be guilty of what she was charged. Though obviously he was dismissed, Barb was pleased to hear a positive comment about herself. There hadn't been many coming out of the South Bend community over the past two years.) And Elaine and I felt positive about the fact that one or two jurors seemed to have had at least some medical understanding.

120

Since Elaine and I were to be witnesses, we were not allowed into the courtroom during the whole week except when testifying, and for closing arguments. We didn't know how difficult that would be until after we had actually spent the whole week in the large atrium outside the courtroom. Elaine did a lot of walking and praying on the second floor of the courthouse. She carried a bag with her daily which included her police interview transcript, "Psalms," a <u>Sing the Journey</u> songbook, three pages of printed out prayers, a small blank legal pad, crackers, and Henri Nouwen's book, <u>The Path of Waiting</u>. I, on the other hand, sat on the concrete bench about 40 feet outside the courtroom door and worked on my Sudoku puzzles. (During the two years prior to the trial, Elaine and I had discovered that crossword puzzles were about the only thing that we could concentrate on together. Many other areas of life just didn't seem as important as before. But since we decided not to sit together during this week, I decided to bring my Black Belt Sudoku book. Elaine hadn't gotten into Sudoku yet.) We were not allowed to talk with anyone about the case. So any conversation was rather artificial, and ignored the huge elephant in the room. As the week wore on, the bench got harder and harder. One day Elaine told me she had found a restroom on the second floor <u>directly over the courtroom</u>. She made a practice of using that restroom whenever necessary, and found a certain glee in the symbolism that represented for her.

Since I was not allowed to be in the courtroom, it was not until <u>after</u> the trial that I was able to really begin the process of understanding what had transpired during the week. Barb shared some of her remembrances, but she was under attack for the whole trial. That's not the best circumstance in which to be alert and have an accurate recollection of all that was said by witnesses. And Jim tried, too, but he also had to be thinking ahead whenever something was said. There was precious little time for him to reflect on anything. Much of the testimony was very technical in nature, sometimes stated with little explanation, and difficult for lay people to understand, particularly in the verbal, quick- paced, and week-long trial. Making it even more difficult to grasp the medical testimony was the fact that prosecution doctors disagreed with each other on many things. It was not until I read through the word for word trial transcripts (every word is recorded) over and over that I could get a better sense of what was actually said by doctors, and what Brant's family said, and how that testimony compared to what had been said two years earlier to the police.

The prosecution obviously didn't like Dr. Fischbach's comments about Natalia's brain injury possibly being due to <u>birth trauma</u>. Or that the injuries were not new, but <u>old</u>. One mystery that we never solved was that Dr. Fischbach's radiology report, made on Natalia's first day (07/27/05) at

Memorial Hospital, stated her brain condition as a possible "sequela of birth trauma." That report was copied at 1:08 pm, 07/27/05 and sent to us as part of the medical records. Another report was copied at 5:08 pm the same day, four hours later, regarding the same examination, and was also sent to us later. This second report, however, was identical to the first report with the exception on <u>one word</u>. The "sequela of <u>birth</u> trauma" had been changed to "sequela of <u>prior</u> trauma." The changing from a possible <u>birth trauma</u>, to a possible <u>prior trauma</u>, had huge implications for a case of this type. Why had that change been made, and who requested it? (We had suggested to doctors initially that perhaps something had happened early in Natalia's life, or during pregnancy, and had been told that was not even in the realm of possibility.) Needless to say, Dr. Fischbach never made it onto the prosecution's team of doctors. They picked only the doctors that gave opinions that fit the prosecution's theory.

The prosecutor in this trial, Ken Cotter, early in his opening remarks indicated to the jury that for <u>precautionary</u> reasons, "<u>a full body x-ray scan was done</u>" (on Natalia at birth). If any defendant has uttered such a falsehood, Mr. Cotter would have excoriated them. The only x-ray ever taken of Natalia at the time of her birth was of her chest, to check for breathing difficulties. Our contention was that there was <u>no baseline</u> full body bone and brain scan done at birth, which makes it impossible to rule out bone and brain problems at birth. (If you don't know what things were like at the start, how can you reliably claim they happened later?) In fact, even the prosecution's doctors indicated that Natalia did have <u>brain damage</u> already prior to birth that was undiscovered until these ER scans were taken three months later. And if she was born with one brain problem, is it not possible she had others? So why would Mr. Cotter say this, and then fail to produce such full body scans in court?

Mr. Cotter went through a list of the various injuries (conditions) that Natalia had. He then listed a number of situations that Barb mentioned to doctors when asked if she knew of anything that could have caused these injuries to Natalia. Next Mr. Cotter attempted to remove Brant from the picture, by saying "Brant really didn't have much interaction with Natalia because <u>he was working</u> so much." And later, "You are going to hear from other individuals who saw Barbara interact with Natalia. (Never any mention that they are all part of Brant's family, and that most of the interaction was of the same few hours of one day.) Finally "Barbara Schrock battered Natalia to the point where now Natalia is going through puberty, she has breasts, she has pubic hair, <u>her brain doesn't work the way it did</u>." (There was never any evidence that Natalia's brain <u>ever</u> worked as it should have. We thought this [precocious puberty] might be evidence that, along with her other brain damage, her brain didn't develop normally in these areas, too. There was a broad range of things that Natalia was suffering from, and all of them were always attributed to <u>Barb's unmerciful beating of Natalia</u> again and again.

Dr. Emenim, one of the Pediatric Intensive Care Unit (PICU) pediatricians, was the first witness to testify. On the surface, Dr. E seems like a prosecutor's dream doctor. He speaks in black and white terms. Ambiguity does not exist. The big, bold statements he makes are good for posters, bumper stickers, and a prosecutor's closing arguments. Every jury member can understand what he is saying. But he has a downside, too. Occasionally he appears to trip over his ego, and makes huge, God-like pronouncements that are just too wild to believe. *At least by most people.*

Dr. E, as you remember, indicated that "it was clear from the <u>very first day</u> ...that this was a non-accidental injury." Now that's not necessarily wild, because many pediatricians believe in the shaken baby theory. But to say, as Dr. E did, that "we can easily recognize it when we see it" and "once you know what it is, it is not hard to pick out at all," when other reputable doctors just as strongly would say it's <u>much more questionable</u>, seems a bit condescending to those other doctors. I will list other <u>statements by Dr. E at trial,</u> comment on some here, and compare the rest with statements by other doctors later:

(1)   She also "had a big gash in her skull". (Dr Cockerill says it was a simple linear skull fracture that spread apart when Natalia's brain swelled three-four weeks earlier.)

(2)   Natalia also had rib fractures, and the "ribs had different stages of healing suggesting they did not occur at the same time." (Dr Cory, the <u>bone injury timing expert</u>, would <u>not</u> say they were fractured at different times when asked. And even the prosecutor, in his closing remarks, indicated they could have been fractured at the same time as the massive brain injury.)

(3)   It's "<u>very difficult</u> for the ends of the bone to fracture." (Dr Cory: "It's just starting to turn from cartilage to bone [at the end of of a bone], and it's <u>easy</u> to fracture."

(4)   In response to whether he examined Natalia's birth x-rays, he said "Yes, I did look at <u>those</u>, too." (Actually, there was only <u>one</u> chest x-ray.)

(5)   "the shear injury tears them (blood vessels) apart so they have lots of bleeding." (He's talking <u>theoretically</u> here [but doesn't say so], because Natalia's brain is too damaged to see any shearing on the scans. He's assuming the vessels have

123

been torn, because that's what the theory states.) "We call it the Shaken Baby Syndrome." *Is there a shear injury in Natalia's brain? None that can be seen.*

(6) "Without referring to notes I do no recall that." (Dr. E has "forgotten" his notes for this trial, and cannot confirm that Natalia had <u>brain damage prior to birth</u>. I've heard from other doctors that they are sometimes coached to not bring notes to trial so they only have to talk about what they want to. The rest they "don't remember.") You'll remember that Dr. E also told Brant at the hospital that he knew nothing about Natalia's missing corpus callosum (in the brain). He did offer under questioning that this brain damage that Natalia had (which he didn't know about) is something that would happen in the <u>first trimester</u> of pregnancy. And while it's absence would not cause Natalia's current brain condition, one wonders if <u>other</u> brain problems might have been present at birth.

(7) Did you tell police the trauma to the brain happened 2-48 hours before ER? "Never said that. You're not going to find that in my notes." *Seems a bit defensive.* (So he <u>does</u> know what's in his notes. Yet, according to police, Dr. E told them "It could have happened an hour before [ER]. Or at 9:30 pm Tuesday evening [seven hours before]. I don't know. There's no way to tell.") *It seems like he's saying both "yes" and "no."*

(8) "Non-accidental injury to the baby. <u>There is no doubt...not one iota</u>." *I speak with all humility.*

(9) What does a seizure look like in a baby? Would the eyes flicker? "Sometimes, yes." Would they look like they were winking at you? "Sometimes, yes." The brain injuries that you saw in Natalia...could they cause seizures? Yes, they could cause seizures." (So if one wanted to know <u>when</u> the injury to Natalia happened, it seems reasonable doctors might take into account <u>when</u> the seizures were observed. But that information was totally ignored.) What about the baby arching its back? "We don't see that. They're not like older children because their brain and nerves are not well formed yet."

(10) "the caregiver who does this to the child...<u>we never get the straight story</u>.....But it is clear from <u>our own medical expertise</u>." (We <u>know</u> what it is. <u>The caregivers all lie</u>. That's the starting point, and the ending point.) *Guilty.*

Next to take the stand was **Dr. Simpson**, the family pediatrician. What follows is a listing of her more significant comments.

Question: What time did you speak with Barb on the phone Tuesday (July 26)?

Dr S: "I don't remember."

Question: Was it during the day, or after hours?

Dr S: "It was during the day." (You will recall earlier that Dr. S told police that she called Barb "after regular office hours" and told Barb to "call her office the next morning to schedule an appointment.")

Question: Did you tell Barb to bring Natalia in immediately, or the next day?

Dr S: "I don't recall."

Now this above testimony highlights a problem that happens throughout the trial. Dr. S gives two "I don't remember" answers, and one totally incorrect answer that contradicts what she said to police just two days after Natalia came to the ER. Barb gave her recollection of those events, which agreed with Dr. S's original statement to police. Sgt. Kaps is sitting at the prosecution table and knows what Dr. S has told police. He interviewed her and knows the "truth." But he says, and does, nothing. So now Barb and Dr. S have different versions of the phone call for the jury. Who will the jury believe.... the child abuser, or the doctor (and police)? In theory their versions should carry equal weight. But in reality--- not likely. And the prosecutor clearly understands this reality. In his closing remarks to the jury, the prosecutor later says, "If you don't believe the doctors, come back and say, 'sorry, we don't believe you.'" *What jury is going to do that?*

Question: What did Barb tell you in that phone call?

Dr S: "All I remember is she (Barb) said Natalia had a low temperature and she wasn't herself, but she was eating and drinking OK."

Question: What was the temperature?

Dr S: "93 degrees."

Question: Did you tell her to come in immediately?

Dr S: "I wasn't convinced that she had the 93 degree temperature because her symptoms didn't match the temperature."

So Dr. S is verifying here that what Barb told the police two years earlier is actually what Barb said to Dr. S. Barb also claimed she mentioned in that conversation that she had been feeling detached from Natalia for a period of time. Dr. S doesn't remember that, but admitted to police earlier that "it was possible that she may have had a passing discussion with Barbara

125

Schrock concerning postpartum depression." At trial, <u>two years later</u>, she is more definite.

> <u>Question</u>: During the course of Natalia's life, did Barb ever tell you she suffered from PPD?
> <u>Dr S</u>: "No."
> <u>Question</u>: And would you have indicated that in your notes?
> <u>Dr S</u>: "Yes."

You will recall that the only record of that call was the original phone note on which Dr. S had written "told mom to make an appointment." Barb also may have called it (what is being referred to as <u>PPD</u>) something else. She used "separation anxiety" with Brant. The term used is much less important than the description given [a feeling of detachment]. But the prosecution preferred using the <u>term PPD</u> because they felt they could make more grandiose claims about Barb.

> <u>Question</u>: What is postpartum depression?
> <u>Dr S</u>: "It's just severe depression."
> <u>Question</u>: Do people <u>say</u> they have postpartum depression when really they're suffering from something else?
> <u>Dr S</u>: "<u>Yes</u>.... I've heard it used in all different ways. And remember there is various degrees. <u>I mean people can be mildly depressed</u>." (Dr. S essentially says people may call it <u>PPD</u> when they are actually experiencing something else.) *But the prosecutor purposely doesn't hear this answer from Dr. S to his own question. Nor from Dr. O later. Nor from Dr. Rutt even later. It would mess up his "evidence" against Barb.*

No one saw <u>severe depression</u> in Barb. Not Brant, or anyone in Brant's family, or in our family. Dr. S was not aware of any depression. Police officers said the house was "very clean and well kept" (with two adults, two children, a dog, and having left in a hurry for the ER.) Severe depression? All testimony points to Barb's keeping Natalia right beside her in the bedroom every night. Not in some other room. Severe depression? On the Sunday prior to the Wednesday 911 call, Barb loaded Natalia into her car and drove to Michigan to visit Brant's grandmother who was dying from cancer. Gary testified that he was ready to bring Bella to Barb's place and that she wouldn't have needed to make the trip. But she did. Why not just stay home if you're severely depressed? In the hospital Barb was concerned <u>both</u> for Natalia's health condition <u>and</u> for her own personal well-being, once the police started making accusations. Members of Brant's family thought she should <u>only</u> have been concerned about Natalia. But isn't it a healthy sign to also care about yourself, too? Severe depression? There simply was no severe depression. Barb consistently described what she <u>was</u> feeling to nearly everyone. But the prosecution recognized that PPD was an avenue to solidify the diagnosis of abuse, and to center on Barb as the abuser. And in the prosecutor's closing to the jury, he referred to Barb's "postpartum depression" heavily.

Next on the witness stand was **Dr. Okanlami**, the other pediatrician who with Dr. Emenim head up the Pediatric Intensive Care Unit (PICU) at South Bend Memorial Hospital.

Question: What was Barb's <u>demeanor</u> like?
Dr O: "I would say she was calm. I mean she was not upset that we asked her questions."
Question: What kind of questions did you ask her?
Dr O: "What brought this child to the hospital? What did you notice at home. Past medical history. What other injuries could the child have been exposed to?" (But even though doctors asked for this information, when Barb [and Brant] suggested possible answers, she was excoriated by the prosecutor for telling all these "stories" and trying to <u>explain</u> Natalia's injuries.)

Question: Talk about the injuries you saw.
Dr O: "She had a skull fracture. She also had an intercranial bleed.....retinal hemorrhages, and a retinal detachment..... fractures in different stages of healing. <u>(The fractures) were not injuries that occurred in the same time frame as the brain injury</u>." *Are you certain?* (Other doctors for the prosecution would disagree later.)

Question: Did she show any other abnormalities?
Dr O: "Well, there was.....what do you mean by abnormalities?" (I believe Dr. O was about to get into the prior brain damage of which she was aware, and then thought better of it.)
Question: Difficulties because of her <u>premature</u> birth? (Natalia's brain damage before birth was not due to prematurity. This allowed her to answer the question in another way.)
Dr O: "It would have been impossible to find those out because she was unconscious, and part of the examination of how appropriate a three month old is considering her prematurity would be interaction of that age. <u>It was impossible to examine</u>." (Dr Cockerill later <u>claimed to have examined Natalia</u> when rendering a time frame for her brain injury.)

Question: Who had postpartum blues?
Dr O: "Natalia's mother."
Question: And Natalia's mother is the one who told you that?

Dr O: "Yes."

Question: Did she explain what she meant by that?

Dr O: "Well, I took it to mean she had some form of a postpartum depression which is very common in women after delivery. But she did mention to me that she did not feel like she had bonded with the child. So in this type of situation, you know, we do get a little concerned. But again, you know, she volunteered this information as part of the history."

Question: Did she tell you whether she was still suffering from PPD?

Dr O: "The impression that I got in talking to her was it something she had and she was over that at that point in time."

Question: Did you determine if this was accidental or non-accidental trauma?

Dr O: "It was my impression that this was a child who had a pattern of being abused......she had a blood clot in her brain, she had a retinal hemorrhage on each side. Those in themselves without a cause was significant enough for me to say this was non-accidental trauma."

Again, this is classic shaken baby theory. If you see these elements, and the caregiver cannot explain how the child got them, the care giver is guilty. The trial becomes a formality.) The other injuries "were at various stages of healing, which demonstrated a pattern here, that this was not even an injury that occurred only at the time of presentation." Dr. O is saying the 24-48 hour "injury" was not the only one. (In fact, it is quite possible that nothing happened at the time of presentation, and that it all happened well before. There is only one minor [questionable] piece of "evidence" for any injury in the last few weeks, that being the few specks of new blood in Natalia's brain.

So we have represented here one of the many "Catch 22's" present in this case. Shaken baby theorists believe that there is an injury (boom!)... and the symptoms emerge immediately (no lucid interval), meaning there is no time between the injury and the symptoms. Hence, everybody's looking at the last two hours before either the ER, or death. Who was there? All you need to do is find who the caretaker was at the time these symptoms of bleeding in the brain, swelling of the brain, and retinal hemorrhages occur, and you've caught the abuser. That's the theory. Now we have doctors testifying that these injuries happened over a period of time. But that doesn't fit the theory. There is not supposed to be a period of time. There is no such thing as a lucid interval in this theory. One might think that doctors would then question the diagnosis. But not so. They've already committed themselves. Now it's just a matter of saying that we have a "serial abuser" here. It's "shaken baby" over and over. Natalia's been abused over a long period of time. Guilty one way, guilty the other. (But watch, as we move through the coming chapters, how the doctors and the prosecutor mix and match different observations, trying to make sense of this dilemma, but twisting themselves into pretzels in the process.)

Question: And did you review the x-rays?

Dr O: "Yes....and of course as you know we defer to the radiologist who gets the final report on all the x-rays."

Question: Did you read the radiologist's report on all of the x-rays?

Dr. O: "Yes.

Question: Were you aware of the reports done by the radiologist that made reference to the corpus callosum in this child?

Dr O: "Yes. I remember that.... (continuing later).... It's not usually a cause for presentation in children unless it's associated, which it also can be, with seizures in some kids."

Question: What type of seizures might a baby have?

Dr O: "Seizures in a baby could be very difficult to diagnose, again to the untrained person, because a baby's seizures could be anything from they stop breathing and have absolutely no movement at all in their body, to stiffening up. (Recall that Dr. E said "we don't see that." He seemed not to want anything to interfere with his diagnosis.)

Question: Could it include the way their eyes flutter?

Dr. O: "Children could have eye movements that range from just staring off in one direction to arrhythmic movement of the eyes."

Note that Brant, Char, Barb, Elaine, and Dan all saw Natalia blink one eye, stiffen and arch her back, and eyes going off to one side at different times throughout Natalia's life. If these were seizures happening, then something was wrong with her brain much earlier than these doctors are talking about.

Question: Did you report to the police what time period this head injury would have taken place?

Dr O: "I probably would have said something of the nature of this injury would be within a 48 hour period or so......this would have been a recent injury." (Dr. O is a pediatrician. Therefore, this injury to the brain occurred very recently. That's the theory, not necessarily the fact.)

Question: Do you know whether the skull fracture was acute (new) or chronic (old)?

Dr O: "Well, there was no bone laid down around that skull fracture, so it was my impression that it was a fresh fracture." (Dr Cockerill, the neurosurgeon, said the skull fracture most likely occurred at the time of the massive brain injury [three weeks old, or more]. Dr. Boll at Memorial

129

Hospital said it was "not new" on his report. And Dr. Cory said it could have been either old or new.) *That's really helpful. Not one of them agrees.*

Question: It would have been acute?

Dr O: "It would have been acute (new)." (She would change her mind about this later.)

Question: Would seizures, knowing what you know about her injuries, be consistent or inconsistent with those injuries?

Dr. O: "It would be consistent."

When doctors use "is consistent with," it simply means that those symptoms may be present with whatever injury or disease you are talking about. It is not out of place. They see it often at those times. The injury or disease does not necessarily cause the symptom, and the symptom is not always present. And if seizures are really present in these cases, when you are timing injuries, wouldn't you want to know if and when seizures were seen? Throughout the trial, is consistent with shaken baby, was used over and over, because there is no causation research. But I seriously doubt if juries pick up this 'slight of hand' usage.

Question: How was mom (Barb) acting?

Dr. O: "Well, the reason it struck me that he (Brant) was distraught ...we usually have distraught moms more often than we have distraught dads. Dad seemed rather distraught and mom....now everybody has their ways of demonstrating grief. And, you know, she just seemed a little bit less emotional about the situation than he was at the time." *Wow. Now there's a foolproof way to determine guilt.*

It is the practice in St. Joseph Criminal Courts to allow jurors to submit questions to the judge, who then reads them to the witness. I like this procedure because, in addition to the juror getting his/her question answered, one can also get a pretty good idea from the question, itself, whether or not the jury is understanding the essence of the testimony.

Question (juror): How much did Natalia weigh when admitted on July 27?

Dr O: "I don't recall. I recall she seemed appropriate for her age."

Question: Is there a weight that you consider appropriate for age?

Dr O: "About the 50th percentile for a three month old would be in the region of twelve to fourteen pounds." (Natalia's weight when admitted to PICU on July 27 was seven (7) pounds, five (5) ounces. A little more than half of fourteen pounds). *You probably should have just stuck with "I don't recall." Adding "she seemed appropriate for her age" only raises more questions about your testimony.*

The next medical witness was **Dr. Cory**, pediatric radiologist from South Bend. Dr. Cory is present because he sees fractures (tiny splinters at the ends of bones) that other other doctors seem unable to see. In addition, he believes he can go back and determine the time that fractures occurred.

Question: So what do you do every day at work?

Dr Cory: "I look at radiographs, x-rays, ultrasounds, CT scans, MRI's... different imaging of the body, and make diagnoses."

Question: How long have Natalia's rib fractures been healing?

Dr Cory: "Somewhere in the range of three to six weeks, possibly longer."

Question: Can you tell whether those different rib fractures occurred at the same time?

Dr Cory: "They could have been anywhere in that range of time." (He does not answer directly.)

Question: Were you able to determine if she had any other fractures?

Dr Cory: "Just below the knee is the tibia (lower leg bone). There is a little piece of bone right here that is detached from the tibia. That's called a corner fracture."

Dr. Cory sees corner fractures (little splinters) of both tibias (lower legs at knee) and one femur (upper leg, also at the knee).

Question: Were you able to determine the age of those fractures?

Dr Cory: "It's a little bit more difficult, but they are more recent than the rib fractures.

Question: They could have occurred the day before?

Dr Cory: "Yes."

Question: How long out could they have occurred?

Dr Cory: "Well, again, about three weeks and beyond you start to see some pretty definite evidence of healing."

Question: Why wouldn't those ligaments (in the leg bones) snap before the bone?

Dr Cory: "It's (the end of the bone) just starting to turn from cartilage into bone. And it's easy to fracture." (Dr E: "It's very difficult for the ends of the bone to fracture.") *Hmmm.*

Question: How do those (posterior ribs) get fractured?

131

Dr Cory: "The only way these can really be fractured in children is by compression." *Shaken baby theory.*

Question: Doctor, did you review Natalia's birth x-rays? (One chest x-ray only.)
Dr Cory: "Yes."
Question: Could you determine whether the fractures you saw (on the full body bone scan) were on her birth x-ray?
Dr Cory: "There were no fractures there (on the birth x-ray)." *Come on!*

This is another devious 'slight of hand' intended to fool the jury. The single birth x-ray was of the chest. It did not even show Natalia's arms or legs. And the jury is not in a position to see details of the x-ray. It seems totally disingenuous to ask and answer a question for which nearly all of the alleged fracture sites are from areas that are not part of the chest x-ray. But, you might say, the birth x-ray did show the ribs. And Dr. Cory says there are no fractures there. *How can he say that? If the ribs had been fractured in the birthing process, they wouldn't have shown up on this x-ray at birth. No callus would have formed by that time.* Dr. Paul Kleinman, for whom the 'Kleinman rib fractures' are named (and clung to so tenaciously by shaken baby theorists) indicates that rib fractures of "are rarely identified radiographically (by x-ray) in the acute (new) phase, and callus formation is usually the first indication of injury (later)." *So this whole line of questions about the birth x-ray is bogus. Why would a medical doctor be a party to this? And why would a prosecutor ask such a question in the first place?*

Question: Did you find the linear skull fracture to be acute (new) or chronic (old)?
Dr Cory: "It's a little more difficult to put an age on a skull fracture, so it could have been either (old or new). There may be more variability in how long it takes to heal."

The final doctor for the prosecution is **Dr. Cockerill,** a neurosurgeon from South Bend. A series of photographs of the parts of the human brain are shown on a screen for the jury.

Question: Doctor, what are we looking at here?
Dr C: "The brain inside the skull---frontal lobe, parietal lobe, occipital lobe, and temporal lobe" (cerebrum--- for conscious decisions, thinking, personality, sensory functions, speech, vision). "You see some of the cerebellum, which is part of the balance and smoothing of motion centers of the brain, and the brain stem, which is a relay center, consciousness center,

breathing center. Most of the housekeeping functions of the brain are located in those areas (brain stem)."

Question: What do you mean by housekeeping functions?

Dr C: "Basic ability to stay conscious, to be able to swallow, to have reflex responses, to be able to stay awake or to go to sleep, hormonal balances are regulated through portions of that structure (brain stem)." (Also "motion of the eyes," "temperature regulation," "sucking," and "crying.")

Question: How protected are the different portions of the brain?

Dr C: "If blood flow is interrupted or the brain is damaged, the portions that tend to exhibit the greatest damage are the more peripheral portions of the brain---frontal lobe, parietal lobe, occipital lobe. Those parts of the brain have a fairly high metabolic (nutritional) requirement. So they require more blood flow than the other portions of the brain."

Question: Do you remember consulting with Dr. O concerning Natalia Benson on July 27, 2005?

Dr C: "Yes. I came up to PICU to see the patient and to review the imaging studies (CT scans)."

Question: Are there MRI's that can also be performed?

Dr C: "An MRI wouldn't really have changed the prognosis or the treatment."

From a medical perspective, Dr. C is correct. An MRI would not have changed the prognosis (outcome) or the treatment. But according to many experts, an MRI is critical in determining if a situation is, indeed, an abuse situation, and when the injury occurred. So moving beyond strictly medical concerns, if it's possible you'll be heading into the courtroom, an MRI is essential. *And was not done.*

Question: Why not do an MRI?

Dr C: "What I saw on the CT scan was a devastating brain injury with almost complete loss of all of the cortical portions of the brain."

Question: Could you determine whether Natalia's brain injury was chronic (old) or acute (new)?

Dr C: "Actually, when I looked at her scans, I saw evidence of both an acute injury as well as a more chronic injury..... There was one very significant event two to three weeks before, and then something more recent as well. [There is] a loss of brain volume. The brain is actually starting to shrink from whatever event occurred a few weeks before. It's causing the brain to shrink away from the skull. We're seeing a brain that looked like it was there, probably relatively normal." *Really? How about the the brain damage occurring during the first trimester of pregnancy and the seizures*

133

witnessed throughout Natalia's life. And in the first three months of life, there is no actual demonstration of the use of this part of the brain for <u>any</u> infant. You indicated earlier that the <u>brain is</u> <u>dead</u>. <u>No brain scans</u> were done at birth. But now you say it was "probably relatively normal." <u>Based upon what?</u>

<u>Question</u>: You've mentioned there was some pretty severe atrophy (shrinkage) within the brain itself, correct?

<u>Dr C</u>: "Correct."

<u>Question</u>: Would there be any visible signs from the outside of that type of injury?

<u>Dr C</u>: "You wouldn't necessarily see anything like bruising of the scalp or anything like that. You might have noticed previous to that some swelling." Also "somewhat irritable," "poor feeding," "frequent vomiting."

<u>Question</u>: Did you consult with other doctors over time concerning Natalia's condition?

<u>Dr C</u>: "I consulted with...Dr. O and Dr. E. But, no, I <u>couldn't</u> consult any of my neurosurgical colleagues. This is a <u>very straight forward </u>case." *Yeah. Taking the time to get a second neurological opinion would have been tough. You had five colleagues several hundred feet down the hall. But one of them might have had another opinion like Dr. Fischbach did. So why muddy the waters?*

<u>Question</u>: Is a detached retina also indicative of shaken baby?

<u>Dr C</u>: "Petechial hemorrhages in the retina are 'consistent with' the diagnosis."

<u>Question</u>: Is it accurate to say injuries---plural---when referring to Natalia's brain?

<u>Dr C</u>: "'Injuries' would <u>probably</u> be more correct in this case."

<u>Question</u>: Is it correct that, in your opinion, there is <u>no doubt</u> that more than one event occurred that hurt this child?

<u>Dr C</u>: "There is evidence to support two events." *Not a ringing endorsement of "no doubt."*

Next we get into a little bit the the medical 'pecking order.'

<u>Question</u>: Dr. Fischbach (who suggested the brain injury might be from a <u>birth trauma</u>) only looked at the x-ray....is that correct? He did not examine and render any opinions concerning the....

<u>Dr C</u>: "No."

<u>Question</u>: (continuing)..CAT scan." *Dr. C can't even wait for the end of the question to answer.*

134

Dr C: "That would be outside his function as a radiologist to examine the patient. He would only provide information on the x-rays themselves. He would look at the CT scan and the x-rays and such, but he does not examine the baby. He does not come up and render a medical opinion. He only interprets the imaging studies." *It sounds like he did give a medical opinion. You may not like it. And, yes, he did not examine the baby, only the scans. But tell us what you found from your examination that enlightened you about your diagnosis and would have made it more relevant than Dr. Fischbach's. Dr. O said Natalia was "impossible to examine because she was <u>unconscious.</u>" And Dr. Cory, the <u>radiologist</u> in this trial (who replaced Dr. Fischbach, the original radiologist who only looks at scans and does not render a medical opinion) --- what did Dr. Cory just say about himself? "I look at radiographs, x-rays, ultrasounds, CT scans, MRI's... and give diagnoses. Is a diagnosis not a medical opinion?*

Dr. Cockerill's answer to a question from a <u>juror</u> is instructive.

Question: Was there more than one event to hurt Natalia's brain?

Dr C: "Based upon the imaging studies, I can say there appears to have been two events."

(Dr. C is basically admitting here that he is making his judgments from looking at the same scan that everybody else is. The scan, and it's interpretation for the timing of Natalia's injuries, is the central piece of evidence in this case. And of the nine doctors that studied that scan, there were it at least five different time frames given for the injuries. I will deal with the timing issue later in the book.)

CHAPTER NINE

Following the testimony of the doctors, the prosecution called several other minor witnesses. One was an EMT intermediate, another a paramedic, and a third was a nurse in PICU. The first two had seen Barb and Natalia briefly on the way to the ER. The PICU nurse had contact over a longer period of time.

The **EMT intermediate** takes the stand first:

> Question (Prosecutor): Who was holding the child...mother or father?
> EMT: "The mother (Barb)."
> Question: Did you tell the parents she is in distress.....she needs to go to the hospital?
> EMT: "I didn't specifically say she was in distress."
> Question: When the ambulance arrived...did she say anything?
> EMT: "She didn't want to go outside without having any shoes on."
> Question: Who got her shoes?
> EMT: "The father."
> Question: Did you describe how imperative it was to get the child into the ambulance?
> EMT: "I urged her that the child needed to be transported immediately. I never specifically told the mother that it (Natalia) was a critical patient."

The prosecutor is trying to say Barb, for whatever reason, is delaying. *She wanted to wear shoes to the hospital?*

> Question: Did she ride in the ambulance with this child?
> EMT: "Yes, she did."
> Question: Did you provide any particular medical help before the ambulance came?
> EMT: "No."
> Question: How long were you there?
> EMT: "A minute and a half roughly."

Next on the witness stand is the **paramedic**:

> Question: What did you do when you arrived?
> Paramedic: "When I arrived...I was met with the firefighters and the child and the mother."

Question: Did you meet them in the house?

Paramedic: "They had walked out to my ambulance. I had just got out of the ambulance when they met me."

Question: Could you see the ground where they walked on?

Paramedic: "Yeah."

Question: What was it like?

Paramedic: "The ground?" (You can imagine that the paramedic is wondering what in the world this has to do with anything. He doesn't know that the prosecutor is still hung up on Barb's wanting her shoes. The prosecutor needs anything...anything at all to convince the jury of Barb's guilt.)

Question: Yeah.

Paramedic: "It was dry."

Question: Was it on a hill?

Paramedic: "No, it was flat"

Question: Was there anything in-between you and the front door?

Paramedic: "No."

The prosecutor decides to go a different direction. *Mercifully.*

Question: What was the condition of the child?

Paramedic: "The baby had good airway...the baby was breathing and there was circulation. The baby seemed distant, didn't move. Eyes open... She actually curled her arms a little bit like 'posturing'."

Question: Is that typical of someone who is suffering a seizure?

Paramedic: "That is typical." (Remember that Brant had told police, "I truly believe that ever since Natalia came home, that she was having seizures.....one eye would wink. We noticed that she would posture sometimes, and we thought it was just her trying to have a bowel movement.") We all saw these things. Remember Char saying earlier:

> Sgt K: "Sounds like posturing with severe brain trauma. They stiffen up and everything goes rigid."
>
> Char: "She did that sometimes...and we always thought she did that when she had to go potty."

Once the doctors described what seizures looked like in infants, we all recognized that Natalia had been doing that all along. But doctors and police seemed to ignore that. It didn't fit the timing of their theory.

Question: What was the mother's demeanor?

Paramedic: "Quiet."

Question: Any crying?

138

Paramedic: "I didn't see any crying."
Question: No further questions, Judge.

Next up was the **PICU nurse**.

Question: Could you describe what you saw in your assessment?
Nurse: "She appeared to be a healthy baby as far as my just looking at her." (This was part of the problem for everyone. Natalia didn't look to be in distress much of the time.)
Question: How was the mother (Barb) acting when you first saw her?
Nurse: "Upset."
Question: Was she crying?
Nurse: "I don't remember."
Question: How about the father?
Nurse: "More distressed."
Question: Crying?
Nurse: "Yes."
Question: Later on, did you see the grandparents?
Nurse: "Yes."
Question: What was their demeanor?
Nurse: "Upset."
Question: Crying?
Nurse: "Yes."
Question: Did you observe Barb over the length of time Natalia was in PICU?
Nurse: "Yes."
Question: What was her demeanor?
Nurse: "I don't really remember."
Question: Do you recall whether she was crying?
Nurse: "She did cry." *You're messing up the prosecutor's whole point here. If Brant cried, he's innocent. If Barb didn't, she's guilty.*
Question: Do you recall her telling you what was wrong with Natalia?
Nurse: "No, I don't think she knew what was wrong with her."
Exactly.

The prosecutor must have been upset with these answers by the PICU nurse. In his closing argument, when he tried to portray Barb as the one who never cried (as if that meant something), he referred back to this nurse. "Now some people couldn't remember too well. The nurse had a hard time remembering because they've had a lot of patients since then."

Question: So the mom told you the child had a temperature of 93...94 degrees?

139

Nurse: "Yes." (As much as they tried to find a place where Barb had lied, they really couldn't. She told them everything. Even details that were not helpful to her case. And remember, Dr. E said they start from the assumption that the caregiver is lying. So they assumed many of the things she told them were lies. But they did choose to believe the things she said that were helpful to them in building a case against her. Those things were true.)

Question: How long was Natalia in PICU?
Nurse: "Roughly three weeks." (Actually 19 days.) *Pretty close.* (Dr. O said Natalia went home in less than two weeks.) *Not as close.*
Question: How often would you see Barb?
Nurse: "Daily."
Question: How often would you see Brant Benson, the father?
Nurse: "I would say daily."
Question: Do you know whether Brant continued to work, or if he talked about his work?
Nurse: "I don't recall." (The prosecutor has been presenting Brant as this person who works 16 hours a day, seven days a week. Therefore, he couldn't be a suspect. He was always working. He just 'happened' to take two weeks off after his father's death. He just 'happened' to be shopping for a thermometer on Saturday, July 23. He just 'happened' to be off the whole day on Monday, July 25. He just 'happened' to be playing with Natalia in bed on Tuesday evening, July 26. He just 'happened to live in the home with Natalia every day. And now the nurse says he was at he hospital with Natalia every day for three weeks. This work thing just isn't holding up.)

Question: Did she tell you she didn't want to be around the child?
Nurse: "Not to me."
Question: What did she say?
Nurse: (from notes) "She had some PPD and did not feel like taking care of her, maybe because she did not bond well to baby being premature. Mom states that depression went away in a couple weeks." (The nurse did not even recognize the prosecutor's question at first because of the 'spin' he put on it. Not feeling like taking care of a baby---and not wanting to be around a baby---seemed like different statements to her.) *And to me.*

The next witness to testify is **Cynthia Lorentzen**, the foster mother. After a lengthy description of Natalia's physical problems she was asked:

Question: What other issues does she have?

Cynthia: "Her brain does not control her temperature. <u>So maybe three or four days out of the week she will drop to below 90 degrees.</u>" *I thought 93 degrees meant organ shutdown.*

Question: Has she gone through any physiological changes?

Cynthia: "She has gone into precocious puberty, which is full development of her breasts, her pubic hair, and she is also going through menopause."

Question: As a therapeutic foster parent, do you have the natural parents ever visit the children that you are taking care of?

Cynthia: "I do."

Question: Have either of Natalia's parents visited her?

Cynthia: "<u>The dad has.</u>"

Question: And that's Brant Benson, correct?

Cynthia: "Yes."

No mention here by either the foster mother or the prosecutor that <u>Barb has been forbidden to visit</u> Natalia, allegedly by the foster mother herself. *Let's just let the jury believe that Barb doesn't care about Natalia, but Brant does.* When asked moments later if she knew that Barb is not allowed to visit, the foster mother replied, "That's what I've been told, yes." *Whatever it takes. Truthful or not.*

Donna Schau, married to Brant's cousin, took the stand:

Question: Did you ever see Barbara interact with Natalia?

Donna: "Once." (At the July 2 party).

Question: What was the interaction like?

Donna: "She (Natalia) was being passed around to, you know, showing off the new baby."

Question: Did Barbara say anything about Natalia to you?

Donna: "She said that Natalia was being really good for the last couple of days, but she picked of all the days to be an a--hole this day at the party, because she was kind of crying."

Question (defense): Do you know how police got your name for an interview?

Donna: "<u>I assume from Char.</u>"

Question: And who is Char?

Donna: "Brant's mother."

Question (from juror): When Barb said Natalia was being an a--hole, what was her emotional state?

Donna: "I would say more frustrated that she kind of wanted her own personal day, and I think agitated."

Question (Prosecutor): She actually used more profanity that day, is that right?

Donna: "Towards Natalia?"

Question: No, in general.

Donna: "Yes." (Barb claims she used that term with Brant because he was pitching horseshoes and not helping. But not with Natalia.)

Next is testimony from **Michelle Schau**, married to Brant's cousin.

Question: Did you have an opportunity to see Barb interact with Natalia?

Michelle: "Not really."

Question: What do you mean "not really"?

Michelle: "The only time I saw her with the baby was at the (July 2) party. And she didn't hold the baby or pick the baby up." (As a social worker, she knows that amount of observation of interaction is best described as "not really.") "I asked to hold the baby and I did for a brief second, or a brief couple minutes."

Question: Had you seen Barbara interact with Bella (Isabella) in the past?

Michelle: "Yes."

Question: Was it appropriate in your opinion?

Michelle: "Yes."

Question: Are you aware of how much Brant worked?

Michelle: "Brant worked a lot of hours...He would stop by the house sometimes on his way home and it would be after I got home from work which was 5:00.....probably 6:00 pm." (Remember, Char told police that Brant would work from 2:00 am in the morning until 10:00 pm at night. *Perhaps just a wee bit exaggerated.*)

Question: Do you know how the police got your name to call you?

Michelle: "I think....... I really don't know." *I think..........she really knows. Char.*

Testimony from **Sara Seiwart,** Brant's cousin, follows.

Question: How many times have you seen Natalia?

Sara: "Two." (Once at July 2 party, once in the ER).

Question: What was Barb saying to Natalia?

<u>Sara</u>: "She had called Natalia an a--hole."

<u>Question</u>: What was Barb's demeanor?

<u>Sara</u>: "Barb was very frustrated, upset."

<u>Question</u>: Did you see Brant at the Ronald McDonald house? (At the hospital.)

<u>Sara</u>: "Yes."

<u>Question</u>: <u>What was Brant's demeanor?</u>

<u>Sara</u>: "He looked like a train just ran over him. He was very upset, crying."

<u>Question</u>: Can you describe what Barbara looked like?

<u>Sara</u>: "<u>It didn't seem like she was that upset about it.</u>"

<u>Question</u>: Was she crying?

<u>Sara</u>: "No."

<u>Question</u>: Was Brant crying?

<u>Sara</u>: "Yes." (Sara mentioned nothing about "crying" observations to the police in her interview five days after Natalia came to the ER.) *Brant cried publicly. Barb not as much.*

<u>Question</u> (defense): Do you know how police got your name?

<u>Sara</u>: "I believe through my <u>Aunt Char</u>, which is Brant's mother."

<u>Question</u>: When Mr. Korpal (Jim) asked you about all those things that <u>the police told you</u> about Natalia's injuries, was that basically <u>because you were asking</u> kind of how she was doing? (Police shouldn't be telling potential witnesses about these injuries. Mr. Cotter recognizes this and offers Sara a possible explanation...but she doesn't take it.)

<u>Sara</u>: "<u>No. I didn't ask.</u>" *I was just told.*

The police did with Sara what they did with all of the potential witnesses. They told them many, many details of the injuries, the people they suspected, who was not a suspect, who was a sociopath, who worked a lot, who should have known things as a registered nurse, when doctors said the timing of injuries were, what the diagnosis was, and even "planted" multiple false stories to steer the potential witnesses in the direction they wanted. Anything to prime the potential witnesses for the trial. And even the doctors entered in to this information sharing orgy. The only thing police didn't do was gather evidence. They just manufactured it. And later the prosecutor would hear much of that manufactured "evidence" repeated in these witnesses' "testimony" at trial.

The next witness is **Gary Mullins**, Char's husband and Brant's stepfather.

<u>Question</u>: How did the process of getting Isabella on weekends work?

143

Gary:"Well, we would actually call and ask to get Isabella."
Question: You and Char would call?
Gary: "Char and I would call."
Question: And you and Char wanted that, is that fair to say?
Gary: "Oh yeah."

This is just a rehash of what Char and Gary told police in their interview. They wanted Isabella, every weekend if they could get her. But you will recall that police, after hearing Char and Gary say this to them, made up a story and told Brant in the brainwashing interview that "She (Barb) set here and she told Randy...Barb told Randy the day she was here that she feels she is a Monday-Friday mom....and that on the weekends she likes to get rid of the kids." *This was never said by Barb anywhere in her interview. The police knew it, and the prosecutor, who was present through the entire brainwashing interview with Brant, knew it, too. Why don't they look for evidence instead of trying to create it?*

Question: Did Natalia go directly home from the hospital?
Gary: "I think they kept her at the hospital.... I can't remember that."
Whoa. He doesn't remember Natalia being in NICU for 19 days. I'm a bit concerned what he will say he does remember.
Question: Why would you keep Isabella, but not Natalia?
Gary: "Probably because she was a preemie and I'm actually afraid to handle babies when they are small. My wife feels the same way I did."

Question: How did Barb interact with Natalia?
Gary: "A couple of times I seen her hold her. I really can't remember how she interacted with her, but she was holding her a couple times."

Question: Where were you when you heard Barb say something to Natalia (at the July 4 party)?
Gary: "We were getting ready to leave, my wife and I and Isabella and Natalia, and we were putting the babies in the car. And I heard....Barbara tell Natalia "why do you got to f---ing cry all the time? Your sister never did that." *Wow. I wonder why he never told that to the police. I guess his memory has gotten better in the intervening years.*

Question: Are there pictures in Barb and Brant's home?
Gary: "Yes."
Question: Are there pictures of Brant?
Gary: "Yes."
Question: Are there pictures of Barbara?
Gary: "I think on the refrigerator I think I've seen a couple."

144

Question: Are there pictures of Isabella?
Gary: "Yes."
Question: Are there pictures of Natalia?
Gary: "I can't recall. I don't remember seeing any." *This is crazy!* (Let's revisit Char and Gary's police interview to see what Gary said to Sgt. Kaps.)

> Sgt K: "Did you notice there was an absence of any photos of the baby?"
> Char: "That's because I didn't have any yet. I always got..."
> Sgt K: "Are you the ones who always took the pictures?"
> Char: "They don't even have a camera."
> Gary: "Wasn't Natalia's picture up by the TV? Didn't you guys see that?"
> Sgt K: "We didn't see any of Natalia. There may have been a baby picture up there from when she was first born, but I couldn't tell if that was Isabella or Natalia. Uh..."
> Char: "But that's why. I always supply all the pictures."

Now two years later, with Sgt. Kaps sitting at the same table as the prosecutor, this whole series of picture questions is asked once more. The prosecutor had to have gotten this picture information from Sgt. Kaps. What kind of a mother would not have a picture of her daughter up in the house? Gary played right along with the whole ruse, totally changing his comments to the police. And later Char would do likewise. Unfortunately, the jury never knew the difference. (One wonders at times if the search for truth ever enters into the process at all?) *Perception, not truth.*

Question: Why didn't you continue to have Natalia at your place after the July 2 party weekend?
Gary: "I don't know. I guess my wife said...thought..maybe something was wrong with her."
Question: Was that based on how she was when you had her that weekend?
Gary: "Yeah. My wife told me...she said there is something wrong with Natalia. She is not active at all." (This is during the July 2, 2005 weekend of the party, and is a very revealing statement. The prosecution has been hard at work trying to 'prove' that Natalia was in tip-top shape during that weekend, when most of us were saying Natalia had problems ever since she came home.)

Question: How was Brant acting when you first arrived at Memorial Hospital? *Oh, no. Here we go again.*

145

Gary: "I never seen Brant like that before. He was just hysterical. He was so upset."

Question: How was your wife acting?

Gary: "Same way, same way."

Question: How was Barbara acting?

Gary: "I didn't see any emotion at all."

Question: You said that Barb asked you (Gary and Char) why you think she hurt Natalia?

Gary: "Yes."

Question: What did you tell her."

Gary: "Somebody did it. And I told her that I knew that Brant wasn't capable of doing this."

Question: What was her response?

Gary: "She (Barb) said 'what makes you think Brant didn't do it,' and I said 'I know Brant wouldn't do this.'" *Come on, Gary. You know that's not true. Barb never accused Brant.*

This trial is being held two years after Natalia went to the ER. The following is what Char and Gary told police two days after ER regarding this same incident. Why has their story changed?

> Char: "Brant came up and got us and said Barb and I want to talk to you. And then after she talked for awhile, she had me convinced that she didn't do this. It's like one side of your brain..."
>
> Gary: "She actually got mad, upset when we started talking about it, didn't she?" *What? Barb got upset just because you told her you thought she severely injured her daughter, when you had no factual basis for that at all.*
>
> Char: "I told her there's only two people...you and Brant. And I know my son didn't do it. So who does that leave? And she says, 'My Mom and Dad know I didn't do it---and---Brant didn't do it.'" (Never any accusations of Brant.... but the jury doesn't know this). *Gary certainly twisted this comment around.*

Question: "After his father passed away, who did Brant work with?"

Gary: "I know Brant worked a while on his own and it got to be too heavy for him as far as work load goes, so Brant accepted a new position."

Question: When you say "got to be too heavy," how often was he working?

146

Gary: "He was working a lot. Every time we would call he would be working. Every time we would see him he would be working." *Does this even make sense?* But the prosecutor continues to try to write Brant out of the script through his witnesses.

Question: At the hospital, did Barb talk about how Natalia might have been injured?
Gary: "Yeah. She said at one point she could have dropped her."
Question: Who could have dropped her?
Gary: "Barb said 'I could have dropped her when I threw her in the air, but I can't remember it.'" *Gary again twists her statement.* (Actual statement by Char to the police with Gary present: "Well, she [Barb] said, 'I could have told them that I accidentally dropped her. But I'm not going to lie about it.'")

Question: What was your relationship like with Barb up until Natalia went to the hospital?
Gary: "We had a good relationship."
Question: Do you believe the two of you were close?
Gary: "Yes."
Question: Do you believe that Char was close with Barb?
Gary: "We both thought that."

Question: Now you mentioned that at the hospital Brant looked like he had been in a trainwreck. (Actually it was Sara, another family member that said this.)
Gary: "He was crying. He was pretty upset." *And again. One more time.*
Question: And your wife was crying. Were you crying?
Gary: "Oh, yes."
Question: And Barbara was calm? *Gotta build that "evidence."*
Gary: "Uh-huh, yes."
Question: Throughout the time at the hospital, what was Brant's demeanor?
Gary: "Brant was upset the whole time."
Question: How was Barbara acting?
Gary: "No actions at all, as far as I'm concerned. I seen her cry once."

Question: You said there were pictures in the house of Brant, maybe Barb, pictures of Isabella, but not Natalia. Is that correct?
Gary: I can't recall no pictures of Natalia." *The prosecutor just wanted to make that extra clear to the jury.*

The defense cross-examines Gary.

Question: Now you said on direct examination that Brant worked all the time. Did he play golf on the weekends?
Gary: "He played golf."
Question: "So it wasn't all work and no play?"
Gary: 'It wasn't all work and no play, but we're talking a couple hours of golf compared to ten, twelve hours of work."

Question: Do you remember the statement to police that your wife had concerns that Natalia wasn't right, right from birth?
Gary: "Not from birth."
Question: You don't remember that statement?
Gary: "I remember her saying she wasn't right, but I don't think that was right at birth."
(Actual statement by Char: "Right from the beginning I told my husband, it seemed like there was something wrong with that baby..... Something just didn't seem right.")

Question: You stated that Barb said to Natalia, "why do you have to f---ing cry all the time?" Do you remember making that statement?
Gary: "Yes I do."
Question: Did you tell that to the police in your statement on July 29? (two years ago.)
Gary: "I can't remember if I did or not." *He didn't. But now, two years later, his memory is quite clear about what Barb allegedly said.*
Question: Do you remember telling the police (concerning Barb's demeanor) that you would be hysterical?
Gary: "I would be hysterical?"
Question: Yeah.
Gary: "If it was me, yes."
Question: Did your wife question whether or not Barb was in some state of shock?
Gary: "Uh-huh."
Pass the witness.

Question (Prosecutor): Do you remember saying "the shock should have worn off by now"?
Gary: "Yes." (This was not said by Gary in the police interview. I can't even quote what he did say, because there is no statement concerning this. The police officer had said something a little like this. But the prosecutor handed this to Gary as a way to diminish the question of shock. And Gary said 'yes.' Actually the only importance of this fabricated

148

statement... is that it <u>is fabricated,</u> and shows again a lack of concern for the truth. The end result, <u>win</u> or <u>lose,</u> seems to be the only thing that really matters here.)

<u>Question</u>: And who would tell you that Natalia was asleep (when they visited)?
<u>Gary</u>: "Barb."
<u>Question</u>: You said Natalia would be in the bassinet with a blanket over her?
<u>Gary</u>: "Yes."
<u>Question</u>: <u>Did you actually see that, or did Barbara tell you that</u>? *Was Barb lying to you?*
<u>Gary</u>: "<u>I walked in the bedroom and seen it.</u>"

Next on the stand was **Charlene Mullins**, mother of Brant Benson.

The prosecutor leads Char through a series of alleged incidents, none of which was ever mentioned to the police during her interview two days following Natalia's trip to the ER. I will cite a few of them.

<u>Question</u>: Did you talk with Barb about her pregnancy with <u>Isabella</u>?
<u>Char</u>: "Yes."
<u>Question</u>: What did she say about that?
<u>Char</u>: "<u>She wasn't very happy.</u>"
<u>Question</u>: Did she tell you why?
<u>Char</u>: "No. The one time when we went to the house she just said that <u>she would be glad to get 'it' our of her.</u>"

This question must have been <u>rehearsed</u>, because the prosecutor asks Char about the <u>wrong</u> daughter, <u>Isabella</u>, but she anticipates it and answers about the correct daughter, Natalia. The prosecutor who is trying to get anything negative about Barb he can before the jury, never even notices his mistake, and continues his line of questioning. But the most grievous part of this interchange is the fact the police <u>planted</u> this very idea during their interview with Char two years earlier:

<u>Sgt K</u>: "From <u>some people we talked to</u>, she didn't want this baby. It was an unplanned pregnancy. <u>She didn't want the baby.</u>" (Barb, Brant, and Elaine are the only people the police have interviewed at this point, and certainly none of them said that. And the police are telling Char this, so <u>she</u> obviously didn't tell them this. Char makes no response to this remark by Sgt. K other than, "There can't be anything

wrong with the baby without her (Barb) doing anything?"
But now, two years later, Char repeats a very similar
statement to the jury, claiming it was said to her by Barb.)
*Should not this be considered witness-tampering? Or is it
okay since it was done prior to Char officially becoming a
witness?*

Question: Was Natalia premature?
Char: "Yes."
Question: Mom had high blood pressure?
Char: "I don't know if that was the problem. She was having
problems."
Question: Was Natalia induced?
Char: "I don't remember that."   *She was induced for three days!*
It's amazing that with all of the alleged negative stuff she claims to remember
about Barb so clearly, Char has forgotten Barb and Natalia both could have
died from the high blood pressure Barb had. That's why they induced her for
several days. Char seems to remember when it helps the prosecution's case,
and forgets when that helps their case, too. More quotes on her memory
follow.
Question: Why didn't you include Natalia when you kept Isabella on
weekends?
Char: "When she first came home the doctor said she had to stay at
home like for a month so she wouldn't be around people, because she was
susceptible to getting colds and stuff." (There is truth to this comment.)
Question: Why not after May?
Char: "Well, one thing...I was kind of afraid, because she was so
little."
Question: What was Barb's demeanor when Isabella was born?
Char: "Fine. She was happy."
Question: What was Barb's demeanor when Natalia was born?
Char: "She wasn't happy." *Char never said this to police in her
interview.*
Question: What did she say after Natalia was born?
Char: "She just....I mean you could tell the look on her face and stuff."
Question: Did she ever discuss Natalia with you?
Char: "Yes.... On the telephone"
Question: Your discussion on the phone about Barb's feelings
towards Natalia... was that before or after the July 2 weekend when you had
Natalia and Isabella?
Char: "I think it was before." (This is significant, but not the answer
the prosecutor was looking for. He asks two more times shortly after this and
gives her hints each time as to what the answer is supposed to be. ["After."]

150

She begins to back away from that a bit. The prosecution has tried to place Barb's feeling of detachment from Natalia after July 2, to coincide with their alleged timing of Natalia's injuries.)

Question: What did Barbara say about her feelings towards Natalia?

Char: "She said I don't love Natalia. And I gasped." *If this were actually said, wouldn't that have been a helpful thing to tell police two years earlier?* (Remember Sgt. K made up a statement for Char and Gary in their interview: "She didn't want the baby.") *Now Char says this.*

Question: Is there more you can say about Barb's feelings for Natalia? *Probably a lot more.*

Char: "It wasn't just what she would say. It was like when we go to pick up Isabella to go to the hospital to see Natalia (in NICU)."

Question: Just after birth?

Char: "Right. I mean she said will you take this milk up there. She said 'I don't feel like going up there.' She had pumped her breast milk and wanted us to take it up to the hospital for the nurses to feed her." (In checking NICU records, Barb was there 15 days out of the 19 Natalia was there. Barb was ill a few days, and didn't have a vehicle a few days. It's not clear which day Char is talking about above.)

Question: Up until that point (July 2) had you noticed anything wrong with Natalia?

Char: "Yes."

Question: What did you notice?

Char: "Well...in June, I mean when I walked in the baby was making these snorting noises so bad and I am like 'what is wrong?'"

Question: When you had Natalia the July 2 weekend, did you get to interact with her?

Char: "See, it wasn't like with Isabella." *Not much interaction.*

Question: How so?

Char: "She wasn't interacting like the same way, but I thought it was just because she was a preemie." *As we all did.*

Question: Did Barb put the seat into the car seat at the party? (Natalia was in a removable seat that snapped into a seat frame in the car).

Char: "Yes, she did.... She kind of slung it in there."

Question: What did she say?

Char: "She said, 'Natalia, why do you have to f---ing cry all the time? Why can't you be more like your sister?" (Words almost identical to what Gary said). *Too identical? Once again, nothing even remotely close to this was said two years earlier in the police interview by either of them.*

151

Question: What did you notice differently in the way Barb interacted with Isabella and Natalia?

Char: "She wasn't happy with Natalia." *You already said that.*

Question: What would make you believe that?

Char: "Well, she didn't pick her up and love on her, or take pictures of her." (Gary testified earlier that Natalia was usually in the bassinet sleeping when they came over. But he *did* see Barb pick Natalia up several times.) *And pictures? Not this again. Is her memory really this poor? Has she forgotten she told police Barb and Brant have no camera? This reeks.*

Question: You talked about pictures.

Char: "Yes."

Question: Did you recall seeing any pictures prior to July 27 in the home?

Char: "No." *None?* (Char gets ahead of where she knows the prosecutor is going).

Question: Any pictures in the home?

Char: "No, not of Natalia."

Question: Any pictures at all?

Char: "Isabella."

Question: You're kind of going a little fast for me. Did you see any pictures in the home? *Work with me here.*

Char: "Yes." *That's better.*

Question: Who did you see pictures of?

Char: "Isabella." *Good.*

Question: Were there some pictures of Brant?

Char: "Yeah." *Very good.*

Question: Some pictures of Barb?

Char: "Yes." *Now we're rolling.*

Question: You said Isabella? *I lost my cue card.*

Char: "Yes." .

Question: Any pictures of Natalia?

Char: "No." *Wow! Barb must really not like Natalia.*

Question: How did Barb interact towards Natalia when you brought her home after the July 2 weekend?

Char: "She held her." *I thought she didn't do that.* "Her and I were sitting on the couch. We were sitting and talking. She held her and all of a sudden she threw her up in the air."

Question: Show me what you mean.

Char: "She just took her and threw her up in the air."

Question: How high up did she throw her up in the air?

Char: "Probably about this far." (I was not in the courtroom, so I shudder to think what Char's description of this looked like. I somehow have this mental image of Barb tossing Natalia to the ceiling and then diving into the end zone to catch her for the winning touchdown.)

Question: Did Barbara tell you that the doctors had told her it was good to throw her up in the air? (Another police-planted accusation originally attributed to Barb, and later to Brant. Both denied it, and correctly so. It was not said.)

Char: "Yes." *Char never told this to police. One more thing that must have clarified as the family talked about it over the years.*

Question: Did she tell you anything else the doctors had told her to do?

Char: "I don't remember." *Surely you can think of something.*

Question: Did she tell you the doctors told her if she was constipated to push her legs towards the chest? *I'm giving you a really big hint here.*

Char: "Yes." *Good job.*

The police had immediately told TV, the press, and later Dr. Simpson herself, that Barb said Dr. Simpson told her to do these things. That is totally and demonstrably false. Then they wanted Brant to agree Barb said to him that Dr. Simpson told her to do this, but he denied it vehemently. Now, two years later, they've finally found someone, Char, who was willing to say Barb told her that "the doctors" told Barb to do these things. *What a devious way to create "evidence"!*

Question: Where did you see Natalia on Sunday, July 24, 2005?

Char: "Barb brought Natalia to my mom's house."

Question: This is your mother who is suffering from cancer?

Char: "Yes..... Gary called to tell Barb he was going to bring Isabella home and she said 'No, I'm going to come up there and bring Natalia up to see Grandma' is what she said."

After seeing Natalia that day, Char felt concerned. Natalia's eye problems and lack of much body movement were more pronounced. Char called Brant the next evening, Monday, and told him of her concern. Brant was home alone with Natalia, and went into the bedroom to take a good look at her.

Char (continuing): "He said, 'Do you think I should take her to the ER?' And I said, 'Brant, I don't know' because I knew they didn't have any insurance. (Char told police two years earlier: "And I said 'I don't know if it is that serious to take her to the ER right now. But she needs to get in to see the doctor.'" *Things change over time. Now it's insurance.*

Question: Do you know how much Brant worked?

Char: "He was working long hours."

Question: My long and yours might be different.

Char: "He was probably working 14 to 16 hours a day.....six or seven days a week." (This almost, but not quite, sounds reasonable when compared to her comment to police two years earlier: "He'd get up at two to three in the morning and go to work, and not come home until nine or ten at night.") *Let's get Brant out of this story any way we can.*

Question: When you arrived at the hospital who did you see?
Char: "Brant and Barb."
Question: What was Brant's demeanor? *If you keep hammering on a point long enough, somebody might begin to believe it's actually important.*
Char: "He was crying and upset."
Question: What was Barb's demeanor?
Char: "Just calm." *Okay. Can we go on to something else?*
The prosecutor led Char through this "demeanor routine" three more times during the remainder of her testimony. Finally, for a little variation, after asking who was crying (Brant first, followed by Gary, Elaine, Dan) he asked about Barb.
Char: "I only seen her cry once."
Question: Do you know what she was crying about?
Char: "Yeah, about her dog."
Question: What about her dog?
Char: "She was just sitting there and she says something about 'I won't be able to take my dog for a walk again' and started crying." *Why in the world would Barb say that?*

Later the questions and testimony changed:

Question: Hang on. You're going too fast.....What did she tell you?
Char: "She was talking about how cute the firemen were, and wished she was dressed better. I think she said something she didn't have any shoes on or something. I don't remember." (Char must have gotten wind of the "shoe" question from someone, but just didn't understand why it was an issue for the prosecutor. It was supposed to have slowed the EMT's down and shown an utter disregard for Natalia's well-being. But Char gets it all confused.)
Question: At some point did you visit (PICU) at different times than when Barb did?
Char: "Yes. But that was after we found out that it was abuse (Friday). We still was believing everything until the male...he was Afro-American doctor (Dr. Emenim). But he took my husband and I, my sister, my sister-in-law, and my brother all into a room and sat and explained everything to us.... He said it's not brittle bone disease, he said it's not a two

and a half year old girl knocking a baby off the bed, <u>it's not a 70 pound dog doing this</u>." *Do HIPAA laws apply at South Bend Memorial?*

<u>Question</u>: <u>Who had mentioned that maybe the dog had done this (to Natalia)?</u>

<u>Char</u>: "Barb." *Translation: Barb was looking for excuses for what <u>she</u> did.*

In actuality, police and doctors were asking everyone what might have caused these injuries. The police had asked Brant specifically about the dog. They had been to the house to search for clues as to what happened to Natalia, but were afraid to enter because of the large dog inside. Brant was called to come and open the house and calm the dog. That's supposedly why his police interview took place later in the day. Two years earlier:

> Lt R: "<u>How about the dog? Was the dog around?</u> I know you have a large canine." (Barb was still being interviewed by Sgt. K when Brant was asked this.)
> Brant: "Yeah. He's about 75 pounds."
> Lt R: "How is he with her? Dogs will do some things. A couple can have a dog for a long time and all of a sudden, they bring a baby home and the dog is jealous."
> Brant: "He's been real good with the kids."
> Lt R: "He never snaps? You've never had to take him away?"
> Brant: "No. <u>Now there's been a couple times</u> where he...he never nipped at her...but he's <u>barked to let her know you're starting to get on my nerves a little bit</u>. Barb and I keep a close eyes on him, because, you know...he is an animal...and <u>animals can snap--- just like that--- at any time</u>."

Police had a conversation with Barb, too, in which the dog came up. As Sgt. K was asking about various possibilities, the following was said:

> Barb: "The ophthalmologist had said something... so Brant said, 'You're telling me she was probably shaken. And he said 'Yes.' That's when him and I just looked at each other like....what's going on here? No. I bumped her head...I told you the whole knee thing with her ribs...I was real concerned that maybe that was something I did. I've <u>never</u> dropped her. I've never hit her head on anything... well, she kinda moved her head around in the sink...never hit hard on anything...
> Sgt K: "Did she ever roll off the bed?"
> Barb: "No. Never rolled off the bed. I had her on the bed once...and<u> the dog jumped up</u> there and kinda clipped the back of her with his paw...</u>"
> Sgt K: "Didn't knock her off?"

<u>Barb</u>: "Didn't knock her off. But she started crying---liked freaked out---but <u>I think it just scared her</u>." *Doesn't sound much like an accusation of the dog.*

Elaine and I were both more concerned with a dog that size running free in their house than either Barb or Brant were. I know he could have knocked me over if he had wanted to. Donna, too remarked to police, "When I first heard it, I kept thinking, 'Did the dog somehow do something?'" And I'm certain the police who were afraid to enter the house felt the same way. But Brant and Barb trusted the dog. So who tried to blame it on the dog? *Barb, of course. We knew she was the one from the first day. "Fry her."*

<u>Question</u>: Now <u>is this Barbara we have been talking about</u>, is that person in the courtroom today?
<u>Char</u>: "Yes."
<u>Question</u>: Can you point out and describe what she is wearing today?
<u>Char</u>: "She is wearing a white top." *A very clinical procedure, with the illusion of certainty. You wouldn't ask this about just anybody. She must be <u>the</u> one.*

<u>Defense</u> questioning:
<u>Question</u>: How many times did you actually see Natalia and Barb together?
<u>Char</u>: "<u>Several</u>." *But I have lots of negative comments, nevertheless.*
<u>Question</u>: Did you notice anything over the July 4 weekend that gave you any pause as to what her (Natalia's) health might be?
<u>Char</u>: "<u>Yeah. But a lot of times I just thought it was because she was premature</u>."
<u>Question</u>: "Well, you <u>gave a statement to the police regarding this case</u>, didn't you?
<u>Char</u>: "<u>I don't remember</u>. <u>It's been so long ago</u>." *She doesn't even remember she had an interview with the police. But all this other stuff is so clear to her?*
<u>Question</u>: Do you recall talking about the pictures in the home with the police?
<u>Char</u>: "You mean the lack of pictures of Natalia?"
<u>Question</u>: Yes.
<u>Char</u>: "Yeah. I think <u>Randy</u> did ask me about pictures because he told me that's when they noticed.... when they went in there." *Randy? Oh, Sgt. Kaps.*
<u>Question</u>: And do you remember your husband inquiring about Natalia's picture on the TV?

<u>Char</u>: "No.... In fact, I didn't get the pictures back until after Natalia was already in the hospital (ER)." *She <u>does</u> remember.*

<u>Question</u>: Right. Well, they're making a big deal about these pictures. <u>The reason Barb and Brant didn't have pictures is that you hadn't gotten them developed.</u>

<u>Char</u>: "<u>Right</u>." If Char were on trial, the prosecutor would be asking her why she waited over three weeks to develop the pictures of Natalia. Does she not love Natalia? (Char must have realized that <u>she had just undercut the whole picture thing</u>, and her memory gets progressively worse following that realization. Finally, when Char didn't remember the answers to <u>six questions in a row,</u> questioning by the defense ended.

<u>Question</u> (Prosecutor): Was Barb's comment <u>before</u> or <u>after</u> anyone alleged that the dog may have done this? (More about the alleged "I won't be able to walk the dog" comment.)

<u>Char</u>: "I would think it was <u>before</u>, but I can't be 100 percent sure." (So Barb is the one who supposedly blamed the dog for Natalia's injuries, but Barb's alleged comment about not ever being able to take her dog for a walk again happened <u>before</u> she blamed the dog.) *Let's just make stuff up here as we go. Whatever comes to mind.*

I had been sitting out in the atrium on the concrete bench working on my Sudoku book and had no idea who was testifying, or where things were inside the courtroom. Several of Brant's family were also on the other side of the atrium. All of a sudden the silence was interrupted by "I done good." Char had just come bursting out of the courtroom and was shouting her relief that she was done.

CHAPTER TEN

The next witness is to take the stand is **Brant Benson,** father of Natalia.

    <u>Question</u>: Was Isabella a <u>planned</u> pregnancy?
    <u>Brant</u>: "Yes."
    <u>Question</u>: Was Natalia a <u>planned</u> pregnancy?
    <u>Brant</u>: "Yes."

<u>Go back two years</u> to Brant's second police interview:

    <u>Lt R</u>: Isabella's pregnancy. Was is planned... or just happened?
    <u>Brant</u>: "<u>Just happened</u>."
    <u>Lt R</u>: The second pregnancy (Natalia)...planned, or something that occurred?
    <u>Brant</u>: "Something that <u>just occurred</u>."

Why do I mention something so insignificant? Let's look at the approach police so eloquently stated to Char and Gary two years earlier on how they would trap Barb. (July 29, 2005: 48 hours after ER).

    <u>Sgt K</u>: "<u>Basically lock her (Barb) in on a story</u>. So once that's locked in, and she's got an attorney, you can't come back later and say, well..... this, that, and this... So either you <u>were lying</u> to us in the first interview..... or when <u>are you lying</u>? Which one is it?"

<u>This is the approach</u>. If you should happen to forget what you said years earlier, there's only one answer for that. You're lying. As Elaine and I watched this process unfold, we were certain that if the police and prosecutor had put the same level of scrutiny on any one of the six of us who were around Natalia most, none of us would have passed their tests. They could have built a similar case against each one of us. So what does Brant's total reversal of answers above mean? <u>Very little when he's not being tried</u>. But if he were the person with charges, it would take on a whole different level of importance. And you could read any sinister meaning into that change of testimony that would support your favorite theory.

    <u>Question</u>: Did Barb voice any concerns to you while she was pregnant with Natalia.
    <u>Brant</u>: "No."
    <u>Question</u>: Did she ever tell you that she didn't want to be pregnant, or anything like that?
    <u>Brant</u>: "No."

Question: How often would you (Brant) visit with Natalia in the hospital?

Brant: "Two or three days a week." (roughly 5-8 days during Natalia's 19 days in NICU).

Question: How about Barb? Did she visit Natalia in the NICU?

Brant: "Sometimes."

Question: Did she visit as often as you did?

Brant: "No." (So, fewer than 5-8 days.) Actual NICU records show Barb was there 15 days.

I really dislike getting sucked into these stupid little games whereby we look at demeanor, or check who crossed their arms, or we count visits, or whatever, to somehow determine who cares about Natalia the most. And the loser of that game is somehow guilty of hurting her. But I don't know how else to show that Brant and his family's feelings are totally coloring their testimony to the jury. Brant's comment above is demonstrably false. *Unfortunately, it's more difficult to prove certain other comments false.*

Question: How did Barb interact with Isabella?

Brant: "She was just a great mother. She would read her books. She would comfort her."

Question: Did she tell her she loved her....things like that?

Brant: "Oh yeah."

Question: Did she act the same way towards Natalia when Natalia was brought home?

Brant: "I would say yes."

Question: Did you feed Natalia?

Brant: "I believe once, after she came home from the hospital."

Question: Where did Natalia sleep?

Brant: "In a bassinet next to the bed."

Question: Did Natalia always sleep in your bedroom?

Brant: "Yes."

Question: How many bedrooms in your home?

Brant: "Three."

Question: Where did Isabella sleep?

Brant: "She slept in the bedroom due south of our bedroom."

The argument that Barb was somehow not taking care of Natalia, rather than just not feeling as close to her as to Isabella, seems false. If she really didn't want Natalia around, why would she keep her right next to her all night? And if she loved Isabella more, why was Isabella sleeping in another room?

160

Question: When you went to work Natalia was in her bassinet, and when you came home, Natalia was in her bassinet. Is that correct? *Nice set up of the question.*

    Brant: "Most of the time.

    Question: How often would you interact with Natalia?

    Brant: "I would play with her when I got home from work sometimes when it was earlier."

There's a bit of a dilemma here for the prosecutor and Brant. They are trying to insinuate that Brant was never around Natalia, and therefore could not have hurt her. On the other hand, they are making all kinds of remarks from what Brant has observed about Natalia's feeding to how she looked at various times. *He was around Natalia a lot, just not enough to hurt her.* (Later on we will hear doctors testify that it takes only seconds to shake a baby. But for now, we don't know that.)

    Question: Did you notice any eating problems with Natalia before July 2, 2005?

    Brant: "No." *I thought you were never home. How could you have noticed?*

    Question: After July 2, did you ever see her spit up anything?

    Brant: "No." *You just testified that Natalia was in her bassinet when you left for work, and when you returned home.*

    Question: What did Barb tell you about her feelings towards Natalia?

    Brant: "She said that she didn't bond with Natalia like she did with Isabella." (Fairly accurate.)

    Question: How did that conversation come about?

    Brant: "It just kind of came about. We were talking....and I asked her then if she felt like hurting Natalia, and she said 'Oh God, no. It's totally opposite. I don't feel the closeness with her that I want to feel.'"

    Question: How about Natalia? Was Barb a loving mother to Natalia?

    Brant: "I felt she was a loving mother for Natalia, too.

    Question: Did she ever use terms of endearment towards Natalia?

    Brant: "Yes."

    Brant (continuing): "When my mom called (Monday evening, July 25, 2005), I looked at Natalia and she didn't seem like there was anything wrong with her."

    Question: Was she awake when you went and looked at her?

    Brant: "Yeah."

    Question: You had said her eyes were hazy (July 4 weekend). Were they still hazy?

Brant: "No, they weren't as hazy as when Barb brought her to me (early in July)."

Question: Did she (Natalia) react when she saw you or anything like that?

Brant: "Yeah."

Question: When your mother told you she thought something was wrong with Natalia, did she tell you to do anything?

Brant: "No. I asked her, 'Do you think I should take her to the hospital?' And she said 'Well, no, I'm not saying that. But I'm just concerned.'"

Now Brant begins to add new things to his previous descriptions of this event.

Question: Your mom wanted to know if Barb was there?

Brant has just said, "She (mom) called and she said that... she asked if Barb was there." [It's almost as if he remembered at the last second to stick this additional phrase in. Brant has described this call numerous times in his first police interview, his second police interview, and in his deposition. Never once did he mention that his mom asked if Barb was there. Nor did Char in her police interview. But the prosecutor builds on it, and Brant accommodates.]

Question: Did she tell why she didn't.... why she wanted to know if Barb was there?

Brant: "Yeah. She was afraid that Barb was going to get upset."

Question: What was Barb's response when you told her your mom called and said this?

Brant: "She said, 'Oh, what now?' She was very defensive."

Again, this last part has all been added to the description of that Monday evening call. The impact of this portrays Barb as a person who is not in control of her emotions, and might erupt at the slightest provocation. *She's out of control. Only God knows what all she did to Natalia.* It also may have been added to explain why Char waited until Monday evening to call. She feared Barb. *Yeah....right.*

Question: Was 6:30 am getting up, and 7:15 pm coming home from work pretty normal for you?

Brant: "Yes." *You probably should tell Char this.*

Question: How many days a week would you work?

Brant: "Six or seven days a week."

162

Question: What did Barb tell you Tuesday evening (July 26) about Natalia?

Brant: "She just said that she ate really well that day....that she had called the pediatrician. The pediatrician called back that evening and said schedule an appointment for the following day..... just so I can get her in to see her." (Partially true, but incomplete.)

Question: Did Barb tell you Natalia's temperature?

Brant: "Yes."

Question: What was the temperature?

Brant: "Ninety-three."

Question: Now, besides being awake, <u>was Natalia lethargic</u>?

Brant: "Actually, I sat in bed and I had Natalia on my lap, and <u>she was moving her arms and her legs and she seemed to be okay</u>. And then all of a sudden, her left eye started blinking by itself." (Dr. Emenim would later imply this is impossible, because Natalia would have been <u>unconscious</u> for the last three to four weeks. And Dr. Okanlami would indicate Natalia would <u>not have been able to eat</u> for the last three to four weeks.) *The doctors have essentially branded <u>everybody who has seen Natalia</u> in the last four weeks as shaken baby prevaricators. That branding is all based on "the theory."*

Question: What was Barb's response?

Brant: "She was puzzled."

Question: Look at slide number 16. You see this book right here?

Brant: "Yes."

Question: <u>Whose book is that</u>?

Brant: "<u>I don't know</u>." *What are you saying, Brant?*

Question: You have never seen this book before?

Brant: "No."

Question: Did Barb ever give you this book to read that (Tuesday) evening?

Brant: "No."

This series of questions is based upon Barb's saying she asked Brant to read this medical book she had gotten just that morning. <u>Brant denies any knowledge of this book</u>. Doesn't know whose it is... where it came from... etc. But the following is taken from Brant's second police interview, two years earlier:

Lt R: "She (Barb) is reading the family medical book."

Brant: "<u>That's the book her mother brought over</u>." *But two years later I don't know anything about it. Never have seen it. Never have heard of it.*

Question: Do you remember <u>what time you went to sleep on Tuesday evening</u>, July 26?

Brant: "Roughly <u>7:45 pm</u>." *Sometimes he seems to say things just to get on to the next question.*

Brant had told police two years earlier:

Lt R: <u>What time did you go to bed Tuesday night</u> (July 26)?
Brant: "I guess it would be safe to say around <u>9:30 pm</u>."
Lt R: "The baby was fine?"
Brant: <u>"She was fine except about 9:00 or 9:30 pm Barb said that Natalia wasn't eating."</u>

Most of these changes in testimony make Barb look like <u>she's</u> not telling the truth. (Remember Sgt. K's "Lock them in on a story," and if they depart from it, one time or the other they're lying. But no such scrutiny was applied to anyone but Barb. And the <u>jury</u> is not aware of the above changes in testimony. In fact, it took <u>me</u> a significant amount of time to search through all of the various records to highlight these testimony discrepancies.)

Question: What did you do (Wednesday morning) after Barb said 'I picked her up and she went stiff' and 'she's holding her breath'?"

Brant: "I said, 'put her in the car. Let's take her down to the hospital'."

Question: Did you look at Natalia?

Brant: <u>"I was worried about getting some shorts and some shoes on</u> and getting her to the hospital." (But when Barb wanted <u>her</u> shoes, it was a <u>huge deal</u>.) *She obviously didn't like Natalia. What about Brant?   Ah...you know how men can be about clothes.*

Question: When the paramedics arrive, do you recall Barbara saying anything to the paramedics?

Brant: "Yes."

Question: Concerning how she was dressed?

Brant: "Yes."

Question: What did she say, and how did that come about?

Brant: "The paramedics took a look at Natalia and said, take her out to the ambulance."

Question: And what was Barbara's response?

Brant: <u>"She said she didn't have any shoes on.</u> *The ambulance was not there yet.*

Question: Did you go with Natalia into the ambulance? (The prosecutor quickly decides to shift questions. Brant didn't go in the

164

ambulance, and that might look bad.) Did Natalia <u>eventually</u> go into the ambulance? *After she was slowed down so horribly by Barb.*

Brant: "Yes."

This is all staged to make Barb look like she was trying to delay Natalia from going to the hospital. <u>Brant had never mentioned Barb getting her shoes before in his police interviews or his deposition.</u> And what did the paramedic say earlier in the trial?

> Question: Had they walked outside, or did you meet them in the house?
> Paramedic: "No. They had walked out to my ambulance. In fact, <u>I just got out of the ambulance when they met me.</u>" *Doesn't sound much like being slowed down.*
> Question: The child was brought out to you, is that correct?
> Paramedic: "Correct."
> Question: <u>That was in the arms of mother</u>?
> Paramedic: "Correct."
> Question: What happened then?
> Paramedic: "She brought the child inside the ambulance, and laid it on the cot."

So all the drama about "<u>Barb's shoes</u>" had nothing to do with delaying anything. *Why does the prosecutor play these ugly games with people's lives? Could it be because he has no <u>real</u> evidence? Is he not aware that a jury could listen to this <u>faux</u> evidence, and be confused into making a decision that might tragically impact the rest of this young mother's life?* (And Brant and his family seem willing to play the game with him.)

Question: How long did it take you to get there (hospital) compared with the ambulance?

Brant: "<u>They got there a few minutes before me.</u> I stayed home and <u>called my mother</u> and then drove down in the car." *Where is the prosecutor on this? Brant <u>called his mother</u> while Natalia was dying. Did he not love her? I mean <u>Natalia.</u>* (A different level of scrutiny.)

Question: Did they tell you why they wanted to do a CAT scan at the hospital?

Brant: "I just thought they were trying to figure out what the problem was."

Question: <u>Are you still distraught</u>? <u>Are you still crying</u>? (At the hospital.)

Brant: "Oh, yeah."

Question: And how about Barbara? Is she crying at this point?

Brant: "No. She was pretty calm." *This is all very clear. I remember every detail.*

Question: The moving of the legs back and forth for gas, did you ever actually see Barb do that?
Brant: "Yeah."
Question: Did you know what she was doing, or what?
Brant: "She actually did that with Isabella (too)." *You mean she wasn't just picking on Natalia?*

Barb did this "bicycling" thing with Natalia's legs to help relieve gas. It became an issue for police, and they stated categorically that Barb said Dr. Simpson had told her to do that. Barb positively never said that. I've check multiple times. But they spread that over the TV, the newspapers, to Dr. Simpson in her interview, and even included it in the "probable cause" document for support of the charges against Barb:

> "Barbara admitted" [she voluntarily shared this with the police] "that she tried to do exercise with Natalia"... [to relieve gas.] "According to Barbara Schrock, she was told by the doctors to do this." (Barb never said this. And neither did Brant. No one ever said that. Actually, Barb read this technique in Parents magazine, August 2005 issue.) But that didn't slow down the police and prosecutor. They used this falsehood over and over, as if it were true. And now, two years later at trial, Brant follows the lead of his mother. He now changes his story, too. *But no one locks him in to his story.*

Question: The throwing her up in the air to check reflexes, did Barb explain what she was doing?
Brant: "She said, 'Well, I'm not hurting her'."
Question: Did she tell you that any medical personnel had told her to do that?
Brant: "She said that. I believe that Dr. Simpson told her that was something to do to check her reflexes." *Brant. You know that's not true.* (While the police knew Barb had not said that Dr. Simpson had told her to do these two actions--- moving Natalia's legs for gas and tossing her in the air for reflexes--- they continued to make that claim. It wasn't on the tape of her interview anywhere. Once they had committed themselves to the degree they had on TV and in the newspapers, however, the next best thing would be if someone in Brant's family would say Barb told them that Dr. Simpson said to do this. They worked tirelessly to get someone to say that. And finally, first Char, and then Brant (years later) both complied. *Why did the police make this up in the first place? It seems so foolish to claim your suspect said something in an interview that is not on the tape of that interview. But in the*

166

end it likely worked for them. Maybe that's why. Nobody caught on. Two years earlier, however, during the brainwashing interview, Brant was still able to resist their attempts:

> Lt R: "When we talked before... about the tossing of Natalia into the air, I think you said before that she had been told to do that."
>
> Brant: "She never told me she was told to do that. She said 'I'm not hurting her. Dr. Simpson told me she's supposed to have that reaction (reflex)'."
>
> Lt R: "She was looking for some sort of reaction to test the reflexes?"
>
> Brant: "I guess.... She never told me that 'Dr. Simpson told me to throw her up in the air'...she never told me that."
>
> Lt R: "She never told you that?"
>
> Brant: "No."

It could not be more clear from the above conversation. Barb never said this. And Brant never said this...... until right now. Now he's changed his story. "Lock them into a story, and if they change it..." *But the police and prosecutor are not locking anybody into their stories except Barb.*

Question: What was your response when Dr. O said the injuries were inflicted?

Brant: "I think my jaw hit the floor."

Question: What was Barbara's response?

Brant: "There wasn't a whole lot of response from Barb."

Question: Were you still crying at this point?

Brant: "I was in shock."

Question: How about Barbara? What was her demeanor?

Brant: "She was very calm."

Question: How did Ace (the 70 pound dog) interact with the children?

Brant: "Great."

Question: Did you have concern about Ace with the kids?

Brant: "Never."

Question: Ace ever growl at the kids?

Brant: "Never." (In Brant's police interview: "Now there's been a couple times...he never nipped at her...but he's barked to let her know, hey, you're starting to get on my nerves. He is an animal, and an animal can snap just like that at anytime.") *I guess growling and barking are different.*

Question: Did you ever catch Ace jumping next to Natalia?

Brant: "He jumped on the bed, I believe, on that Tuesday night. But he didn't jump on Natalia." *Hey, that's what Barb said, too.*

167

Question: Did you go and speak with the officers?
Brant: "Down at the Homicide Unit, yes."
Question: Did you speak with Lt. Richmond then?
Brant: "I believe so. Steve?"
Question: Yeah. Randy Kaps didn't speak with you, is that correct?
Brant: "I don't think Randy spoke with me." *Steve and Randy? Sounds like Brant was a real suspect.*

Question: Did you talk with Barbara after doctors said the injuries were inflicted?
Brant: "Yes."
Question: What did she say?
Brant: "She said she didn't do it."
Question: Did she say how Natalia could have suffered these injuries?
Brant: "She said she thought it was something medical."
Question: Did she make any suggestions on what medically could have been wrong with Natalia?
Brant: "She had said something about meningitis."

(Now police were not interested in having meningitis become part of this case, because they already "knew" what the diagnosis was--- "shaken baby," and who the guilty party was--- "Barb." So they always got rather defensive when some other possible cause of Natalia's condition came up.)

Question: Who brought up that term first?
Brant: "Barbara." *Once again Brant implicates Barb.* (Brant's Police Interview: "Dr. O told us there was a blood sample they found had some bacteria growing in it.... And there could have been an infection there. I said 'Could the infection cause meningitis?' and she said 'yeah, it could.'") *But now the answer is "Barbara." Who else? She's on trial.*

And in Char and Gary's police interview two years earlier:
Sgt K: "Did you hear anything about something that has to do with meningitis?"
Char: "They said there was a fungus in her (Natalia's) blood that could have caused this."
Sgt K: "Who, who, who told you that?" *Defensive?*
Char: "The doctor."
Sgt K: "What doctor?"
Char: "The black lady (Dr. O). They're going to do a meningitis test today."
Sgt K: "Obviously, her duty is just to inform the parents and nobody else." *Yeah. What's she doing talking about this?*

168

It's __my__ duty to inform everybody else. How can we ever build a case this way?

Back to Brant's testimony:

Question: At what point did Barbara first mention meningitis?

Brant: "I believe it was <u>after three or four days</u> at the hospital." (Not only has he "forgotten" <u>who</u> brought up meningitis, but now he has forgotten <u>when</u> it was brought up. Dr. O had mentioned this to Char and Gary before their Friday, July 29 [first 48 hours] interview.)

Question: Did you ever see Barbara <u>cry</u>?   *Oh, my. Again?*

Brant: "Yes."

Question: When was that?

Brant: "I believe I seen her cry once at Natalia's bedside and once when we were in a glass room where they trained some of the nurses."

Question: Did anything occur just before she cried?

Brant: "She just started crying."

Question: Did she ever talk about your dog, Ace?   *How about a little help?*

Brant: "That was one of the times she cried."

Question: What did she say?

Brant: "I don't remember exactly. Just something about Ace." (Never said by Brant before.)

Question: Why didn't you go back to your own home after you quit sleeping at the hospital?

Brant: "Because I knew I had nothing to do with what had happened. And I told her (Barb) I have to separate myself because I knew I didn't do anything wrong." *A more truthful answer would have been: "because the police told me to <u>separate</u> myself from her."*

Question: Who did you think had done something?

Brant: "There was good chances that Barb had done something." *At least that's what everybody you talked to, besides Barb, was telling you.... that <u>she</u> was guilty.*

Question: You mentioned morning and afternoon shifts at the hospital. What did you mean?

Brant: "Well, I didn't really want to be around Barbara. So we just decided that we would have shifts to be at her (Natalia's) bedside."

Question: Did Barb ever question you on whether you could have hurt Natalia?

Brant: "No." *She said <u>nobody she knew</u> could have done that to Natalia. Not a very helpful stance to take <u>if you knew you, yourself, had hurt Natalia</u>, but were trying to deflect suspicion onto somebody else.*

Question (defense): Was there a time right after your father's death when you took off work for <u>two weeks</u>?
Brant: "For <u>one week</u>."
Question: Do you recall telling police that you were off for <u>two weeks</u>, and money was tight?
Brant: "Okay. If it was a week or two. <u>It may have been two weeks</u>." *But I was never home.*

Question (defense): Now you said Barb didn't realize she was pregnant (with Isabella) until four months had gone by?
Brant: "Correct."
Question: And you said she had some concerns about that, correct?
Brant: "She had been drinking and smoking before she found out she was pregnant."
Question: Now when you use the <u>term drinking</u>, what do you mean?
Brant: "<u>A few beers</u>."
Question: And when she found out she was pregnant, she stopped?
Brant: "Yes, she did."

Question (defense): Did she have her tubes tied at that time (right after Natalia's birth)?
Brant: "Yes she did."
Question: And was that a discussion you had with her and agreed to that?
Brant: "It was discussed that with the complication, yeah, that was the decision that Barb wanted, and I backed her with it."

Question (defense): And you talked about some point in time Barb's asking you if Natalia's eyes looked normal?
Brant: "Correct."
Question: Do you have any idea when that conversation occurred?
Brant: "It was July 3 or 4, <u>right after the July 2 party</u>."

Question (defense): Did you get a <u>call on June 25 from Elaine</u> that Natalia, who was staying in Goshen with the Schrocks, was having problems?
Brant: "Yes."
Question: And what were the problems?
Brant: "She said Natalia's not doing well. She's having difficulties breathing."

Question: Did you guys immediately make an appointment with the doctor?

Brant: "I said, 'Natalia has a scheduled wellness visit with her pediatrician on Monday.' She said, 'This can't wait.' So I hung the phone up, Barb called the doctor's office, and Dan and Elaine came to the house with Natalia, and we went to the doctor's office."

Natalia started a 10-day dose of an antibiotic for sinusitis on that Saturday. On Monday, June 27, (two days later) Natalia kept her wellness appointment.

Question (defense): Were you aware that she received seven immunization shots on that date?

Brant: "That's what Barb instructed me that had taken place."

Question: Were you aware that Barb called the doctor's office in the middle of July because of a problem with Natalia's bowel movements?

Brant: "Barb said that she contacted the doctor, yes."

Question: Did you have a conversation with her prior to contacting the doctor?

Brant: "She said that Natalia was constipated and that she was going to call the doctor."

Question: And are you aware of what the doctor told her?

Brant: "I believe I had to go and get some Karo syrup."

Question (defense): You talked about one time when Barb threw Natalia in the air. Now when we're talking about throwing her in the air, like, did this child go to the ceiling?

Brant: "No. She probably went that far out of her hands (indicating)." [I was not in the courtroom to see this indication.]

Question: Just out of her hands?

Brant: "Yep." (He said 5-6 inches in the police interview. I'm hoping his indication here agreed.)

Question: And you answered some question about pushing up the legs to alleviate gas. And you said she did that with Isabella, too?

Brant: "Correct."

Question (defense): Do you remember telling police that you had asked Dr. E about the absence of Natalia's corpus callosum in her brain?

Brant: "Yes."

Question: And what was his response?

Brant: "He didn't know what I was talking about." *That's what Dr. E said.*

Question: And did that surprise you?

Brant: "Yeah." *Why were you surprised? Prenatal brain damage could cloud the whole "shaken baby" diagnosis. But don't feel too bad. I trusted these people, too.*

Question: And did that surprise you because Dr. O told you about that, and they were partners?

Brant: "Yes."

Question (defense): Did the police tell you that it was a good idea if you separated yourself from Barb?

Brant: "Yes." *So it wasn't just because "I knew I had done nothing wrong" as he said above.*

The prosecutor resumes questioning.

Question: Now Mr. Korpal asked about Barb drinking and smoking during Isabella's pregnancy. Did she drink and smoke while she was pregnant with Natalia?

Brant: "Not that I was aware of."

Question: Were you home all the time and around her?

Brant: "No, not always." *Well, if you weren't home all the time, we know the real answer.*

Question: Was Barb mad at you for getting the generic formula instead of the regular?

Brant: "She was mad that she didn't want to switch the formula."

Question: Was she mad at you that day when you brought it home?

Brant: "Yeah." *We've got an unstable woman here. Mad at everyone.*

This is just another clear example of Brant's "brainwashing" by the police. But there are so many, many other examples where he totally changed his story after the police wore him down with untruths, and he, himself, ended up in the ER. Let's look at what Brant said about the generic baby formula several times two years before to Lt. Richmond during his police interview:

> Brant: "And I read the ingredients, and it was the same thing. So I brought it home and Barb went 'Oh, you got generic formula.' And she said, 'Well, OK.'"

> Brant (continues): "I brought it (generic formula) home and Barb said 'I wish you would have bought the Enfamil' because Bella had done so well on it. She (Barb) looked at it and said, 'You know what? These ingredients are real similar...so let's give it a try.' My mom was told...and Tara

172

and Traci (cousins) were told ...that there was a <u>big fight</u> over the generic formula. <u>That's not true.</u>" *I wonder <u>who</u> told all these people there was a <u>big fight</u>? Maybe somebody trying to get witnesses rounded up by being deceitful.*

<u>Lt R</u> (later in the same police interview): "That's why she blamed you for the purchase of the generic formula."
<u>Brant</u>: "Well, she (Barb) <u>didn't really blame anybody</u>."
Can't Lt. R hear well?

You can see how "mad" Barb got in the above exchanges about the generic formula. Lt. R was trying anything to get Brant to turn against Barb. And as Lt. R, himself, likely <u>would have said</u> during his brainwashing of Brant, "We've had gals come in here and call that '<u>witness tampering</u>.'" (There's something seriously immoral, and highly unethical with this approach. But apparently it is legal. How can it be permissible for police to tell people totally false stuff and hope someone will get angry enough to become a witness. Nor should it be permissible for the prosecutor, who is very much aware of all this chicanery that has transpired, to then ask questions of these same witnesses in the courtroom and get the very same answers back that were <u>fed</u> to them earlier. It may work...it may even be legal... but it's clearly dishonest. The prosecutor clearly had no qualms about Brant's <u>change of story</u>, even though the police talked about "locking people in to their stories." As much as I'm disgusted with what Brant is doing by changing his story multiple times this way, I also have to feel sorry for him. He had become a <u>victim</u> of this process just like the rest of us.)

<u>Question</u> (defense): Mr. Benson, looking back at that July 2 party, Barb had every right to be upset with you, correct? You're never home, you're working, you're playing golf, and you're not helping with the kids at this party. That's what this is about, correct?
<u>Brant</u>: "<u>Possibly</u>."

<u>Question</u> (juror): When did you begin to disbelieve Barb's denial of wrongdoing?
<u>Brant</u>: "It probably was <u>a year and a half</u> that I really had to stop and think about it, you know, and trust in the doctors and of what they said...what they told me. It took me a long, long time."
<u>Question</u>: For you to begin to disbelieve what she had said. Do you understand the question?
<u>Brant</u>: No, I guess I don't."
<u>Question</u>: When first, and why, did you begin to disbelieve what she had said when she said she didn't do wrong?

173

Brant: "About a year and a half after Natalia was admitted. Just thinking back on all of the comments that were made and things that were said" (*and imagined*), "and the doctor saying there's no other way." (*Shaken baby.*) "There's no other reason. There's no other way it could happen." (Brant believed the doctors. It was him or her.   What do you do and think when the situation is framed in that way?)

Question (juror): Did you give permission for the medical personnel to disclose to your family the assumed abuse?

Brant: "I guess I don't quite understand the question?"   *HIPAA laws. I (Dan) understand.*

Question: Well, some of your family members have testified to talking with doctors about her conditions. Natalia's condition. I think the question is, "Did you give permission for the doctors to talk to your family about Natalia's condition?" (Brant responded that he was unaware of any medical information release consent.)   *Somebody on the jury had some medical understanding here. That's a good sign. According to testimony, Doctors were flagrantly giving information to everyone in the extended family. Now if there were only someone on the jury with an understanding of police ethics. Or isn't there such a thing?*

CHAPTER ELEVEN

In a trial of this type, the prosecution has the burden to prove guilt beyond a reasonable doubt. But since the shaken baby theory has inherent within it both the diagnosis of a crime, and the guilty party (the one most recently with the victim), there is really no possible way to show your innocence. The two questions: (1) is there a crime?... and (2) who did it?... are already basically decided before you get to trial. Although our family had very serious questions whether a crime had been committed, we had no way, other than stating things that did not fit the theory, of challenging that. As for who did it, we could only hope to show that several people had the opportunity. So as defense witnesses, we would have only marginal impact on the outcome. We did feel, however, that we needed to have someone knowledgeable speak to what postpartum depression is, and whether Barb suffered from that, or not. And also what role, if any, a person's demeanor plays when reacting to a tragic incident. There seemed to be major confusion (purposeful?) and disproportionate significance surrounding these areas.

Elaine and I were witnesses, simply to reiterate what we saw happening with Natalia over the three months before the ER. Also we could share what we observed in Barb as a mother. Obviously, as family members, there would likely be assumed as bias on our part. But we wanted to be witnesses, nevertheless. Whether to have Barb take the witness stand was a bigger question. She did not have to testify. And after observing how the police and prosecution twisted, exaggerated, and even totally made up statements during police interviews, plus applying a level of scrutiny to Barb that none of the rest of us could have passed, we had reservations about having her on the witness stand for several hours. Would she hold up any better than Brant did in his second police interview? We were impressed that Barb had told a consistent story to doctors and police, and one that meshed with Brant's and our observations. But she has only an average memory. What would she say after two years under intense questioning? "Lock her in on her story" kept ringing in my ears.

Elaine, I, and Jim Korpal (our attorney) were pondering the wisdom of putting Barb through that ordeal. Barb, however, never considered anything else. "I don't know what the outcome of this will be, but I'm not going to face my girls at some later date, knowing that I didn't do everything I could for them." So she never really entertained the option of not taking the witness stand. In light of that, I got out the word-for-word transcript that I had made of her two-hour police interview and said you need to memorize what you said to police. (It's been our feeling all along that the statements to police two hours after Natalia arrived at the ER were the most accurate rendition of the truth). So what she answered two years later needed to reflect that earlier interview. Barb, on the other hand, is a more spontaneous person. She quickly glanced over the transcript of the two-hour interview. Her basic response was, "God will give me the words." My inner thought was, "They're right here in front of you." But I didn't say that. Instead I said... "Good luck with that. I hope you're right." Actually, I prayed that she was right. Perhaps she had more faith than I did at that point.

The first witness for the defense was **Carl Rutt**, psychiatrist.

Question: Could you explain to the jury what postpartum depression is?

Dr R: "Postpartum depression occurs after childbirth. It's partly hormonally induced. Preexisting personality traits might influence that.... a difficult childhood, a person with preexisting depression, a person with a preexisting PPD would be more likely to have one when the next baby is born also."

Question: Are there different severities?

Dr R: "Yes. They are sometimes called mild, moderate, and severe. Certainly severe can merge into postpartum psychosis."

Question: Is it unusual for a woman who has given birth to have thoughts of distance between them and the child?

Dr R: "That is not unusual."

Question: If the child was born premature and kept away from the mother for a period of time, would that impact those feelings?

Dr. R: "This is a significant issue for the neonatal nurseries where the baby is kept one, two, or three weeks.... So it's an unfortunate setup for difficulties in parent and child bonding."

Question: Could it cause a person to think they are a bad mother?

Dr R: "It could."

Question: Let me ask you straight out. Is PPD mostly self-reported (as Barb did)?

Dr R: "I think officially it's a diagnosed term. But a parent might say they have it as they read about it and so forth."

Question: How is it diagnosed?

Dr R: "It's diagnosed according to standard procedure. The psychiatric manuals, the diagnostic manual used by psychiatrists and accepted by the medical profession as well."

Question: How many times have you talked to Barb about it?

Dr R: "I talked to her seven times (starting a year after ER)."

Question: What was your evaluation?

Dr R: "I felt that (PPD) was was not the most accurate term. I called it NOS, which means not otherwise specified. It's a category slightly

176

different than major depression. PPD fits within the major depression category."

Question: Now when you talked with her, she had been charged with a crime, correct?

Dr R: "That is correct."

Question: Were you able to differentiate depression she was feeling now (from the current situation) from what she told you about after Natalia was born?

Dr R: "There had been an accumulative total which difficulty (current) has taken on her certainly. She felt steadily burdened down by the legal situation."

Question: Can you tell the jury what "shock" is?

Dr R: "It's sort of a lay term in some ways....There is a medical term called shock which means the blood pressure drops to practically zero. But if we're talking about sort of a psychological shock, I think of it as a kind of numb state where a person is not fully responding as they normally would."

Question: How would that type of shock show itself?

Dr. R: "A person might not be moving about as they normally would. They might stare straight ahead, they might speak less, they might even be saying things they don't remember later on."

Question: Would crying or hysteria be a part of that shock process?

Dr R: "It could be. People express shock in different ways."

Question: Do people handle stress and anxiety differently?

Dr R: "Yes, they do."

The prosecutor then briefly cross-examines Dr. Rutt. He seems mainly concerned that Dr. Rutt, who has watched the tape of Barb's police interview, might comment about her truthfulness. "That's for the jury to make a determination" says Mr. Cotter to the judge in a sidebar conference.

Question: When she told you about her feelings (distance from Natalia), was that roughly the beginning of July?

Dr R: "You mentioned July. I'm not sure it was July."

Question (juror): In your opinion would feeling detached change the reaction of major events regarding the child?

Dr R: "A person can feel detached and still react appropriately to the child's needs I would say."

The next witness for the defense was **Daniel Schrock**, father of Barb and grandfather of Natalia and Isabella. I have not included much of my formal testimony, since most of it has come out by way of commentary in this writing. But I did have a few things to say, and observations to make, that I have included here.

Question: What did you think of the relationship between Isabella and Barb?

Dan: "It seemed like a very good one. They both cared about each other, and Barb seemed to be a natural kind of mother in a sense. She subscribed to Parents magazine and would read that and apply those things, and buy books and try to educate her (Isabella) to the numbers and alphabet and things."

Question: Did you have experiences with Natalia of being able to hold her and be with her?

Dan: "Yes. She took her formula well. She sucked a lot, but didn't swallow much. It just kind of ran down the sides of her mouth and she would always end up with a wet shirt top."

Question: Do you recall any problems with Natalia eating?

Dan: "Well, just as I described. But when I was holding her to feed her, she arched so intensively that I was afraid she was going to pop herself out of my arms. So I soon learned I had better be sitting down and in a secure place when I fed her. For her size she just really arched and clenched her fists and stuff early on right through the two months that we were able to help her."

Question: Did you and your wife talk about this?

Dan: "Yeah, we were aware of it. Again we always had trouble sorting out ...is this because she is premature or not, you know."

Question: Now you had her the weekend of July 16. Anything odd about the way Natalia acted?

Dan: "Well, I was feeding her...and she was taking down the whole bottle, and I thought this is good. And all of a sudden it just all came back up all over me. It wasn't a little spit up. It was almost everything she had taken in."

Question: Did you notice anything about her eyes?

Dan: "Yeah. They were always a little different from early on. But that time--- I remember Brant saying, you know, these eyes are going off to one direction--- and so when I held her I looked at her, and her eyes when [when I held her] they were this way (indicating) and would go off to this side. But then you hold her this way (indicating) and they would look right at you like you felt she was making eye contact with you. But in all honesty, I don't think she ever made eye contact with us."

Question: On July 27 at the hospital, how were people acting? What was their demeanor?

Dan: "Well, I guess all of us were stunned. Some were crying, some were just sort of numb... different responses. But it was a heavy time for all of us. What we were gathering was that Natalia was very ill and likely to die. And then, just a little later they said 'and we think one of you did it,' and those two things were pretty heavy."

Question: Did the police ever interview you, Dan, about this?

Dan: "No, they didn't." *I wasn't in their 2-48 hour time frame.*

Question: Did you ever observe Brant or Barbara do anything to either your grandchildren that you would call abusive?"

Dan: "No, not at all."

Question (prosecution): You talked about when Elaine came home July 26 and told you she had concerns about Natalia, is that fair?

Dan: "Yes."

Question: She told you her (Natalia's) eyes were worse than ten days ago?

Dan: "Yes, she felt they were worse than ten days ago."

Question: That wasn't the only thing she told you though, was it? Didn't she also tell you that she took Natalia's temperature and it was 93 degrees?

Dan: " No, she didn't tell me that."

Question: She didn't tell you that?

Dan: "No."

Now this apparently stunned the prosecutor. He went into this long line of questioning about what school nurses do. But he simply had difficulty imagining that Natalia's temperature was not the most important concern on Elaine's mind at that point. And I'm not certain he even gets it today. That's why he charged Elaine. The temperature. The same temperature that was reported to Dr. Simpson. The same temperature that Dr. Simpson felt was inaccurate because of the other vital signs. The same temperature that Elaine did not believe was accurate, also due to vital signs. But Mr. Cotter could not conceive of anything more important than a thermometer reading. After a while, the prosecutor dropped this line of questioning. Apparently he figured he would get what he wanted later from Elaine.

The next witness for the defense was **Elaine Schrock**, mother of Barbara, and grandmother of Natalia and Isabella.

Question: Were you in the delivery room?

Elaine: "Yes."

Question: Was it you, your husband, and Brant?

Elaine: "Yes."

<u>Question</u>: Can you describe what Natalia looked like when she was born?

<u>Elaine</u>: "She was very small and very blue. The obstetrician was surprised... called her a 'peanut' when she came out. They weren't expecting her to be so small."

<u>Question</u>: Do you know how long she was in NICU?

<u>Elaine</u>: "I think it was 19 days." (First person to get this accurate).

<u>Question</u>: And were you present when she came home?

<u>Elaine</u>: "We used our van to take her home, yes."

<u>Question</u>: Had you had any experience with the care of premature infants at all?

<u>Elaine</u>: "<u>No, I had never held one before</u>."

<u>Question</u>: Did you have any discussions with Barb about how she felt about Natalia?

<u>Elaine</u>: "Yes. Barb said she felt less attached to Natalia than she remembered with Isabella because she didn't have that bonding time right after Natalia was born. That's the way she described it."

<u>Question</u>: Did you tell her anything to do about that?

<u>Elaine</u>: "Well, I asked her if she felt like hurting Natalia or herself. And she said 'no, no...it's not like that.' It's just not feeling bonded. And I said, you know, if it ever is like that to be sure to tell somebody...tell me."

<u>Question</u>: As you think back, did you notice anything wrong with Natalia when you kept her the weekend of June 7, 2005?

<u>Elaine</u>: "It was pretty much like the visit before (in May). She had the snorting. She was sleeping a lot, feeding a lot, always had some formula come out of her mouth somewhat when she was sucking. But it was not more of a concern than before."

<u>Question</u>: Did you notice any improvement?

<u>Elaine</u>: "<u>No</u>. I expected <u>that</u> time, and the other times that she would be --- <u>I didn't know</u> <u>whether to expect with a preemie</u>---she would be improving in terms of focusing her eyes, holding her head.... and those things did not change. They were still like a very newborn baby."

<u>Question</u>: The weekend of June 24 you again kept Natalia and you became concerned. Why?

<u>Elaine</u>: "Well, we got her Friday night. With the feedings that night she was choking some and I thought there must be something wrong with the nipple. So I went out and bought another one, but that didn't change. It seemed to me that she was having a hard time breathing and taking any formula at all, so I was concerned all night about her breathing."

<u>Question</u>: Did you stay up most of the night with her?

<u>Elaine</u>: "Probably, yeah. Off and on... I decided during the night we had to do something, so in the morning early I called Barb and Brant and I

180

said I think this is a crisis, and either I need to take her --- it was Saturday so there weren't office hours--- I either take her to the ER in Goshen, or what I thought would be better, if there is somebody on call at Navarre Clinic (South Bend) where she usually went and where her records were."

Question: Did you and Dan take the child back to South Bend?

Elaine: "Yes. Barb called and found that there was a pediatrician on call at Navarre, so we decided that was better. So Dan and I went back (to South Bend) and picked up Barb and Brant, and we all went to the Navarre Clinic (Saturday, June 25)."

Question: She was diagnosed with sinusitis--- a sinus infection?

Elaine: "Yes."

Question: Were you aware that Natalia had a well visit scheduled for Monday, June 27?

Elaine: "Yes. I did not think they should wait until Monday with the situation."

Question: And are you aware of what happened to Natalia at that June 27 visit?

Elaine: "She was still on antibiotics for sinusitis, and she was given all her immunizations, probably about seven of them on that visit."

Question: When you had Natalia (in Goshen) the weekend of July 16, were you aware that Barb had called Dr. Simpson's office concerning a problem she was having with Natalia?

Elaine: "Yes. She hadn't had a stool in five days, so Barb was supposed to put Karo syrup in her formula."

Question: Did you notice anything different that weekend?

Elaine: "Again, she hadn't progressed. One thing was different--- she did vomit her formula a couple of times."

Question: Did you notice anything different about her eyes?

Elaine: "Well, again like other things about a preemie, I wondered if she could see. And I wanted her so much to have eye contact with me. She never did smile as though she saw me. Never, that I could see, tracked any movement. So in the back of my mind, that concerned me. But, again, I thought if she had been born at a normal time she would be a very, very young baby."

Question: Did you talk to Barb after these incidents of throwing up?

Elaine: "Well, yeah. I talked to her on the phone, but also then when we took Natalia back I knew that she had done that at home, too. And the strange thing was, then you get another formula bottle ready and she takes it and keeps it down. So I didn't have the concern about her not getting her nutrition because she would. But it always seemed strange."

Question: Have you ever witnessed any frustration or anger (by Barb) towards Natalia?

Elaine: "I've never seen it towards either child, no."

Question: You described your daughter as sensitive in some ways. What did you mean by that?

Elaine: "Well, she is sensitive with people, and I saw her very sensitive with her children.... She is sensitive, but rough around the edges. I would see that more with her choice of words sometimes."

Question: And did you make arrangements with her to come to her house July 26, 2005?

Elaine: "Yes, we had made the arrangement the week before, because she had a hair appointment."

Question: Did Barb tell you why she was going to call the doctor about Natalia (July 26)?

Elaine: "Well, there were several things --- the vomiting, the eyes looking different-- she and I both decided it was time to call and check."

Question: And when you got there (Tuesday, July 26), did Barb leave?

Elaine: "Yes... Her hair appointment was canceled by her hair dresser. But she did leave. I said I'm here to stay with the children, you might as well go out anyway."

The police and prosecutor were told by doctors (my best guess is Dr. E) that Natalia, according to the shaken baby theory of "no lucid interval," would have been in dire straits at this point. Consequently, Barb's heading out as mentioned above (and Elaine's suggesting it) were more than the shaken baby theorists could comprehend. Obviously Barb and Elaine were people who had little concern for Natalia's well-being. All throughout the questions and comments by police and prosecutor is the assumption that Natalia is lying here at her home near death. *And they did nothing to help her.*

Question: Can you tell us what you observed?

Elaine: "When I first got there Barb was giving her a bottle and I said, well, 'I will finish this.'

And so she took that bottle fine and I burped her and so forth. And while she was gone I watched her. Barb had said before she felt cool-- and she did kind of feel a little cool-- so we went outside, wrapped her up and went in the sunshine because Isabella likes to go out anyway. And her color looked okay. I did check her pulse and respiration. That seemed okay. And I had a thermometer along. I did check her temperature."

Question: What kind of thermometer did you have?

Elaine: "Oh, it was a little cheap home thermometer. The 3-5 dollar digital kind."

Question: How did you take the baby's temperature?

Elaine: "I took it axillary, under her arm."

Question: Do you remember what the temperature was?

Elaine: "It was between 91 and 92 (degrees)."

Question: Did that concern you?

Elaine: "I thought, well, that isn't right. I knew axillary is at least one degree lower, and I also knew it is the least specific. I mean it can vary so much. And I also knew the kind of (thermometer) I brought isn't very accurate either. I knew that from home and from school, so I thought, well, I will take it several times. So I waited a while."

Question: Did the temperature actually go up?

Elaine: "It went up some."

Question: When Barb came home did you tell her you thought she could call the doctor?

Elaine: "We were planning on calling the doctor when she came home." (This had been decided earlier. Elaine would observe, and Barb would call.)

Question: Did she call the doctor?

Elaine: "She went away again and came back, and then it was nearly noon, and she thought the doctor's office was closed over noon, so she called--- we decided what things were important to report-- and then she called around 1:00 pm, I guess."

If you believe what the Lt. R said to Brant, "Your girlfriend... or fiance.. turns home from her morning of galavanting off to the hairdresser, or whatever the hell else she did that morning," you would then believe that Barb and Elaine both had a callous disregard for whether Natalia lived or died. Conversely, these actions could be viewed exactly as Elaine and Barb described them--- the situation involved continuing concerns about Natalia that now needed to be reported to the doctor---- but no emergency. And when they did report this to Dr. Simpson, she came to the same conclusion as Elaine and Barb, and asked Barb to set up an appointment the next morning.

Question: And did you hear the conversation Barb had with the doctor's office?

Elaine: "Yes, I heard everything because I was standing right at the door (when Barb called)."

Question: Was the doctor's office told about the temperature?

Elaine: "Yes."

Question: What else did she say?

Elaine: "She's not responding like she usually does, she is feeding. I had given her another bottle at noon. She said her eyes weren't right, weren't looking right."

Question: And did they tell you the doctor was going to call back?

Elaine: "Yes."

Question: Did you leave then?

Elaine: "Yes, I was planning on taking Isabella anyway, so I left right away at that point knowing that she would just have one child and could go to the doctor whenever they called and said 'come'."

Question: Did you talk to Barb later that evening?

Elaine: "She said the doctor called back and said to call in the next morning for an appointment."

Question: Do you understand why you were charged with neglect of a dependent?

Elaine: "As I understand it, it was a charge that because I'm a registered nurse that I should have known that I put my granddaughter in danger, because I should have gone to the emergency room rather than call her pediatrician to report her condition, and that I did that intentionally."

The prosecutor now cross-examines Elaine. This is an important moment for him. He has charged Elaine, not based on any factual evidence of neglect, but on the basis of a theory. He has never met Elaine. He has never spoken to Elaine. He just knows she is a central figure that needs to be dealt with if his theory is to hold up. And he clearly wants it to hold up. So he jumps right into Natalia's temperature reading that Elaine had gotten on Tuesday, July 26, 2005.

Question: And before you became a school nurse, where did you work?

Elaine: "I worked with home health care which is mostly 80 year olds, and before that as a school nurse in Egypt and Kuwait. And before that I was a college nurse, and one year in a hospital in adult medical."

Question: So you did have have young kids, is that correct?

Elaine: "First grade to twelfth grade, yes."

Question: And what type of training did you have"

Elaine: "My training is a bachelor's degree of science in nursing."

Question: Now is it fair to say that a person who has a temperature of 93 degrees is not healthy?

Elaine: "You know, I don't know that for sure. I don't know. I never in..." (cut off by prosecutor)

Question: You don't know that a person who had a temperature of 93 degrees is sick?

Elaine: "I never had that in my whole life of nursing, not once." (Not an actual 93 degrees. She had gotten numerous inaccurate readings in that range.)

Question: What is a normal temperature for a human being?

Elaine: "Orally?"

Question: Yes.

Elaine: "Ninety-eight point six."

Question: And if a person had a 101 degree temperature, is that person sick?

Elaine: "Yes."

Question: That's three degrees different from 98.6?

Elaine: "Yes."

Question: So if you reverse three degrees, that would be 95, correct?

Elaine: "Yes."

Question: You didn't think that while three degrees higher--- they're sick--- then three degrees lower they must be sick too. That didn't register?

Elaine: "It doesn't work that way."

Question: Doesn't work that way! Would it surprise you if I told you that a person's organs can shut down when they get a low temperature. (Remember, the foster mother said Natalia's temperature was below 90 degrees three or four times a week. And she was still alive).

Elaine: "Like with hypothermia, that's right."

Question: What was the first temperature you took?

Elaine: "The first one was between 91 and 92."

Question: That's even lower than 93? *I hope he knows the answer to his own question.*

Elaine: "That's right."

Question: That made you nervous, right?

Elaine: "No."

Question: Her temperature didn't make you nervous?

Elaine: "No.... First of all, it was axillary, which is not very specific. And secondly, it was a thermometer---I mean at school I have used those orally and they're sometimes 94, 95 degrees--- and they go back to class. So the issue was the kind of thermometer and the accuracy of the site that it was taken (axillary), plus I didn't know that was an important issue with a preemie." (As I stated earlier, Elaine had asked the head of the school nurse leadership team for the Westview Corporation to go back through Elaine's records for the two school years immediately prior to Natalia's trip to the ER. She found that 39 students had a temperature reading in this same range as Natalia's, taken on a similar thermometer, and none of them had serious consequences. Most went back to class.)

Question: You took her temperature because you had concerns about her in the first place, correct?

Elaine: "I took her temperature. I wanted to be sure she didn't have a fever, actually."

Question: Did she feel hot to you?

Elaine: "No, she felt cool. That happens with a fever."

Question: Wasn't there any concern about Natalia's health when you took the temperature?

Elaine: "It was not an emergency in my mind. It was a reason to call the doctor and report it and see, but it was not an emergency."

Question: A temperature of 91 doesn't raise any higher concern in your mind?

Elaine: "I'm saying it <u>did not</u> because I didn't think that could be accurate. But we <u>did</u> report it when we called it in."

Question: You took her temperature a second and a third time, correct?

Elaine: "Yes. Between 93-94 the second time, and between 92-93 the third time."

Question: Do you normally take a child's temperature three times?

Elaine: "No, I don't. But the reason I did is because I didn't think it was accurate."

Question: There was some kind of concern it was inaccurate?

Elaine: "Yeah. Because it didn't make sense. She was taking her bottle, her color was good. It didn't make sense."

Question: You didn't have any other concerns about Natalia except for the temperature?

Elaine: "<u>The temperature was not my main concern.</u>"

Question: My question is 'you didn't have any <u>other</u> concerns about Natalia'?

Elaine: "<u>I did</u>." (And then the prosecutor finally shifts directions).

In addition to sometimes making statements rather than questions, the prosecutor also uses a lot of pronouns without known referents. And other times he states questions in the negative, or uses double negatives. All of this, whether done intentionally or just sloppily, makes it very difficult to answer correctly when on the witness stand. And an <u>incorrect</u> answer can become a really big deal. The following is an example:

Question: "And they told her that was normal of a preemie baby is the lungs were underdeveloped and as they grow the lungs---"

Elaine: "They did not say that."

Question: "Well, she didn't tell you they told her that, correct?" *What?*

Elaine: "Pardon me?"

Question: "She didn't tell you that they told her that, is that what your saying?"

Another example:

Question: "Many children are born with a vacuum, is that fair to say?" (He most likely means they are delivered with the assistance of vacuum extraction.)

Elaine: "I don't think that's fair to say."

Question: "You don't think that's fair to say."

Elaine: "No."

Question: "Would it surprise you if I told you that the percentage is roughly 30 percent of children that are born?"

Elaine: "That would surprise me."

Question: "That would surprise you. Would it surprise you if I told you that there are probably people in this room who had children that had the vacuum used?"

Elaine: "I don't know how to answer that."

Question: "You don't know how to answer that." *Where are we going here?*

Trying to answer questions phrased like these above is very difficult, particularly with the natural nervousness of sitting on the witness stand. You don't know when you're being led into a trap, or just the victim of a poorly worded question.

Question: You thought she was unusual because she was blue when she was born, correct?

Elaine: "I was asked what I noticed when she was born, and she was blue, yes. That's not usually a good sign."

Question: And they took her (Natalia) to NICU?

Elaine: "Yes."

Question: And they released her a few days later?

Elaine: "Nineteen days later."

The prosecutor now shifts to postpartum depression (PPD).

Question: Did Barbara tell you they talked to her about postpartum depression at the NICU?

Elaine: "I think she used the term PPD. And when she was asked what that meant, it had to do with bonding and feeling attached to a child."

Question: That's what she told you?

Elaine: "Yes. That's what she said about every time she talked about it."

Question: Didn't she tell you it could be some kind of depression, too?

Elaine: "Like I said, she used that term (PPD), and when asked what she meant, she said it had to do with bonding with her child. She did not feel bad about herself."

187

Question: Didn't she tell you she was feeling a <u>deep</u> postpartum depression?

Elaine: "<u>No</u>." (This was another <u>favorite trick</u> of the prosecutor. Ask a question that is almost correct, but add a significant dimension that you want to get on the record, and hope the witness doesn't notice the incorrect part). *But Elaine noticed.*

Question: You don't remember talking to the officers and telling the officers that 'but she did have some kind of a depression and a <u>deep</u> postpartum depression'? You didn't say that? (The prosecutor acts as if he is reading from her police interview. He knows that Dr. Rutt, the psychiatrist, has said that <u>severe</u> PPD <u>with psychosis</u> can be the dangerous kind, and now he wants the jury to believe Elaine is denying what she said in the police interview. <u>Perception, not truth.</u>)

Elaine: "I did not say <u>deep</u> postpartum depression. What I said was she used the term PPD. And when I asked her what that was, she said it had to do with bonding and feeling attached to the baby. (Elaine had studied the transcript of what she had told police, and it was beginning to irritate the prosecutor.)

Question: You don't recall ever using the word <u>deep</u> PPD? *Why would she? It didn't happen!*

Elaine: "To repeat, I used the word postpartum depression, saying that she (Barb) used that, and this is what it meant. I never put the word <u>deep</u> with it.

Question: That's my question. You didn't use the word <u>deep</u>?

Elaine: "Never." *Could you be a little bit clearer, please?*

Question: That is inaccurate? (His unspoken challenge to the jury: Are you going to believe the prosecutor [who <u>appears</u> to be reading from the police interview transcript] or this woman who has felony charges against her?) *This type of trickery seems unconscionable. Are there no ethical requirements in this line of work?*

Elaine: "That was not in there." (In the police interview transcript.)

Question: Did she tell you that she actually did feel that PPD?

Elaine: "She said she had trouble feeling attached to the baby."

Question: My question is, did she ever tell you that she was feeling PPD <u>and</u> she had bonding problems with Natalia? (He tries a slightly different approach---PPD <u>and</u> bonding problems.)

Elaine: "She told me she had bonding problems, but not depression."

Question: "She never used that term? *This has been answered five or six times. Are you going to try until you get the answer you want?*

Elaine: "She used that term. And when I asked her what that meant, she said it meant bonding."

Question: When she told you that, did she tell you <u>when</u> she started feeling that?

Elaine: "Yeah. I think already at the time that Natalia came home."

Question: She told you that right when Natalia came home?

Elaine: "Within the first week of being home."

Question: That's when she started feeling the PPD? (He seems unwilling to use any other term than PPD, even though everyone who talked with Barb heard her describe it as something else, and the psychiatrist said it was something else.) *Hammer it into the juror's heads.*

Elaine: "That's when we talked about it first."

Question: And when she talked about that with you, did she later on talk about it again?

Elaine: "Yes."

Question: How often?" *This was over two years ago.*

Elaine: "Oh, maybe two or three times."

Question: Do you recall when you talked with her about postpartum depression?

Elaine: "I did not talk about PPD. I talked about her being attached to her child."

Question: How often did you talk about the attachment? *He didn't say PPD! Amazing.*

Elaine: "The first week she came home. And I remember probably some time in June. And I remember talking to her when we were on vacation, which was the first week of July. She said, 'You know, I'm starting to feel more attached to Natalia now.' And I thought, 'Wow, that's a good sign.' I don't remember talking about it after that."

Question: So the last time you talked about it was right around July 4?

Elaine: "No. It would have near the end of that week. We were on vacation. It was by phone."

Question: Now the other two times --- did you ask her if she felt she was going to hurt Natalia?

Elaine: "Yes."

Question: And she was unequivocal. "No, I don't feel that way"?

Elaine: "No. 'That isn't it at all.'" (Correcting the prosecutor on exactly what Barb said.)

Question: Why did you ask that?

Elaine: "Because I knew that sometimes that is a part of it, and I wanted to take precautions for her to get some help if that were the case."

Question: You weren't sure she was going to do that, were you?

Elaine: "That she was going to get help?"

Question: If she actually felt that?

Elaine: "Yeah."

Question: Did you?

Elaine: "Yeah. I felt that. I thought she would, yes. That's why I asked."

Question: Do you remember being asked by the officers that if she had done something like this, would she be honest to herself?

Elaine: "Yes."

Question: And do you remember your response?

Elaine: "Yes."

Question: And what was your response?

Elaine: "My response was, 'I don't know. I would hope so.' Because you can never answer a question like that for someone else." *Right. But Char and Gary answered it for Brant anyway.*

Question: Didn't you actually say on this question, 'Do you think she would be honest enough with herself?' And your response was, 'I don't know.' Do you remember that?

Elaine: "I said, I don't know. And I said I hope so, also." (This comment agrees word for word with the transcript of the police tape.) At least the prosecutor just left out the second half of her response as he tried to set up Elaine into looking like she didn't trust Barb. He didn't change her words to the extent the police did when they told Brant: "I asked her mother that flat out....... and her mother (Elaine) said 'probably not.'" And when Brant seemed astounded at this, Lt. Richmond once again told the whole story which ended with her answer being "probably not." And the prosecutor was present when the police did that interview with Brant. But neither the prosecutor, nor the police seem to have any moral compunctions about playing fast and loose with the truth here. The prosecutor continues:

Question: Did you (say, "I hope so.")?

Elaine: "Yes."

Question: Okay. I will keep looking. Do you remember what part of the conversation?

Elaine: "It was the same place." (Now he is aware that she knows in detail what she told police. But he keeps trying to trap her). *Is this what "justice" is all about?*

More questions from the prosecutor, this time about Natalia's eyes and "tracking" (following things).

Question: You didn't see her tracking at all? You're sure about that?

Elaine: "I never tried to see if she was [tracking] before that (July 26)."

Question: Don't you remember that eight days before she (Natalia) actually looked at you and you thought to yourself, "Oh, my gosh, I'm glad she recognizes me." You don't remember any of that?

Elaine: "I said, 'she looked at me and I really couldn't know for sure if she was, you know. You hope so.' I think that is what I said."

Question: You thought it was, but you said, "well, maybe it's just my wishful thinking?"

190

Elaine: "That's not tracking though. That's eye contact."

Question: Okay. So you believe then she had eye contact?

Elaine: "I said I was hoping. I wanted to imagine that. I didn't say I knew for sure." (Actual quote to police: "She didn't have the kind of eye contact that a baby should have at that point. But I remember I said, 'she is looking at me now...sort of.' You know, you try to imagine things like that."

Once again, Elaine had been totally truthful with her responses. And once again, one doesn't know how the jury perceived all the disagreements between what Elaine said, and what the prosecutor claimed she said. Were they able to see what the prosecutor was doing, or were they simply watching what they thought was an alleged felon get tripped up by the prosecutor's skillful quoting from the police interviews? How could they possibly know what was true?

The prosecutor, however, knew. He needed to expose Elaine as a liar if he wanted to convict Barb. And it wasn't working. He had not been successful in getting Elaine to change what she had said to police about Natalia's temperature. He could not get Elaine to change what she had said about Barb's description of what she meant by postpartum depression, nor the timing at which this PPD (lack of bonding) occurred. He had failed to get Elaine to say what he wanted her to say about whether Barb would be truthful if confronted. And now he has been unsuccessful in getting Elaine to say Natalia's eyes were okay the weekend of July 16. These were all central to his charging Elaine in the first place. Had he checked the police tapes more carefully early on, perhaps charges would not have been filed. But now he was running out of options on how to challenge Elaine. He apparently decided if this doesn't go the way he has planned, he had better at least protect Brant, who was present in the home for at least some part of each day over the last three months.

Question: Now during that whole time period, Brant worked a lot, correct?

Elaine: "Yes."

Question: Brant was gone a lot?

Elaine: "Yes."

Question: He was working twelve, fourteen hours a day?

Elaine: "I don't think he was working that much."

Question: You don't think he was working that much?

Elaine: "But I don't know how much. There were days that he took off, but he was gone a lot."

Question: Did Barbara ever voice any frustration about Brant's not being around enough?

Elaine: "She voiced to me that she felt so fortunate that they could work this out, that she could stay home with the children. I knew they both wanted to do that. And while she felt bad that he had to work that much, I think that's why we kept the girls sometimes so they could have some time together."

Question: Natalia <u>did</u> cry normally throughout the time which you took care of her, is that fair to say?

Elaine: "I wouldn't say she cried <u>normally</u>. She--- because she was a preemie--- it was a very small cry."

Question: Do you remember telling the officers that I had her just last weekend, and she cried very normally?

Elaine: "Yes."

Question: So did she cry normally?

Elaine: "Normal for a very, very small child, yes."

At this point the state of frustration that he had planned for Elaine has reached the boiling point ---but not in Elaine---- in himself. Mr. Cotter is getting nowhere with the circumstantial stuff. Elaine knows too well what she actually said. But he apparently feels he still has one final option remaining on the table----the nuclear option. The one that you use when you've played a long, hard chess match--- and all of a sudden you realize you're in deep trouble--- so you "accidentally" bump the chess board and the pieces go flying in all directions, leaving no other option but to start over. And he decides to use it. The prosecutor continues with the following question/statements:

Question: Oh, I see. You had an opportunity to review your statement quite often, haven't you? (In other words--- I don't seem to be able to trap you.)

Elaine: "I have."

Question: As a matter of fact, not just your statement, but you had an opportunity to hear what other witnesses had to say in this courtroom, isn't that fair to say? (This trial has the 'separation of witnesses', which is why Elaine and I were not able to be in the courtroom. Upcoming witnesses are prevented from hearing previous witnesses and then changing their own stories accordingly to help their side of the case. That is precisely why I went to the trouble of transcribing all of the police interviews. Because of those transcriptions we knew what had been said by us, and by the others, and would be able to be consistent with our previous statements to police.)

Elaine: "No. I have listened to the police reports of the other people." (The prosecutor now moves from his table into the gallery.)

Question: Who am I standing next to?

Elaine: "My sister-in-law."

Question: Is it not fair to say that during the course of the trial she would write things down and go and show you what she wrote things down about?

Elaine: "No."

Question: Oh, she didn't. Would it surprise you if other people saw her doing that?

Elaine: "Yeah. Because she didn't show me."

Question: Do you remember your husband out in the hallway writing things down after she had come out and talked with him? *Uh-oh. Now I guess I'm identified as the secretary of this conspiracy.* (Fortunately I didn't know anything about this until the next day when the defense rested. But who would have accused us of something like that? Or was this just another prosecutorial machination with the truth. Now that I have the trial transcripts in hand, I have a better understanding of who prompted the prosecutor to push the red button for the nuclear option.)

Elaine: "No."

Question: No. Not at all. Was he writing anything in a notebook while you were out there?

Elaine: "Was he writing anything? He was doing Sudoku." (Once again, totally true. It was one of the things I did to keep my mind at least half-way sharp at my age. And it seemed to make the time go faster while sitting hour after hour on those hard concrete benches in the atrium of the courthouse.)

Question: So he wasn't writing anything in note pads?

Elaine: "No, not that I know of."

Question: Now is there another individual that looks somewhat like your husband in the courtroom? *Is this another trick, like pretending to read from the police interview?*

Elaine: "That looks like my husband?" (Elaine was wondering what in the world is going on here?)

Question: Yeah.

Elaine: "I don't think so." *Nobody in the world looks like me.*

Question: Wearing a green shirt, not in here now?

Elaine: "I don't think so."

Mr. Korpal: "Your honor, may we approach?"

(Sidebar conference)

> Mr. Korpal: "I don't know what this is about. What is the relevancy of these questions? Where are we going with this?"
>
> The Court (Judge): "Tell me about this."
>
> Mr. Cotter: "Sure, Your Honor. Originally there were some concern and I voiced it to Mr. Korpal and I don't remember if

I voiced it to the court." *He doesn't remember whether he voiced it to the court. It's only been a day or two. I guess he wouldn't stand up very well under his own scrutiny regarding "memory."*

The Court: "You did not. I will bring that absolutely to your attention." *The judge remembers.*

Mr. Cotter: "Mr. Korpal's client had been talking to her parents about the testimony." *Now it's Barb telling Elaine and me something. I thought it was my sister informing Elaine. Or was she informing me? I can't keep up.*

The Court: "Hey, folks. Can I have you park the jury in the jury room for a couple of seconds, please." *Yeah, after hearing all these accusations about Elaine.....leave.*

(Recess taken: No jury present; Visitor's gallery still present; Attorneys back to their tables)

The Court: "Speak freely."

Mr. Cotter: "Concerning?"

The Court: "What were we just talking about?"

Mr. Cotter: "I'm not sure which issue you wanted me to address first."

The Court: "Well, the line of questioning is implicit. You believe she has been discussing testimony with someone else and you began to explain to me while you began to ask her questions and point to specifics suggesting that. Do you want to tell me where we are going... what we have?

Mr. Cotter: "Certainly, Your Honor. At the beginning of this trial I have been advised by other individuals in the courtroom that the defendant had been talking to her mother and her father about was said during the trial."

The Court: "Who told you that?"

Mr. Cotter: "Paula Muhlherr, who is the CASA, who is in the courtroom at this time." *Paula? Neutral Paula? Unbiased Paula? The one who sits right behind the prosecutor's table? The one who sits with Brant's family during all breaks in the atrium? What would she have to gain by alleging this?*

The Court: "Okay."

Mr. Cotter: "I advised Mr. Korpal. I said, Mr. Korpal, please advise your client not to do that."

The Court: "Yeah."

Mr. Cotter: "After that, Ms. Muhlherr, along with Wendy Nowicki (the prosecutor's assistant), sitting next to me had observed the lady who I identified in the courtroom as well as the other gentleman who is currently not in the courtroom, writing information down throughout the course of the trial (which is perfectly legal), going out to both Dan and Elaine Schrock, telling them what was said in the courtroom (not legal), and Dan writing

194

things down. Now they did not notice Elaine writing things down, but they did notice him writing things down, so that was the purpose for the line of questioning." *Had I known at the time, I would have turned in my Sudoku book to them. But now I simply have it as a souvenir in one of my large boxes of trial materials.*

The Court: "Let me ask you a question in passing. She (Elaine) said 'no.' Do you propose to ask Ms. Nowicki and the CASA lady to impeach her on whether or not she talked to the people?" (Elaine was sitting there listening to all of this, not knowing what was going on. When she heard the word "impeach," she thought "what does that mean?" She had only heard of that term related to President Clinton, and didn't understand how it related to her.)

Mr. Cotter: "Yes, your honor." *That is his plan. Upset the chess board. Impeach her. Start over.*

The Court: "Well, can I ask you a question? If you asked me for separation of witnesses and you believe in good faith there is a violation, don't you think you have some reason to tell me about it? I'm just curious."

There is much more in the transcript that represents a judge that is basically seething at what the prosecutor has done. According to those in the courtroom, the judge dressed down the prosecutor with scathing sarcasm for not playing by the rules. "I'm trying to run a trial that gets tried one time--- not two or three." This continued for a considerable time. In the midst of all of this commotion, Elaine was still sitting on the witness stand, totally confused. The judge was trying to be fair, but he simply didn't know what to do. The prosecutor had left a real mess for him to clean up.

Let me interject here that we definitely did not do the sharing of information that was alleged:

> (1) because integrity is important to us;
> (2) because, even if we were scoundrels, for the last two years we had known everything that was said to police in the interviews. We didn't need to cheat;
> (3) if you check what the prosecutor was questioning Elaine about, no sharing of information would have helped (this topic had not been discussed by others); and
> (4) Elaine never changed her story. So what good would knowing what was said inside the courtroom have done?

But as I said earlier, probably none of the above matters. What is relevant, however, is that the prosecutor was likely totally frustrated with how his questioning was going with Elaine. In his mind he apparently had no other option.

So now, after all this delay, the jury is brought back into the room. No explanation is given to them. They simply are expected to continue listening as if nothing has happened. The last thing they heard before leaving the courtroom was the prosecutor ranting about how Elaine was able to answer the prosecutor's questions, ostensibly because she had a "mole" in the courtroom who was passing information to her. Who will they believe---the prosecutor---or the woman with felony charges? And so, we never get to know how large a part this debacle played in the jurors' minds. But you can bet it was something that was not ignored. The trial resumes with the judge saying, "Bring them in. Have a seat, folks. Counsel." Mr. Cotter: "Thank you, your Honor."

Question: Was she (Natalia) snorting after the antibiotic treatment?
Elaine: "She snorted her whole life."
Question: So the snorting was not part of the sinus problem?
Elaine: "No."
Question: When Natalia went for her wellness check on June 27, did Barbara tell you that the doctor said everything was okay except for the sinus problems?
Elaine: "Yes. There was some question on something, whether she had a social smile, I believe, or something like that."
Question: That's what Barbara told you."
Elaine: "No. I saw the records."
Question: You saw the records for the wellness check?
Elaine: "Yes."
Question: And everything was okay, isn't that correct?
Elaine: "Except for that one area."
Question: Except for the social smile?
Elaine: "Which has to do with vision."
Question: Okay. Did the doctor put in there that we have a concern about her vision?
Elaine: "About a social smile." (This checks out to be true. The June 27 medical record, which is the only record from June 8 to July 27, indicates under social smile--- "not sure," and is left unchecked.)

Question: Did the doctors note any concern on the records about her cognitive ability to be able to understand things? *Does he understand how old Natalia is?*
Elaine: "Cognitive ability?"
Question: Yes.
Elaine: "A baby.... no."
Question: There weren't any indication whatsoever?
Elaine: "No."

196

Question: Now, granted for a baby there is not going to be a lot of that, correct?

Elaine: "I don't think there would be any cognitive ability, no."

Question: Part of cognitive ability, wouldn't it be fair to say, that's recognizing things around you?

Elaine: "Not for an infant."

This above interchange highlights a major part of the problem with a trial like this one. Police, prosecutors, judges, defense attorneys, juries, and most non-medical witnesses normally have very little, if any, understanding of anatomy, physiology, medicine, and psychiatry. Most just try to "wing it" and hope they don't come out looking too ignorant. The doctor is king/queen in this kind of trial, and the conviction rate is, therefore, extremely high. It also underscores the fact, as Dr. C, the neurosurgeon implied, that the part of Natalia's brain damaged and atrophied on the brain scan was largely the cognitive part, the part largely unused by a three month old preemie. So there was no empirical evidence that part of the brain ever was normal. And there were no brain scans to show it was normal at birth.

Question: Was she (Barb) going to call the doctor until she talked with you?

Elaine: "She was planning to call, and I said I will just add my observations to it since I was going to be there."

Question: So you guys were going to decide what you were going to tell the doctors?

Elaine: "We were going to add up what I saw and what she saw, yeah."

Question: And when Barb called she just spoke with somebody in the office, but not the doctor?

Elaine: "That's what I understand."

Question: Did you urge Barb to take Natalia to the hospital?

Elaine: "No."

Question: Did you even think that may be necessary?

Elaine: "No, I didn't."

Question: You didn't have any concerns about her health?

Elaine: "I had concerns about her health, which is why we called the pediatrician, yes."

Question: Did Barbara borrow a book from you? (The medical book.)

Elaine: "I brought a book that I had from school--- on well baby things--- that day I think."

Question: Did she ask you if she could keep it?

Elaine: "I left it there, so she must have. I'm not sure."

Question: Just so we're clear, State's 31, is this the book? *More "evidence".*

Elaine: "Yes."

Question: And it's entitled Your Child's Health?

Elaine: "That's right." (Elaine's questioning is ended.)

CHAPTER TWELVE

The final witness for the <u>defense</u> was **Barbara Schrock**, mother of Natalia and Isabella.

Question (defense): Were you satisfied with Dr. Simpson as your family pediatrician?

Barb: "I was. I trusted her a lot."

Question: Did you begin to have problems during your pregnancy with Natalia?

Barb: "Yes. I was sick a lot of the day, sick a lot at night, headaches, constant headaches. I didn't eat very well and couldn't hold my prenatal vitamins down."

Question: Was there a time when you became more sick?

Barb: "Toward the last two months I started developing high blood pressure. I was even at the doctor's one day and they wouldn't let me leave until I laid on my side for a while until my blood pressure went down."

Question: Was there ever a time right before Natalia's birth that they decided to keep you and put you in the hospital?

Barb: "Yes. About three days before her birth I was at the doctor's office not knowing I was going to give birth in three days. But they said 'you need to go to the hospital now.' And I said, 'my fiance and child are at home. I need to go home first'," (she had their one vehicle) "so they have a way to get here. So I went home and we went straight to the hospital."

Question: Did they come and show you Natalia after she was born?

Barb: "Yeah. I didn't get to hold her for very long. Brant got to see her, and my mother and father. If I recall correctly, Brant's mother and stepfather came in and took some pictures of her and then they said we pretty much have to take her now."

Question: Did you talk with Brant about having your tubes tied?

Barb: "Absolutely."

Question: Were you able to visit Natalia every day in the NICU?

Barb: "I recall about two or three times that I did not go there. The rest of the time I would go when Brant would get home from work." (You will remember that NICU records showed that Barb was there <u>15 of the 19 days</u>. Char gave testimony that Barb didn't go very often, and Brant said he was there <u>more than Barb</u>. According to Brant, <u>he</u> was there between 5-8 days.)

Question: You still had Isabella at home?

Barb: "Yes."

Question: At that time you still had one car?

Barb: "That's correct."

Question: Do you remember the day she was allowed to come home?

Barb: "Well, from April 23,---- 19 days. So, no, I'm not good at math. I couldn't tell you that date." *She's right. She's not particularly good at math. But she got the basics right.*

Question: What were the instructions on how to take care of her?

Barb: "He told us that it is necessary to keep Natalia away from large groups of people. And if anyone were to pick her up, to make sure they're washing their hands, and to try to keep her in a quiet, dark area so she could rest. Technically she wasn't born yet is what they kept telling us."

Question: Did there come a time when you started to have concerns that you weren't getting close to Natalia?

Barb: "Yes. With Isabella, they gave her to me right away and I breast fed her right after she was born. With Natalia, I didn't get that time. So I was really anxious to get her home. When she came home we had that long period of not being able to bond together. So as happy as I was to have her home, I didn't feel the same way that I felt previously with Isabella."

Question: Was she a more quiet baby than Isabella?

Barb: "Yeah."

Question: She slept more than a regular baby?

Barb: "She did."

Question: What was it like to care for Natalia?

Barb: "Natalia was a sweet baby. She wasn't fussy at all. She slept a lot, and she ate, but a lot of times would not keep a lot of her food down. She seemed to have issues with gas. Not outwardly to where she would be fussy. Just you could kind of look at her and tell she may be not feeling well."

Question: Was she generally easy to take care of?

Barb: "Oh, yeah."

Question: There has been some discussion about Isabella going to Brant's mom and dad's quite often. Was that at their request?

Barb: "Oh, yeah. They loved Isabella. Brant is technically an only child, so his mother and stepfather were just ecstatic about having Isabella at their house."

Question: And the weekend of July 2, 2005. Who kept Natalia that weekend?

Barb: "That weekend Gary and Charlene Mullins, Brant's mother and stepfather, kept both of the girls."

Question: Now is that the first weekend that Natalia was out in public in terms of around a lot of people?

Barb: "Yes."

200

Question: And at the July 2 party, were you upset with Brant that day?

Barb: "Yes."

Question: And could you tell us why?

Barb: "His mother and stepfather said they will bring the girls as long as we go to the party, because it's a lot of work for two children when you have one that wants to run, and the other one is an infant. So we went there and I said to Brant, now, I haven't had a chance to see a lot of your family members. So when we get there I would like to be able to socialize, too, not just you always socializing...... Long story short, Brant was not holding his end of the bargain, so I was annoyed with him."

Question: Did you call him a name?

Barb: "I did."

Question: Between doctor visits, did you call Navarre Pediatrics?

Barb: "Yeah. She hadn't had a bowel movement for what seemed like a week."

Question: Any other phone calls to Navarre?

Barb: "I called one other time, too, because she had problems with her formula. It wasn't just general spitting up. She would throw up her entire bottle."

Question: On Sunday, July 24, you went to Brant's grandmother's house with Natalia. Did Char say anything to you about Natalia's welfare that day?

Barb: "They were just all kind of holding her and looking at her." (Nothing was said.)

Question: On Monday, July 25, did you leave Natalia with Brant?

Barb: "I did. Isabella and I went to long John Silvers in Niles (Michigan)."

Question: And how long were you gone?

Barb: "At least an hour an a half."

Question: When you got back, did you have a conversation with Brant about a phone call?

Barb: "Yes. [His mother said that on Sunday] Natalia just didn't look right and she thought something was wrong."

Question: Did she think the child should go to the doctor?

Barb: "I don't recall if she thought that or not."

The next morning Elaine came to babysit while Barb was supposed to get a haircut. She brought a thermometer and a medical book from her school. A call is received indicating that the haircut has been canceled. Barb went with her friend, anyway, to have breakfast and go to a used clothing store.

Question: When you came back, did your mother express concerns about Natalia?

Barb: "Yes, her eyes didn't look right. She <u>had</u> eaten. She (Elaine) took her temperature and said it was 93 degrees. She didn't think that was alarming, but at the same time the way she was looking and kind of acting didn't seem quite right."

Question: When did you call the doctor's office?

Barb: "Around 12:30 or 1:00 pm."

Question: Can you tell the jury when the doctor called you back?

Barb: "The doctor called me back at approximately 5:30 at night."

Question: Did you have a similar discussion with the doctor as you had with the receptionist?

Barb: "Yes. She had eaten well that day, her temperature was 93 degrees, but I was concerned about her eyes, and she just seemed to be just kind of laying there. There wasn't a whole lot of action."

Question: And what were you told to do?

Barb: "She said, 'Well, she is eating well?' And I said 'yeah, she's eating fine.' And she said 'Well, why don't you go ahead and call in the morning, or just come in the morning.'"

Question: Did you feed her before you went to bed for the night?

Barb: "I think I fed her around 7:30 pm again, and she had eaten really well. Then around 9:30 pm I tried to feed her again and she didn't really want to take much."

Question: During your statement you talked a lot about small incidents that happened with Natalia. <u>Why did you feel a need to explain those small things to police</u>?

Barb: "The reason I told the police that is because as a parent, if I had done something to hurt my child, I wanted to know that, and I also wanted them to know that."

Question: Have you ever harmed Natalia?

Barb: "No."

Question: Did you ever shake her with such force to give her brain damage?

Barb: "No."

Question: When was the last time you saw Natalia?

Barb: "Two years ago."

Question: Are you still allowed to see Isabella?

Barb: "Once a week if her father or family doesn't cancel that visit."

Question: Are you given updates by CPS concerning Natalia's condition?

Barb: "There is a social worker that originally started out with Natalia, and her name was Katie Coronado, and she was helpful. And I called her a lot and asked her questions. When her sister took over, Kelli, this last year--- to be honest with you, when the foster parent came in yesterday that was the first time I had found out anything about Natalia--- excuse me--- and Natalia's condition in probably the last six months."

<u>Cross-examination</u> of the witness by the <u>prosecutor</u>.

<u>Question</u>: Now when you talked about throwing Natalia in the air, how far would she leave your hands?

<u>Barb</u>:   "From here to here (shows). I mean <u>the length I can reach my arms up</u>. So it was like that."

<u>Question</u>: Show me like this. <u>It's about a foot</u>? *Barb wouldn't know that.*

<u>Barb</u>:   "I'm not good at that stuff. I couldn't tell you."

<u>Question</u>: People voiced concerns about that, correct?

<u>Barb</u>:   "Yes."

<u>Question</u>: And you said, oh, <u>I'm just checking her reflexes</u>, correct?

<u>Barb</u>:   "<u>Correct.</u>"

Now the prosecutor begins to play with Barb's memory from two years ago in a very deceitful way. The police and prosecutor have said publicly on multiple occasions that Barb has told them Dr. Simpson told her to throw Natalia in the air. It was on the TV evening news, it was in the newspapers, it was even in the document to support probable cause of felony charges against Barb. And, yet, she never said this. It is not in her police interview anywhere. And the police and the prosecutor <u>knew</u> this. So they had asked Brant, and he responded categorically to police that he had <u>not</u> said Barb told him that Dr. Simpson had said Barb should do this. But after they took him through that multi-hour brainwashing session and turned him against Barb, two years later <u>Brant changed his testimony in this trial</u>. Now the prosecutor, as he had with Elaine, is tricking Barb into believing (and the jury into believing), that he is reading from her police interview. <u>She answers that she did not make that assertion</u>--- that the doctor had told her to throw Natalia in the air--- but the prosecutor proceeds to get her to believe that her memory is just bad, and that she is changing her testimony from what she told police. *I'm certain this prosecutor and these police officers must have some way of rationalizing these "techniques" in their own minds so that they are able to sleep at night.*

<u>Question</u>: <u>Did the doctor tell you to do that</u>?

<u>Barb</u>:   "<u>No</u>."

<u>Question</u>: Did you tell Officer Kaps that the doctor told you to do that?

<u>Barb</u>:   "I don't recall telling him that."   (She didn't.)

Question: If you told Officer Kaps, would that have been accurate then?

Barb: "I guess if I told Officer Kaps that, then it must have been accurate."

Question: Today you do not recall?

Barb: "I do not recall that."

The prosecutor will continue to use this "technique" multiple times later in the questioning of Barb. *Truth is not the goal. Winning is.*

Question: Where did you get the term postpartum depression?

Barb: "Well, probably reading one of my parenting magazines, or from television."

Question: Did you ever watch a show on Lifetime about a woman who had PPD? That doesn't stick in your mind? (Actually, the police had planted this idea in Char and Gary's minds, and two years later Brant came out with it in the courtroom.)

Barb: "Not necessarily. I remember watching the Oprah Winfrey show with Brooke Shields in it, and she was talking about how she suffered from PPD. That's what I recall."

Question: The show I'm thinking of is about a woman who injured her children and alleged she suffered from PPD. *The planted story.*

Barb: "I don't remember."

Question: You don't remember? (Implication: You don't want to remember.)

Barb: "No, I'm sorry." (The bigger question is how the jury understands this stuff.) Perception, not truth.

Question: You're telling her (Elaine) you're suffering from PPD. She says are you feeling like you want to hurt your child, and you say "no"?

Barb: "I guess the way you phrase the question, I'm not sure if I fully understood what postpartum depression was." *A fair statement.*

Question: I wasn't asking if you actually suffered from it. You just said you suffered from it. *There's really no question whether you suffered from PPD. You said you did. What else matters? Certainly not the psychiatrist's diagnosis that you did not have PPD.*

Barb: "Yes."

Question: You saw the tape, right?

Barb: "I read over my statements yesterday, yes."

Question: Is that the only time you ever watched that tape or read the statement?

Barb: "I tried to watch it before. It was kind of hard to hear. (The tape audio was not of good quality.) Not yesterday, but at home."

Question: How many times did you try to watch it?

Barb: "Once."

Question: Just one time? *Where is he going with this?*

Barb: "Yes."

Question: When was that? *What was the day in the last two years? Look out.*

Barb: "I don't remember."

Question: How long have you had that tape? (He seems to be trying to get a feel of how well Barb knows the tape of the police interview. He doesn't want to make up statements he claims are on the tape if she knows the tape well enough to expose him. Elaine already burned him on that. Unfortunately, Barb didn't know the tape well enough. And he took advantage of her because of it.)

Barb: "I don't know that either."

Question: When you were talking about PPD, you didn't want to have much to do with Natalia, correct?

Barb: "I felt more a separation with her. Not that I didn't want to have anything to do with her."

Question: Do you remember telling Officer Kaps it (PPD) came on three weeks or a month ago, and then I didn't want to have a lot to do with her?

The above statement is true. Barb did give that timing to police. But she also gave other timings previously. The following are some of the other answers given to the timing question:

> Dr. Rutt: "In general, at some point following the birth of Natalia." (But it was not PPD.)
> Elaine: "Within the first week of (Natalia's) being home."
> Brant: "I believe it was when Natalia was in the NICU."
> Barb (at trial): "There was a little bit before, and then after Natalia came home."
> Nurse Spratt: "Mom (Barb) went through PPD." [from notes]
> Char and Gary: (Char and Gary did not know about PPD. Sgt. K mentioned it to them five separate times throughout their police interview.)
> Dr. Okanlami: "The impression I got was it was something she had, and was over it at that point in time (July 27)."

So the prosecutor has picked his timing from a "buffet list" of timings, because that particular timing works best into his theory. But hardly beyond a reasonable doubt. And Barb tries to answer honestly his timing question:

Barb: "I don't remember, but if it's down there."

Question: Would that be accurate?

Barb: "That would be accurate then."

Question: At those times you would feed her, put her back down, and not deal with her otherwise? (Not accurate.)

Barb: "I would feed her, and bathe her, and care for her, and put her back in the bassinet, correct."

Question: You didn't feel like you wanted to hold her?

Barb: "I _did_ hold her some, but there wasn't a bond there."

Question: But my question is, did you _feel_ like you wanted to hold her? _Not whether you actually _did_ hold her._

Barb: "I don't remember how I felt at the time. But if I had said to Officer Kaps that's how I was feeling, then that's how I was feeling." _Barb trusts this man too much._

Question: You were annoyed by his mother? (Because of Char's Monday evening, July 25 call to Brant).

Barb: "Yes."

Question: For?

Barb: "Well, I had asked what it is that she thinks is wrong with Natalia. And he (Brant) said 'I don't know, she doesn't look right.' I don't know what that means." (Barb didn't talk with Char directly about it.)

Question: Weren't you worried about Natalia?

Barb: "Of course I was worried about her. She is my child."

Question: You cut short your outing because 'I'm worried about Natalia and, you know, I really need to find out what is going on.' Isn't that how you were feeling?

Barb: "I guess it was."

Question: It's not _my_ emotions. It's yours. _There's some question about that._

Barb: "You're reading it verbatim, aren't you?" (Barb is under the impression that he is reading this word for word from her police interview. And for good reason. The prosecutor never answers, but leaves that impression. She can't remember every feeling, and timing of feelings, from two years ago. So go with what the prosecutor is "reading" from the police interview. What I said back then was true, and I trust the prosecutor is being honest now.) _Not always a good assumption._

Question: Does that sound accurate?

Barb: "It does sound accurate."

Question: Did you think something was wrong with her?

Barb: "I didn't know if there was anything wrong. I was a little bit suspicious of the way she was acting that morning."

Question: When you got back home that morning didn't you start kind of investigating?

Barb: "I spoke to my mom about her temperature, and what she had thought she noticed, and then I called the doctor."

Question: The something about the eyes--- was that different than what you told us before?

Barb: "With the gazing and winking."

Question: Even more different than we talked about before?

Barb: "Probably more pronounced. She was doing it more often than she had done it in the past----either that---or I did not notice it in the past like I did at this point."

Question: And if the temperature was 100 degrees, would you believe the child was ill?

Barb: "Yes."

Question: But low you didn't think anything was a problem?

Barb: "The doctor told me that she might go under that (98 degrees) just a little bit. But as far as knowing that 93 was low to the point that Dr. Simpson had said, no, I never knew that. A high temperature concerned me more."

Question: So temperature was not a concern? It's the eyes that are gazing differently?

Barb: "She is just staring off and then she is not eating (Tuesday evening), and she is kind of laying there."

Question: Let me shift gears a little bit. Let's talk about the way you dealt with her gas, moving her legs around?

Barb: "I would move her legs in a bicycle motion, sometimes just press them gently against her stomach, and then pull them back. And push them forward again, and pull them back."

Question: That was to help relieve gas?

Barb: "Yes." (This method, as mentioned, was suggested in Parents magazine, August 2005).

The prosecutor begins questioning about the Medical Book that Elaine brought with her Tuesday morning.

Question: You recall giving him (Brant) that book?

Barb: "I do not recall giving it to him. He might have taken the book himself, but I don't remember giving it to him."

Question: So you told him, 'Hey, Brant. I want you to read this book. But you don't know whether he read it or not?

Barb: "I don't know whether he read it or not."

Question: You just told us, I think, that you didn't physically hand him the book?

Barb: "Correct."

Question: Do you recall telling him, hey, there's a book there that I want you to read?

Barb: "I'm sure I mentioned to him there is a book and you should read some of the things in it."

Question: But you don't recall whether he read them or not?

Barb: "I don't recall that."

You will remember that Brant denied on the witness stand ever knowing whose book this was, that he had never seen it before, or that Barb asked him to read it. According to Brant, <u>the book never happened</u>. Except that he had told police two years earlier:

Lt R: "She is reading the family medical book, trying to figure out what's wrong with Natalia?"

Brant: "Yeah, that's the book that her mother (Elaine) brought over."

The prosecutor moves on with a poorly worded question that causes some confusion. And when there is confusion, the defendant is usually assumed somehow to be "covering up."

Question: Did <u>you</u> actually take Natalia's temperature on Tuesday, July 26? (The correct answer is "<u>no</u>." Elaine took those temperatures.)

Barb: "I don't remember." (Barb is likely trying to remember if she, herself, had taken those temperatures as the prosecutor appears to be asking).

Question: You said a 91, then 93, and then a 95?

Barb: "<u>I don't remember if I did or not</u>. (Take the temperature.)

Question: <u>You don't remember telling the officer that</u>? *She didn't tell him <u>she</u> took the temperatures.*

Barb: "I don't."

They're talking past each other here. The problem is that whether this is trickery, or simply lack of clarity by the prosecutor, Barb comes out looking like she's intentionally "forgetting" what she did.

Then the prosecutor moves on:

Question: Did you tell Dr. Simpson about your PPD? (He continues to use <u>PPD</u> to imprint this on the jury, even though that's not what Barb had).

Barb: "<u>I think I spoke to Dr. Simpson about feeling detached from Natalia.</u> I don't recall if I used PPD or not." (This could possibly explain why Dr. Simpson responded to the police PPD question as she did. Perhaps Barb talked about her <u>feeling of detachment,</u> and didn't use the label PPD that time. <u>But the prosecutor is more interested in the label</u> than in what Barb was actually feeling.)

Question: Do you recall telling the officers, 'well, I told her (Dr. Simpson) about it yesterday. I said I thought Natalia was withdrawn because I wasn't paying enough attention to her because I went through PPD.' And she said, 'well I want you to bring her in so I can look at her.' That's not accurate?

Barb: "Yes. Again I apologize. I can't remember what I said two years ago. If I told Officer Kaps that, then that's the truth."

Question: Does that help your memory on whether you told Dr. Simpson about PPD?

Barb: "I'm sure I spoke to Dr. Simpson about it. I trusted her and shared a lot of things with her." (Unfortunately, Dr. Simpson did not remember Barb saying this. Dr. S also forgot almost everything else, including those things that police had <u>documented</u> her as saying.)

Question: Is it accurate to say then that your PPD feelings, or what you called PPD, started right around the last week of June, first week of July?

Barb: "It's probably a little more accurate to say that. <u>I'm not always great on my timing</u>, so I could have been off." *You're right, Barb. Your timing of these feelings is not great.*

Question: Was it when she got home?

Barb: "I don't recall exactly at what time or moment that I started feeling those feelings."

Question: Was it a day later, or a month later, two months later, you just don't know?

Barb: "A couple of weeks, maybe a month, I don't know."

Question: Well, could it have been two months?

Barb: "<u>I really can't give you timing on that. I had three months with my daughter</u>."

Question: At the July 4 weekend party, you were upset with Brant, correct?

Barb: "Correct."

Question: You called him names, correct?

Barb: "I did."

Question: Do you remember voicing any concerns or anger towards Natalia?

Barb: "No."

Question: Did you call her a little a--hole?

Barb: "No, I didn't."

Question: So that's inaccurate?

Barb: "I called Brant an a--hole."

Question: But you didn't call Natalia that? Did you say why can't you f---ing act like your sister?

Barb: "No."

Question: That's inaccurate?

Barb: "That's inaccurate."

Question: How many times did Brant.... was Brant alone with Natalia when you were not there?

Barb: "I walked out of the house all the time. There were lots of..."

Question: When you were gone any appreciable amount of time? *How much time is that?*

Barb: "Once, maybe twice." *You probably shouldn't have answered a question like this one.*

The prosecutor goes one by one through Natalia's list of injuries, and after each one asks Barb if she believes Natalia suffered from this. And each time Barb says "yes." Then he asks:

Question: Do you believe that the cause of these was trauma, or some birth defect?

Barb: "When you say 'birth defect,' .... was she born with that.... I don't know. I don't think so. Could something else come about. That's a possibility. I don't know."

Question: Like what? *Barb is supposed to name the medical condition?*

Barb: "I don't know. They didn't finish doing some tests on her, so I don't know if..."

Question: So you think it's brittle bone disease?

Barb: "I don't know if it's brittle bone disease. There are some other things that can be wrong with infants other than just the two things you mentioned to this court today." (Actually, this is exactly what the medical controversy over shaken baby today is all about. Barb didn't know about the controversy at the time, but there are diseases and conditions that mimic shaken baby.) "I don't know. All I know is I didn't do anything to my child. So I don't have an explanation for her condition that she's in."

Question: Are you saying that you do not know what could have caused those injuries to her?

Barb: "I am saying that I do not know."

Question (juror): Were you upset about the dog at the hospital?

Barb: "I don't even know what they were talking about. I apologize. I don't even know what that is about."

Question (juror): Why didn't you stay at the hospital the whole time Natalia was in NICU?

210

<u>Barb</u>:   "I had a two year old. At the time Isabella was two. And so Brant had to work, so somebody had to go home and care for Isabella while he worked. It was our only means of income at the time, so I would go back and forth to the hospital from home."

The defense rests its case. **Closing arguments** will be next.

CHAPTER THIRTEEN

In the closing arguments, Mr. Cotter, the prosecutor cites those "facts" that have been testified to during the trial, which he believes have the most impact for convincing a jury of the defendant's guilt. And so he starts out immediately with the doctors. This is a shaken baby trial, and the doctors occupy the central position in it. There is no crime unless the doctors give such a diagnosis. Once the diagnosis of non-accidental injury had been made, a crime has been committed. And when this type of crime has been declared, the rest of the shaken baby theory takes over. There is a crime, symptoms occur immediately with no "lucid interval" in which the victim is conscious, and the person responsible for the injuries is the one caring for the child at the time of the 911 call and/or death. It's so neat and tidy.

"Let's start with the people who know what they're talking about," says the prosecutor. The idea here for the jury is--- no matter what you may question concerning the rest of the witnesses--- these doctors are the ones that really know the truth. They are beyond questioning. He says that Dr. Okanlami, Dr. Emenim, Dr. Cory, and Dr. Cockerill all tell you "purely and simply that Natalia suffered from nothing else but non-accidental trauma. Unequivocally every time those doctors voice their opinion" *(and that's just what it is)* "based upon the radiology reports, the CAT scans, and their own evaluation of Natalia, what did they tell you? That she was hurt non-accidentally." (Actually they knew nothing concerning causation from the evaluation. As Dr. O said, Natalia was in a coma. All of the doctors based everything on the CD of the brain and bone scans. Nothing other than that was testified to in court, with the exception of a report from the ophthalmologist that indicated retinal hemorrhages.)

The prosecutor continues. "The coin phrase from Dr. E is 'Let's call a spade a spade'. This was not accidental." The prosecutor flashes up a picture of Natalia onto the screen. "That's Natalia. That's Natalia in the hospital." (She is a small, adorable, preemie with tubes and machines hooked up to her in a hospital bed, and appropriately eliciting sympathy. But can anybody know from this picture what happened, or who allegedly hurt her? This is how you play the game as a prosecutor. You work on the jury's emotions. This is why you must have a jury, and not just a judge.) *Perception, not fact.* After listing her injuries, he then goes on. "You have to believe things beyond a reasonable doubt. And in this case you had four folks (doctors) who really know their stuff." *Are you honestly going to doubt them? Need we go any further?* "They told you how it happened. What they told you was this is <u>shaken baby syndrome</u>." (Even though they weren't there, and couldn't see shearing of vessels in the brain on the scans.)

"What do you know for sure. What do you know literally <u>without any doubt</u>? You know she suffered serious bodily <u>injury</u>". (Actually, we know that is the opinion of the four doctors the prosecution chose for their team. Are we ready to say that doctors never misdiagnose, particularly when that diagnostic opinion is based upon a theory that is still in progress?) "We know at some point she was placed in some type of injury---some situation to endanger her life or health. We know she was placed in that area by somebody. We know <u>that</u> according to the doctors. <u>If you don't believe the doctors, come back and say, 'Sorry, we don't believe you'.</u>" *You have two options. The doctors are either <u>telling the truth</u>, or they are <u>lying</u>. Which will the jurors choose?* (Actually, there <u>are other options</u>. The doctors on this team believe strongly in this theory. That doesn't necessarily mean it's true in this instance, <u>or</u> that they are lying.) But the prosecutor has set up his own construct for the jury. *Will they accuse the doctors of lying? Not likely.*

"We know that whoever did this could not have <u>accidentally</u> done that. Not a chance. Too much force necessary. Force to drop somebody from five stories; force to be in a high speed auto accident; force that would crack those bones." *Has anybody questioned how little seven pound Natalia dropped the equivalent of five stories and is still living two years later? Does that even make sense?*

"We know that Ms. Schrock had a legal obligation to take care of her (Natalia). We know that. By law, <u>mother and father</u> are supposed to take care of their children. Keep them safe. The only issue then is 'was it Barbara Schrock?'"

"Let's talk about <u>reasonable doubt</u>. A reasonable doubt is a fair, actual, and logical doubt. It's a doubt based upon reason and common sense, not a doubt based upon imagination or speculation. It has to be beyond a reasonable doubt in your mind that it arises after impartial consideration of all the evidence."

"You start with when a witness takes the stand, they swear an oath to tell the truth." (Unfortunately, <u>only the witnesses raise their right hand</u>. That leaves others in the justice system apparently free to manipulate the truth like play-doh. As I said earlier, a person of integrity shouldn't have to swear to tell the truth. It's one of several parts of our justice system I don't understand. The suggestion seems to be that it's okay to lie except when you're under oath. I actually prefer the Sermon on the Mount model from Matthew where it very simply says "Let your <u>yes be yes</u>, and your <u>no be no</u>." In other words, telling the truth is not something that you turn on and off). "You start with the presumption that <u>they are telling the truth</u>. That's where you start." (That isn't quite where <u>Dr. E</u> starts. He says: "The caregivers who do this to the child...we <u>never</u> get the straight story." So he starts with the presumption that the <u>caregiver is lying</u>. Is it fair to say that's where all shaken baby proponents start? Is it ever possible for a caregiver to break through that wall of cynicism if their story were true?)

The prosecutor continues once again. "And then you start looking at, well, do they (the witnesses) have a <u>bias</u>, do they have a reason why they want to not tell you everything that is accurate. Every witness that you heard from, whether it's the <u>defendant</u> who took the stand <u>because she has a right to do that</u>..." (He seems to be flipping the tables here. The defendant took the witness stand, even though <u>she had a right not to</u>.) "Every witness, you start there. And then you start to narrow it down if there is a conflict between those witnesses." *Let's see. Were there any conflicts in testimony here? And do they have a bias?*

"The only issue really in this case is did the defendant do this or not." (The doctor's <u>diagnosis</u> of shaken baby has removed the question for the prosecutor of whether indeed Natalia has an injury, or is suffering from a condition.) "We know <u>somebody</u> did it. So, was it the defendant? Well, let's talk about her. Look at her <u>demeanor</u>, <u>motive</u>, <u>opportunity</u>, and <u>stories</u>." The prosecutor puts up an impressive power point image onto the screen. *Motive and opportunity seem relevant. But demeanor? And stories?*

"What do I mean by demeanor? What was her demeanor after the 911 calls? What did the paramedics tell you? What did Brant Benson tell you? When the paramedics got there, how was she? Calm. <u>My child was so bad I had the father of the child call 911</u>." *This is pitiful! Can you imagine if Barb had handed Natalia to Brant so she could make the call? The line would be "She wouldn't even hold her own dying child, but made Brant do it." Another Catch 22. <u>You cannot do it right.</u>)* He goes on. "If Natalia is so bad, and if Barb is that concerned when she is asked to carry the child out to the ambulance, what does she do? I'm not going out there. <u>I have no shoes</u>." (Brant, according to his own testimony had gotten his shoes on earlier while Barb was taking care of Natalia. But the prosecutor knows who his defendant is. And it's not Brant. From day one it was Barb.)

"You heard that from the paramedics. That wasn't just Brant Benson telling you about that, the paramedics. Her child is so bad off she doesn't want to take the time to drive the child there, she just wants to call 911 and she pauses at the door to get her shoes on. She is not crying. She is not upset." (Actually Mr. Purcell, the paramedic testified that when he got there with the ambulance, "I was met by the firefighters and the child and the mother. I just got out of the ambulance when they met me." No delays here as the prosecutor wants the jury to believe. *Another made-up story.* And where was Brant? No mention by the paramedic.)

Now what about at the hospital? "What do all the witnesses tell you about her demeanor at the hospital? Was she crying? No, she was calm. She was calm." *So if you ever take someone you care about to the hospital, make certain you're never calm or rational. Always go ballistic and hysterical for your own protection.* (Nurse Spratt said she saw Barb cry. Brant testified to that, also. Elaine and Dan did, too. Most of Barb's showing of emotions, however, was in private. This whole concept is so senseless, but I feel that with the prosecutor using this as one of his four main areas for proving Barb's guilt, I can't simply ignore it. As Dr. Rutt, the psychiatrist testified, people respond to the same situation in a wide variety of ways. Most of us know that. However, apparently not everybody.) "Her demeanor when she was at the hospital and according to the family members who were there as well.... she didn't cry. She wasn't upset. She was talking. That's what her demeanor was at the hospital." *Whoa! Talking?*

"What else? The interview itself. Watch the body language. Watch the times that Officer Kaps confronts her about certain things and she crosses her arms like that." *Woe be unto you that cross your arms.* And here the prosecutor chooses from among the variety of options given for the time frame of Barb's detachment (PPD) from Natalia. "That was about a month ago. And she specifically said in the interview, yeah, but it went away a week ago. Now that wasn't, well, it was there for three weeks, you know, it was there for a month at some point and then three weeks later is stopped like she tried to tell you on the stand. But she tells the officer that day. Watch the video." (That day is intended to convey that she said this to police the very day Natalia came to the ER, so this was the most fresh rendition of the timing of her detached feelings for Natalia. But actually she had talked to both Brant and Elaine weeks before the police interviewed her, and they each testified to different time frames than the one given to police. Also, Nurse Spratt interviewed Barb the same day as police, but prior to the police interview, and she stated another different timing. So using the police interview timing as if it were the most accurate one given, has no particular merit other than it seems to fit their theory.) He continues. "Now isn't it ironic. When did Dr. Cockerill tell us that Natalia first suffered the most traumatic injury? And you know when he said that was? About a month

216

before she presented (at the ER)." *Wow. It just fits. Well, okay, it fits the timing alternative we chose.*

"Do you remember what Dr. O told you that she called it? She (Barb) didn't call it PPD. She called it postpartum blues." (Careful listening would have helped the prosecutor here. Dr. O said the following: "And her mom (Barb) reported to me that she had what you call postpartum blues after the baby was born." Two things; (1) Dr. O is the one calling it that, not Barb, and (2) the timing is "after the baby was born." But the prosecutor plows on, making another linkage that seems ridiculous.) "Do you remember the book she had there? What do they call that? Postpartum blues. What does that tell you?" *I don't know. What does it tell us?* "She started looking in the (medical) book to get excuses about why Natalia was hurt. That's exactly what she was doing." *Isn't that why we all use family medical books— to look for excuses. This guy is really hurting for evidence.*

"Listen to what she says. Listen to it. Listen to it again. See and watch how she answers all those questions. Her demeanor was not accurate." *So now there's an "accurate demeanor" when your child is near death? You'd better learn what it is, folks.*

"Let's talk motive. Let's talk about that PPD. She told the medical personnel that, she told her family that, she told us all in the interview." (And she told each one of them what she meant by that.) "That's what she called it. That's what she called it." *You said the "word." Na-na-na-na-na-na.* (Apparently the label is more important to him than the description of what she was feeling. He must feel that she was telling the truth about the label, but lying about the description of her feelings. Why anyone would do that is beyond me. Or was it that he liked the label because he thought he could attach it to severe PPD with psychosis and the murder of children, even though the psychiatrist testified totally to the contrary.) *These are his facts?*

"She also said she was disconnected from Natalia." (No. This is what Barb described each time she explained what she meant by PPD. There was no "also" involved. But now the prosecutor is trying to make it sound like there was PPD and this. It was always this, not PPD.) "Isabella— great mom (Barb) according to what everybody is telling us. She was a great mom. And what everybody else are telling us is they thought she was a good mom for Natalia except when she told people about having that disconnect. She is not Isabella. She didn't love her like she loved Isabella. It wasn't just different. It wasn't as much." (Four points here; (1) Not everyone said she was a good mom to Natalia except when she had that disconnect. Brant didn't. Elaine didn't. It was just Brant's family that said that. No one else.

217

(2) When <u>was</u> this disconnect? Multiple times are given. (3) Brant's extended family, except Char and Gary, only saw her for a few hours of one day during Natalia's life. And (4) it was Char, on the stand and nowhere else, that said Barb <u>didn't love Natalia like she loved Isabella</u>, not Barb. Barb said <u>it was different.</u> And the prosecutor said <u>it wasn't as much.</u>) *This is Barb's motive to abuse Natalia repeatedly over time until she nearly died?*

"How about her <u>opportunity</u>?" The prosecutor here goes into the various <u>injuries</u> (<u>we</u> still leave open the strong possibility that they are <u>conditions</u>) that Natalia has, and <u>recites the timings</u> that the doctors have given for them. But the timing of injuries is <u>anything but an exact science.</u> The prosecution's own doctors have said this. In fact, they called it an <u>inexact science.</u> The more I see and hear about the amount of disagreement in dating injuries, the more I believe calling it an inexact science is very <u>charitable.</u> Different doctors seldom come up with the same timing. (I will include a chart of the different timings and discuss them later in this book.) But for a prosecutor who is trying to prove a point, these timings take on almost <u>magical qualities.</u> At the minimum they become "fact." (All non-scientists <u>know</u> that science is infallible, even if it is an inexact science.) Anyway, the prosecutor uses these <u>timings</u> to try to show that Natalia's injuries occurred multiple different times. This makes Barb, as a stay at home mother, a more likely suspect.

Then the prosecutor introduces another term--- "<u>appreciable time.</u>" This term is supposed to represent the concept that one needs appreciable time to commit an act of injury. Mr. Cotter goes on. "Now according to what Ms. Schrock herself tells us from the stand, Char and Gary, Brant's parents.... had Natalia alone for any <u>appreciable time</u> two times. Are any of those two times within that 48 hours that Dr. Cockerill talks about?" (The answer is <u>no</u>. Char and Gary were not around Natalia within the last 48 hours--- <u>within the last 60 hours</u>---would be closer.) But one needs to ask <u>where the 48 hour timing came from</u>. It comes from Dr. Cockerill, the neurosurgeon, who said there was a "massive brain injury that occurred <u>a few weeks ago, potentially even a longer period of time before [the ER]</u>." He characterized this injury in different ways: "a devastating brain injury," "all cortical areas were completely dark," "very extensive," "dramatic," "overwhelming," "almost the entire brain severely injured," "very significant event," "basically a dead, dead brain," "loss of brain volume," "a dark, damaged brain." So a few weeks or longer before Natalia came to the ER, she suffered this <u>totally massive brain injury</u>. This is not what the prosecutor wanted to hear. Too many people have been around Natalia when you go back that far. In fact, there were well over 20 people at the July 2, 2005 party alone. The police were focused <u>from day one on the last 2-24 hours, and later 24-48 hours</u>.

218

Remember how Sgt. K wouldn't even consider Brant's time with Natalia on Monday evening (30 hours earlier) as relevant? Now the prosecutor has to deal with "a few weeks, potentially longer" (possibly sometime in June) as his time frame.

Dr. Cockerill, however, then gives a questionable opinion that appears to partially bail the prosecutor out. He did see a few specks of new blood that showed up on Natalia's brain scan and would "support" another event of some type. How does he refer to this "event?" "Some sort of event," "something more recent," "a more recent trauma," "some type of bleeding," "probably more correct to say 'injuries' in this case (than to say one injury)," "appears to have been two events." (This is clearly waffling from the other absolute statements being given by doctors in this trial.) Where does he get this critical bit of information? He has previously undercut his radiologist colleague, Dr. Fischbach, by saying he doesn't really do anything but look at scans and imaging studies. Dr. Cockerill, however, examines, listens to the history, and treats the patient. He has the total picture. But when asked if there was more than one event that occurred to Natalia's brain, he responds, "Based upon the imaging studies, I can say there appears to have been two events." So he uses the exact same tool that Dr. Fischbach used to make his determination. Remember he dismissed Dr. Fischbach's statement of a possible "birth trauma" because all Dr. Fischbach does is look at images. A more correct way of saying this is that Dr. Fischbach does this all day long, every day. Dr. Cockerill is basically a surgeon. He looks at scans as a small part of his job. (But this time there was no good way of examining Natalia in a coma.) So Dr. Cockerill sees these few specks of new (acute) blood and gives a time frame of 24-48 hours for the possible second event. And now we can fit it back into the shaken baby theory. *Except for the three week lucid interval between the two events, which in shaken baby theory is impossible.* (Doctors in this trial who have bought into the shaken baby theory really didn't know how to deal with all of this. It simply didn't fit. But they certainly tried to make it fit. Dr. E even went so far as to say later under oath:

> Dr E: "This child (Natalia) would not maintain well, it's not going to be awake (unconscious)."
> Question: "I just want to make certain I understood you...You were talking about the massive injury to the brain?"
> Dr E: "Yes." (So Dr. E, in trying to make this fit the theory, says Natalia was unconscious for the last three to four weeks. *You know, "no lucid interval."* And Char, her mother, Gary, Brant, Barb, Elaine, Dan, and possibly 20 plus other people at the July 2 party just didn't notice she was unconscious.) But Dr. E later at trial doesn't back down. "It (Natalia) would

be so different that <u>you really would have to be from outer space</u> not to realize that." *So now everybody that saw Natalia in the last month is an alien.* Just to be certain Dr. E is not misunderstanding something here, the question is rephrased to ask whether he is referring to "changes of behavior resulting from an injury like <u>this first brain injury</u> of Natalia?" No misunderstanding here. Dr. Emenim responds, "<u>Yes, that's very correct</u>."

But back to Dr. Cockerill. His characterization of the <u>few specks of new blood as supporting a</u> <u>second event</u> is the <u>single most significant and controversial piece of testimony</u> in the trial in my mind. More than a year later I send the same brain scan, the one that Dr. Cockerill based his possible "second event" comment on, and a copy of Dr. Cockerill's testimony about that scan, to another neurosurgeon from out of state. He observed both the brain scan and the testimony, and then said largely what Dr. Cockerill did about the massive, dramatic brain injury that had occurred. He agreed with the basic timing of that injury---- probably three to four weeks prior to Natalia's coming to the ER. The basic gist of his comments indicated that he felt Dr. Cockerill had timed the initial massive injury rather correctly. He also stated that the way the brain looked on the scan is "consistent with," but "not proof of" shaken baby. But then he commented about the <u>few specks of new blood</u>. This neurosurgeon said that since the brain has been damaged that much, it is easy for the brain to gradually ooze blood over time. The vessels have been stretched and compromised, and will bleed again very easily. <u>This could quite reasonably have been a single event with "ongoing bleeding</u>." When I asked if he has ever seen <u>spontaneous</u> bleeding after an injury like this one, he said "Sure. All neurosurgeons have." His final comment was "<u>there is absolutely nothing that you can say definitively about how those few drops of blood got there</u>."

Apparently the prosecutor realizes the significance of Dr. Cockerill's comment, too. Throughout the trial, even though the massive, overwhelming brain injury of three to four weeks earlier was an accepted fact by the prosecution, and restated frequently, the prosecutor normally <u>made a point of first referring to Natalia's questionable secondary brain injury as the acute injury in the last 24-48 hours</u>, and followed up with the major injury three to four weeks earlier. <u>He needed that recent time frame, no matter how questionable it was</u>.

Let's return to the "appreciable time" concept. According to the prosecutor, Char and Gary had two such times. (But neither of those times fell in to 24-48 hours prior block, <u>so he rules them out as suspects</u>.) Elaine

220

had five times. One of those was during the 24-48 hour time frame. But he says "Elaine did not show any other signs except she really cared about the child. And she is a nurse. Did Elaine commit this? That seems pretty clear I think to everyone here." So he rules Elaine out (in spite of the fact that he charged her with a felony for doing "nothing.") "Dan? Dan didn't have much to do with Natalia because that was Elaine's job." *Hey. How about a little respect?* "Now Brant certainly had some appreciable time alone with Natalia on the July 25 (Monday), two days before she presented to the hospital. So I guess on the outside" (What's outside about this? It's totally within the 48 hours) "Brant could have done that. But, if you recall not only from his demeanor" *(he cried a lot....a whole lot)* "and how he testified, was he appropriate when we're asking about different times with Natalia." *I'm not certain what he means here.* "Isn't that something that a father would react to thinking about her?" *He even cried here at trial. He must be innocent.* "And what about the other time? The other time was in May" (Brant's other appreciable time). "It was substantially earlier. It wasn't certainly within the three to six weeks that would have required the perpetrator to have been with Natalia." (Dr. Cory is a diagnostic radiologist--- one of those doctors that according to Dr. Cockerill just looks at images--- who rendered an opinion that the rib injuries were three to six weeks old. Dr. Fischbach, also a diagnostic radiologist, rendered an opinion that the brain injury may have happened at birth. Apparently one radiologist's opinion is valid and the other radiologist's opinion isn't. Regardless, the prosecutor rules out Brant. His appreciable times didn't fit with the dating of the injuries. Unless, of course, you believe the prosecution's own doctors, and the National Shaken Baby website as well, that state "it only takes a few seconds to shake a baby." Brant lived at home every day that Natalia was there.) *That pretty much exposes the "appreciable time" hoax for what it is.*

But let's see now. Who's left? Oh, yeah. He continues. "So who is the person who is taking care of this child? Who is the person suffering from postpartum depression, even though Dr. Rutt (the psychiatrist) doesn't think she actually suffered from that? Who is the only person who had the opportunity to do this? BARBARA SCHROCK."

"And what does Barbara Schrock have to say about these things? Do you remember the different stories that she gave? What were the different stories that she gave? The defense listed--- I think I counted 19 different, well, could have been this, could have been the mobile, could have been the faucet, could have been throwing her in the air, could have been kicked by Bella, could have been the dog did it." *He must have pulled 19 out of somewhere. I won't even venture a guess where.* (Actually, the defense did not mention any stories by Barb at trial, let alone list them. Only the

221

prosecutor. He appears to be putting up an imaginary "straw man" here to knock down. <u>Brant and Barb were asked by doctors for possibilities</u> of how Natalia could have gotten this way. Since Barb and Brant had been watching her closely for several weeks because of her increasing symptoms, they shared their observations. As Dr. E noted, "<u>Sometimes parents are non-medical people and they may not know what is important</u>," and also "She....<u>they</u> asked about all the possibilities including, you know, minor traumas that could have explained this." So there were no stories being made up to <u>sell</u> to the doctors or to the jury, and Barb was not the only person asking about whether certain things could have caused Natalia's condition).

"Let's talk about the mobile for a second, folks. What does Dr. Cockerill and Dr. Okanlami say? Absolutely not. No way. Oh, no. This thing could not have done those injuries. The faucet? That faucet there. Remember she bumped her head and she got a little bruise there. Maybe that's what could have done it. Dr. E and Dr. Cockerill, Dr. O, absolutely not. It doesn't work. No, no, no." (Perhaps it would clarify what the prosecutor is doing here if we quoted from Dr. O, who later said under oath:)

<u>Question</u> (prosecutor): When she (Barb) <u>told you</u> about the skull fracture, did she tell you about hitting Natalia's head on a mobile above the bed?

<u>Dr O</u>: "It came up as a question....could this be due to? She <u>did not know</u> that the child had a skull fracture in my discussions with her. <u>She was not informing me</u> that this is how these happened, <u>she was asking me</u>, could the injury have been caused by that?"

<u>Question</u>: Did she ever talk to you about <u>meningitis</u>?

<u>Dr O</u>: "<u>I</u> would have <u>talked to her</u> about meningitis." *It doesn't sound like <u>Barb</u> is making up stories. But it <u>does</u> sound like someone else is.*

<u>Question</u>: Do you recall her reaction when you told her they (incidents like Barb asked about above) were not consistent with those injuries?

<u>Dr O</u>: "<u>She did not really exhibit a lot of emotion at that time</u>. And I have to say that in my 20 something years of taking care of critically ill children, <u>parents exhibit a wide range of emotional responses</u>...from <u>totally stunned and non-responsive</u> to being <u>uncontrollably distraught</u>."

Mr. Cotter continues with his closing argument. "A fall from a significant height comparable to extreme motor vehicle crash, or fall from extreme height. That's what her doctor tells us. We could go on and on and on about these different ones (stories). But really Dr. Emenim said it best. You have to be ducking the issues not to see this. This was abuse. <u>This was shaken baby syndrome without any doubt.</u> 'Not one iota.' Nobody wants to

222

believe that a parent would do things like this to a child. It's a difficult thing for us to acknowledge, but sometimes parents do things that are horrible. And in this case what's horrible is on more than one occasion Barbara Schrock hurt her child."

Defense Closing Argument (Jim Korpal):
"Natalia Benson was born April 23, 2005, and she was born premature. Three pounds, 11 ounces. And during the course of 95 days things happened to this child that have made the rest of her life nothing but misery. And you are here to decide who, if anyone, did this to her. Now I've been around a long time.... heard a lot of doctors testify. And the problem that I have when doctors testify is they are very absolute about everything they say. It's 100 percent. And when you think about it, well, could it have been something else? All of us have been in a situation where we heard, or our own family members, or people have said, well, maybe I ought to get a second opinion. And so I asked them (doctors) about other possibilities for the problems that Natalia was suffering. And it was quite obvious that Dr. Emenim had made his decision immediately. And there were no other possibilities other than shaken baby syndrome with regard to this child."

"When approached by Brant Benson and asked about the absence of her corpus callosum, Dr. Emenim said 'I don't even know about that.' So that concerns me when a doctor does that. That concerns me that he is so confident in his diagnosis by looking at this child and looking at x-rays.... that's the only thing that this could possibly be."

"Now these injuries happened over a long period of time. And when you talk about bone diseases, we heard a lot about brittle bone disease. But some of them like rickets of prematurity have to be tested immediately (at birth) because the child grows out of it, as the doctor said, with proper nutrition. So the ability to know if that was in fact there, is gone because they said this is what it is. This is what it is. It can't be anything else." (Recent vitamin D deficiency studies at the U. of Pittsburgh Medical School are a good example of this. A lack of Vitamin D is associated with preeclampsia and with weaker bones. In Natalia's case, no vitamin D testing was done at birth. It was too late once she went to the ER.)

"And Mr. Cotter talked about the shaken baby and ribs... and the ribs would be the place you would grab them, but the rib injuries were older. They were three to six weeks old." (Why no brain injury six weeks ago, if Natalia were shaken hard enough to break her ribs?) " And Dr. Cockerill talked about the brain injury being in the last 48 hours, and then up to three weeks prior to that." (But no rib injuries since the first ones.) "So then I start

223

thinking, well, if the rib injuries happened, why are they so old? The doctors are very sure of what they say. They are very sure that this was the only thing that could have caused the injuries to this child." (The Sept/Oct issue of AARP has an article referring to the rash of misdiagnoses nationally, written by Jerome Groopman, M.D. He states, "About 15 percent of all patients are misdiagnosed, and half of those face serious harm, even death, because of the error." Most errors are not mixups of records or lab specimens, but "due to mistakes in the mind of the doctor." Dr. Groopman says there are three questions that doctors need to keep in mind forming a diagnosis: (1) "What else could it be?" [Prevents settling on a diagnosis too quickly]; (2) "Could two things be going on to explain the symptoms?" [Doctors are taught to look for a single cause]; and (3) "Is there anything that seems not to fit with your working diagnosis?" [Rather than ignoring things that don't fit, in order to make the diagnosis work.])

Jim said that according to the foster mother, there are physical issues that keep arising with Natalia. "I can't be certain that is exactly what caused these injuries of the child. Because there are still questions out there. And you can't sit here and say whatever the doctors say is gospel. Because that's not the way it happens in life."

"Dr. Emenim said this was shaken baby syndrome. The police are there. Two days later Barb Schrock is charged." (Error: the charging took place one month and two days later.) "Two days later Brant Benson is no longer a suspect." (Barb was actually the suspect from day one according to police.) "Two days later (Error: One month and two days later) they charged Elaine Schrock with neglect of a dependent because she took a temperature of a child, and she is a nurse, and that temperature was reported to a doctor who said bring the child in the next day."

"She (Barb) has been described as many things. Maybe mouthy, talks too much. And Dr. Rutt testified that everybody handles things differently. And I have to go back to Brant Benson, because he said on his testimony that it took him a year and a half to finally decide in his own mind that Barb had done this. A year and a half. And he gave a statement to the police the same day Barb gave a statement, and he told the police that Barb was a good mother, that she was loving and nurturing to both of the children. [He said] that Natalia was an easy baby to take care of. Wasn't screaming all the time. She cried very little. She ate and she slept. She was premature."

"When she (Barb) talked about being disconnected, that was part of the problem because a premature baby doesn't do anything. Doesn't coo at you, doesn't laugh and giggle. That took time. That took a lot of time to

224

develop. She came home. She weighed three pounds 15 ounces. She ate and she slept. But Brant said that Barb was great with the children. In the first statement to police he couldn't understand how this could have happened. He questioned himself. He questioned everybody around. But he couldn't understand because there were no bruises, there were no dislocations. He didn't understand, and he 'believed Barb 100 percent.'"

"But then the police brought him back on August 6 to talk to him again. And the police told him things.... people have told us that Barb's a party girl. 'I don't know anything about that.' Did they ever tell you who said that? 'No.' People have told us that Barb never wanted this baby. 'Well, I didn't know that.' Did they ever tell you who told them that? 'No.' Barb was so happy this baby was out of her, she was ecstatic. Did they ever tell you who said that? 'No.'"

"And then they said Barb's mother (Elaine) said when she came to the house on July 26 the baby's eyes were going off in different directions, and he (Brant) got mad. He got mad. If Barb's mother had seen that, why wasn't that baby taken to the hospital immediately? Why did she only say when I came home the baby's temperature was low and we need to watch her? Then things change for Brant. They told him lies and he believed them, and the more lies came, the madder he got. And who did he get mad at? He got mad at her (Barb.)"

"Let's talk about Char and Gary who gave their statement together, and again... 'Barb would never have done this.' They asked what about brittle bone disease? 'We already tested for that. It's not that.' How could this have happened? 'She is the only one who had the opportunity. Your son is not a suspect. We are looking at Barb.' And then what did Char say? 'She (Barb) should fry.' And then she took the stand here and testified, and things she never told the police started coming out. 'Oh, Barb was screaming and outraged at Natalia for being a cry baby. She cried too f---ing much.' That's what she said at the party. What else did she (Char) say? 'She is a boozer and a drinker. A drinker and a smoker....that's the problem.' Just out of the blue."

"And then they talked about pictures. She (Char) told the police that the reason they (Barb and Brant) didn't have any pictures in the house was because they didn't have a camera, and she is the one who took the pictures and she hadn't given them any yet. But on the stand she made it sound like 'I couldn't understand why they didn't have any pictures of Natalia in the house.' This is just crazy. Brant lives in the house. So this is an issue that there are no pictures of Natalia, and that's going to be another dig into Barb Schrock."

"And the part about the EMT's....she waited around to put her shoes on. But the EMT said the minute the ambulance pulled up she came out with the baby. So what is this about? <u>He didn't stand here and say we had to wait five minutes to put her shoes on</u>. 'When we pulled up she came out.' They (the prosecution) have to put it in because there are barbs that have to be thrown. <u>She has to be made to look bad</u>. <u>To look like a horrible person</u>. And her demeanor. You saw her take the stand. She is what she is. And Dr. Rutt testified that some people are hysterical, and some people aren't hysterical. And that she cried, and Brant said she cried. She cried twice. And the mother (Char) says, oh, she was only upset because she was never going to be able to walk the dog again. And the fireman was a hot guy. Now, I understand that they want her to fry. <u>Tell the truth</u>. Tell the truth about the person. <u>Don't make up stuff to make her look bad</u>."

"Nurse Spratt said <u>both of the parents were upset</u>. And then they bring the ladies from the party where Barb freely admits she called Brant an a--hole. That gets turned around. And the police station got their names from Char and some relatives came and said she referred to the baby as an a--hole.

Little things. <u>When you don't know who it is, it's little things</u>. And they dig and dig and dig until you think that is enough. <u>Well, it's not enough</u>."

"<u>Did anybody testify that they ever saw her do anything</u>? No. They testified these little innuendos, and these little stories to make you think that she is a bad person. But that is not what this case is about. The state had decided to base this case on circumstantial evidence as to who did these injuries to Natalia. And the court is going to instruct you where <u>proof of guilt is by circumstantial evidence only, it must be so conclusive and point so convincingly to the guilt of the accused that the evidence excludes every reasonable theory of innocence</u>."

"Barb was very upfront with the police. She told the police 'I felt detached from my child.' She told her mother that, she told Brant that. She had a conversation with her mother, who testified that if you ever have more serious problems than simply detached, you call somebody. She (Barb) said 'no, it's nothing like that.' She told that to the police."

"And then Mr. Cotter talks about all the excuses she gave. Well, ladies and gentlemen, you have to think about this as human beings. And would you not think to say to yourself, 'Oh, my God, did I do something to harm this baby?' You're the baby's mother. This baby they say it's now been injured. 'My God, did I do something wrong?'"

"In every case---every criminal case the burden is <u>beyond a reasonable doubt</u>. And in this case, because this is a circumstantial evidence case, the <u>burden gets even a little bit higher</u>. You have to be truly convinced in your mind that there is no one else who could have done this except Barb Schrock, and you have to be totally convinced in your mind <u>this is the only reason this child has these injuries</u>. She is not guilty, and I would ask you to find her not guilty. Thank you."

<u>Prosecution</u> Rebuttal (Ken Cotter):
"Isn't it ironic that the fractures are at the legs where the child is crying or doing whatever, and you are just frustrated, grab the child and you jerk the child? <u>Maybe</u> Barbara got upset because, hey, Isabella had all these facial expressions and was reacting, and Natalia is not. <u>So I don't know</u>. You know, it really doesn't matter. What matters is we know that's what happened. She (Natalia) has scoliosis of the back because her brain is dead." *Everything that Natalia has is because her brain is dead. Even scoliosis.* "I mean how many times are we going to look for an excuse <u>before we look a spade in the eye</u>? A <u>spade is a spade</u>, <u>without one iota of a doubt</u>, absolutely <u>this is shaken baby syndrome</u>." *Is this gobbledygook.....or is he in another realm?*

"Who tells you that she is this great mom? <u>People who see her interact with her children, right</u>?" *Who else could tell you.... somebody that hasn't seen her interact?* "Who sees her interact with these children when it is her and Isabella and Natalia? Nobody but Isabella and Natalia." *Under this assumption, there is no such thing as a good mother. Who knows what they do behind closed doors? You just turn it off and on, depending whether you are in public or not. Can someone spell "cynical" for me?* "Brant believes she is a good mom. Brant worked twelve to fourteen hours a day, six and seven days a week. And, frankly, when he decided I'm working my tail off and I need to golf, I need to do something. <u>I'm just going crazy working so much</u>." *That might even cause enough stress that when he came home and the baby was crying and he just wanted a little peace and quiet.....* (This may be a good place to interject that when our attorney, Jim, said that in order to clear Barb, we would need to show that Brant, also, could have done this to Natalia. Elaine, Barb, and I were very clear with Jim that we did not believe that either Barb or Brant had done anything to Natalia, and that we didn't want Jim to portray Brant as a bogeyman. He agreed that he wouldn't do that, but said that the police and the prosecutor would be trying everything they possibly could do in an attempt to write Brant out of the picture, and Barb into it. *We had no idea, however, that they would make stuff up.* We did agree later that he could at least <u>correct the record</u> when statements that "Brant was nowhere around" kept being put forward. So now we have all these claims by the prosecutor that Brant worked all the time, with Char ratcheting it up even more by telling police that Brant "got up at two or three o'clock in the morning to go to work, and did not return home until nine or ten o'clock in the evening." If the police and prosecutor had decided to apply the same level of suspicion to Brant as they had to Barb, then the reality of Brant's working 20 hour days might have struck them differently. Brant could well have been totally stressed out when he came home to a crying baby, and therefore harboring a potential reason [<u>motive</u>, as the prosecutor would say] for shaking Natalia. Even the prosecutor here is talking about Brant's <u>going crazy</u> from all the work. And if they had asked him, as they had Barb, about alcohol and abuse in the family, they likely could have put together a case at least as compelling as the one they built against Barb. But as Sgt. Kaps said, "we knew from <u>day one</u> it was Barb," and "we need to just clear Brant's name out of this.") *Some investigation!*

The prosecutor continues on with his rebuttal. "So is he (Brant) home very much at all to be able to see how she is <u>really</u> interacting with the children when things aren't perfect?" *We just don't know what happens behind closed doors. But you surely can imagine.* <u>Perception, not fact.</u> "Isn't it normal for a parent when you take your children to your relatives... you're not going to smack them if that's what you do at home." *You obviously don't know Barb. She doesn't hide her real self from anybody.* "You're not going to yell and scream at them if that's what you do at home. You're going to be on your best behavior. They are going to frustrate the heck out of you sometimes, knowing what kids do. I have two of them. I know that feeling. Everybody has that feeling. But it doesn't give her (Barb) the right to grab her and shake her, because that's what she did. <u>I don't know why</u>... and frankly I don't have to prove why she did it. <u>I don't have to prove a motive.</u>" *Then why did you spend all that time on insisting that she had PPD, when she didn't? And why did you list "motive" as one of your four major factors, along with demeanor, stories, and opportunity?*

"I don't know and I don't care (about her motive), but what I do care about is the <u>evidence is real clear</u>. She did this. She hurt this child. You need to find her guilty for that. The doctors are "real clear....it's shaken baby syndrome. Bone disease does not affect the brain. So I suppose that not only had she suffered from bone disease, she had to suffer some kind of catastrophic brain injury." *Gosh.... <u>two things</u> going on at once? Who ever heard of that?*

"Mr. Korpal talks about 93 degrees and is flabbergasted that Dr. Simpson said 'call me in the morning.' What was Dr. Simpson told? Dr. Simpson was told she had a 93 degree temperature and that she was moving--- she was otherwise moving and she ate. That couldn't be according to Dr. Simpson." *Once again, Barb, Brant, and Elaine must all be lying. Actually, when everybody in the world seems to be lying, maybe it's time to take a good look at yourself. Might you just be misreading something? Perhaps your theory isn't quite as perfect as you had imagined.* "If she is 93 degrees, she needs to be rushed to the hospital right away." (Once again, the assumption here is that the temperature is correct, and Barb and Elaine, are lying about the movement, eating, breathing, circulation, voiding, etc. And Brant must be lying about playing with Natalia in bed that night. No one ever asks if the temperature might be wrong. No one, other than Elaine and Dr. Simpson. You don't get incorrect temperature readings in the intensive care unit.) "Who took the 93 degree temperature? Grandma (Elaine) knows something is wrong." (If you think Elaine and Barb knew something was seriously and critically wrong with Natalia, and were trying to cover it up, why would they call in the 93 degree temperature? Just say it's 98. Or don't call at all.) "Grandma is stuck in a trick box. We're not here to try grandma. That's for a different day. What we're here to say is...judge her credibility when she took the stand. She knows she's in a trick box. Ninety-three degrees. I hope nothing is wrong. I hope nothing is wrong. I know that is bad. I know that is bad. She is telling us on the stand that she doesn't know that a 93 degree temperature is bad." (She'd seen these kind of temperatures on a similar thermometer tens of times, and the situation was never serious. The thermometer was always wrong. The other vital signs in Natalia's situation indicated the same thing. But she still had Barb report this when she called the doctor.) "She wants us to believe she didn't know something was real serious about that. Credibility...judge that." *(Oh. And I left out that fiasco where I accused Elaine of passing information outside of the courtroom in violation of court orders. You didn't hear anyone say anything to refute that, did you? She clearly did that. This woman is not to be trusted.)*

"The (police) officers were not jumping to any conclusions. They are gathering evidence. As a matter of fact, it doesn't make sense anyway because the officers talked to Brant again on August 6." *The prosecutor was present at Brant's brainwashing interview and knows very well Brant was not there because he was a suspect.* (That interview, as was pointed out earlier, happened the day after police sent the probable cause document for charges against Barb and Elaine to the prosecutor. The main agenda for that interview was to turn Brant against Barb.) "Do you remember that? Nobody is jumping to conclusions." (Lt R: "The very first day...even we come into these cases...you know, it's just like...BARB." Sgt. K [first 48 hours to

Brant's parents]: "We can rule Brant out for sure. I feel comfortable, and my partner feels comfortable, that Brant didn't do this.") "What they were doing is painstakingly going through, okay, who could have done this, what could have happened. They waited until they had all the information about her injuries and what the doctors were saying about the injuries, and somebody did it, and then put it together to find out that lady there did it. Nobody else did it." *Yep. That's just the way it happened. That's the true story, and I'm sticking to it.*

The prosecutor goes on to say that Mr. Korpal spent a long time on the inaccuracies of the prosecution witnesses. He (the prosecutor) then says Barb had the most inconsistencies with her statement, but does not give any examples. Not one. *Just trust me. She lied.* And then back to the demeanor again. "The tears that you saw (on the stand) weren't the same when she was in the hospital learning about how bad she (Natalia) was hurt." *She cried here at the trial. She must be guilty.* "But holy smokes, folks, look at the demeanor."

"We know a person did this, unless you decide you're not going to believe Dr. Emenim, Dr. Okanlami, Dr. Cory, and Dr. Cockerill, all four of them." *And who would do that?* "Unless you decide you are not going to believe them that somebody did this act, that somebody (Barb) talked to Officer Kaps that day and she hasn't been able to get her story down pat yet. And so when she testifies on the stand, those two stories don't fit." (Two things here: (1) The prosecutor once again gives the jury two options--- believe the doctors, or say you don't believe them [they're lying]. For the second time in this closing statement the option that they may have made a misdiagnosis is not an option. What if we said our family doctors were lying every time they made a misdiagnosis? We don't do that. We know they can make errors like anyone else; and (2) The prosecutor again talks about Barb's story and testimony as conflicting, without giving even one instance where that occurred.) *Just say it enough times, and maybe they'll believe it.*

"It is a sad day that we're here because we have a child who is hurt for the rest of her life and is going to be literally a vegetable." *Actually, we prefer to think of Natalia as a person.* "Everybody is sad about that. It doesn't mean because we're sad about that, that this poor mom...we don't want to prosecute her. Look at the facts. Don't throw out your emotion. You can use your emotions." *He's counting on it.* (Beginning the closing argument with a photo of Natalia all hooked up to tubes, and ending with encouragement of the jury to use their emotions. This is why we wanted a bench trial, and why the prosecutor denied it. You don't need to deny a request like that if you actually have facts.) "But you have to look at it rationally. You have to look at, okay, what would happen here. Your common sense is the one that puts stuff together. And while nobody ever wants to believe that a mom can do this to a child, more than once, that's exactly what happened. Mr. Korpal is flabbergasted. I'm disgusted. Thank you." *All in a day's work.*

The jury is given instructions for deliberation (approximately 6:00 pm, Friday, September 28, 2007).

CHAPTER FOURTEEN

The trial of Barb went from Monday afternoon jury selection through Friday afternoon. For those of us in the atrium outside the courtroom, the waiting was painful. But nobody in the courthouse went through more pain during this trial than Barb. She sat there the whole week listening to Brant's family, with whom she had been very close, as they said what was necessary to make certain Brant was not held responsible for actions against Natalia. And finally Brant, himself, said what he needed to say. There were those in the South Bend community who "knew," even before the trial, of Barb's guilt. A trial would have been unnecessary for them. For those people, Barb was a young mother with no feelings. How else could she have done what they all knew she did. Barb, however, had little concern for those people's thoughts. They could think what they wanted to think. They didn't know her. But with Brant's family there was a feeling of abandonment by those she had grown to know and love. And one by one they came through the courtroom to share whatever morsels of "evidence" they could muster.

Barb actually held up rather well through all of this, largely because she wanted to be reconnected with her girls. When we reminded her of how difficult it would be to take care of Natalia in Natalia's current state, she claimed, possibly naively, to be ready for that. And Isabella was a huge loss. They had developed such a deep, loving relationship in the nearly three years they were together at home. Also, after listening to Brant in the courtroom, she knew he would likely never be close with her again. And that, too, was a loss. Much of this would be somewhat hypothetical, however, depending upon the outcome of the trial. Would things ever return to even semi-normal?

Out in the hallway, Elaine and I went our separate ways most of the week. We felt the tension of what must have been happening inside the courtroom. But we had much support from our church, other friends, and family. A different minister from College Mennonite Church was inside the courtroom each day of the week. Friends from most of the groups of which we were a part attended as regularly as their work schedules would permit. And my sister, her husband, and daughter were present all week from Michigan and Washington, D.C. Elaine's spiritual director was there, spending much time with her in prayer. And I did a lot of Sudoku puzzles, which must have seemed unusual at least to somebody in the courtroom. But we were well supported, and continue to be thankful to this day for that support. Barb also appreciated it, and said at one point later, "I don't know how I would have made it through the week without being able to look back in the gallery of the courtroom and see those supportive friends."

The one really awkward part of being out in the atrium was the way the two families divided into opposite sides of the fairly large area. Not too long ago we were friends with Brant's family and interacted together on various occasions. Now we were in this very visible division of two groups, theirs a good bit larger than ours. At the first of the week we had made attempts to at least recognize them as persons. We would say "Hi" or give some other acknowledgment of their presence. That didn't get a response, however, and their eyes would never meet ours. Finally, we stopped trying. But that really didn't feel right. Somehow we should have been able to do something better than we did. The anger from them was palpable. It felt as if we had had a sign around our necks that said "unclean."

So now the jury is out for deliberation. Many in our group headed up the street to a small restaurant for supper. We had no idea of how long it would take for the jury to come to a verdict, so we moved rather briskly. Inside the restaurant we all squeezed into a large corner booth, and in a few minutes ordered sandwiches. Nobody felt much like eating a large meal at that point. Most of us were operating on automatic pilot. We were trying our best to act as normal as possible. There was some laughter, but mainly small talk. The huge elephant in the room was largely ignored. When our orders came, we ate, and headed back to the courthouse.

It had been about an hour since the jury had left for deliberation. We reentered the courthouse atrium. Someone had come up with a few chairs to go with the concrete benches. On the other side of the atrium was Brant's family. Not even a glance was sent in our direction. They had commandeered the larger table that attorneys and their clients sit at for conversations, and the chairs that went with it.

On our side of the atrium the little group of about twelve people sat quietly in silence and reflection in the loose semblance of a circle. My sister, husband, daughter, friends, Tim (one of our ministers from church), Elaine, Barb, and I waited....and waited. Occasional one-on-one conversations were happening, but very little group banter. Elaine had been reading a short booklet entitled "The Path of Waiting" by Henri Nouwen, and passed it around for others to read. Periodically many of us prayed individually and inwardly as we waited. Elaine visualized the jury and prayed for them. When I prayed it was the same theme as for the last two years----please make clear what happened to Natalia. The overall mood of our little group was somber, indeed.

Across the atrium, Brant's family was sitting around the large table. Brant, Char, Gary, other family members, Paula (the CASA worker), police, and Mr. Cotter were all part of their group at various times throughout the evening. The mood there was quite different. There was much banter and some laughter. Occasionally someone would say shhh....be quiet...when things got a bit raucous. We hoped that it was out of respect for us. But there was clearly a huge chasm in the 30 feet between our groups. We wanted "truth." They wanted "justice." And while both of our groups thought we knew what those terms meant, neither group actually knew whether the clarity and fulfillment of those two terms would ever come to fruition.

As time dragged on, the internal tension increased. I knew this case pretty well, and I was certain the facts were on our side. But I also knew the emotions that are conjured up in a trial like this. While I thought our chances for acquittal were good, I also knew any outcome was possible. The thought of how we would get Barb's car home from South Bend if she were convicted struck me for the first time. I quickly realized that would be one of the lesser worries if we were to lose the case. At about 10:00 pm Barb asked if we could join hands in a circle and pray. It seemed like a good idea, but we also realized it could be interpreted on the other side on the atrium as an "in your face" move, or as "posturing." And we didn't need any possible jeering from them to add fuel to the division of families. So we all moved outside the courthouse to the front steps. It was dark, and no one was at the courthouse other than the two families, the jurors, judge, and attorneys. Cars were passing by on the street. But there on the courthouse steps we held hands in a circle and individually prayed aloud for the various concerns that each of us felt. And we also listened. After we had shared with God our needs and feelings for some time, Tim closed the prayer time. We embraced each other, and headed back into the courthouse with a bit more courage for what might be ahead.

At about midnight, Barb was called back into the courtroom with Jim Korpal, Ken Cotter, and Judge Chamblee. The message to Barb was that the jury was having difficulty coming to a decision. Apparently they were struggling with just exactly what does "beyond a reasonable doubt" mean. *Does anyone really know?* The jury apparently suggested that they go home and reconvene the next morning. Barb and Jim both agreed that the jury should continue to deliberate, and Mr. Cotter and Judge Chamblee concurred. A note to that effect was sent back to the jury.

All of us were waiting tensely outside the courtroom to find out what was happening. Barb came back and explained what the issue was. So we waited some more. Everyone was getting a bit weary by now. Finally, shortly after 1:00 am, Barb was called back in to courtroom. The jury sent back a note to the judge indicating they were not making any progress. They were deadlocked. Judge Chamblee declared it a <u>hung jury</u>.

Barb and Jim came out of the courtroom and headed for our group. Ken Cotter headed for Brant's group. (Those of us in the atrium still didn't know at this point what had happened.) Jim looked over at the other group, and then waved us outside onto the front steps. We followed him as he stomped across the atrium. This didn't look good. He seemed to be angry. Once we all got outside onto the steps, Jim said the trial resulted in a hung jury. After waiting over seven hours, we were numb. Just what does that mean? Will there be another trial? What do we do now? Jim was rather short and somewhat curt. Don't ask any more questions. We'll meet next week after the prosecutor decides if he wants to retry the case. I'll see you guys next week. Call me. Now go home and get some sleep. *Sleep? We're supposed to sleep.*

So there we were, standing on the courthouse steps at 1:30 am in the morning. We talked briefly about what we thought might happen next. Friends then said goodnight and headed back to Goshen. My sister and her family had planned to head back home to Michigan that evening. They had said goodbye to the hosts where they were staying in Goshen for the week. But now it seemed a little late for them to head out. They also weren't certain whether they should just leave us at that point. Where would they stay at this time of night? Their daughter, Val, had been staying downstairs with Barb at our home during this week, so that was not a problem. But what should Nancy and Ron, my sister and husband, do? Tim, our minister, was standing there on the courthouse steps as we discussed this. Out of the blue he said to my sister and husband, "Why don't you stay with us? We have room." They didn't know quite how to respond. Nancy and Ron wanted to stay somewhere, but they didn't know Tim, and felt they would be intruding, particularly at this time of the night. He responded quickly, "No. It's no intrusion. I'll give Jan a call." And just that quick he had his cell phone out calling his wife at 1:30 in the morning. "Hi, Hon," we heard him say. "I have some guests that are looking for a place to stay overnight, and I offered our place." A few seconds later, while still on the phone, he asked my sister and husband, "What are your names again?" And just like that, Nancy and Ron had a place to stay in Goshen. And we had one more finite example of the infinite warmth and love that surrounded us.

In the morning (Saturday) we had Nancy and Ron over for breakfast before they left for Michigan. It was soon evident that we were all still in limbo, just like for the last two years. Nothing had been decided or clarified. We also recognized that politically the prosecutor likely would need to be asking for another trial. Society demands answers.... no matter how ill-founded those answers might be. But for now we had the weekend to recuperate. We went to church Sunday morning for worship, and refilled our tanks with the essence of life. I was energized by being with the MYF youth group again during the Sunday School hour. Sunday noon we had a carry-in meal for Goshen College students. Much time this whole morning was spent conversing about the prior week's trial activities with the many people who cared. Sunday afternoon we watched the Indianapolis Colts game with our friends. On Monday Barb thankfully headed back to her work at Goshen Hospital. Elaine had just retired from her school nurse position, so had far too much time just to think about the multiple tragedies surrounding this whole situation. And I was pleased to be back attending a girls' soccer match Monday evening. Things weren't back to normal yet.....but we sometimes pretended they were.

Thursday we went back to South Bend (we were developing a real dislike for being in that community, but recognized we were probably biased) and met with Jim. He was still upset about the verdict, but did share that his attorney colleagues were congratulating him on getting a hung jury in Barb's trial. That's almost considered a victory with the nearly automatic conviction rate in most shaken baby cases. However, he slowly and painfully shared two things: (1) there <u>would</u> be another trial; and (2) <u>he would not be able to serve as our attorney</u> in the new trial. The hung jury evidently divided 6-6. Normally that would cause a prosecutor to have serious second thoughts about having another trial. It's one thing if the jury is divided 11-1, or even 10-2. There you can figure that with a little more effort the possibility of getting a unanimous verdict is thinkable. But a 6-6 split doesn't usually play out that way. Half of the people weren't convinced. Apparently the prosecutor's ploy of accusing Elaine of passing information in the trial apparently led at least some jurors to believe Elaine may have been more deeply involved than it seemed. So this 6-6 split gave the prosecutor an opening to charge a <u>conspiracy</u> between Barb and Elaine. *He can get them both that way.* Consequently, a new trial made sense to him, and it was set for April 21, 2008. Jim, on the other hand, had been representing both Barb and Elaine in the first trial. Given the framework the prosecutor was planning to use in the second trial, Jim felt he could not represent both of them again in the new trial. He would have to choose either Barb or Elaine. And he felt is was an ethical dilemma to choose one over the other. Jim could end up working <u>against</u> the one he did not choose. Anyway, the bottom line was that we needed to not only find a new attorney, but <u>two</u> new attorneys. *Bad news. Really bad news.*

I recognized immediately that this was not a good thing for our side. To go into a second trial when the prosecutor has already been through a "trial run" (another unintended pun) and knows exactly what everyone testified, and what needs to be shored up, and the defense with a new attorney who knows very little about the previous trial and has to start from scratch, is a scary thought. But I had no real idea of just <u>how weak</u> a position that put us in. Anyway, we thanked Jim and asked him if he would give us recommendations of attorneys that I might check with. He obligingly did that. (I also want to say here that we found Jim to be a competent, experienced attorney, a person of integrity who cared about his clients. He worked hard for us, and we appreciated that.)

I looked over the six names Jim gave me, and some of the comments he made about each. But the only criminal attorney I had ever known was Jim. And we had rather accidentally come across his name on the internet. So how was I going to make a selection of not just one, but two new attorneys. We talked as a family about what type of attorney we needed for Barb, and what type for Elaine. I had some related experience in hiring, since I had interviewed several hundred potential employees for the Mennonite Board of Missions during my 13 years in personnel work there. But somehow this was different. I did have ideas of what personal and professional characteristics I was hoping to find in an attorney. Integrity, ability to relate, and caring about us as people were important personal characteristics for our family. But we also needed to know professionally about their criminal trial experience, how hard will they work, how good are they in the courtroom, how much medical knowledge do they have, and how easy/difficult is it to get in contact with them when you need them. And while I felt confident in my ability to ascertain personal characteristics, assessing professional skills in an interview was another matter. You simply find that out once you're into the trial itself.

I narrowed the group of six attorneys down to four, and set up appointment times with each of them. All four were kind enough to humor me with a one hour interview. These interviews were very helpful in getting a feel of who these attorneys were and what their personal relational styles were like. Once again, however, their professional skills for a case like ours was far less easy to determine. In the end, the process was less similar to my personnel hiring experience, and more like the choosing of our daughter, Barb, as a one-month old from the orphanage in Iran. You looked for ten fingers and ten toes, and checked whether she appeared to be healthy or not. Beyond that, it was in God's hands. So, too, with the attorneys. I reported back to our family my findings, and we later hired Jeff Sanford as Barb's attorney, and Charles (Chuck) Lahey as Elaine's.

Elaine, Barb and I met with Jeff and Chuck several times during November and December, preparing for the April 21 re-trial. Since our attorneys were new to the case, they both needed a copy of the trial transcript from Trial One. All of the testimony is included in the transcripts and therefore essential to prepare for a new trial. In talking to the trial recorder, our attorneys found out it might take until January 1, 2008 for the transcripts to be ready. That would make it a bit of a scramble to be ready by the April trial date, but everyone thought it would be possible. When January 1 rolled around, however, there were no transcripts. We started asking questions about who has the authority to get this done. There didn't seem to be an answer to that question. Apparently the court recorder has no immediate superior, and simply functions according to her own timetable. Finally, on March 6, we received the transcripts. Unfortunately, that was way too late to do the necessary preparation for the April trial. The word "continuance" reared its ugly head again, and the trial had to be reset. Barb, Elaine, and I were nearly apoplectic at this point. It felt like this nightmare would never end. We lobbied hard for a May or June date at the latest, but were finally assigned a new trial date in September, 2008. Once you get out of line on the court calendar, you start all over at the bottom of the priority list. And once again, it wasn't of our doing.

It was clear that the delay would also have a significant financial impact for us. Barb was still paying $160 a week to visit with Isabella. Other costs were mounting, too. The court transcripts, that caused this latest delay, came through with a charge attached: $3,900.00. The sticker shock of this whole judicial experience had left us numb. We were now well over $100,000 in expenditures with no end in sight. And nothing was settled. Just "continued." I thought back to Jim's earlier statement that "no client of his has ever been hurt by a delay." It was all rather depressing. But we did have the transcripts. So the attorneys were now able to get on board, and I was able to start digging, too.

Two things on the legal front happened between November and May that did elevate our spirits. First, Elaine had found out about a doctor from Stanford Medical School who was doing a research study on infants with a vitamin D deficiency and bone formation. Unfortunately, Natalia had not had a test for vitamin D at birth, so couldn't be part of this study. But the doctor graciously agreed to look at the brain/bone scan CD that had been used by the prosecution's doctors throughout the first trial. She had been looking at scan images for her research study. We had recognized early that this CD was the central piece of evidence from which all allegations had been made against Barb and Elaine. No matter what the prosecutor tried to intimate, there <u>was no other evidence</u> in this trial. So we sent this CD to the Stanford doctor. She looked at it carefully, and sent an e-mail back to Elaine.

Excerpts from that e-mail follow:

> I have some good news and some terrible news for you.

> Natalia has bad brain damage, the type that occurs during the pregnancy, or in a premature infant. Because of changes that take place in the newborn brain, periventricular leukomalacia does not occur after 40 weeks gestation (or the time a normal term infant is born) so the timing of this damage is either during pregnancy up to the time she spent in the NICU. Secondly, she has metaphyseal irregularities at her wrists, knees and ankle. These are the classic locations and classic metaphyseal changes we see in metabolic bone diseases.

> If they did not do an MRI yet, they must get one now, as this damage was not done by you. Dr. Patrick Barnes is a pediatric neuroradiologist here at Stanford and I will ask him to review the imaging for you. I also need all the imaging that was done in the NICU, including any head ultrasounds they might have done, and all brain imaging that has ever been done.

Although this news was likely of little help for Natalia, it was <u>HUGE</u> for us. We had been hoping that someone outside of South Bend might take a deeper look at this case. Now these doctors were saying that <u>we didn't do this to Natalia</u>. This was not news to us, but the affirmation was totally heartening. And we just happened to stumble onto perhaps the most experienced and influential authority in the country related to infant brain conditions. Once I looked online and read through Dr. Barnes' 60 page vita, I recognized we were in contact with someone with unique qualifications. His speciality of pediatric neuroradiology centers on the the brain imaging in young children. In addition to editing several textbooks on this subject, he had chaired a national child abuse task force, and written concerning non-accidental injury and its mimics, congenital brain anomalies, child abuse in evidence-based medicine, and the medical ethics of these areas. He has worked extensively with the shaken baby theory, having testified for both the prosecution and the defense in numerous national cases.

According to the other Stanford doctor, Natalia's bones had "irregularities" at the metaphyses (the bone ends.) No mention of fractures. Since we no longer had custody of Natalia, getting an MRI for her was next to impossible. And there was no other imaging to gather, with the exception of one chest x-ray, which was taken in the NICU. So getting them additional

240

information was not possible. The Stanford doctor later responded again to our return email.

> Dr. Barnes looked at the brain images (CT scan) this weekend and was quite shocked. He feels something went wrong during the pregnancy and/or birth. We need to get ALL of your daughters prenatal and birth records reviewed by a pediatrician (do you have one working for you?) Dr. Barnes wants to help in this case if you're interested. He has incredible credentials (currently a professor and chief of pediatric neuro imaging at Stanford, and before that, a similar position at Harvard.)
>
> Also, he was part of the committee that put together the recommendations for imaging newborn brains under certain conditions, and he feels this standard of care was not followed in your case.
>
> I believe the bone changes are metabolic, but there's so much that can go wrong when a child has this much brain injury. Also, in addition to checking the billing records during her birth admission, I would check ALL her billing records to look for that MRI or any other imaging they may have. Dr. Barnes cannot believe that they did not do an MRI with the extent of injury on the CT.
>
> I concur, and believe there is more imaging out there somewhere.

Once again, there was no other imaging that was done on Natalia. As for finding a pediatrician who would review the prenatal and birth records for these Stanford doctors, that's a story in itself. For six months I worked diligently at finding such a pediatrician. I soon found that most pediatricians at that time were so invested in the shaken baby theory that they would not challenge another colleague. The three local pediatricians who had seen Natalia were all on the prosecution team of doctors. Since then, Natalia had been moved miles away to another part of the state. And we had no access. But another local pediatrician could have reviewed the records. None, however, could be found. Some knew the South Bend pediatricians involved, and did not want to undercut them. Others simply didn't want to question the "theory."

Not many doctors want anything to do with the courtroom. Their understandable interest is in medical practice. But I found a doctor from Cincinnati, Ohio who listed himself as a medical expert for trials. When I talked with him, I asked if he was familiar with the shaken baby controversy. He responded "What controversy?" I didn't go any further. Any medical person who is totally unaware of the controversy about shaken baby theory is either severely uninformed about the field, or is playing games like Dr.

Emenim and his comment "what corpus callosum problem? I don't know anything about that." Anyway, the overall resistance to helping us was unmistakable. It seemed to us that a doctor would not have to disagree with the shaken baby theory in order to review the medical records for the Stanford doctors as we were asking. But apparently we were wrong.

After three months, we finally found a doctor at Michigan State University who agreed to review the records. We were so pleased that someone would actually look at these records objectively and relay to the Stanford doctors the information they needed, and possibly take the witness stand to relate what had, and had not, been done medically in Natalia's case. We sent all of Natalia's medical records as requested, the CD of the brain/bone scans, and the $1000 he wanted in order to peruse them. Things were looking up at last. However, we were needing a response fairly soon. The April trial had not yet been canceled. But it took him nearly three months to get around to reviewing the records. One day in June he called Chuck, Elaine's attorney, and talked for an hour. While we had simply wanted him to review the records and consult with the Stanford doctors, he gave an indication that if he were to write an opinion, (which we didn't want) it would be that this was a shaken baby syndrome case, and that the brain injury happened within an hour or two before Natalia went or the ER. He did seriously question why there was only one x-ray taken during Natalia's 19 day NICU stay, and also found it very unusual that no MRI was taken before charging abuse. But we decided not to have him write an official report.

What a letdown. We paid a thousand dollars for something we were not even asking him to do. Not only that, but we received another bill for an additional $300 for the phone call to Elaine's attorney. Shaken baby theory had apparently taken over his mind completely. No lucid intervals. Symptoms appear immediately. To this day, I seriously doubt he even looked at the CD of the brain/bone scans. But he knew the theory. I believe he simply looked at what the other doctors at South Bend Memorial had said. We didn't want another opinion. We wanted him to review the records and relay necessary information to the Stanford doctors. Chuck, however, was just getting on board with this case, and felt we should have him write an official report of his unofficial findings, since it would totally absolve his client, Elaine. With this "report," the only persons who could have hurt Natalia would have been Brant or Barb. Elaine was long gone by that time this doctor felt the injury occurred. Elaine and I had to work pretty hard to convince Chuck that this "unofficial" opinion was ludicrous, and would not stand up in court. It wasn't until many months later that Chuck thanked us for steering him away from this tempting, but extreme (except in shaken baby theory) opinion.

All of this was bitterly disappointing. But even more disappointing was the fact that somehow during this three month delay, we had lost contact with the Stanford doctors. Back in January the Stanford doctors had requested to be in direct contact with our attorneys. That contact was established and several e-mails were exchanged between them. Then the long, unsuccessful wait for a pediatrician to review our case for them happened. As that time of waiting for a pediatrician dragged on, the Stanford doctors undoubtedly had other demands on their plate. So that remains one of the great, painful mysteries for us in all of this. Did our attorneys drop the ball? Were we lost in the heavy schedules of these Stanford doctors? Did our inability to find a pediatrician to help us review Natalia's records end our connection with the Stanford doctors? We hoped and prayed for a renewal of that connection right up until the start of the second trial. That didn't happen, however, and to this very day that question continues to gnaw at us. We just don't know what happened.

Perhaps this is a good place to let you know one of the reasons why we continue to question the absoluteness and sanctity of shaken baby theory in Natalia's case. First the "crime" is diagnosed. As you know by now, this theory assumes that the last caretaker of the child is the perpetrator. Since in this theory there is no such thing as a lucid interval, everything works out very neatly and cleanly when there is one person who was clearly caring for the child at the time of the development of the life-threatening symptoms. So when a doctor can't explain what is wrong with a child with certain "consistent with" symptoms, it offers a quick and clean answer. (I wouldn't call it an "accurate" answer, though "possible" might fit.) But what happens when it is not clear who the caretaker was at the time of the injury? Or even when the injury itself happened? Then another "science" kicks in-----the timing of the "injury." A doctor, or doctors, are called in to tell everyone "when" this injury occurred. They do this by looking at the various scans that have been taken. What they testify to a jury sounds very "scientific" and is often carefully couched in "ranges" of times. But those ranges vary significantly from doctor to doctor, and even vary when the same doctor is looking at the same injury at a later date. All too frequently these ranges are viewed as absolute. So if you don't understand something yourself, you tend to believe whoever is an "expert" in the field. Jurors are no different. They have nothing else to go on. "Tell us what to believe." Computer technology, medicine, law, aerospace, and economics are a few examples of fields for which this is a problem. But for people working inside of these fields, there are plenty of differences and controversies at play. They recognize these are not absolute answers.

Over the course of roughly two years, <u>nine different doctors</u> viewed Natalia's brain/bone scan CD. The following is a listing of their conclusions as to <u>when</u> this massive "brain injury" happened. (Remember, they are looking at the <u>same scans</u>):

<u>Mich St. U. Dr.</u>---- **Pediatrician:** <u>1-2</u> hours old
<u>Dr. Okanlami</u>------- **Pediatrician:** <u>24-48</u> hours old
<u>Dr. Emenim</u>--------**Pediatrician:** "Could be an hour before." "You won't find 24-48 hours in my notes." In coma ever since <u>first</u> brain injury; <u>(Unclear)</u>
<u>Dr. Cockerill</u>--------**Neurosurgeon:** <u>3-4 weeks</u> old or longer; also a possible second recent 'event'
<u>Out of State Dr.</u>-----**Neurosurgeon:** <u>2-4 weeks</u> old;
<u>IU Med Sch Dr.</u>-----**Neonatologist:** "<u>Old</u>" injury
<u>Stanford Dr.</u>---------**Ped. Neuroradiologist:** Around <u>birth</u>
<u>Stanford Dr.</u>---------**Ped. Radiologist:** At or around <u>birth</u>
<u>Dr. Fischbach</u>-------**Radiologist:** Possible <u>birth</u> trauma

What are the patterns you can observe from the above timings? There is obviously very little agreement. Look at the three <u>pediatricians</u>. Two say it happened in the last few hours. The third, Dr. Emenim waffled all over the place by saying to police, "Something could have happened an hour before. I don't know. There's no way to tell." But at trial he said, "you won't find 24-48 hours in my notes." And then he said the child would have been <u>unconscious right after the first massive injury</u> (3-4 weeks before). The two <u>neurosurgeons</u> said the massive brain injury happened somewhere between three to four weeks ago, or longer. Dr. Cockerill felt the <u>few specks of new blood could also indicate a possible second "event" 1-2 days before</u> ER. The out-of state neurosurgeon said the massive brain injury was two-four weeks old, but there is <u>absolutely nothing conclusive that can be said about the few drops of new blood</u>. "It could have simply been oozing from the original injury." The <u>neonatologist</u> just said the brain injury is "old." How about the three <u>radiologists?</u> Two said the brain injury happened around the time of Natalia's birth, and the third said it <u>possibly</u> happened at birth.

It would certainly make an interesting study to see what these doctors are taught in their specialties at medical school about shaken baby, and the timing of injuries. But the <u>bottom line</u> from these nine doctors is this: <u>Natalia had something occur to her brain sometime between just before her birth, and one hour before being taken to the ER</u>. Or to sharpen it up a bit....this brain event <u>happened</u>. I can't help but follow this up with a hypothetical question: <u>If someone accused you of allegedly hurting your</u>

child, would you like to have the verdict and prison sentence to be based upon the precision of this "scientific" method of dating brain 'events'?

I mentioned earlier that there were two things that happened in the case against Barb that lifted our spirits as we looked toward the second trial. After receiving the transcripts from the first trial, I was not only able to put together the variations in timings from the nine different doctors, but I also was able to take just the timings given by the prosecution's own team of doctors and enter them on a chart showing that every one of Natalia's "injuries" could have occurred during the first week of July. That time frame, of course, included the July 2, 2005 party with Brant's extended family, the first time Natalia had been with a very large group of people since birth. The various timings of injuries come so quickly at trial, and can go right by you without ever seeing how they intersect. And while I realized that these timings by the doctors were very "inexact," it was also very clear that the prosecutor was using them as "exact" timings. These timings didn't fit the traditional shaken baby theory. Given that, the prosecutor fit them into his newly created theory that this was shaken baby, shaken baby, shaken baby, and shaken baby. Multiple times of shaken baby. An ongoing abuse of Natalia. But nobody ever even tried to explain how there would have needed to be multiple lucid intervals (or one very long one) for this to be the case. Or why the ribs broke one time (with no brain injury), then later the massive brain injury (with no broken ribs), and then leg "fractures" at yet another time. And finally the occurrence of a few drops of blood in the brain that were highlighted as a possible second brain injury. Pediatricians pounced on the possible recent brain injury because it fit the traditional shaken baby theory. But there was no scalp bruising or swelling. And the skull fracture was not new. Nothing really added up, unless everything happened at one injury time about 3-4 weeks earlier, and the few drops of recent blood were not a second injury at all, but oozing of blood from the original injury.

By putting these timings on a chart, however, one could see visually what you could not understand simply by listening to several days of testimony. What sounded good in the courtroom did not look so good on a chart. I have included a copy of that chart here. I showed this chart to Jeff first. He looked at it for a while, and then said we had something really significant. It should be a game-changer. Later Chuck viewed the chart and asked, "Do you realize what you have here? We don't get something this explicit very often." So I felt good. But would the jury be able to comprehend it quickly? There is a lot of information on one page.

Essentially, this chart shows **Dr. Cory**, the prosecution expert's timing the various bone injuries, giving the following timings:

Rib injuries------- "the range of June, <u>early July</u>, perhaps earlier"
Leg injuries------- "<u>early</u> to mid-<u>July</u>"
Skull injury------- "unable to date"

Dr. Cockerill, prosecution expert for the brain, <u>dating the massive brain injury</u>:

Major brain injury--- "<u>3-4 weeks before July 27</u>" (<u>early July</u>)
Skull fracture-------- "same time as massive brain injury" (<u>early July</u>)
[He also testified to a <u>possible brain event</u> "within 24-48 hours," based upon the few specks of new blood present on the scan.]

Testimony from **all witnesses** concerning the major increase in Natalia's symptoms:

Symptom increase---- "after the July 2 party" (<u>early July</u>)

The chart shows how <u>all of these different "injuries" intersect</u> at the <u>first week of July</u>. The only timed injury not falling within this week is the possible "second event" to the brain, which was put forth by Dr. Cockerill to explain the few drops of acute blood visible on the brain scan. He could not say anything else about that possible brain injury except that it would have taken <u>much less </u>force and may have been <u>accidental,</u> Other doctors say it's impossible to determine definitively why those few drops of new blood are there, whether they were caused by abuse, a sneeze, or simply bleeding spontaneously from the earlier injury. (In other words, this possible second injury is <u>very</u> questionable.)

Below the chart are listed the weeks, and <u>segments of the months</u> prior to Natalia's going to the ER. And at the very bottom are the <u>persons with access</u> to Natalia during the various time segments.

It seems <u>impossible</u> one could determine from these timings that <u>beyond a reasonable doubt, more than one time of injury</u> occurred. Certainly there <u>is</u> Dr. Cockerill's theory that a second minor brain injury <u>may</u> have occurred. This potential injury, however, is simply anything but clear.

But let's assume for a minute that we ignore the obvious (<u>the first week of July</u>) intersection for all of the injuries. What about the possible new injury to the brain 24-48 hours before ER. Who was around Natalia during that time? <u>Barb, Brant, and Elaine</u> each spent significant time alone with her. Remember, it takes "seconds" to shake a baby.

246

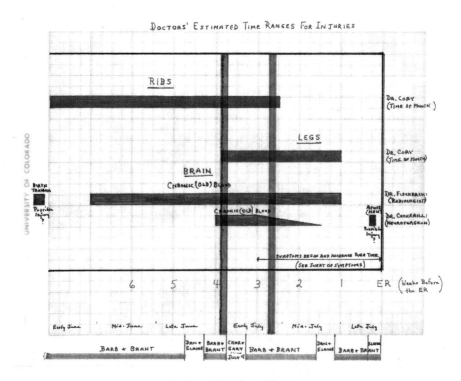

Injury Timing Chart

One needs a <u>gigantic stretch</u> of the imagination to believe the idea put forth by doctors and the prosecutor that Barb shook Natalia hard enough to break her ribs sometime in June, but not hard enough to give her a brain injury. Then she shook her again the first week of July so hard that she had a massive brain injury, but no broken ribs or retinal hemorrhages. Then her legs were apparently broken at another time with no other injuries happening. And then she shook her again 24-48 hours before ER, causing only a few drops of blood in her brain, but retinal hemorrhages in her eyes, and no broken bones. Elaine saw Natalia take her bottle twice on Tuesday (during this period of time). And while Natalia's temperature registered low on the thermometer Elaine was using, her other vital signs seemed fairly normal. Barb fed her another bottle at 5:30 pm Tuesday. Later that night Brant played with Natalia in bed. And yet, Dr. Okanlami said Natalia wouldn't be able to eat after a massive brain injury. And Dr. Emenim says Natalia was unconscious for the last three to four weeks, and yet nobody noticed. *Does any of this make sense?*

How could anyone believe all of those things <u>beyond a reasonable doubt</u>? Or for that matter, that Brant was eliminated as a suspect because:

247

(1) He "cried."

(2) He was "totally stunned."

(3) He told officers "the child was in the care of her mother."

(4) He "worked a lot."

We eagerly awaited the <u>second trial</u> to see how the prosecutor would explain all of this, and whether any jury would buy his explanation.

Our two attorneys were preparing for trial. But Jeff knew Barb's trial was more imminent than Elaine's, so he had to get ready sooner. None of our three attorneys had significant medical knowledge. I say this not as a criticism, but as a reality. The preparation of criminal attorneys does not include medical knowledge any more than the preparation of neurosurgeons includes criminal law. Criminal attorneys get very few trials that require a deep understanding of medicine and injuries. Consequently, they simply cannot prepare for every possible type of specialized knowledge that may be necessary. Elaine and I were aware of that very early. Although this was one of the criteria I was looking for in my attorney interviews, it really wasn't present in any of them to the degree we had hoped. That's probably not unusual in any city the size of South Bend. But it meant that Elaine and I would need to try to help our attorneys get comfortable with at least some basic anatomical and medical understandings necessary in a trial like this. *Not that we were all that medically knowledgeable ourselves.* Our attorneys, to a person, were open and receptive to anything we could provide for them. We were grateful for that. They could have seen it as a sign of weakness on their part to accept help. Actually that was another factor I tried to ascertain as I interviewed. Do these people listen? And we found that <u>our attorneys did.</u> But the learning curve in medicine and medical terminology is steep, and we were not the best ones to be teaching them. So we <u>limped together</u> in our preparation for the trial.

Jeff felt strongly that we needed to give the jury a choice of others who had the opportunity to have done this to Natalia. That's normal procedure in a murder trial. Why not in this case, too. They needed an option. He didn't want to challenge the <u>diagnosis</u> without doctors on our side. So, unfortunately, we had to start out with the assumption that this <u>was</u> shaken baby syndrome. All we could challenge with this approach was "Who did it?" *I didn't like it, but it <u>was</u> our reality.*

Studies done at the University of Pittsburgh Medical School since Barb's first trial established that <u>pregnant women with a Vitamin D deficiency</u> were <u>five times more likely</u> to develop preeclampsia. That is significant, since there's a much stronger likelihood that Barb, having had

248

preeclampsia, had also had a Vitamin D deficiency (which was never tested in either Barb nor Natalia). And consequently, Natalia would not have had normal bone development. But if we don't challenge the diagnosis, how do we make the jury aware of this study? You will recall one of the Stanford doctors believed Natalia's "bone changes to be metabolic." Neither Stanford doctor, however, would be present to testify. So we were limited to showing that Barb was <u>not the only one</u> who could have injured Natalia.

Earlier we showed how much the doctors disagreed on the <u>timing of the brain injury</u>. Now let's look at whether the doctors agreed or disagreed about the <u>timing of the bone injuries</u>. (Timing is determined by how much healing has taken place.) Bone injuries:

LINEAR SKULL FRACTURE

Dr. Okanlami: No new bone laid down, so it was my impression that it was a **fresh fracture**. It would have been acute **(new)**.

Dr. Boll: **Not an acute** fracture **(not new)**.

Dr. Cory: Could have been **either** acute **(new)** or chronic **(old)**.

RIBS

Dr. Cory: There are rib fractures that I would estimate to be **3-6 weeks old, possibly older**. Could have occurred anywhere in that range of time.

Dr. Boll: There are **old, healed** rib fractures.

LEFT RADIUS AND ULNA (At wrist)

Dr. Cory: **Corner fracture of both** radius and ulna.

Dr. Boll: **No definite fracture**.

RIGHT TIBIA (Below knee)

Dr. Cory: Fracture. **Doesn't show evidence of healing.**

Dr. Boll: There is a **healing fracture** of the right tibia.

Dr. Okanlami (from Lt. Mark Reihl interview report): **Healing fracture.**

LEFT TIBIA (Below knee)

Dr. Boll: There is probably also an **age indeterminate** fracture of the left tibia.

Dr. Cory: Comer fracture of the left tibia **doesn't show evidence of healing.**

Dr. Okanlami (from Lt. Mark Reihl interview report): **Healing fracture.**

RIGHT FEMUR (Above knee)

Dr. Cory (from Sgt. Kaps report): Spot on right femur **could be a fracture, but can not be sure** with these particular x-rays.

Dr. Cory (same doctor at trial, looking at <u>same x-rays</u> two years later): **corner fracture of her right femur.**

Dr. Boll: **No definite fracture** evident.

Once again, the <u>lack of agreement is astounding</u>. Not only is the timing different, but some see fractures, and some do not. And Dr. Cory, the bone expert, <u>didn't see a fracture of the femur</u> on July 28, 2005, but <u>two years later in the courtroom saw a fracture</u> from the same bone scan. Added to this is the Stanford doctor who refers to all of the arms and legs as metaphyseal (end of bone) "irregularities" and "changes," not fractures.

As we "snailed" towards the September trial, I found I needed a break from preparing my part of this case. In June of 2008, I spent a week with the MYF high school age youth group from College Mennonite Church on a service project in Kentucky. The seven to eight hour trip in our vehicles was filled with picturesque hills, valleys, trees, and small towns. Five adults and about 22 youth carried out various work projects in four or five different modest homes in one small town. The owners often joined in with our work

250

crews. It was a good chance to connect with local people, to help them with a project they could not have done otherwise, and to bond as a youth group. The weather was hot and the work was hard, but I heard very few complaints from the youth the entire week. Perhaps they were too tired to complain. Property owners seemed genuinely appreciative. The group of six that I was in built an addition onto a small home. Digging in hard ground, pouring concrete, cutting and nailing joists, nailing flooring, framing in the sides, hooking into the existing roof, and marking and laying shingles kept us busy all week. Both girls and guys were using power saws, electric drills, and mixing cement. We slept on the floor of a local church there each night. No trouble going to sleep. It was a great week, and a good opportunity for me to get away from the heaviness at home. Two years later I would have another opportunity to do a similar thing with the MYF in Denver. I have really good feelings about the youth of our church and hope that the next generation in this country will all be as high spirited, caring, and responsible as these young people.

As we approached the September 15, 2008 trial date, it actually seemed that we would not need another continuance this time. Finally. Elaine and I spent a week at a church camp about four hours away in Michigan in July. We had been going there each summer for about 22 years, but had skipped some years recently after this tragedy struck. Now we returned there and had a somewhat relaxing time. But we realized that we could never totally relax during the past three years. We always had to wait for the next crisis situation, and be prepared to try to work it through.

Jeff, our attorney, was also taking an August vacation to the west coast. We had hoped he might be fully rested and ready to go when he returned. Unfortunately, while he was on the west coast, his house in South Bend suffered severe fire damage. He returned home to the mess that was before him. At our next meeting Jeff told us that he had so much to do at home, there was no way he could be fully ready for the September trial date. *Nuts!* Our choice was to either ask him to go into the trial less than fully prepared, or go for another continuance and allow him more time to get prepared. One of the things that we learned through all of these years of legal hassling was that attorneys seldom really prepare in depth much before a week or two prior to trial. There are so many continuances that if they prepared earlier, it would be wasted effort. Trials seem much more likely to be continued than held. So would he have adequate time to prepare? He was saying "no." We could hardly stand the thought of going to the back of the court docket line for a ninth time. It might be another six months or more until we could get a trial scheduled. In the end we suggested that Barb use Elaine's trial time in October. (Each time a trial date was continued for Barb,

Elaine's trial date also was changed to a later time.) We were able to satisfy both Jeff and the Court by moving Barb's trial date to <u>October 13</u>. This meant a four-week delay, but that was much better than any other alternative.

In some ways , the past year has really seemed to move in slow motion. And yet, we're now ready for a second trial. It <u>did</u> get here. We had experienced the hung jury. What kind of jury will this one be? Will they acquit or convict Barb? <u>Very little will be different in this trial except the jury</u>. Which way will it go? Questions abound. This time I will <u>not</u> be sitting in the atrium outside of the courtroom all week. Jeff has asked me to be his "Witness in Chief," which means I will be sitting with him at the defense table, with Barb in between us. At least I won't have to wonder what's happening inside the courtroom.... and maybe I can help. *Besides, I had already finished my Sudoku book.* Jeff is convinced that I know what this trial is about, with its various details. But since the jury for the first trial was unable to reach a verdict, it seems more than likely the prosecution witnesses will just <u>ratchet up the rhetoric</u> in this trial. <u>There will be no new evidence.</u> Actually, <u>there wasn't any old evidence either</u>. I will not be a witness for the defense on the stand unless for some reason I'm needed. Dr. Rutt, the psychiatrist, will be back again. And we will have the Lead School Nurse from the Westview School Corporation as a witness to clear up the whole 93 degree temperature fiasco. Elaine and Barb both plan to testify. But clearly, the <u>jury will be the key</u>. *Is there anyone left in South Bend that doesn't have a strong opinion about this case?*

Sunday, October 12, we went as usual to church. While our minds were on the upcoming trial, we <u>were</u> able to appreciate the sermon that morning. Apparently we were not the only ones there thinking about our trial. Following the sermon Klaudia, one of our ministers, asked Elaine and me to come forward to the circle at the front of the church. There she announced what most members already knew--- that jury selection for our trial would be starting the next day. As we stood there with Klaudia, she gave an invitation to anyone who wanted to come forward and lay hands on us during her prayer. We were humbled when many from the congregation came forward and did exactly that. Immediately following her prayer for courage, truth, and God's presence with Elaine, Barb, and me, as well as with all persons who would be part of the trial directly or indirectly, including Isabella, Natalia, and Brant's family, we all sang "Rain Down," one of our favorite songs, as the people continued to keep their hands on us. <u>Rain down your love on your people</u>. What an expression of support. We were now ready for whatever lay ahead.

CHAPTER FIFTEEN

It was quite different to observe the workings of the judicial system from the inside of the courtroom. Our first task on Monday was to select a jury. This, again, was somewhat like our choosing Barb from the orphanage. You have some idea of what you would like to find in a juror, but you are limited to what they say. Are they being totally honest? Only they know. We did end up with a jury of twelve, plus two alternates. My biggest concern was that there appeared to be little to no medical experience represented. You choose from among the jury pool that is drawn for that trial. But we have a jury, so let's go.

Mr. Cotter is back as the prosecutor. He started his opening remarks with the jury by telling them that Natalia had a bone x-ray in NICU at birth. (He still doesn't know, or perhaps want to know, that it is an x-ray of the lungs.) And he also told them that Brant "didn't see Natalia very often." *Get him out of the picture early.* Then he talked about doctors comparing Natalia's x-rays that were taken in the ER (July 27) with the "x-rays that had been taken when Natalia was first born." *Apparently it isn't going to be any easier to get at the truth in this trial than in the first one.* Next the prosecutor told the jury that when the doctors told Barb about Natalia's injuries, they (jury) will hear a whole lot of stories from Barb about what could have caused them (injuries). And the doctors will say "no way" those events could have caused these injuries.

The first witness in Trial Two is **Dr. Cockerill,** neurosurgeon, from South Bend.

> Question: How long have you been a brain surgeon?
> Dr C: "Since 1995." (Roughly 13 years at the time of this trial.)
> Question: How many patients have you had under the age of two?
> Dr C: "I would say probably ten or less." (Fewer than one a year.)

Hmmmm.

> Question: Do you have an opinion as to what she (Natalia) may have been suffering from?
> Dr. C: "Yes. My opinion, based on the CAT Scan and evaluation was that this most likely represented non-accidental trauma." (In other words, he talks to the other doctors, asks about the history, and then interprets the CAT Scan. The information he gathers colors what he sees on the scan. The danger in that is that he no longer can look at the scan objectively.)

Dr. C (looking at scan): "That's a fracture (skull fracture). What that suggests is a fracture that occurred a few weeks before" (old).

Dr. C (continues): "a fairly extensive trauma to the brain... 10, 14 days, three to four weeks, some place in that neighborhood.....has caused those portions of the brain to start to die."

Dr. C (after 24 pages of testimony): "Also, one point I would like to make. There is a little acute (new) blood here as well, suggestive of a possible second injury, that would have occurred probably within a day or two prior to admission." (Dr. C has talked about the massive brain injury at some length, and then adds, almost as an afterthought, that there is this little new blood that could represent a possible second injury. It doesn't seem like his heart is really into these few drops of new blood, but the prosecutor will swoop in on this because it's the only "injury" left that is supposedly in the 24-48 hour time frame.) *One by one the other injuries all have been determined to be weeks old.*

Question: In Natalia's case, was there a shear injury to her brain? (Dr. C has just explained the shaken baby theory which says a shear injury occurs that pulls apart the nerve pathways in the brain.)
Dr. C: "There was.....probably (a shear injury). I cannot definitively say that based on the CAT scans." (He believes the theory, but he cannot support it with the evidence.) *The problem throughout the case is when shaken baby theory, itself, is used as evidence.*
Dr. C (continues): "Usually what you'll see with a shear type injury...it's petechial. That means very small, focal areas of hemorrhage inside the brain in multiple areas.
Question: Now is there a syndrome that is used for this?
Dr. C: "Yes. It's called shaken baby syndrome."
Question: Did Natalia have petechial hemorrhages?
Dr. C: "Most likely after the injury." *Because I believe the shaken baby theory.* "But, again, I can't document that on the CT scan." *Darn, the evidence on the scan just isn't there.*

Dr. C (continues): "The petechial hemorrhages start to resolve, to go away....the white little dots inside the brain on the CT scan tend to go away, and the brain itself tends to die, to become shrunken, smaller. And that's what we see on the scan."

Question: When would the skull fracture have occurred?
Dr. C: "It would have occurred most likely at the same time when the (massive) brain injury occurred." (Three to four weeks, or longer before ER.)

254

Question: Was the massive brain injury the only injury to her brain?

Dr. C: "There also appeared to be some evidence of a more acute (new) injury. There was some more acute hemorrhage inside the brain that should have resolved from an accident a few weeks before. More likely it represented a second episode. (Again, a pretty weak endorsement of a second injury.)

Question: And can you tell from the CAT scan there's fresh bleeding?

Dr. C: "Yes." (Fresh bleeding, or unresolved blood from the prior injury?)

Dr. Cockerill indicates that the ophthalmologist's report cites evidence of retinal hemorrhages.

Question: Is retinal hemorrhaging consistent with shaken baby syndrome (SBS)?

Dr. C: "Very consistent with SBS..... Retinal hemorrhages really nail down shaken baby syndrome." *It seems clear from previous testimony that he believes the retinal hemorrhages happened during the massive first brain injury.*

Cross-examination by Jeff Sanford.

Question: Would it be accurate to say that SBS can happen in as little as five seconds?

Dr. C: "It takes usually, in my experience, more than one brief shaking." *His experience? He's actually watched this?*

Question: Well are we talking about ten, fifteen minutes?

Dr. C: "Well, 20, 30, 40 seconds or more."

Question: You said there was a possible newer brain injury, 24-48 hours old?

Dr. C: "That blood (from the massive first injury) should not have hung around for three to four weeks." (There are serious questions about this. I have read in brain surgery articles that the blood takes from three weeks to two months to resolve. The time varies significantly from person to person.)

Dr. C (continues): "The bleeding usually occurs at the time of the event. It doesn't continue to bleed for long periods of time." *How about rebleeding later?*

Question: So how long would it take for those little dots (specks of blood) to go away?

Dr. C: "On a CAT scan, usually anywhere from ten to 14 days, maybe a little longer, you start to see those go away." *When are they gone?*

Question: Is it possible that the specks of "new" blood could have come from the earlier injury?

Dr. C: "Most likely not. I think it would have been gone by then."
(Again, he doesn't seem overly convinced. And the question of oozing blood over time is not addressed.)

Question: How much force would have been required to produce that secondary injury?

Dr. C: "That's much harder to say when the brain has been so damaged by the initial injury. It would be more likely to become injured again."

Question: Much more easy for it to become injured again?

Dr. C: "Yes."

Question: Less force than the first injury 10 days to three weeks prior?

Dr. C: "Three to four weeks (prior).

Question: You don't agree with Dr. Fischbach's report that this injury may have been birth trauma?

Dr. C: "No. The problem with radiology is that you're basing your opinion on an isolated study. You're not looking at the entire situation. You're just looking at the image." (The radiologist looks at the images (scans) and writes into his report what he sees. Dr. C looks at the history and projects what he learns into what he sees on the images.)

Question: You're saying the radiologist's opinion is somewhat subjective?

Dr. C: "To some degree. All he can say is that you see severe diffuse brain injury. As far as the mechanism, he can't say that." *He's just a radiologist.*

Question: But isn't the whole theory of shaken baby based on some study a radiologist did?

Dr. C: "To some degree." *I don't believe he knows.*

Question: It's based on a radiologist's interpretation of that study, isn't it?

Dr. C: "I'm not familiar with that study." *Thank you for your honesty.*

Question: But it was a radiologist who first came forward with that shaken baby theory, right?

Dr. C: "That's my understanding, yes." *So how can you believe this theory if it was originally proposed by a lowly radiologist?*

Question: Now in regards to this secondary brain injury, can you say that some very minor trauma couldn't have caused that injury?

Dr. C: "It's hard for me to put a figure on that." *Force unknown.*

Question: Can you say for certain if this secondary brain injury was intentional or accidental?

Dr. C: "I cannot say that." (Dr. C knows he is on shaky ground in this whole secondary brain injury thing. He can't really say anything definite

256

about it.   Yet it will continue to be the prosecutor's most significant "evidence.") *Beyond a reasonable doubt.*

The <u>prosecution</u> resumes questioning.

Question: Mr. Sanford was talking early on about if you could quantify the kind of force that would be necessary to cause that injury. Do you remember that?

Dr. C: "The skull fracture, like that?"

Question: No. <u>Including the brain as well.</u>

Dr. C: "This type of injury is <u>most consistent with</u> a violent shaking <u>you see</u> during a shaken baby episode." (<u>Three things</u> happened in this answer:

> (1) Dr. C <u>shifts away from</u> the force required in the possible <u>secondary brain injury,</u> to the earlier massive brain injury. Jeff only asked about force needed for the second possible injury.
>
> (2) More "consistent with" language.
>
> (3) Dr. C once again <u>seems to have seen</u> violent shaking going on regularly.)

Question: You were uncomfortable saying whether the secondary brain injury was accidental, or intentional. Correct?

Dr. C: "Correct. <u>I couldn't say.</u>"

Question: You couldn't say?   *Pleeeease?   The prosecutor really wants this questionable injury to be* <u>*intentional,*</u> *but we're not even that sure it* <u>*was*</u> *a second* <u>*injury.*</u>

Dr. C: "I can't say."

Question (juror): If the brain is shrinking, what is the cause of the increased pressure?

Dr. C: "The <u>pressure was present after the initial injury.</u> What <u>we're seeing now</u> (on the scan) is there is <u>no pressure.</u>" (Scan was taken July 27, 2005)

Question (Prosecutor): When you examined Natalia July 27, 2005, <u>was there still swelling</u> then?

Dr. C: "All I can say is <u>there had been</u> significant amounts of <u>swelling in the past.</u>" (Not now.) *Obviously Dr. C and Dr. E disagree totally on this. And both looked at the same scan.*

The next witness is **Dr. Okanlami**, pediatrician, in the PICU.

Question: What other injuries did you find?

Dr. O: "We did discover a number of rib fractures that were in <u>different stages of healing</u>. We also discovered fractures of her tibia (leg) that were not new."

257

Question: What did Barb Schrock tell you when you asked about Natalia's history?

Dr. O: "The child had not been feeding well (after July 4) and had been throwing up for about three weeks."

Question: Did Natalia have complications at birth?

Dr. O: "She stayed in the NICU for a short while, purely because she needed to gain some weight. She was not feeding well at birth." *Yeah. She bulked up from 3 pounds, 11 ounces at birth way up to 3 pounds, 15 ounces during her 19 days there. Maybe there were other reasons, too, why she was kept in NICU.*

Dr. O (continues): "And the mother did report to nursing that she had 'postpartum blues.'.... Many women go through a period of time after the delivery of a child where they have a form of depression."

Question: Did she tell you that she just didn't feel like taking care of Natalia?

Dr. O: "I don't recall her telling me that. I recall her saying she didn't quite bond with the child, which again is not an unusual phenomenon when a baby is born early and spends a significant period in the NICU." *That's how Barb nearly always described it.*

Question: Did the mother ever tell you when that (PPD) occurred?

Dr. O: "During the period of time that the child was in the NICU. And it went away in a couple of weeks."

Dr. O (continues): "And I did share with her the injuries that we found, the skull fracture, which was not fresh (not new). The brain injuries, the bleeds, which were fresh..... She said she would need to position her on her belly to help her go to the bathroom and asked if, you know, ...could that have caused those injuries? To which I said 'no'.... She was not informing me that this is how these (injuries) happened, she was asking me, could the injury have been caused by this?" (But the prosecutor will still continue to use Barb's questions against her as stories she told.)

Question: What was her demeanor when you were talking about these injuries?

Dr. O: "She was rather emotionless."

Question: What was the father's demeanor?

Dr. O: "Pretty distraught."

Dr. Okanlami then states that she has seen a "wide range of emotional responses from parents whose children are critically ill....from non-responsive and stunned to uncontrollably distraught." (But that testimony, again does not slow down the prosecutor from continuing his "demeanor" evidence pursuit.)

258

Dr. O (continues): "Natalia had a skull fracture that did not have what we call soft tissue swelling above it. If a child hits her head, you get a goose egg over the area where there's a cracked bone. Well, that's a <u>recent injury</u>. She (Natalia) <u>didn't have that</u>." [<u>In Trial One</u>, Dr. O said: "There was no new bone laid down around that skull fracture, so it was my impression that was a <u>fresh (new) fracture</u>."] *Now the doctors are not only disagreeing with each other, they're <u>disagreeing with themselves</u>. First trial <u>new</u>, but second trial <u>old</u>.*

Dr. O: (continues): "If a child sustains an injury of significant force as to crack their skull, they would be very irritable. <u>They won't eat.</u>" *So now Natalia <u>hasn't eaten for the last three or four weeks,</u> according to Dr. C's timing of the massive brain injury and skull fracture. And Dr. Emenim says Natalia <u>was unconscious during the same three to four week period</u>. What a one-two punch. How do you overcome this type of radical testimony? No wonder Barb and Elaine were charged with felonies. There should have been a whole bunch of other people charged if you are to believe these two pediatricians. And yet not one of the multiple people who saw Natalia during this time, saw what these doctors are alleging. This <u>shaken baby theory</u> causes some otherwise intelligent people to assume some very strange things.*

Dr. O (continues): "In a child's brain (Dr. O uses the example of an <u>egg</u> to describe the brain) that includes blood vessels that bridge the yolk to the white, <u>which snap</u>, which are <u>responsible for some of the retinal hemorrhages</u> that we find behind the eyes." (This would happen with a "significant" brain injury, [like the <u>massive brain injury</u>].)

Question: Are Natalia's injuries <u>consistent with</u> shaken baby syndrome?
Dr. O: "They are." *That's all we need to know.*

<u>Defense cross-examines Dr. O.</u>
Question: You were talking about getting a history from the parents?
Dr. O: "That's correct. Part of my care of the child includes my asking the parents some questions. And that did occur in this case."
Question: And so Barb is going through a list of things that she thinks might have caused the problem?
Dr. O: "When I told her some of the injuries, <u>she asked me</u> how do I think that could have happened, could it have been... you know. <u>She at least did not seem to have any</u> knowledge of how those injuries occurred, is the impression that I got from her asking me those questions."
Question: Now Mr. Cotter refers to that as <u>rationalization</u>, but she's really responding to some of the statements you're making, correct?

Dr. O: "She asked me some of those questions in response to my informing her of the injuries that were found." *No selling, no rationalizations, no explanations, no excuses.*

Question: Now Mr. Cotter seemed to take some stock in how she reacted...

Mr. Cotter: "Judge, can we approach?"
The Court: "Make a point."
Mr. Cotter: "I object to how he's commenting and discussing how I ask questions." *He seems to be very thin-skinned here.*
Mr. Sanford: "I'll rephrase it. I'm sorry if I offended Mr. Cotter."

Question: You said in handling people who are in a similar situation that Barb found herself in that day, that there's a whole gamut of emotions, correct?

Dr. O: "That's correct."

Question: How long would it take to shake a baby? A matter of seconds?

Dr. O: "Yes. I would say a matter of seconds."
Question: And in reference to the more recent bleeding in the brain....can you say how that injury resulted?
Dr. O: "No. I wouldn't be able to say."
Question: Could the recent blood be a result of those injuries that happened four weeks ago?
Dr. O: "Not the fresh bleeding, no. It would have to be reinjured for fresh bleeding to occur." *She doesn't know about continuous oozing and spontaneous rebleeding either? That must not be a part of shaken baby theory.*

Question: Can you tell me how much force would be necessary for this new blood to show up?
Dr. O: "I don't know if it's possible to quantify it. But I can say that if you have a previously injured brain... it would quantitatively take less force the next time around because you have already compromised the brain."
Question: And this acute bleeding could be the result of either intentional or accidental injury?
Dr. O: "It could be intentional. It could be accidental. But it would not be compatible with normal handling of the baby that's three months. That's the distinction I would like to make." *Where did she get that?* "None of the forces required to cause that second injury would have been compatible with normal handling of a three month old."
Question: What study would you base that on, Doctor?

Dr. O: "<u>Oh, just 28 years of practice</u>." *She "knows" from experience that a severely injured brain will not bleed again unless the force is <u>beyond normal handling</u>? Dr. Cockerill "knows" from experience that it takes <u>more than one brief shake</u> to shake a baby. What are they doing and observing to gain this experience, and why haven't they given these findings to the scientific community?*

Dr. O (continues): "<u>I'm sure that we cannot find a study</u> that would tell you quantitatively how much force it takes to injure a previously injured brain. <u>We can't do that kind of study</u>." *So I just say, "force beyond normal handling." That seems to work okay.*

Question (Prosecutor): Was there a reason why you did not ask questions of the father?

Dr. O: "Because he was not in the hospital that much."

Question: Okay. Was it because you had any concerns that the father had done this, or anything like that? (The prosecutor is asking Dr. O obliquely about whether she thought Brant <u>had hurt</u> Natalia <u>or not</u>, and if this is <u>why she didn't ask him</u> questions?)

Mr. Sanford: "Judge, I'm going to object to the question."

The Court: "Well, you're right. <u>The objection is sustained</u>."

Question: When <u>Mr. Sanford asked you what force is necessary</u>, I'm going to focus on <u>shaken baby syndrome itself</u>, to cause brain injury. <u>What force is necessary?</u>" (The prosecutor, just as he had done earlier with Dr. Cockerill, <u>shifts</u> "the amount of force required" question <u>to</u> the first massive brain injury, and <u>away from</u> the possible secondary injury, which was not at all what Jeff had asked. But it serves to confuse the jury.) *And Dr. O.*

Dr. O: "<u>I said it doesn't take much</u>. However, it is force that is <u>beyond the normal</u>." (Dr. O <u>misses the shift</u> the prosecutor is trying to make, and answers again what she said to Jeff. The prosecutor obviously doesn't like this "force required for the secondary brain injury" question. <u>She was supposed to reinforce</u> the fall from a skyscraper or the 100 mph Ferrari crash. But once again, the answer she gives is nearly unfathomable.... "<u>force that is beyond the normal</u>," as if that were some known quantity. It would have been more honest just to say what she had earlier, "<u>We can't do that kind of study</u>." Perhaps if you think that people believe the three story, or five story, or ten story fall is a <u>fact</u>, why not "force beyond the normal" as a <u>fact</u>? It all makes sense... <u>if you believe the theory</u>.)

Question: The first brain injury, is that <u>consistent with shaken baby syndrome</u>?

Dr. O: "<u>The child did not present to me at the end of the first injury</u>. The child presented at the point in time where what I was seeing were

261

the findings consistent with a healing injury. *So Natalia came to the ER with a healing injury? Unbelievable.*

Question: The healing injuries you observed, were they consistent with shaken baby syndrome?

Dr. O: "That would be more difficult for me to answer, you know, yes or no."

Question: What is your opinion on whether the first injury was accidental or non-accidental?

Dr. O: "My conclusion was that the child had a first injury. I cannot speculate on the nature or the force that caused that injury. (Basically no comment on the first injury.) *It doesn't fit the theory. I don't believe in lucid intervals.*

Dr. Okanlami had testified just a few minutes earlier in the trial:

> Question: Are Natalia's injuries consistent with shaken baby syndrome?
> Dr. O: "They are."

So how are we to understand this reversal? Did she simply change her mind in the past few minutes? Or is she saying the first definite, massive brain injury has questionable consistency with shaken baby syndrome, but this possible secondary brain injury is consistent with shaken baby syndrome? We don't know. What we do know, however, is that she and Dr. Cockerill view this all very differently. He was definite that the early massive injury was consistent with shaken baby syndrome, but not even totally certain if there was a second injury. He said it was "possible," but could make no conclusions beyond that. Dr. Okanlami, however, is committing to nothing as it relates to the first injury....not if it was shaken baby, not if it were intentional or accidental....nothing. The second "possible injury," if there indeed was one, is the one she apparently thinks is shaken baby. It must fit her theory better. But she also just said the second possible injury could have been either an intentional or accidental injury. Can "shaken baby" be accidental? These doctors seem to be testifying in riddles.

The prosecutor still has only established this secondary brain injury (within 24-48 hours) as a "possible injury" with no known force requirement, and no commitment on whether it would be an intentional or accidental injury, and no certainty whether the person caring for Natalia at the time of this "injury" was the same one who caused the earlier massive brain injury. This won't pass muster. He has not been able to firmly establish any definite injury in the last three weeks. Consequently, the conversation turns to the retinal hemorrhages, for which the ophthalmologist who wrote the report is not present at the trial.

Dr. O (continues): "She had a <u>second injury</u> for which she was presenting, and she now had <u>bilateral hemorrhages</u> with retinal detachment. Those were <u>more recent injuries</u>. That is <u>highly consistent with a shaken infant</u>." (So this partially clarifies her stance. This second possible injury is "consistent with" shaken baby syndrome. If there are retinal hemorrhages present---it's shaken baby.) *Even though she doesn't know if it was an intentional or accidental injury. And clearly it was recent. The theory says so.*

Question (Defense): <u>Can you date the retinal hemorrhages?</u>
Dr. O: "No." *But you said they were recent.* "Except that <u>they were described</u> as acute. They were <u>fresh bleeds</u>." *So the ophthalmologist must have described them as acute* (recent).
Question: Can you date them?
Dr. O: "No." *She's said this twice now. No, she can't date them.*
Question: Wouldn't you expect to see a broken neck before you saw hemorrhages in the eyes?
Dr. O: "No. <u>A significant enough brain injury</u>...when the <u>blood vessels are snapped</u> and you see bleeding inside the brain, you have a <u>chance of seeing retinal hemorrhages</u> in the back of the eyes." *And which was the massive injury that would have torn the blood vessels? The three to four week old one, or the possible recent one?*

Question (juror): "Is the <u>retinal injury</u> associated with the <u>first brain injury</u> or the <u>second?</u>" *Excellent question. I'm eager to hear this answer and reasoning.*
Dr. O: "From the description of the <u>ophthalmologist's report</u>, which <u>described these retinal hemorrhages as relatively fresh</u>, (now they're described <u>not as fresh</u>, but <u>relatively</u> fresh) I would <u>guess</u> that they were <u>associated with the second injury</u>." (This is likely why Dr. O believes that this second "injury" is much <u>more definite</u> and <u>more serious</u> than Dr. Cockerill does. The second injury is the one associated with the "<u>fresh</u> retinal hemorrhages" in her mind. Note, however, that Dr. Cockerill also referred to the ophthalmologist's report, but did not associate the retinal hemorrhages with the possible second brain injury.) *I wonder why?*
Dr. O (continues): "<u>I was just looking (on the report)</u> at the retinal hemorrhages as described by the ophthalmologist just to see <u>if</u> he mentioned anything that would relate to the retinal hemorrhages." *If he mentioned anything? You just said he described them as fresh. Then relatively fresh. Did you make that up?* "He <u>does not</u> say anything about <u>old</u> retinal hemorrhages. So they <u>sounded like</u> they were acute (new)." *They sounded like they like they were new? Wow! If you say you own a car, and you don't say it's old, obviously it must be new. This is ridiculous!* (All that Dr.

263

Okanlami has said about the new blood in the brain and it's being "consistent with" shaken baby, seems to have based on these <u>retinal hemorrhages</u> that she has <u>wrongfully remembered the</u> <u>ophthalmologist calling acute.</u> She will need to change her thinking again, just like she did for the <u>skull fracture</u> which she <u>earlier thought was fresh, too.</u> One doesn't have to look very far in medical literature to find that it is <u>very difficult, if not impossible, to determine the timing of retinal hemorrhages</u> with any degree of precision.)

<u>Question</u> (Prosecutor): When you were talking about the <u>retinal bleeding, you said that it was</u> <u>acute bleeding</u>, correct? (He's desperate to get something in the last 24-48 hours.)
<u>Dr. O</u>: "<u>Yes</u>." (Even though no one else, including the ophthalmologist, has said this. And what she thought was in the ophthalmologist's report, wasn't there. And after she twice said she couldn't date retinal hemorrhages.)

This is probably the appropriate time to recognize that Dr. Okanlami is a pediatrician. She doggedly believes in the Shaken Baby Syndrome. So when an injured child like Natalia comes into the PICU, she starts from that premise. As Dr. Emenim said, the <u>caretakers never tell us the truth.</u> Given that mindset, Dr. Okanlami lets that theory influence her understanding of the injuries. She said in the <u>first trial</u> that the <u>skull fracture</u> was <u>fresh</u>. Why? Because the theory says that <u>everything happens in the last 24-48 hours</u>. Consequently, the skull fracture was new. You will remember, however, that in <u>this trial</u> she said the skull fracture was <u>not fresh</u>. Somebody must have informed her of that during the intervening year. But if the skull fracture is not new, how does all of this fit the theory? Next she tries the <u>retinal hemorrhages</u>. Dr. Okanlami says she can't date retinal hemorrhages, but the <u>ophthalmologist described the retinal hemorrhages as "acute."</u> Now she can keep her theory. But when she read the report again on the witness stand, the ophthalmologist never said they were acute. So now, in response to a desperate prosecutor's question, Dr. Okanlami decides to date them herself. <u>THEY ARE ACUTE</u>. Now she can hold on to her theory again.

<u>Question</u> (Defense): You said <u>you would guess</u> that the retinal detachment was associated with the second injury?
<u>Dr. O</u>: "I say that because-----<u>the examination of the retina is in the jurisdiction of the pediatric ophthalmologist</u>"---- *Really?*---- "who made a <u>definite notation</u> about it in his consultation, about the fact that this-----this----he <u>did not make any notation</u> about these being <u>old</u> hemorrhages. They were <u>described as multiple hemorrhages</u>." *So do we have <u>any definite injury</u> in the last 24-48 hours? Beyond a reasonable doubt?*

264

Next, **Dr. Cory**, pediatric radiologist, takes the stand. He goes through a number of scans and describes various fractures that he sees.

Question: What fractures were you able to observe based upon this x-ray?

Dr. Cory: "There's a small fragment of bone here which represents a fracture." (This is true for many of the bone "fractures" in this trial. They are tiny fragments of bone at the end of the leg or arm bones that look like a little splinter, and are very hard to see. The doctor from Stanford Medical School called them "irregularities.")

Question: Is that the only fracture you observed?

Dr. Cory: "The left tibia (lower leg at the knee.) There's also a little bit of a linear---very thin fragment there that's a similar type of fracture---and that's the femur in the right leg."

Question: The right leg had femur and tibia fractures?

Dr. Cory: "Yes" (This is interesting because when Sgt. Kaps showed Dr. Cory this same bone scan on July 28, 2005, Dr. Cory said he "could not be sure the right femur was fractured with these particular x-rays." *Apparently the x-rays got clearer over the years.*

Question: You told us before that you can get an idea of when various fractures occurred, right?

Dr. Cory: "Yes. Well with bones such as the ribs, there's a fairly predictable pattern of healing." As the bone heals, "you get what's called callus around the area.... And generally that process takes somewhere between three weeks and six weeks to get to that stage." *So there's at least a three week window during which the ribs were fractured. And those are the predictable ones.*

Question: If you know the start date is July 27, when would Natalia's rib fractures have happened?

Dr. Cory: "I would say in the range of June to early July, and perhaps earlier than that."

Question: When would the fractures to the tibias (legs) and femur (leg) have occurred?

Dr. Cory: "Those are a little more difficult because they are more subtle (most doctors can't see them) and so dating them is a little more difficult. But it does not appear to me that these have completely fused with the bone that they've broken off of. And so I think these are probably more recent (than the ribs). In the range of two to three weeks."

Question: Would these leg injuries have been at different times?

Dr. Cory: "I think it's likely that they occurred at the same time."

Question: Is it your opinion that the rib injuries occurred at a different time from the leg injuries?

Dr. Cory: "Yes. It is."

Question: Could the leg fractures happen with little force?

Dr. Cory: "It takes a lot of force." (In Trial 1, Dr. Cory said: "Well, again, this is where the bone grows (at the end of the bones)....It's just starting to turn from cartilage into bone. And it's easy to fracture.") *Time changes testimony.*

Question: And do you have an opinion as to the age of the skull fracture?

Dr. Cory: "I don't. I can't put a date on it."

Now Mr. Cotter shows Dr. Cory the lone x-ray taken at Natalia's birth. It is a chest x-ray of her lungs. And he asks the following:

Question: "As a matter of fact, looking at that whole x-ray, were you able to determine whether this child had any fractures on April 25, 2005 (Natalia's birth)?"

Dr. Cory: "There were no fractures visible at that time." *Wait a minute! Not again.*

The deception in this exchange is total. There's no way to give the prosecutor the benefit of the doubt here. This is the same chest x-ray as in the first trial. The jury cannot see the details from the jury box. Once again, to say there are no visible fractures is completely misleading. Of course there aren't any visible fractures. First of all, none of the areas in question (legs, arms, skull), with the sole exception of the ribs, are even included on this x-ray. And any possible fractures of the ribs would not have shown up on this birth x-ray, since new fractures to the ribs would not show up on an x-ray until they start developing callus. There is nothing else to call this stunt except a charade for the jury. *Perception is king. Truth is just a jester.*

Question (Defense): Well, we have a range for the ribs of three to six weeks, and a range for the legs of two to three weeks. So I don't understand, Doctor, how you can say that there isn't a possibility that those injuries didn't occur at the same time?

Dr. Cory: "I can't say that it is impossible." *Dr. Cory is allowing for my case of one injury time for all injuries.*

Question: The radiology report from Dr. Boll (radiologist) says there is no definite fracture of the right femur. Would you agree with that?

Dr. Cory: "No." *He did agree three years ago.*

Question (juror): Would a person caring for a child know when those fractures occurred?

Dr. Cory: "Not necessarily." *The prosecutor thinks they would, and has said so.*

Question (Prosecutor): What do you mean, not necessarily?

Dr. Cory: "Unless you have an x-ray, you wouldn't know that a rib (or any other fracture we talked about) is broken." (This is an important point, since the prosecutor likes to point out that Natalia had all of these "broken bones," and no one did anything to help her.)

Anthony Van-Es, now a paramedic, and **Eric Purcell**, another paramedic, both took the witness stand. Essentially they said nothing different from the first trial. The prosecutor brought up demeanor and shoes again, but didn't seem to get far with that. Jeff simply asked the paramedics if it was more helpful when they were trying to gather information about the crisis situation to have the parent be hysterical and crying, or more calm. They responded that calm was more helpful. Then he asked if Barb's getting her shoes before she went to the ER with Natalia delayed them in any way, and the answer was "no." *But trust me, the prosecutor will raise these non-issues again (and again).*

Cindy Lorentzen, foster mother, and **Dan Nowicki**, police officer, also testified briefly, but added nothing significant to their previous testimony.

Next on the stand was **Dr. Emenim**, pediatrician in the PICU.

Question: Can you tell us about Natalia's physical condition on July 27, 2005?

Dr. E: "Well, when I came on, the child was deathly ill, on life support, on the ventilator. She had a serious brain injury that put her in a coma where she was not responsive. The brain of the child was severely swollen and threatening to end life."

Question: Were all of Natalia's injuries suffered at one instance, or on multiple instances?

Dr. E: "Looking at the x-rays, it was clear that all of the injuries did not occur at one time." *Everything is always clear to Dr. E ......except Natalia's missing corpus callosum.*

Question (Defense): You testified that when you saw her, her brain was swollen?

Dr. E: "The brain was severely swollen and was threatening to herniate..... having so much bleeding in the brain that it was threatening to push the brain through the hole out of the base of her skull." *No downplaying of the description here. The answer is "yes."*

Question: Would that be noticeable?

Dr. E: "Certainly. No matter who the observer is, you should be able to tell that there's something wrong with the baby."

Question: <u>Immediately after the injury that caused the brain injury,</u> correct?

Dr. E: "These injuries were very severe. The <u>degree of injury</u> this child had....was <u>so massive</u> that you really <u>have to be from outer space</u> not to recognize that there's something wrong with this child." *We've got a whole bunch of space aliens around.*

Question (Defense): The skull would have been swollen, is that correct?

Dr. E: "The <u>skull</u> may not have been swollen because, depending on the injury, but the fact is that <u>this child would not maintain well</u>.....is <u>not going to be awake</u> (unconscious)."

Question: I just wanted to make sure I understood you because <u>you were talking about the massive injury</u> to the brain? (The first brain injury.)

Dr. E: "<u>Yes.</u>"

Question: You said somebody <u>would have to be from outer space</u> not to notice that?

Dr. E: "Yes."

Question: So the behavior would be different?

Dr. E: "It would be so different that <u>you really have to be from outer space</u> not to realize that." *He seems in love with that line. But does he <u>understand the implication</u> of what he is saying?* Evidently, some of the jurors must have been wondering the same thing?

Question (juror): "Doctor, in your opinion, would a person acting as primary caregiver be able to <u>note changes in behavior</u> resulting from an injury like the <u>first brain injury</u> sustained by Natalia?"

Dr. E: "<u>Yes. That's very correct.</u>"

Question (juror): "Did you notice any bruises or cuts on Natalia?"

Dr. E: "No."

Question (juror): "The jury has heard that the brain was atrophied...<u>shrunk</u>. Was it still swollen when you saw her?"

Dr. E: "The brain was <u>not shrunk</u> when we saw this child. The brain was <u>massively swollen</u>."

(Dr. Cockerill, who said her brain was <u>atrophied</u> and <u>not</u> under pressure (not <u>swollen</u>), saw Natalia and the brain scan when Dr. Emenim did. They were looking at the same scan and the same child. Disagreement between the team of doctors that the prosecution had rounded up, let alone outside doctors, was a major concern. Even on Wednesday, July 27, 2007 [day one] Sgt Kaps alluded to this problem in his interview with Barb.

Sgt K: "They're (the doctors) all pretty good at what they do. The problem is <u>getting then all to agree on one thing</u>." *I wonder if Mr. Cotter is a bit nervous about all of the medically conflicting remarks from his own team.   He* <u>*should*</u> *be.*

CHAPTER SIXTEEN

The next witness to take the stand is **Dr. Simpson**, family pediatrician.

Question: Did you talk on the phone with the mother of Natalia on July 26, 2005?

Dr. S: "Yes. Natalia's temperature was low, she was eating, but not quite acting normally."

Question: I didn't hear the last part of your answer.

Dr. S: "Her temperature was low grade. She had a temperature of 93 degrees according to this (telephone note of call)."

Question: Okay. So she called, correct?

Dr. S: "Yes."

Question: Left a message?

Dr. S: "Yes."

Question: Did you ultimately talk to her? Did you call her back?

Dr. S: "I don't remember how it went, but my note is that I told Mom to make an appointment."

Question: If you were advised, and <u>all</u> you were advised, is that a person has a 93 degree temperature, what is your thought?

Dr. S: "<u>The only time I have seen a temperature that low is if a patient has some type of organ shutdown, or they're exposed to extreme hypothermia (extreme cold)</u>." (Remember that Elaine said the same thing about hypothermia in Trial 1. Dr. Simpson could have added "an <u>actual</u> temperature" that low, because there are lots temperatures taken that are <u>incorrect for a variety of reasons,</u> as Elaine's records at school confirmed. And Dr. Simpson also later confirms that.)

Question: If I call you on the phone and say, Doc, I got a 93 degree temperature, what are you going to tell me?

Dr. S: "You <u>ask the patient how they are doing</u>."

Question: Well, <u>if all I know</u> is it's a 93 degree temperature, that's my question?

Dr. S: "<u>I would just have to question what's going on</u> because I mean they probably would not be doing very well at 93."

Question: What would you advise me to do if I had a 93 degree temperature, and that's all you knew?

Dr. Simpson: "Well, first of all, we check to<u> make sure it's okay,</u> because I mean that's extremely low."

The above interchange between the prosecutor and Dr. Simpson is further indication of the <u>major problems in a medical trial of this type.</u> For <u>non-medical people,</u> the question being asked seems so simple. "What would you tell them?" But Dr. Simpson's responses are appropriate. You hear 93 degrees, you don't tell them anything. You start asking more questions to help determine if the temperature is accurate. As Dr. Simpson said, you just don't see that kind of temperature in normal situations. And when you do, it's typically a mistake. So nearly everyone in the courtroom thinks like the prosecutor is thinking, and wonders why Dr. Simpson doesn't just answer his question. She actually does answer the question over and over and over, but the prosecutor can't hear the answer because he has a different hypothetical situation in mind. Consequently, he continues.

Question: Doctor, I can't hear you. *Or I don't understand you.*

Dr. S: "You re-check ----because sometimes they tell you it's 93 degrees and it's actually 98.3 or something like that. So we want to make sure that it's not an erroneous value."

Question: My question isn't good enough, and I've got to make sure I'm limiting it, because I don't want any other variables. You know, doctor, that I have a temperature of 93 degrees. What are you going to have me do? (The prosecutor is asking Dr. Simpson to answer a question to a situation that she would never encounter, because she would ask other questions first. The prosecutor imagines a life without variables----black and white. But the doctor finally answers his hypothetical question.)

Dr. S: "Come in immediately."

Question: You said, well, I'm going to check it and I'm going to ask you other questions. Why do you say it like that?

Dr. S: "Because a 93 degree temperature is----is not believable hardly, you know. I mean the patient who is eating usually doesn't have a 93 degree temperature."

Question: Why? What else is happening to the body when somebody has 93 degree temperature?

Dr. S: "As I said before, they have some organ shutdown, severe hypothermia."

Question: Now you were advised that she had a 93 degree temperature, right?

Dr. S: "Yes."

Question: And you told her to do what?

Dr. S: "To come in."

Question: When did you tell her to come in?

Dr. S: "I don't have the exact time here, so I can't say. But it would have been soon."

And so the temperature question is left dangling. As is the time that she told Barb to make an appointment. It certainly appears that what Dr. Simpson is saying, and what Barb is saying, conflict. Barb has said Dr. Simpson told her to call in the morning for an appointment. Here again, who will the jury believe? The woman accused of child abuse, or the doctor? (We know what the truth is in this situation because of the police notes. Sgt. Kaps, sitting at the prosecutor's table, and who interviewed Dr. Simpson, knows the truth, too. It's contained in the police interview with Dr. Simpson on July 29, 2005. "She suggested Barbara call her office the next morning to schedule an appointment for Wednesday, July 27, 2005.)" *But the jury never hears this. Who did they end up believing?*

The prosecutor then directs the questioning to Natalia's constipation. (Barb called in to Dr. Simpson's office mid-July about Natalia's constipation---the record of that call is part of the trial evidence.)

Question: Would you advise a patient to take the legs and push the legs towards the chest (for constipation)?

Dr. S: "No."

Question: Would you advise the parent to squeeze the kidneys areas?

Dr. S: "No."

The obvious implication of this above interchange is that Barb told police Dr. Simpson told her to do these things. Once again, Barb never said that to police, and the prosecutor never produced any evidence that she told them that. *There is none. It just wasn't said.* But he continued to act like she had said this throughout both trials. And this was not the first time Dr. Simpson heard this either. Remember that police wrote in their report that Dr. Simpson denied four things that Barb supposedly said to police that Dr. Simpson either told her to do, or that Barb had talked with her about. Three of those things were never said at all. The fourth accusation was that Barb had said she mentioned on the Tuesday evening phone call (July 26) with Dr. Simpson that Barb had gone through a time of not feeling attached to Natalia. Barb did tell police that. And Dr. Simpson said to police "it was possible that she had a passing discussion with Barbara" concerning that, but that she normally makes a record of that. Since this was not said in the context of a well baby visit, but on the phone, the only record of the phone call was the original phone message slip on which Dr. Simpson simply wrote "Told mother to call for appointment." (Ironically, Barb's total police interview was played in the courtroom, with a transcript provided to the jury, but no questions or points of emphasis were allowed. One could only hope that the jury was alert enough to notice that Barb never said any of the first three things police attributed to her.) *But there's so much information to absorb. My guess is they didn't notice.*

Once the prosecutor got his innuendos into the trial record, he shifted to postpartum depression. You may remember his obsession with PPD in the first trial. Now he questioned Dr. Simpson, a pediatrician, at length on this topic, knowing that the <u>psychiatrist</u> would testify later for the defense that <u>Barb did not have PPD</u>. And then it was back to the question of <u>whether Barb was lying</u> about <u>mentioning</u> to Dr. Simpson that she had <u>gone through a time of feeling detached</u> from Natalia.

Question: Do you routinely ask how parents are feeling about children?

Dr. S: "Yes."

Question: Did you do that same routine for Barbara Schrock?

Dr. S: "Yes."

Question: Did she ever advise you during the <u>course of your treatment</u> of Natalia that she was suffering from PPD? *Barb didn't mention this in Dr. Simpson's office during the course of treatment. It was on the July 26 phone call. Barb's police interview indicates this.*

Dr. S: "No."

Question: That would have been in your notes.....is that fair to say?

Dr. S: "Correct."

Question: And is it in your notes?

Dr. S: "No." *So, obviously, Barb is assumed to be lying. For what reason she would lie about this, no one knows. But that doesn't matter. The doctor has spoken.*

<u>Cross-examination</u> by Mr. Sanford now begins.

Question (Defense): If you thought Natalia was being abused, doesn't state law require you to report that?

Dr. S: "Correct."

Question: But you didn't notice any problems, correct?

Dr. S: "Correct."

Question: Did you see any evidence of abuse, Doctor?

Dr. S: "No."

Question: Without any sort of variable thrown into the situation, if you knew a child's temperature was 93 degrees, you would say "come in immediately," correct?

Dr. S: "Correct."

Question: That's without knowing anything else. But in real life, if you get a call like that, you would start asking questions, wouldn't you?

Dr. S: "Correct."

Question: And in this case, you did ask questions, or your receptionist asked questions, correct?

Dr. S: "Correct."

Question: And you learned she was eating?

Dr. S: "Correct."

Question: Okay. So you had some questions about that, because you told mom to make an appointment the next day, right?

274

Dr. S: "I don't know when. She should have come in the same day, but...."

Question: Well, let me show you the phone message that's dated July 26, 2005. Do you recognize that?

Dr. S: "Yes"

Question: And what does it say?

Dr. S: "Tell mom to make an appointment. And that's my initials. A.M."

Question: Well, is it your initials, or is it "make an appointment in the A.M.? What time did you call her?"

Dr. S: "I don't remember."

Question: Was it 6:00 in the evening? (She told police 6:00 pm, and said that she told Barb to call in the morning.)

Dr. S: "I don't remember." *Rats! What are the odds that her initials would be A.M.? Now they won't believe Barb for sure. And the police report that contains the truth will never see the light of day.*

Question: If you got a call about somebody with a 93 degree temperature and they were eating, would that indicate they were in a coma?

Dr. S: "Not necessarily, no?"

Question: Well, certainly, if they're eating-----if somebody's in a coma, they're not able to eat, correct?

Dr. S: "Correct." (From the prosecution's point of view, however, the temperature is correct and Natalia is in a coma. Natalia couldn't be eating. Dr. Emenim said she would have been in a coma, unconscious, not awake for three to four weeks. And Dr. O said she would not be eating. So all the people (30-40) who say otherwise are prevaricators. But the prosecution never answers this dilemma in their case. They insist Natalia was not able to eat. Or play in bed. Or kick her legs. She was just lying there for weeks.)

Question (Prosecution): Mr. Sanford asked you whether you saw any signs of neglect or abuse to Natalia by Barbara Schrock, right?

Dr. S: "Yes."

Question: Would you consider what had happened to her that caused her to go to the hospital on July 27 to be abuse or neglect? *What does this have to do with Barb's guilt or innocence? It's purely to inflame the jury.*

Dr. S: "Yes."

The witnesses from Brant's extended family, **Donna Schau**, **Michele Schau**, and **Sara Siewert**, added little to their previous testimony. The accusation that Barb called Natalia an a--hole, that she had her tubes tied, and that she didn't cry in their presence at the hospital, were all reiterated once again.

Next on the witness stand was **Gary Mullins**, Brant's stepfather.

Question: How did Natalia look, besides being small?

Gary: "She was never crying or moving or anything. It was just a baby laying there like she was half asleep or whatever. She was never no actions or nothing."

Question: Did you see Barbara interact with Natalia?

Gary: "I seen Barb hold her a couple of times. Yes."

Question: Was there a time that Natalia stayed with you guys?

Gary: "Yes. That was the July 4 weekend. We kept both babies that weekend."

Question: Was she moving when you guys tried to play with her?

Gary: "Very little. Very little. There was not much movement at all (July 4 weekend)."

Question: What was Barb's demeanor at the pool (July 4 party)?

Gary: "She was pretty upset."

Question: What did she say?

Gary: "She was talking about Brant, that she was pretty upset with him because all he wanted to do was come up there and have fun, and not help her with the kids."

Question: Was Natalia crying, was she loud, was she quiet?

Gary: "Not a word, that I can recall."

Question: Well, was Natalia talking then? *She's two months old!*

Gary: "I never heard Natalia talk at all."

Question: She was making any noises that you heard?

Gary: "Not that I heard."

Question: How did Natalia get to your vehicle when you were ready to leave the party?

Gary: "I believe Barb carried her there."

Question: Did you see Barb carry her there?

Gary: "I think so, yes."

Question: Did you see Barb put her into the car?

Gary: "Yes.... She was still pretty upset.... She was still mad at Brant...and Barb asked Natalia, 'Why do you f---ing cry all the time? Your sister never did that."

Question: Who else was around when Barbara said that about Natalia?

Gary: "I think my wife was off to my left."

Question: Where was Brant?

Gary: "I don't think he was around the car at the time we were leaving."

Question: He wasn't with you guys?

Gary: "No."

276

Question: The times you saw Natalia between the time of the party and the ER on July 27, how was she acting?

Gary: "The same way. She wasn't much active at all."

The prosecutor then goes through the demeanor at the hospital questions again.

Question: Did you see Barbara at the hospital (PICU)?

Gary: "At first, yes, until we started going at different times." (Remember, they started visiting in shifts after Char and Gary's police interview on July 29, two days after ER.)

Question: When you say at first...roughly how many days?

Gary: "First week or so."   *A pretty shaky memory.*

Question: What was Barbara's demeanor during the first week or so when you saw her?

Gary: "She was never upset."

Question: Did you ever talk with Barbara during that week or so?

Gary: "Yes."

Question: Did she ever tell you what was wrong with Natalia?

Gary: "No, not at first. She really didn't know."

Question: Was there a time that she did start talking about what was wrong with Natalia?

Gary: "After a couple of weeks...after a week or so she did."

Question: What did she tell you?

Gary: "Well, when they (Barb and Brant) found out that the doctors had told my wife, Charlene, and I..."

Question: Okay. I'm going to stop you. You can't talk about what other people told you except for her."

The prosecutor cuts off Gary here. First, Gary brings up "they" (meaning Barb and Brant). Earlier Dr. Emenim had also said "they (Barb and Brant) asked about all the possibilities including minor traumas?" But the prosecutor doesn't want to hear the word "they." He doesn't want his own prosecution witnesses to be saying that Brant was hearing and asking and saying the same things that Barb was hearing and asking and saying. The other awkward part also arose previously. Doctors were telling Brant's extended family about Natalia's injuries and how she got them. This raises serious questions regarding the HIPAA laws. The prosecutor cuts off Gary, and tries to limit the variables.... Barb, not anybody else (just as he tried to do with the 93 degree temperature...no other variables.) Once again, the selective scrutiny is on Barb.

Gary then starts talking about the various things that Barb supposedly told him about how Natalia could have gotten these injuries.

(According to Gary, she told him this after "a couple of weeks." But they weren't seeing Barb then. They were visiting in shifts after the first two days.) *Never mind the details.* And then the prosecutor moves through a laborious series of questions about everybody's <u>demeanor</u> again, before indicating "no more questions."

<u>Cross-examination</u> by the defense.

<u>Question</u>: So when you say Barb didn't have any outward manifestation of crying or being hysterical, as you describe your step-son as being, <u>you don't know what was going through her mind</u>, do you?

<u>Gary</u>:   "<u>No</u>."

<u>Question</u>: And do you have a degree in psychology or psychiatry that would make your <u>demeanor comment</u> anything more than a hunch?

<u>Gary</u>:   "No, I have no degree."

<u>Question</u>: Now you talked with Officer Kaps in your police interview, right?

<u>Gary</u>:   "Right."

<u>Question</u>: He was investigating potential criminal activity, right?

<u>Gary</u>:   "That's correct."

<u>Question</u>: Now you testified here that Barb said, "Why do you have to f---ing cry all the time...your sister didn't," or words to that effect, right?

<u>Gary</u>:   "That's right."

<u>Question</u>: You never told police that, did you?

<u>Gary</u>:   "<u>I can't remember</u>." (He clearly <u>didn't</u> say anything about this to police.)

<u>Question</u>: Oh, you can't remember.

<u>Gary</u>:   "No. I can't."

<u>Question</u>: Well, would it refresh your recollection if you had a chance to review the tape?

<u>Gary</u>:   "I could have said it."

<u>Question</u>: You could have said it?

<u>Gary</u>:   "I don't remember."   *Should we play the tape, or will the jury fall asleep if we do?*

<u>Question</u>: Were you at the hospital when Natalia was born?

<u>Gary</u>:   "I was in the hospital, yes."

<u>Question</u>: Did you know that Barb had some complications?

<u>Gary</u>:   "No."

<u>Question</u>: You didn't know that? Nobody ever talked to you that?

<u>Gary</u>:   "No."   *What <u>does</u> he remember?*

<u>Question</u>: I'm a little confused. You said earlier that you saw Barb every day for the first week or so, but after that you didn't see her.

278

Gary: "She would go at different times, yes."

Question: Then you said she started telling us stories of what might have happened to Natalia, after that first week or so. But if you weren't seeing each other after the first week or so, how could you have a conversation with her?

Gary: "That was before we split up, started going at different times."

Question: But you said after the first week or so, Barb tried to explain how this could have happened to Natalia. You also said you weren't talking to her at that point. How could you have had that conversation if you weren't talking anymore?

Gary: "Maybe I mixed up on my....maybe one or two days difference there."

Question: Okay. All right. And so when you say that Barb is saying these things, they are in response to questions the doctors are posing, right?

Gary: "No. Barb told us this (reasons Natalia might have injuries) before we talked to the doctors." *He's already said she told them after the doctors talked to them. How could the jury possibly make any sense out of anything Gary had said?*

The next witness is **Charlene Mullins**, mother of Brant.

Question: Now how was Natalia doing when she left the hospital after her birth?

Char: "She was fine."

The prosecutor goes through a series of questions to show that Char has been around a lot of babies and is a capable evaluator of how they are doing. He is trying to show that there was never anything wrong with Natalia until Barb repeatedly hurt her sometime after the July 2, 2005 party. And then he continues:

Question: Other than her size, did you notice anything different about her compared to the other....

Char: "Just that she was awfully little."

Question: And the time from birth to the July 2, 2005 party, did you notice anything unusual about her then?

Char: "Just little." *My, how we forget.*

Char had said the following to the police investigators in her interview three years earlier:

Char: "Right from the beginning I told my husband it seemed like there was something wrong with that baby. I didn't know..."

Sgt K: "Was that just in the last couple of weeks?

279

Char: "No. After she came home in the beginning. I said I hate to even say this, but I was thinking that she was going to be retarded or something.... There was just something. Something just didn't seem right." (So which time is she telling the truth? The time when she talked to police and had nothing to gain by lying. Or at Trial Two when now it's either her son or Barb?) *Sometimes I wonder if Brant's family was coached on what to say, and other times I think maybe they just got together before the trials and decided what needed to be said to "fry her."*

Most of the testimony given at the trials by Brant's family bears little resemblance to what they said to the police.

Question: Did you ever have Natalia overnight up until the July 4 weekend?

Char: "No."

Question: Why not?

Char: "Because my mom was diagnosed with cancer, and I was taking care of her sometimes on weekends."

At Trial One, Char had answered the very same question:

Char: "Well, I was kind of afraid." *But now in Trial Two she's no longer afraid. If she were afraid now, it might indicate something was wrong with Natalia after all.*

But back to Trial Two:

Question: Did you have Natalia on the weekend of the July 2 party?

Char: "Yes."

Question: Why that weekend?

Char: "I wanted to get her and take her to the party." *Did her mother's cancer go away?*

Question: How was Barb acting before you went to get something to eat (at the party)?

Char: "She wasn't doing much. She was just lying by the pool."

Question: When you came back, after you talked to Gary, how was she acting?

Char: "She was really upset."

Question: How did you know?

Char: "Because she had been hollering and screaming about Brant."

Question: What did she holler and scream?

Char: "She was mad because he was playing horseshoes."

Question: What did she say?

Char: "Just cussing."

Question: When you left (the party) how did you leave?
Char: "In our car."
Question: How did Natalia get to your car?
Char: "I carried her." *Gary just said Barb carried her. You need to get your signals straight.*
Question: Did Barb go to the car with you?
Char: "We had to go get her."
Question: Why?
Char: Because we couldn't get the seat snapped into the safety seat in the back."
Question: What was Barb's demeanor when you saw her at the car?
Char: "She was screaming at the baby."
Question: What was she screaming?
Char: "She said, 'Natalia, why do you have to f---ing cry all the time. Why can't you be more like your sister?"

Of course, none of this was said to the police by Char. But this story is fairly similar to what Char said in the first trial. She embellished it some this time by adding "Barb was screaming at the baby," trying to ratchet up the impact it might have on the jury.
Question: Who was around when she said that?
Char: "Me, Gary my husband, Isabella and Natalia, and Barb.

Question: What did Barb do? (Referring to later, when Barb and Char are at Barb's home.)
Char: "We were just sitting there talking, and all of a sudden she just took her (Natalia) and threw her up in the air."
Question: You said she threw her in the air. What do you mean?
Char: "She just threw her up in the air (indicating)."
Question: Then you kind of showed, when you did that, your palms were up?
Char: "Yeah. She just went like that and threw her up in the air (indicating)."
Question: Did she catch her?
Char: "Yes." *That was lucky.*

Let's go back to what Brant said about this to the police three years earlier:
Question: How high would she throw her?
Brant: "She wouldn't throw her that high. She'd probably come out of Barb's hands about that high...underneath the armpits... and then catch her."

Question: She'd release her, and be down by her upper legs or lower legs....and then catch her again?
Brant: "No. I believe she'd catch her underneath the arms."
Question: Her hands would be down by her upper legs, or lower legs?
Brant: "Probably not even that far. Maybe like her waist."
Question: Five to six inches?
Brant: "Yeah. Right."

I trust Brant's description of this more than anyone else's, because he was measuring every day in his work as a finish carpenter. But if you consider an 18-inch child, the distance from armpit to waist is likely even less than Brant's description (probably 3-4 inches at most). And as time goes on, Char is increasingly becoming the queen of verbal histrionics. *Palms up? Come on.*

Question: Did you continue to have Isabella for the weekends (from July 3 to July 27)?
Char: "Yes."
Question: Would Natalia come with Isabella?
Char: "No."
Question: Why not?
Char: "I was taking care of my mom." *Cancer.*

Question: What was Natalia like on Sunday, July 24?
Char: "She was very lethargic." *Like Gary described her the weekend of July 2.*
Question: What do you mean by lethargic?
Char: "She wasn't moving her arms or her legs or anything. And her eyes were kind of going off to the side."
Question: Were Natalia's eyes opened or closed during that visit?
Char: "Her eyes were opened, but they were kind of off to the side."
Question: You thought that was unusual?
Char: "Yes."
Question: Why didn't you talk to Barb then?
Char: "Because Barb gets too mad." *This was not part of the story to police three years ago.*
Question: Do you remember when you called Brant on Monday?
Char: "It was in the evening. And he said Barb and Isabella had gone to Long John Silvers to pick up supper."
Question: And did you suggest to Brant that Natalia needs to be looked at by a doctor?

282

Char: "Yes. That was Monday night (July 25)." (This is when Brant went in to look at Natalia and said she 'looked fine.')

Question: Tuesday, July 26, the day before Natalia went to the ER, did you talk with Barb?

Char: "I think I did." *Wrong!* (No record of this anywhere.)

Question: Did you talk to her about Natalia?

Char: "No."

Question: Did you talk to Brant about Natalia?

Char: "No." (Clearly, as concerned as she claims to have been, she would have asked about Natalia if she had talked to either Brant or Barb the next day. One wonders why she didn't call to check how Natalia was doing?) *Or wasn't she as concerned as she says she was?*

Question: Did you talk with Barbara Wednesday at the hospital about what was wrong with Natalia?

Char: "They just said she wasn't breathing." (Brant and Barb said this.)

Question: Okay. I'm only going to talk about what Barb told you. Did Barb tell you what was wrong with Natalia?

Char: "Yes. That she wasn't breathing." (Now only Barb said this.)

Next Char begins to recite the list of things she says Barb told her could have happened with Natalia. She begins by saying Barb may have done it when throwing Natalia in the air. When asked if Barb said that just to "you guys," or in front of the doctors, Char responds, "in front of the doctors." Strangely, however, no doctor ever reported her saying that to them. And Char goes on about brittle bone disease, Isabella could have done it, and the dog could have done it. Again, no doctor was saying these things. Apparently Barb just shared all of this with her special confidante, Char. But as Dr. Emenim said, "They were asking what could have happened." Both Barb and Brant were asking lots of questions, not telling the doctors what happened. But Char tells it otherwise, since it might implicate Brant to see it any other way.

Question: When the doctors told you (Char) in front of Barbara, that Natalia had brain problems... brain injury... what was Barb's reaction?

Char: "That's when she was talking about brittle bone disease." *In relation to the brain injury?*

Question: Was Brant there as well?

Char: "Yes."

Question: How many times were you there when the doctors came and talked about Natalia's condition?

Char: "I don't remember."

Question: More than once?

283

Char: "See, in the beginning, they took Barb and Brant in the back. But then the one doctor--I can't remember his name--- he was an Afro-American (Dr. Emenim), took my husband and I, and my sister and my brother, and sister-in-law into a room... *Just busting HIPAA laws all over the place....*

Question: Okay. I'm only asking about when Barbara was with you when the doctors talked about Natalia's condition, okay? (This is the third time this issue has come up concerning Dr. Emenim's telling anyone who wanted to listen about Natalia's injuries, and what caused them. And once again the prosecutor stops the comment. It's unclear if he knows the laws, or he simply wants to focus on when Barb was present.)

Question: How many times did you talk with Barbara about Natalia's condition?

Char: "Not much after that."

Question: After the first day, or second day?

Char: "Roughly the second day." (Because after that, they visited in shifts and didn't see each other.) *In spite of what Gary testified.*

Question: Were there any other times?

Char: "Not after the second day."

Mr. Sanford cross-examines Char. Jeff repeats nine different things that Char has just testified that Barb said and did. None of them was intended to be complimentary to Barb. After each of the nine things that Jeff repeats, he asks Char whether she told these things to the police in her interview three years earlier when her memory was still fresh. Seven of the statements Char responds with "I don't remember." All seven of those statements that she couldn't remember if she shared with the police---the record shows she did not share with them. The other two statements, when asked if she made them to the police, Char responded "Yes, I think I did tell police that." In checking each statement with her police interview transcript, the two she thought she told police about---she had. So each time she used "I don't remember," it was an attempt to cover the fact that she had not told police. Each time she thought she did tell police, she did. The bottom line is Char used this technique, and stuck to it rigidly, to avoid the truth. *Did she figure this out own her own, or was she told to use this technique by somebody?* You will recall that Barb often said "I don't remember," but added if it was on the police transcript, then it was true. And while this was an honest approach, the prosecutor took advantage of it and pretended to be quoting things from the police transcript that Barb never said. And sometimes she appeared to agree with what the prosecutor said because she thought he was reading from that transcript.

One other brief exchange highlights <u>Char's frequent tendencies toward hyperbole</u>.

<u>Question</u>: Wasn't her father (Dan) on the internet looking things up?

<u>Char</u>: "Her mom and dad was on the internet <u>the whole time they were at the hospital</u>."

Actually Elaine and I did check on the internet at the hospital the first day or two for ideas of what could be going on. None of this made sense to us, and the police had not used their "techniques" on us to convince us of something other than we had seen with our own eyes. But to say we were on the internet the whole time we were at the hospital is ludicrous. We were at the hospital 13 days while Natalia was there. After the first two days we no longer saw Char and Gary, or any of Brant's family. We were visiting in shifts. But this is part of the mythology that continues to grow to this day in Brant's family concerning Natalia's tragedy and its surrounding circumstances.

CHAPTER SEVENTEEN

On the witness stand now is **Brant Benson.**

    <u>Question</u> (Prosecution): How many vehicles did you have when Isabella was born?

    <u>Brant</u>: "Two."

    <u>Question</u>: Did you continue to have <u>two</u> throughout the course of the relationship?

    <u>Brant</u>: "Yes."

This little interchange between the prosecutor and Brant illustrates one of the problems of getting at the truth. This question is relevant because Brant has testified that Barb was not at NICU every day when Natalia was born. She contended that part of the reason for that was they only had <u>one</u> vehicle, and Brant had used that for work. Now this question is posed, and Brant answers it honestly. *Well, sort of honestly.* They did have two vehicles during this time. Had the question been, "Did you have <u>two vehicles that worked</u>?" the answer should have been "no." In essence, there was only <u>one</u> vehicle available during Natalia's lifetime, until they purchased another one July 12, 2005, two weeks before Natalia was taken to the ER. The jury, however, never knew this. *They just knew that Brant and Barb disagreed about the number of cars they had.*

    <u>Question</u>: After your father passed away, did you have much interaction with Natalia?

    <u>Brant</u>: "No."

    <u>Question</u>: Why not?

    <u>Brant</u>: "I was <u>never</u> home." *The perfect excuse.*

    <u>Question</u>: But when you <u>were</u> home, was Natalia awake or asleep?

    <u>Brant</u>: "Asleep."

    <u>Question</u>: How long were you and Barb at the July 2, 2005 party?

    <u>Brant</u>: "I'd say around three hours." (Donna testified that it was six hours.) *Whatever.*

    <u>Question</u>: Did you see Barbara interact with Natalia that day?

    <u>Brant</u>: "Yeah."

    <u>Question</u>: What did you<u> hear her say</u>?

The prosecutor seems aware that Brant is about to testify <u>that Barb said something to Natalia,</u> so leads with this question. Remember that <u>Brant never once in his four different times of being questioned</u> ever mentioned that Barb had said anything negative to Natalia. <u>Brant is about to change his testimony</u>. And the prosecutor sets him up for it.

>Brant: "<u>I heard her call her, Natalia, a little f---ing bitch.</u>"   *Join the rest of your family.*

>Question: And how did that come about?
>Brant: "<u>She was putting Natalia in the car.</u>"
>Question: Whose car?
>Brant: "<u>My mom and Gary's car.</u>"

The prosecutor apparently knows this severe change of testimony (above) is coming, but has not said anything to the defense about it. This statement from Brant has a <u>major emotional impact on everyone in the courtroom, including the jury.</u> Char and Gary have said something similar before, but their testimony throughout is totally suspect. Brant seems to have been at least partially credible up until this point. But now this. He's talking about the alleged language used to Natalia when Barb was putting her in Char and Gary's car seat. <u>Let's look first</u> at what Brant told police in his <u>August 2, 2005 police interview.</u>

>Brant: "<u>Why wasn't any of this brought to my attention</u> about <u>Barb talking nasty to Natalia?</u>"   (So <u>he clearly didn't know about any nasty talk by Barb</u> towards Natalia three years ago. He was even <u>angry</u> that no one had told him about this alleged nasty talk.)

Now let's look at what Char has testified about this alleged incident, and <u>who was there</u> to witness it.

>Char: "She said, Natalia, <u>why do you have to f---ing cry all the time?</u>"
>Question: <u>Who was around</u> when she said that?
>Char: "<u>Me, Gary, Isabella, Natalia, and Barb</u>."   *Brant? Not around.*

And now Gary's rendition:

>Gary: "And Barb asked Natalia, '<u>Why do you got to f---ing cry all the time</u>'?"
>Question: <u>Where was Brant?</u>
>Gary: "He was there (at the party) somewhere. I don't think he was around the car at the time we were leaving though."
>Question: <u>He wasn't with you guys?</u>
>Gary: "<u>No.</u>"   *Brant? Not around.*

So not only is this a <u>dramatic change of testimony</u> which the prosecutor <u>knew</u> was coming, but also <u>both of Brant's parents</u> say that Brant was <u>nowhere</u>

around when it happened! Brant was not there! No wonder he didn't quite get the line down the way Char and Gary alleged it was said. This also highlights something that I have referred to earlier. I believe that over the three year time period there was so much rehearsing and embellishing of what happened, that even Brant and his family no longer knew what was true. *Anything they say at this point has questionable truthful value.*

Question: Did Barbara talk to you about what she said to Natalia?
Brant: "We didn't really talk about it." (Does this make any sense? He was incensed when hearing from the police about Barb allegedly talking nasty to Natalia. But now that he untruthfully testifies that Barb did say something really nasty, he just says they "didn't really talk about it.") *Whatever it takes to convict.*

But Brant doesn't stop there. (He evidently senses the emotional commotion he has engendered with his last comment.) *Why not try for another? This is heady stuff.*
Question: Did Barb ever tell you about her feelings towards Natalia?
Brant: "Yes. She said she didn't feel a bond with Natalia like she did with Isabella."
Question: "When did she tell you that?"
Brant: "I believe that it was when Natalia was in the NICU."
Question: After your father passed away and before the July 2 party, did Barbara talk about her feelings towards Natalia?
Brant: "Yeah. She said something to the effect that 'can't we just get rid of her?'" *Brant!*
Question: Can't what?
Brant: "Can't we just get rid of her? Can't we put her up for adoption?"

So now Barb wants to get rid of Natalia and put her up for adoption. *My prediction that Brant and his family would ratchet up the negative assertions for this trial seems to have been a huge understatement.* Again, a massive shift in testimony. How does one defend against this type of statement, other than to point out that this is Brant's fifth time of making statements on the record, but the first time he has said this. Either Brant has been told, or he figured out himself that much stronger statements are needed if Barb is to be convicted. *Is there a chance that the jury believes what he is saying? I fear that there is.*

Question: Did you look at Natalia when your mom called Monday evening, July 25, before Barb got home?
Brant: "Yes. She looked fine."

Question: Did you go to work the next day (Tuesday)?

Brant: "Yes."

Question: That night did you interact with Natalia?

Brant: "Yes, I did."

Question: How did Natalia look?

Brant: "She looked fine." *According to doctors, she's supposed to be unconscious.*

Question: Did you look at Natalia that night then?

Brant: "Yes, I sat on the bed and I had her on my lap, and <u>she was kicking her legs</u> and she looked fine."

Brant has made statements on numerous occasions over the past three years that Tuesday evening, July 26, Natalia was "<u>kicking her legs</u>," "<u>squeezing my pinky</u>," "<u>I was playing with her in bed</u>," and "<u>she</u> was moving her arms and legs</u>." This is the <u>supposedly unconscious Natalia</u>, the one who wouldn't have been able to eat, the same child that Barb and Elaine <u>were thought to be lying about</u> concerning her <u>taking her bottle several times</u> earlier in the day. This is Natalia, who had a massive brain problem three to four weeks or more earlier. This is Natalia, whose brain scan was looked at by a doctor at I.U. Medical School very familiar with child abuse and who commented unofficially that <u>without a direct witness or a confession</u>, this case would not even come to trial in Indianapolis. This is Natalia, the infant who was <u>squeezed into the shaken baby theory</u>, even though the theory didn't fit. And this is Natalia, the baby for whom no one in authority took the time or trouble to investigate further the family observations like Brant's above, or the witnessing of seizures throughout her life by numerous family members. How do you simply ignore these various observations of Natalia, and instead plug in the ill-fitting shaken baby theory?

<u>Cross-examination</u> of Brant by Jeff Sanford.

Part of why we hired Jeff Sanford as Barb's attorney was that we thought he <u>could be a bit edgy</u> in the courtroom <u>if he felt someone were playing games</u> with him. So far in the trial I had not seen any of that, although he was a little bit feisty when Char continued to use "I don't remember" multiple times. But now that Brant had made these highly charged statements out of the blue, Jeff was mad. A controlled mad. Barb and I were mad, too. How can you pull a stunt like that when the police and prosecutor hammered so hard against "change of testimony" over the last three years. So Jeff went after Brant's obviously false testimony.

He quoted the comments that Brant had made, and then, one by one, challenged Brant if he had made these same comments in the other statements that he had given. And one by one, Brant said "no," he had not made these statements ever before. (At least he didn't say "I don't remember.") After a lengthy procedure of getting Brant to admit that these were totally new comments, Jeff one more time asked, "You never testified to that (earlier), did you?" Brant responded, "Well, over a three year period you tend to remember some things that happened." (With that, Jeff's clipboard hit the floor. Rather hard. I think it was a non-accidental drop.) "Sure. Your memory gets better as time goes on. I understand." (More than a hint of mockery was present here.) And while it felt good to us that somebody was finally challenging this kind of garbage, I had to wonder if the jury might react against this mini-tirade. But then Jeff moved on.

Question: I'm kind of curious, sir, since you spent little or no time with your daughter as you testified, how would you know about her physical condition?
Brant: "From what Barbara was telling me."
Question: Well, you testified that you observed some of these things and yet then you testified that you weren't around her that much?
Brant: "I did live in the home." (This is an important admission. The impression has always been otherwise. You know, "Brant was never around.") It takes "seconds" to shake a baby.

Question: And when you got to the hospital, as you testified before, both you and Barb started asking questions about what was wrong with Natalia?
Brant: "Yes."
Question: Did Barb respond to what Dr. Okanlami was saying when she talked to the two of you?
Brant: "Yeah. She wanted to know if she could have done...caused the injuries."
Question: She's trying to figure out what happened?
Brant: "Yeah."

Jeff paused to look at some information at his table. I may have suggested something to him. I had police transcripts with me. During the pause, Brant wanted to ask a question.
Brant: "Can I ask the Court a question?"
Court (Judge): Not right now, Mr. Benson.
Barb whispered to me that Brant was looking at me just before he asked that question. He probably wondered why I was at the defense table. Sometimes I did, too. I don't think I was all that helpful.

Question: So as time progressed, and you got further and further away from that time, your memory got better. Is that what you're saying basically?

Brant: "Yeah, that's what I'm saying."

Question: Barb wasn't living with you after September 2005, was she? Didn't you throw her out of the house in September?

Brant: "I believe it was----yeah, what, four months." (Actually four weeks after ER--- in August.)

The next witness for the prosecution is Sgt. **Randy Kaps**, police investigator.

Question: How did Dr. Cory get involved in this case?

Sgt Kaps: "I had contacted a person, her name is Dr. Roberta Hibbard. She is professor at the I.U. School of Medicine specializing in pediatrics. She is an expert on child abuse. So I contacted her to see if she knew anybody who specialized in pediatric x-rays, or had any special training. She suggested I call a few people."

Question: Do you recall when you did that in the course of your investigation?

Sgt Kaps: "It would have been following day one or two. I think it was July 28."

Cross-examination of Sgt. Kaps by Mr. Sanford (Jeff).

Question: How long were you involved in the investigation?

Sgt Kaps: "I was involved July 27, 28, and 29."

Question: And were you the officer that interviewed Charlene and Gary Mullins?

Sgt Kaps: "Yes."

Question: And had you learned at that point that there is a major head, brain injury that Dr. Cockerill had testified to a couple days ago? Did you know the timeline of that yet?

Sgt Kaps: "Yeah. They suggested the older injury, the older brain injury." (Three to four weeks old.) *Did he really know? I don't think so.*
Here's what Sgt. Kaps told Char and Gary about the head injury in their interview referred to above:

> Sgt K: "But the head injuries didn't happen---the head injuries--- were about two days before, at the max." (Either he is not telling them the truth, or he doesn't know yet about the timing of the major brain injury.) *So did he know? Even though he was certainly not averse to being untruthful, I believe, based on all of the references made of "2-48 hours" to the various witnesses, that he did not know. But as he, himself, would say, "Lock them in on a story." Then if they change it, one of the two times they are lying.*

292

Question: And did you ascertain, as of July 29, the amount of people who might have had access to Natalia during that three-four week period?

Sgt Kaps: "Yes. It would have been Barbara, her mother and father, it would have been the Mullins [Char and Gary], Brant, and it would have been whoever was at the party [July 2]." (Then why did he say "from the first day..it was like...BARB." And also in this above interview, "We need to eliminate Brant however we can."? *No mention of the others.*

Question: And would you agree with the doctors on the amount of time it would take to cause those injuries? (Seconds.)

Sgt Kaps: "I'm going to leave that to the medical people to say." *What else can he say?*

Question: Did you tell Char and Gary during their interview that you completely ruled out Brant as a suspect? (on Friday July 29.)

Sgt Kaps: "Yes."

Question: And why was that?

Sgt Kaps: "We weren't getting the red flags with Brant that we were with Barbara?"

Sgt. Kaps then goes into the red flags that caused him to conclude on day one that Barb was guilty, and that Brant should be dismissed as a suspect. He refers to six red flags:

(1) Her demeanor (didn't cry enough);
(2) She said she spoke to Dr. Simpson about PPD. We found out that wasn't true (lies);
(3) Excuses as to what could have happened to Natalia (stories);
(4) Access to Natalia (appreciable time and timing of injuries);
(5) Ongoing pattern of abuse (more than one injury); and
(6) Detachment (PPD), and timing of PPD she gave that corresponded with increase in symptoms (the PPD she didn't have, and the timing they chose.)

Most "red flags" have already been dealt with in this book. But to review these briefly one-by-one:

(1) The demeanor of persons varies drastically in crisis situations. This was testified to by several of the prosecution's own doctors, and the defense psychiatrist.

(2) Dr. Simpson's memory is not something to write home about. But she did say to police two days after the alleged phone conversation Tuesday evening that it was possible that she could have talked about the detachment (PPD) in passing. (Also, Barb may not have referred to it as PPD, since sometimes she used that label, and other times she described the feeling.) *Sgt. K never even mentions the other three statements about Dr. S*

293

they claimed Barb had made. Obviously he knew Barb had __never made__ any of them.

(3) The two pediatricians at PICU both testified that Barb <u>was not giving excuses,</u> but <u>responding</u> with possibilities <u>to their questions</u> about what might have happened to Natalia, and <u>asking</u> if any of those could have been responsible. <u>Brant</u> also did this.

(4) <u>Access</u> relates to the <u>timing</u> of the injuries. As you have seen,and as even the doctors noted, timing of injuries is a very <u>inexact science.</u> The police and prosecutor obviously didn't know that shaking a baby takes <u>just seconds,</u> or they would not have talked about "appreciable time" with Natalia as hours or days. Brant lived at home, too. The other thing missing here is the strong <u>possibility that all of the injuries occurred at one time,</u> three to four weeks earlier. The police were <u>certainly not aware</u> of that the first day.

(5) Here, again, <u>ongoing abuse</u> assumes <u>more than one incident.</u> That certainly was never established conclusively. Dr. Cory said his opinion was more than one injury, but that the other opinion of <u>one injury only</u> was <u>also possible.</u> Dr. Cockerill thought there was <u>likely</u> a second event, but <u>would not conjecture how much or how little force it would</u> have taken, nor whether it would have been <u>accidental</u> or <u>intentional</u> in nature. The <u>police knew none of this trial testimony</u> the first day.

(6) It was <u>never established</u> that Barb had <u>PPD</u>. The psychiatrist said <u>she did not.</u> At times Barb labeled it PPD, but always described it as a detachment from Natalia. (Remember that Sgt. Kaps said, "When you hear the word <u>depression,</u> you automatically think that somebody wants to <u>hurt themselves</u> or ....[others]") Is it any wonder that he considered this a <u>red flag</u>? The police and prosecutor <u>believed her label</u> rather than <u>her description</u> of what she was feeling. *If she had labeled it <u>"whooping cough,"</u> but described it as a soreness in her ankle, would they have believed she had whooping cough?* As for the timing that these feelings occurred, many timings were given. Remembering the beginning and ending of feelings is nearly impossible. So the police simply chose the timing option they liked best.

All of these <u>red flags</u> that Sgt. Kaps talks about <u>on day one</u> may have meant something to him at the time, but almost <u>all</u> should have been <u>non-issues,</u> as even the prosecution doctors considered them. The remaining ones were either erroneous, or questionable assumptions at best. Yet this is how they settled on Barb the very first day.

<u>Question</u> (defense): Your calling Barb's answers to the Doctors' questions "excuses," that was your interpretation, correct?

<u>Sgt Kaps</u>: "<u>That was my interpretation,</u> correct."

Question: That was a very subjective interpretation of what she was trying to do, right?

Sgt Kaps: "That is correct."

Question: You have no way of reading her mind?

Sgt Kaps: "Absolutely not."

Question: When you went to the house, things were fairly neat?

Sgt Kaps: "Oh, absolutely, yes."

Question: Do you recall telling Char and Gary that generally we get confessions. Generally the perpetrator for shaken baby is a male figure, probably in 80 percent of the cases, usually a boyfriend or father. Those are the two top ones. Then the babysitter or caretaker. The mother actually falls in to the lower range as far as Shaken Baby?

Sgt Kaps: "Yes." (Yet, in spite of this, he chose Barb the first day as his suspect.)

Question: And is that based upon your experience in investigating these cases?

Sgt Kaps: "Well, yeah. It's experience plus I did extensive research. These cases are definitely not easy to investigate." *So we pick a suspect and try to lock them into a story.*

Question: Now you asked Barb at different times during her interview if she dropped Natalia, or did she ever fall, or did she get hit, or did the dog hit injure her, or did you have blackouts, or was she in daycare, or had she fallen off the bed?

Sgt Kaps: "Yes."

Question: And what was the purpose of those questions?

Sgt Kaps: "Generally in interviewing possible suspects of shaken baby syndrome we will try and minimize, or throw out accidents and see if somebody will bite on that?"

Question: And Barb didn't bite, did she?

Sgt Kaps: "No, she did not."

Question: She didn't bite on any of that stuff?

Sgt Kaps: That is correct." *She wasn't looking for "excuses."*

Question: And Lt. Richmond interviewed Brant on July 27 and August 6?

Sgt Kaps: "Yes. He interviewed Brant on two separate occasions."

Question: Did either you or Lt. Richmond do any further investigation with Char and Gary Mullins after the July 29 interview?

Sgt Kaps: "No, neither one of us did."

Question: Because on the July 27 you were pretty confident you had your person? (Day one.)

Sgt Kaps: "Yes, I was very confident." *Barb.*

295

The prosecutor now resumes his questioning of Sgt Kaps.

Question: During July 27 – July 29, had you learned who was the primary care giver of Natalia?

Sgt Kaps: "Yes. It was Barbara Schrock." *Apparently the person around Natalia the most is the guilty one. That makes it easy.*

Question: You learned there were two separate injuries to the head and brain?

Sgt Kaps: "Are we talking July 27, or are we talking July 29?"

Question: Let's talk about July 29.

Sgt Kaps: "By then, yes." (Again, why on this same day does he tell Char and Gary "two days max" for the head injuries, if he knew differently?) *Some serious doubt about this recollection.*

Question: Had you learned of the acute retinal hemorrhages in her eyes? (Dr. O's testimony has just established that the ophthalmologist did not call these retinal hemorrhages "acute" on his report. But the prosecutor needs at least some injury to be recent, so he uses the adjective "acute" to describe the retinal hemorrhages, further distorting the record. *In fact, such distortions may be the reason Barb is the defendant in this trial.*

Sgt Kaps: "Yes." *Somehow, Sgt Kaps thinks they are acute also. Did neither of these guys read the ophthalmology report? Or do they just know the "theory?"*

Next the prosecutor lists all of Natalia's injuries separately and asks Sgt Kaps if he was aware of these, too. Sgt Kaps replies, "yes."

Question: Why had you ruled Brant out to Char and Gary?

Sgt Kaps: "Because of the ongoing pattern of abuse. Not only by my partner talking with Brant, by talking with relatives, by talking with Barbara herself-----Brant was never home." *So how could Brant have had time to do this? He was never home. Except all of the times that he was home. It takes "seconds." And was it really ongoing abuse?*

Question: Now you gave percentages of who generally commits shaken baby. Do you recall the question?

Sgt Kaps: "It wasn't --- I didn't give you out any percentages. I listed the persons responsible in order." *Really?* (Sgt Kaps: "Generally the perpetrator of shaken baby is a male figure, probably in 80 percent of the cases.") *He agreed that this was his quote just five minutes ago. He would never pass his own "lock them in to a story" scrutiny for lying.*

Question: How many cases have you investigated concerning shaken baby syndrome?

Sgt. Kaps: "It's over five." *Impressive!*

296

Question: Do you know whether she was clinically diagnosed at the time with PPD?

Sgt Kaps: "Not to my knowledge, no."

Question: Did that make any difference to you in making your determination?

Sgt Kaps: "No." *Why would facts change what I think?*

Question: Why not?

Sgt Kaps: "Well, she admitted she was having the postpartum depression." *Apparently this man believes you admit to illnesses, rather than being diagnosed with them.*

Question: Why wasn't Brant Benson's interview at the same time as Barb's?

Sgt Kaps: "We needed someone to do something with their German Shepherd so we could get our evidence guy [into the house] without getting hurt. So Brant was taken by Lt. Reihl over to the house so he could secure their dog and then he was brought back to our office at which point he was interviewed." *Sure, sure. Blame it on the dog. Let on like he's dangerous. No..... wait. This isn't Barb talking. This is Sgt Kaps.*

Question (defense): So you could have easily interviewed Brant Benson first and had Barb go down to take care of the German Shepherd, right?

Sgt Kaps: "Yes." *But we knew, even before any interviews, who we needed to interview first.*

At this point, the prosecution rested its case.

CHAPTER EIGHTEEN

There was a break for lunch just before Sgt. Kaps had testified for the prosecution. Following Sgt. Kaps the prosecution rested its case. But during the lunch break, Elaine, Barb, Jeff and I went to a little restaurant to eat. As we were eating, Jeff let us know that he did not feel we needed to have <u>any</u> defense witnesses take the stand. We were planning to have Dr. Rutt, Elaine, the Westview Corporation School Nurse Leader, Barb, and possibly me as witnesses. Jeff felt quite certain, however, that the prosecution had not proved their case. While without our own doctors we could only tangentially challenge the basic "crime" that was diagnosed by the doctors for the prosecution, the question of <u>who</u> then hurt Natalia was the only real question up for debate in this trial.

As long as there was a reasonable possibility that Brant, or anyone else besides Barb, could have done this, the jury couldn't convict. <u>And Jeff was clear that Brant had not been ruled out.</u> The prosecution would have to show that Barb is the <u>only</u> person who could have harmed Natalia. The injury timings from the doctors, rather than firm, were more like jello. There could have reasonably been only <u>one injury time</u>. And Brant's "<u>not me</u>" <u>defense</u> of "I cried," "I was never home," "I was totally stunned," and "The child was in the care of her mother," certainly didn't eliminate him. He lived at home every day, slept at home every day, ate at home every day, and was around the kids every day. Barb was outside of the house numerous times for fifteen to twenty minutes on a daily basis, some days for an hour or more, while Brant was home. It takes just "seconds" to shake a baby. And Brant was highly stressed from working long hours. Brant was <u>not ruled out</u> beyond a reasonable doubt, and Barb was <u>not ruled in</u> beyond a reasonable doubt. So Jeff leaned toward not putting anybody on the stand. Barb, however, went with her inner feelings. As in the earlier trial, she felt she could never face her girls if she dodged the witness stand. Elaine and I felt that if Barb were going to testify, we should at least probably put Dr. Rutt on the stand to rule out PPD for the jury. And perhaps the Westview Lead School Nurse to talk about thermometers, temperatures, and her investigation of Elaine's school records regarding temperatures over the past two years. **Barb** took the stand after Sgt Kaps was finished.

<u>Question</u> (defense): Where are you working now?
<u>Barb</u>: "I work at Goshen Hospital."
<u>Question</u>: What do you do there?
<u>Barb</u>: "I work in housekeeping."

Question: Are you going to school?
Barb: "I am going to EMT school."
Question: How long have you been going to school?
Barb: "I did my medical terminology. I finished that. And now I'm four months into my EMT school."

Jeff then leads her through the history of this case.

Question: What did you think of Dr. Simpson?
Barb: "I liked her a lot."
Question: Did you trust her?
Barb: "Yes, I did."
Question: Did you trust her opinions in regards to health matters relating to both children?
Barb: "Absolutely."
Question: Were you ever diagnosed with postpartum depression?
Barb: "No."
Question: How did that particular subject come up?
Barb: "I had watched Brooke Shields on television...this was years ago...talking about her bout with PPD and kind of how she felt."
Question: When you talked to your mom about this, what did you say?
Barb: "I just told her I felt a little separated from Natalia. There were times when I would just feel like feeding her, bathing her, kind of putting her back down in her bassinet."
Question: Was Natalia responding differently than Isabella did?
Barb: "Yeah. The doctors at Memorial kind of told me it was important for her to get rest, quiet, not be around a whole lot of people."

Question: How long do you think you slept that night (Tuesday, July 26, 2005)?
Barb: "Oh, all together, maybe an hour."

Question: Why did you get upset at the July 2 party?
Barb: "Because he (Brant) was goofing off and we had two children."
Question: Had you guys had a discussion about watching kids on your way up there?
Barb: "Yeah. We had several discussions about parenting."
Question: Was there some sort of agreement that you came to about watching the kids?

Barb: "I just said to him, 'Brant, you know you just can't screw off all day long while we're there. We have two children there. These are <u>our</u> children.'"

Question: Did you call Natalia an a--hole at the party?
Barb: "No."
Question: Did you use that term?
Barb: "Yes."
Question: In reference to whom?
Barb: "Brant."
Question: Why was that?
Barb: "Because he was."
Question: Did you ever call Natalia a f---ing bitch?
Barb: "No."
Question: Did you ever tell Brant, "Let's just get rid of her. Let's put her up for adoption?"
Barb: "No."
Question: Now you heard Char testify that you "just threw Natalia in the air." Did that happen?
Barb: "No."
Question: Would you ever lift her up?
Barb: "Yeah. I would do this kind of thing. Like, you know, <u>she didn't leave my hands</u>."

This above action had become a major part in the prosecution's "fact" arsenal. Brant and Barb were in close agreement about the description of the two or three incidents of this that we know were observed. Brant said Barb's hands moved from Natalia's armpits to her waist. His judgment was 5-6 inches. Realistically is must have been even less than that, given Natalia's size (18 inches overall). But the question is this; <u>Is Natalia leaving Barb's hands if her hands slide from Natalia's armpits to her waist?</u> Barb had said to the police three years earlier during her interview, "it's not like she's leaving my hands." But once Char and Gary got into the story, Natalia was soaring in the air like a bird. And later the prosecutor in his closing statement was looking to spot what he thought was an inconsistency in Barb's story anywhere he could. His obsessive concern with this action appears to be threefold. One, it made good media fodder. Two, it made Barb <u>look totally irresponsible</u> with callous disregard for Natalia. (Why would you throw a young baby way up into the air?) *And tell the police that your doctor told you to do this?* And three, Barb's response to the police question "Was it a foot?" for how far Natalia left her hands was, "I'm not good at that (distances)." (So that meant to the prosecutor <u>she was now lying</u> because if Natalia didn't leave her hands, why did she answer what she did? He neglected to cite her other earlier response in the same police interview of "it's not like she left my hands.") *Somehow this was a major inconsistency for _him_.*

Question: What did you and Brant decide to do after Char's call Monday evening, July 25?

Barb: "I said that my mom was going to come over the next day, that I would have her kind of take a look at her and see what she thought, and then we would call the doctor and kind of give the doctor an idea of what we were talking about so we could be a little more detailed with the doctor about it."

Question: Why was it important for your mother to take a look at her?

Barb: "She is a nurse, and I thought maybe she would have an idea, a better way for me to describe to the doctor some of the symptoms that we were seeing."

Question: Tuesday night, after she was not eating, how did you keep an eye on her?

Barb: "Well, Brant was back in the bedroom then. He had played with her a little bit. I was basically up all night.

Question: In your bedroom?

Barb: "Yeah, in my bedroom."

Question: And the bassinet was right next to you?

Barb: "Right next to us."

Question: What did you do as you sat in the bedroom?

Barb: "I was reading a book that my mom had brought over (family medical book)."

Question: What was your purpose in reading the book?

Barb: "I wanted to look at what symptoms she was having and look them up in the book and see if I could figure anything out." (The prosecutor says she was looking for excuses.)

Question: Did you figure anything out?

Barb: "Not really."

Question: "Did you ask Brant to read the book?

Barb: "Yeah. I had marked a few pages in there that I wanted him to look at."

Question: Describe to the jury what that ambulance ride was like, what you were seeing, what are you looking at?

Barb: "It was awful. I was seeing my little girl, and I will never forget it, in her pink dress, an a big cart shaking around while they had oxygen on her. It was terrible."

Question: Was it loud?

302

Barb: "It was extremely loud. The sirens were loud. They had to honk the horn. Naturally on #31 [Route] there was a lot of traffic and I just remember her kind of being jostled around in there because she was little. And that's how it is on those beds. You can only strap them down so much, obviously. An infant you're not going to strap down completely."

Question: Were you holding her hand, or touching her?

Barb: "I was playing with her feet, touching her feet because they were concentrating--- they gave her oxygen."

Question: You testified earlier that when she came back after the July 4 weekend she looked a little different. Why didn't you do anything then?

Barb: "Do anything?"

Question: Weren't you concerned about that then?

Barb: "I was concerned about it, but not---it wasn't alarming to me. I mean she just looked different. She was acting different. And again, it's always---remember she is a preemie, she is not going to look like other children, don't expect the same things from her that you did from your other child--- so we would kind of recognize it as that on occasion."

Question: There's been much made of the fact that you didn't get upset, or at least that's how it's been characterized. Would you care to talk about that?

Barb: "Well, yeah. I was terribly upset. I mean---I guess I'm not really clear on what people mean when they look at me and say I'm not upset. Nobody knows me, nobody knows how I am. I cried every night in that room wondering what was happening, what was going to happen with my child. That's my general personality."

Mr. Cotter asks the judge if he may to go to the restroom. The judge declares a brief recess. When they come back, the judge has made a decision. "We're going to call it a day now." I feel sorry for Barb. She has to come back tomorrow knowing that Mr. Cotter will be coming at her full blast with anything he can conjure up. And he has a whole night to prepare, instead of needing to do it immediately. Things do seem to be looking good for us, though. Jeff feels we're in a good place, too.

At the beginning of this trial week I went to College Mennonite Church to borrow an old overhead projector to show the injury timing chart that I had put together several months earlier. We tried it out at home, and it seemed to work all right. Not high tech, but functional. So it, along with all of the transcripts, notes, medical reports, etc. was put in our minivan Friday morning to take with us on the one hour trip to the South Bend Courthouse. Elaine again led a devotional time on the way, as we recognized obliquely that it was possible Barb may not be returning with us that evening. That was a sad and sobering thought. When we got to the courthouse, we unloaded the overhead projector and other materials near the front steps where my sister and husband were waiting for us. I parked in the parking garage and walked back to the courthouse. Then we dragged this projector up the steps, through the doors, and through security. Since we were early, I was able to put the projector near the table where Barb, Jeff, and I sat inside the courtroom. Whew. We had technology available. But just in case a bulb blew, or the projector for some reason wouldn't function, I had made about 20 color copies of the injury timing chart that could be handed to jurors.

As we stood and the Judge entered, we found out that **Dr. Rutt,** the psychiatrist, would be on the stand first before Barb was cross-examined by Mr. Cotter. Most of Dr. Rutt's testimony was similar to his Trial One testimony.

Question (defense): What were some of the common denominators in the treatment of people who had been convicted of child abuse?

Dr. Rutt: "Frequently they have been raised in abusive homes, frequently they were very isolated folks, frequently they had unrealistic expectations of children, frequently maybe there was poverty or alcoholism, or stress and abuse between the parents."

Question: Did Barb have those traits?

Dr. Rutt: "Barb did not have the traits of abuse as a child. She had perhaps some financial stress, but not significant poverty, and there was not abuse going on between her and Brant."

Question: As you viewed the tape of Barb's police interview, what are your thoughts on her emotional reactions.

Dr. Rutt: "It's difficult at times to know whether people are---what it means when they react. People react to stress in different ways."

Question: There isn't a standard way that somebody would react in a given situation, correct?

Dr. Rutt: "That is correct. There tends to be a range of reaction. Some are stoic, and some are very dramatic."

At this point Mr. Cotter objects. The judge calls the two attorneys forward, and they talk. Mr. Cotter is concerned about the psychiatrist commenting on demeanor, and goes on at length about his concern. The summary of his concern is encapsulated in the single comment that follows:

> Mr. Cotter: "I think it's the province of the jury to determine whether her demeanor is appropriate for one matter or another." *Facts about demeanor only mess that up.*

Mr. Cotter has just asked Sgt. Kaps about Barb's demeanor, and prior to that has asked multiple times every one other than the security people out front for their thoughts on Barb's demeanor. But now he objects to the psychiatrist, who has <u>watched her entire police interview twice</u>, giving his view of her demeanor. Later Mr. Cotter objects to Dr. Rutt, who has had seven sessions with Barb, giving a description of Barb's personality. *Go figure.*

<u>Cross-examination</u> of Dr. Rutt by the prosecutor.

Question: You noted a reaction (from Barb) when Sgt. Kaps (during Barb's police interview) mentioned Natalia had broken legs, correct? (Barb had no previous knowledge of the broken legs, so <u>reacted with feeling</u> when they were mentioned for the first time.)

Dr. Rutt: "That's correct."

Question: You didn't note much of a reaction when Sgt Kaps talked to her about this child was severely ill, did you? (The prosecutor here either forgets, or is obfuscating the fact that Barb had already heard about all of these other injuries from the doctors previously---except the broken legs--- and is therefore not surprised when they are mentioned.) *Or is she supposed to grimace each and every time these injuries are mentioned?*

Dr. Rutt: "I think the reference I made was a comment about possible brain damage. I don't think she reacted intensely at that point."

Question: Did you note at any time whether after Sgt. Kaps mentioned this child has severe brain damage, or broken legs, that Barbara noted a concern or an interest in, oh, my gosh, what is wrong with my baby?

Dr. Rutt: "She would periodically, as I recall, be asking herself how could this have happened, that kind of question."

Question: And she (Barb) is a fairly intelligent person, would you say?

Dr. Rutt: "Yes."

Question: She told you that Natalia <u>cried</u>?

        Mr. Sanford: "Judge, can I approach?"

        The Court: "Yeah. Come on up."

        Mr. Sanford: "This goes beyond the <u>jury</u> question." (In response to one of the juror's questions, Dr. Rutt said that Barb told him Natalia <u>cried</u> in relation to something.)

        Mr. Cotter: "She told you <u>there was times when the baby cried</u>. That is a pretty straight forward question. The reason, judge, so you know, the reason why is during the interview (with police) <u>Ms. Schrock on a number of occasions</u> said the baby <u>never cried</u>. So [now] she is saying <u>the baby did cry</u>." *Stop it! Get off this kick. You've just listened to the whole police interview in the courtroom, and had printed* *transcripts made for each juror. Listen. Read. It's not there. It was a figment of Sgt Kaps' imagination and passed on to Char and Gary first, and then to the you. There are references throughout the interview that indicate <u>Natalia cried</u>. And still you drum this up as another one of your "facts."*

Question: Doctor, in reference to one of your questions, did you tell us that Barbara told you there were <u>times when Natalia would cry</u>?

Dr. Rutt: "Yes, I think she would describe it as sort of like <u>she cried less</u> than Isabella."

Question: Sure.

Dr. Rutt: "She would cry, but <u>her cry was weaker and less frequent</u>, and not quite like Isabella's."

Next on the stand for <u>cross-examination</u> was **Barbara Schrock**, the defendant.

Question: And there were times when Natalia was just with Brant, correct?

Barb: "That is correct."

Question: But you were the primary caregiver?

Barb: "Yes."

Question: When Natalia left the NICU, did the doctors tell you she had any medical problems?

Barb: "They had taken a chest x-ray and just said------no, you're right. They did not say she had any medical issues."

The prosecutor asks a series of questions related to Natalia's doctor checkups, which yielded no indication of any serious medical problems. But, just as doctors testified that a pediatrician <u>would not have necessarily been able to detect any outward signs of abuse</u>, the <u>same holds true for detection of any outward signs of non-abuse physical conditions</u> which might have been present in Natalia at that point. (It wouldn't have been detected either.) It was indicated earlier that <u>any brain condition that affected Natalia's cerebrum</u> (the part shown to be affected on the brain scan) <u>would not</u> have changed her actions or activities at her age. And any bone sliver "fractures" likewise <u>would not have been visible</u>. So the whole line of questioning seemed rather futile, except for playing to the jury. Neither Doctor Simpson, nor any family member, noticed a <u>serious</u> problem.

Then the prosecutor shifts to the call to Dr. Simpson's office that Barb made on Tuesday, July 26, 2005.

Question: The first call (at 1:00 pm) you left a message?

Barb: "Yes. With Lynn the receptionist."

Question: That's when you told the receptionist about the low temperature of 93 degrees, right?

Barb: "Yes. I think what I said was she has a 93 degree temperature, but she is eating."

Question: You also said the way she was acting. It <u>wasn't lethargic,</u> but she didn't seem interested in following anything?

Barb: "Correct."

Question: When Dr. Simpson called you back sometime later, did you convey that information to her?

Barb: "Yes."

Question: What else did you tell the doctor?

Barb: "Dr. Simpson asked me how I was doing."

Question: That's right. Because <u>you told Dr. Simpson that you didn't know if the way she was physically was a reaction to your feeling of being detached from her</u> (Natalia)?

Barb: "<u>That's correct.</u>" (Her brief conversation with Dr. Simpson about the detachment that Barb sometimes labeled as PPD. Dr. Simpson could not remember this.)

Question: After the 9:30 feeding (Tuesday evening) where she didn't feed, that's when you started reading it pretty diligently (the medical book)?

Barb: "<u>I looked through it, yeah.</u> I don't know if <u>diligently</u> is the right word to use. I was looking at things."

Question: You were looking for symptoms?

Barb: "Correct."

Question: <u>Lethargy</u> was one of them, right? (The relevance of this is minimal, but the prosecutor wants to get this into the record since he plans to use "lethargy" in his closing argument.)

Barb: "If I said that, it must be true." (Here again, the prosecutor has Barb assuming that he is reading her police interview. He has just a few minutes earlier said that she told Dr. Simpson Natalia was <u>not lethargic,</u> but <u>didn't seem interested in following.</u> Later that night Natalia may have gotten less active (lethargic), but both Brant and Barb testified that they played in bed with Natalia Tuesday evening.)

Question: So what you told Sgt. Kaps, if that's what you told him, must have been true?

Barb: "Absolutely. <u>If I told him that, that must have been what I said at the time.</u>"

Question: You are having a hard time?

Barb: "Sorry. It's been three years. I apologize."

Question: I think you had told Sgt. Kaps that after the July 2 party, you started noticing Natalia's eyes getting worse, correct?

Barb: "After the July 4 weekend I remember saying that observing her and thinking that she looked different."

Question: Part of that was her eyes?

Barb: "Correct." (Brant told police he noticed this, too. He indicated that the eye problem would come and go.)

Question: At some point then she started throwing up instead of just spitting up, correct?

Barb: "Correct."

Question: Was it like projectile vomiting?

Barb: "I think a couple of times from what I seen. It was my first time seeing that in a baby. I'm assuming that's what they would refer to it as." (Remember in Brant's police interview that he said: "Barb didn't even know the word. I said 'projectile,' and she said 'she's not shooting it across the room---but it's not just dribbling out either.'" Barb referred to spitting up/vomiting four different times in her police interview, and never once called it projectile vomiting. But the prosecutor is setting up to his closing argument again.)

Now the prosecutor continues to try to develop his closing argument by going over the various times that different individuals had Natalia in their care. He attempts to rule them out, and Barb in. He works his way through each one, and finally comes to Brant.

Question: Brant. There was one or two times where Brant was alone for any appreciable time with her, is that fair to say? (The prosecutor is back with his "appreciable time" concept, whatever that means, since doctor testimony reveals it takes "seconds" to shake a baby.)

Barb: "I want to clarify something with that. Brant lived in my home. We lived together. He was with his daughter every day."

Question: That's not my question though.

Barb: "Okay."

Question: My question to you is there was only one or two times when Brant was alone for any appreciable time?

Barb: "What does that mean? Is that like 20 minutes, 30 minutes, 15 minutes, five minutes?"

Question: Let's say an hour. *How does an hour have any relevance to anything?*

Barb: "There were times I was downstairs doing laundry for a certain amount of time, or outside mowing for a certain amount of time."

Question: Let's say two hours. *Whatever it takes. I need there to be only two times.*

Barb: "I'm sorry. I don't know how to answer that without sounding like I'm trying to be smart. To tell you my every day schedule--- there were times I was outside for an hour or more and Brant was inside the house. I mean I ran to the store on occasion. And so I don't really know what that means when you ask me that."

Now here we get into how this prosecutor thinks and plots and works to set his traps.

Question: Do you remember giving a sworn statement last year? (He's not supposed to refer to the fact that their was another trial that resulted in a hung jury. So he asks the question in a rather open ended, unclear way. Last year?)

Barb: "I don't remember when I did, but I must have." *If you say so.*

Question: Do you remember giving a sworn statement?

Barb: "Yes."

Question: In that sworn statement, do you remember me asking;

Question: "How many times was Brant alone with Natalia when you were not there?"

Answer: "I walked out of the house all the time. There were lots of....." (cut off.)

Question: "When you were gone for any appreciable amount of time?"

Answer: "Once, maybe twice." Do you remember that? *Truth is not the object here. Trapping you is. "Lock them in to their story." You didn't ask what appreciable time meant the last time. Why would you ask this time? Okay--- well, maybe you did---- so I cut you off. But the point is, you said "once, maybe twice." Don't try to change it now.*

Barb: "'There were lots of'.... that sentence wasn't finished. What was my finish to the sentence with that? There were lots of times that I was gone and Brant was there, or what? I'm sorry. I'm not trying----it confuses me when you guys read those things sometimes. It sounded to me like I didn't finish my sentence." *You didn't. He cut you off. Confusion is the name of his game.*

Mr. Cotter continues:

Question: Did anybody else from July 3 until July 27 have Natalia for any appreciable amount of time when you were not around? *Again, what is appreciable time? He keeps using it.*

Barb: "Other than?"

Question: Other than the ones we talked about?

Barb: "No."

Question: Every time you saw Natalia after those individuals had Natalia--- Gary and Char, your parents, Brant, including the <u>inappreciable amount</u> of time when you were outside or down in the basement--- did you notice any differences in Natalia? *Now there's a question to try to answer after three years, particularly when no one saw any major changes in her problems at any one time except right after the July 2 party.*

<u>Barb</u>: "I couldn't tell you specifics on each occasion that each person would have had her if I noticed something directly after she was with them."

The prosecutor shifts again to an extensive line of questioning that again attempts to read Brant out of the story. He worked lots, the kids were always sleeping when he got home, he would <u>never</u> hurt Natalia. Then he runs through a series of questions intended to show that Barb is <u>upset</u> all the time; with Brant, with Char, and most certainly with Natalia. He shifts yet again and explores in minute detail the testimony about "throwing" Natalia in the air.

Question: Did you throw her up in the air?

<u>Barb</u>: "<u>She didn't leave my hands</u>."

Question: She didn't leave your hands? Do you recall giving a sworn statement? (Mr. Cotter <u>reading</u> from Trial One transcript):

> Question: "Now when you talked about throwing Natalia in the air, how far would she leave your hands?"
>
> Answer: "From her to here (witness indicating.) I mean the length I can reach my arms up. So it was like that."
>
> Question: "Show me like this. It's about a foot?
>
> Answer: "<u>I'm not good at that stuff</u>. I couldn't tell you."
>
> Question: "How often would you do that?"
>
> Answer: "Oh, I did it a couple of times."
>
> Question: "My couple and your couple?"
>
> Answer: "Two."
>
> Question: "People voiced concerns to you about that, correct?"
>
> Answer: "Yes."
>
> Question: "And you said, 'Oh, I'm just checking her reflexes, correct?"
>
> Answer: "Correct."
>
> Question: "<u>Did the doctors tell you to do that?</u>"
>
> Answer: "<u>No</u>." (Remember that the police and prosecutor <u>have told the world</u> that Barb said Dr. Simpson told her to throw Natalia in the air, and she <u>clearly did not</u>. The tape of that interview has just been played for the jury, and Barb said no such thing.) <u>Mr. Cotter suddenly stops his reading</u>. But

why? Here's what comes up next in the Trial One transcript that he doesn't want to read aloud at this trial:

> Question: "Did you tell Officer Kaps that the doctor told you to do that (throw Natalia in the air)?"
>
> Answer: "I don't recall telling him that."
>
> Question: "If you told Officer Kaps, would that have been accurate then?"
>
> Answer: "I guess if I told Officer Kaps that, then it must have been accurate." (Here again, Barb trusted the prosecutor and what he seemed to have in front of him. Except it wasn't in front of him. He was just pretending for the jury in Trial One. And he used this same technique multiple times in this current trial. But now this jury has just listened to the tape of Barb's interview, with a full transcript in hand. One would assume by now they know Barb did not say any such thing. This is the nastiest of tricks, intended only to entrap, certainly not to get at the truth. And unethical to the core. The prosecutor knows full well that she did not tell Sgt. Kaps that. Yet a gigantic issue had been made of the "fact" that she has said this. So now Mr. Cotter must cover up deviousness in Trial One by abruptly halting his reading.) *Whew! I almost read too far.*

Apparently, Mr. Cotter was concerned about this above trickery in Trial One might have been exposed, so he declined to read that part. The jury might have noticed. *Hopefully, though not for certain.* But he continues on now in a fairly similar manner.

Question: So it is your memory today that Natalia never left your hands, is that correct, when you threw her in the air?

Barb: "I would do this (indicating)."

Question: Not lift her in the air?

Barb: "Not lift her in the air. I would be like this. I would go like this, but I don't recall her leaving my hands."

Question: Her body never left your fingers, that's your memory today?

Barb: "That's my memory today."

Question: Do you recall talking about throwing her up in the air to Sgt. Kaps when he interviewed you on July 27?

Barb: "I remember him asking me some questions about that."

Question: You don't recall telling Sgt. Kaps that you threw her in the air?

Barb: "I don't recall the specifics. <u>If you said that I said that</u>, then I must have said that. I apologize. Again, it's been three years."

Now why didn't Mr. Cotter just read what Barb said to Sgt. Kaps in that interview. The videotape was just viewed by the jury. The transcript of the tape was handed to the jury. Hopefully they will read through this during deliberations and see just what the prosecutor is doing here. But since you readers don't have a transcript of her comments to Sgt. Kaps--- here they are:

> Barb: "It doesn't hurt her. <u>It's not like I'm throwing her up in the air</u>....I'm just kinda doing like that (shows Sgt. Kaps).

And you will recall Brant talking to Lt. Richmond about this same incident described Barb holding Natalia under the armpits and Natalia went up until Barb's hands were at her waist. <u>Is she leaving Barb's hands if her hands are sliding from her armpits to her waist</u>? *How many angels can sit on the head of a pin? Is the prosecutor this desperate to find a flaw in her testimony?* The prosecutor mercifully moves on to other territory. But he will bring this up again in the closing argument.

Question: My question, ma'am, I think was, did you believe at the time that the 91 degree temperature was <u>dangerous</u>?
Barb: "<u>I just knew it wasn't normal</u>."
Question: Did you know it was <u>dangerous</u>?
Barb: "<u>No</u>. I just knew it was abnormal."
Question: And I take it 93 degrees would also be abnormal, but you didn't know it was dangerous?
Barb: "I called Dr. Simpson and asked her, and I assumed in her voice, or she would have told me to take her to the hospital if it was serious. That's what I based my feeling on was what Dr. Simpson said."
Question: So I take it that the 93 degree temperature, you didn't think it was dangerous, you didn't know?
Barb: "I didn't know."

Now the prosecutor starts a line of questioning that is designed to have Barb <u>explicitly time</u> the feeling of detachment she had with Natalia. For the prosecutor, in a case like this with no hard evidence, he wants <u>exact timings</u> so he can make <u>logical</u> conclusions. That's why he is frustrated with doctors who tell him that the <u>timing of injuries</u> is an "inexact science, at best." He <u>needs</u> black and white. And when the testimony regarding the timing of Barb's detachment with Natalia varies from <u>at birth to a week before ER</u>, it's not the black and white answer that he needs. When the family testifies that now that they know what seizures look like, they believe Natalia has been having seizures ever since she came home from the NICU, it doesn't "work" in his timetable. Again, it's not black and white. It <u>detracts</u> from shaken baby theory. And when Dr. Cockerill is hesitant about the possible second injury to Natalia's brain, the force required to cause it, and whether it was intentional or accidental, Mr. Cotter starts talking <u>even more forcefully and definitively</u> about those factors. All of this appears to be an attempt to make up for the black and white evidence that he lacks. *Everything is gray!*

<u>Jeff</u> questions Barb once again.

<u>Question</u>: Would it be fair to say that when you thought there was a health problem with Natalia, that you would contact the doctor?

<u>Barb</u>: "Yes."

<u>Question</u>: And did anybody from your pediatrician's office instruct you to take Natalia to the doctor?

<u>Barb</u>: "No."

<u>Question</u>: Did you tell your doctor of your daughter's condition?

<u>Barb</u>: "Yes."

<u>Question</u>: Did she tell you to go to the ER?

<u>Barb</u>: "No."

<u>Question</u>: Or to bring her in right away?

<u>Barb</u>: "No."

<u>Question</u>: And you had a relationship with Dr. Simpson for as long as Isabella had been a baby, correct?

<u>Barb</u>: "Correct."

<u>Question</u>: And you trusted her opinion, correct?

<u>Barb</u>: "I did."

Now the <u>prosecutor</u> returns, but is near the end of his questioning. <u>He becomes quite confused and confusing with his dates and times.</u> Of course that makes answering his questions just that much more difficult.

<u>Question</u>: Well, I guess I'm a little confused about your definition of lethargy because is it fair to say when you came home on July 26, she was <u>lethargic</u>, or <u>not lethargic</u>? *The prosecutor seems to love these terms like <u>appreciable time</u>, and <u>lethargy</u>, which have wide ranging meanings and characteristics to most people. But he treats these concepts as if they are crystal clear (black and white) and universally accepted, rather than terms best measured on a <u>continuum</u>.*

<u>Barb</u>: "On July 26?"

<u>Question</u>: After you went out to breakfast and Plato's Closet?

<u>Barb</u>: "She wasn't acting normally."

<u>Question</u>: Was she <u>lethargic</u> based on your definition? *Don't we all have a standing definition for "lethargic"?*

<u>Barb</u>: "<u>I guess</u>."

313

Question: What did you mean when you testified yesterday then when you said you played with her after you came home?

Barb: "Exactly that, that I played with her." *Just like Brant did. Why not ask him what he meant?*

Question: What did you do when you played with her?

Barb: "I sat there on the bed with her and played with her. I don't know how you play with a three month old. I talked to her, I looked at her. I actually got one of the little toy things out that has dangling things on it that babies can use. That's what I did with her."

Question: By then though, you already talked with Char, right? (Here's where the prosecutor accidentally or purposefully begins to fade in and out. They have been talking about Tuesday evening, July 26. Although there was some confusion three years later, Barb never talked with Char from Sunday, July 24 until Natalia was in PICU, July 27.)

Barb: "I guess. I don't remember talking to Char that day." (Barb is too quick to please, by saying "I guess." But at least she follows it up correctly. There was no conversation with Char on this day.)

Question: I meant on July 25, when Char was with Natalia and said, hey, something is wrong with Natalia. (Now it gets really confusing. Char was with Natalia on Sunday, July 24. She called Brant on Monday, July 25, to say that she felt Natalia didn't seem right. So how do you answer questions like this?)

Barb: "Are we talking about Monday or Tuesday? Which day are we talking about?"

Question: Right now I'm talking about July 26 (Tuesday). You had already talked with Char about...."

Barb: "Correct." (Now he has Barb confused. Char didn't talk with Barb. Char talked with Brant Monday evening on the phone, and with neither Brant nor Barb on Tuesday.)

Question: Right?

Barb: "Correct."

Question: And then Brant told you that she calls again, right... or she calls? *Now, I'm confused. Char called Brant Monday evening. That's the only call she made.*

Barb: "She calls, correct." (Monday evening.)

Question: "And something is wrong with her (Natalia). And you said, look, 'I got this motherly instinct'." *Barb never said this to anybody.* "'I don't see something that is immediate. We will call the doctor in the morning,' right?" (Barb never talked with Char to say anything.) *What a horrible sequence!*

Barb: "I didn't say it like that, but something similar to that." (Actually it wasn't all that similar. Barb knew Elaine was coming Tuesday morning to babysit, and felt Elaine, as a nurse, could look at Natalia during the morning hours before Barb called Dr. Simpson. She told Brant that Monday evening, after his mother called him.)

Question: You didn't call the doctor in the morning, did you?

Barb: "I called her after my mom got there."

Question: You called her after your mom got there. Was that in the morning?

Barb: "Tuesday morning my mom stayed with her. And when I got home at one o'clock I called Dr. Simpson's office."

Question: That's not in the morning, is it? *Another "fact." She called an hour after morning.*

Barb: "No." *Gotcha!*

The inference that Mr. Cotter appears to be trying to make above is that Barb waited too long to call the doctor. After Char saw Natalia on Sunday afternoon and felt Natalia didn't seem right, she waited until Monday evening to call Brant to let him know of her concern. When she called, Brant went into Natalia's room, looked at her, and said she looks fine to me. Brant tells Barb about Char's concern when she gets home later Monday evening. Barb says my mom is coming over tomorrow morning, and I will have her observe Natalia, and then I will call the doctor. Barb came home Tuesday noon and called her pediatrician at 1:00 pm, and now the prosecutor derides her for not calling in "the morning" (an hour earlier). According to doctors, however, this call is totally irrelevant. Dr. Cockerill said that when there is an injury as devastating as Natalia's first massive brain injury, (weeks earlier) "there is very little we can do" in terms of treatment. Dr. Emenim says Natalia would have been unconscious for the last three to four weeks. Dr. Okanlami says Natalia would not have been eating for the last three to four weeks. The prosecutor is basing much of his case upon the statements of these doctors. This, of course, creates the "fact" that everybody who has seen Natalia in the last three to four weeks is lying to him. So why pursue the timing of this call to Dr. Simpson? Because, in addition, he needs to try to degrade Barb and her testimony in any way he can to hopefully sway the jury. (Mr. Cotter will bring this up again, including all of the wrong dates and times, in his closing statement.)

This ended the cross-examination of Barb. As hard as the prosecutor hit the temperature question, it seemed to me that calling the Lead School Nurse from Westview for clarity would have been helpful. She would have put that whole debate in the proper context. Jeff, however, felt that we didn't need any more witnesses for the defense. The prosecution simply had not proved it's case against Barb beyond a reasonable doubt. And with the significantly higher standard required for circumstantial evidence only, Jeff felt comfortable as to what the outcome would be. His experience and

315

understanding in criminal trials was well beyond anything else we had to rely upon. So we did not put either Elaine or the School Nurse on the stand. The defense rested.

A recess for lunch was taken, with closing arguments to begin an hour later. Elaine, Barb, and I, along with my sister and family, and a few other friends went to a nearby restaurant called "Le Peep." We felt under some pressure to be back to the courthouse in less than an hour, and I wanted some extra time to set up the overhead projector. So Barb, Elaine, and I ordered first. I couldn't tell you if I had salmon or pancakes or asparagus soup. My mind was focused elsewhere. So was everybody else's. We arrived back at the courthouse with time to spare. I set up the overhead projector, got the timing chart ready, and had the printouts of the chart in case something happened to the projector. It became clear that the prosecution also was planning to use a timing chart, but a quite different one from ours. With the abundance of medical testimony, injury timings, and the comparisons of who said what---and in which police interview, deposition, or trial--- it seemed reasonable that the jury would appreciate any attempt to pull together these elements in a way that made sense. Certainly the prosecution knew how to use "show and tell." And we needed to have our alternative to reach the jury.

CHAPTER NINETEEN

As the people began gathering once again in the courtroom, and the start of closing arguments was nearing, Jeff leaned over to me and said, "Don't be too surprised if I decide not to use the timing chart." *Whoa. When did this happen?* Obviously he had been spending his time over the lunch break putting his closing argument together. Perhaps this chart wouldn't fit in with the time that was allotted to him. Perhaps he didn't feel comfortable with his command of the information on the chart, and how to explain it. Perhaps he felt he had come upon a better way of reaching the jury. Regardless, I hoped and prayed that something good could come out of this potential change of plans.

It wasn't until I became more intimately involved with the workings of criminal attorneys that I developed an appreciation for the difficulty of their task. (This is likely true for prosecutors as well.) They really have comparatively little time to slice through the meat of a case. Consequently they look for "sound bites" and images that will stick in a juror's mind. The prosecution, however, seems to have a significant advantage in a case like this. When doctors are willing to say, "There's <u>not one iota of</u> doubt in my mind that this is shaken baby," or "You'd have to be from <u>outer space</u> not to see" what was wrong with Natalia, or "She would not have been able to maintain---she <u>would not be awake</u> (unconscious)" for the last three to four weeks, or she would <u>not have been able to eat</u> for the last few weeks, or witnesses say "She <u>called Natalia an a--hole,</u>" or "Can't we just <u>get rid of her,</u>" or the police bring up to potential witnesses "<u>Andrea Gates,</u>" the woman in Texas who had severe postpartum depression with psychosis and killed her children, or the prosecutor asks "Who had <u>appreciable time</u> with Natalia?"--- <u>these things resonate and stick with jurors.</u> But none of these "facts" indicated that Barb was the only one who could have hurt Natalia (if indeed she was hurt). Some speak to whether or not there was a crime. Others are a "he said, she said" kind of evidence. There is no <u>hard</u> evidence that a crime has been committed. There is a "theory." There is no <u>hard</u> evidence that Barb hurt Natalia. There are people saying things against Barb, many of whom would be suspects in the own right if those things were not said. They have much to gain by saying them. All of the "evidence" is <u>circumstantial</u> evidence. And this makes it next to impossible for the defense to <u>prove innocence.</u> You may be among those who still believe that the defense does not have to prove innocence. It's the prosecution that has to <u>prove guilt.</u> But unfortunately, that is another "theory" in a case like this. Since there is no <u>hard evidence,</u> that also means there is no DNA to <u>exonerate</u>

the accused. And there is no <u>bloody glove</u> to allow for a "If it doesn't fit---you must acquit" slogan. There is <u>nothing</u> available to the defense to use except to try to look honest, to tell the truth, and to show that others also had opportunity to hurt Natalia. But with the police and prosecutor trying to make you look dishonest at every turn, and making false statements designed to erode credibility, that's an enormously difficult task.

The prosecutor begins his closing argument by once again <u>flashing up a picture on the screen of</u> Natalia, tiny Natalia, all hooked up to tubes, monitors, and machines. It is a sad, sad picture. Everyone in the courtroom is justifiably moved deeply by this picture. But does it lend anything to proving who <u>caused</u> this situation, or is it simply to inflame the public and the jury. "This is Natalia" says the prosecutor. And he runs through the list of injuries that doctors say Natalia has had. "We know that there were <u>more than one incident</u> that caused that (brain) injury." (Again, Dr. Cockerill spoke of a "possible" second event that was "suggested" by the few drops of new blood in Natalia's brain. The "facts" surrounding that possible "second injury" are highly questionable. We've covered that before.) Mr. Cotter continues. "Let's first talk about the significant, the chronic brain injury. You heard from Dr. Cockerill. You heard him tell us the most significant brain injury occurred roughly <u>three to four weeks</u> before she presented on July 27. We know that."

"We know that Dr. Cockerill tells you there was a second injury, the acute injury. <u>That is the injury that caused the bleeding in the eyes</u>." *Whoa!* (Dr. Cockerill never said this possible second brain injury <u>caused the retinal hemorrhages</u>, nor did he ever <u>even attempt to give a time that the retinal hemorrhages occurred</u>.) *This is not a good start. The prosecutor is spreading manure again.* Then the prosecutor says Dr. Cory identifies the leg injuries and rib injuries. "His opinion is <u>clearly they occurred at separate times</u>." (That <u>was</u> his opinion, but it was <u>anything but clear</u>. In fact he agreed "it was <u>possible that they (bone injuries) all occurred at one time</u>.") *Does the jury remember this?* "We know that Barbara Schrock is the primary caregiver." *No dispute here.*

Now the prosecutor switches to talk about the <u>timeline</u>, the calendar. "<u>Who is around</u> Natalia when those (injuries) occur? <u>More importantly</u>, who tells Sgt. Kaps when she talked to him that same day, July 27, that <u>she is suffering from postpartum depression</u>?" *Barb's saying she felt <u>detachment</u> from Natalia is even <u>more important</u> than who had <u>access</u> to Natalia?* (This likely serves as an indication of how little confidence the prosecution has in it's "access to Natalia" evidence.) Mr. Cotter then attempts to link the timing of her feelings of detachment from Natalia to the timing of the injuries. "She

318

tells Sgt. Kaps it (her feelings) started three week to four weeks before. Then it ended roughly around July 20." (Two points: (1) You have already seen the wide range of timings of her feelings that were given. The police chose the one that fit their theory; (2) If these feelings were actually the reason Natalia was hurt, what happened with the alleged 24-48 hour injury which happened well after the prosecutor says her feelings stopped? You can't use the timing <u>for</u> your case in one instance, and <u>avoid</u> the timing in another. *Well, maybe you can. But it doesn't make sense.* The strongest thing this theory of the prosecutor has going for it is that it is <u>on a chart in front of the jury</u>, which <u>gives it the appearance of hard data.</u> In fact, the timings both of Barb's feelings, and the timings of the injuries to Natalia are very soft, subjective data from an "inexact science.") *But how will the jury view this?*

"We know Brant was there. We know that Brant had <u>one time</u> when he had any <u>appreciable time</u> away from Barbara. The other times---yeah, she would go down in the basement, or she might go outside." *Never mind seconds to shake a baby. We're back to <u>appreciable time</u>. So Brant <u>couldn't</u> have done anything.* "The other people who watched Natalia; Char, Gary. We know that Char and Gary had her on the [July 4 weekend]. We know Elaine had her on the July 16 weekend. Those are the only individuals, those are the only other people besides Barbara Schrock who had Natalia." (In addition to ruling Brant out because of <u>appreciable time,</u> he also ruled out Elaine, who clearly <u>also</u> had Natalia alone for four hours on Tuesday, July 26.) *This is not just sloppy "who's in, and who's out" work. It's insulting to the listener, even if you were to figure that there <u>was</u> a <u>recent injury</u> in the picture. Glossing over potential access in this way makes a mockery of this whole exercise. Of course, <u>without the possible recent brain injury</u>, <u>everybody</u> is a suspect.*

"First one happens, the ribs and maybe at the same time the skull fracture and the <u>acute</u> brain injury." (Here Mr. Cotter confuses <u>acute</u> (new) with <u>chronic</u> (old). *He must know the difference by now---I think.* The doctors' timings and statements indicated that the <u>ribs, skull fracture,</u> and <u>chronic massive brain injury</u> from three to four weeks ago could all have happened <u>at the same time.</u> Even the prosecutor has said this in the past. This is all hard enough for a jury to follow. But to switch <u>acute</u> and <u>chronic</u> injuries on the jury at this point in a trial like this is <u>totally confusing</u>.) Then Mr. Cotter follows this error with another: "What does Dr. Emenim tell us about <u>that acute brain injury</u>? 'You had to be from outer space' if you were around this child not to notice the difference.'" (Not only has the prosecutor confused the jury about the <u>concurrent timing of the different injuries,</u> he now has Dr. Emenim referring to the <u>incorrect brain injury</u> for this infamous quote. Dr. E was referring to the first massive brain injury (the chronic one.) *How can the jury possibly put all of this together?*

"Who is the primary caregiver? Barbara Schrock. And Barbara Schrock does <u>nothing</u>." *Just another general jab at Barb. Nothing personal.* "Again, if Barbara Schrock, having the care of Natalia, takes her to get care, she doesn't get hurt again. Again, <u>if you're not from outer space</u>, you know something is wrong. Barbara Schrock does nothing. <u>She placed her in that position</u> and that place <u>so</u> she can get hurt again and again." (The prosecutor is making <u>several assumptions</u> here: (1) That Natalia was <u>hurt more than one time</u>. That has been addressed before; (2) That it was <u>obvious to Barb that something was seriously wrong</u> with Natalia. Notwithstanding Dr. Emenim's outrageous comment (*which one?*), none of the dozens of people who saw Natalia believed she needed to go to the emergency room, and none was from outer space; which leads to assumption number (3) That <u>Barb caused these injuries</u> to Natalia. That's the only way you can interpret the prosecutor's comments. Expecting Barb to "do something" assumes she <u>knows</u> there is something to be done. Even the doctors didn't <u>know</u> about the bone "fractures" until a bone scan was done. And Natalia <u>was not</u> unconscious for weeks, no matter what Dr. Emenim alleged. So the prosecutor <u>attempts to prove</u> Barb is the guilty party <u>by first assuming</u> Barb is the guilty party.)

"Did she (Natalia) get placed by Barbara Schrock in a situation that would endanger her life and health? Yes, she did. <u>Beyond a reasonable doubt</u>. Beyond <u>any</u> doubt." *Absolutely none.* "Her job is to protect that child. She certainly didn't do it. <u>First Char talked to her</u> (Barb) on July 25, and then called Brant the next day." (Once again he is <u>confused, and confusing</u>. Not only does he have the wrong day, but <u>Char never talked to Barb about this matter regardless of which day it was</u>. Remember that earlier in this trial the following exchange took place between the prosecutor and Char:

> <u>Question</u>: Why <u>didn't</u> you talk to Barbara then (Sunday, July 24)?
> <u>Char</u>: "Because Barb gets too mad." (Char <u>never claimed</u> in any setting that she talked with Barb about this concern.)

The prosecutor continues. "What does she (Barb) say? I got the <u>motherly instinct</u>. <u>I know when my child is injured</u>." (This reference is very obliquely taken from the prosecutor's questioning Barb about <u>her feeling of separation</u> from Natalia. One can only faintly ascertain her original words given in a totally different context.)

> <u>Question</u>: And because you were feeling what you described as postpartum blues back then, you would feed her, put her back down, and not deal with her otherwise?

320

<u>Barb</u>: "Yeah. It wasn't an everyday thing. There were days when I did hold her. But, yeah, that was basically what it was. <u>I knew my mothering skills</u>, and <u>I knew what I needed to do to care for her</u>."

The prosecutor has taken her response to his earlier question, twisted it beyond recognition, and applied it to a totally different conversation about injuries---a conversation that never even happened. Then he continues. "Well, she <u>certainly didn't know</u> her child had acute brain injury. She <u>certainly didn't know</u> the child had the leg fractures. And she <u>certainly didn't know</u> the child had that chronic (old) brain injury. <u>Beyond a reasonable doubt, you bet</u>." (Amazingly, he now states that she <u>didn't know</u> all the things that earlier he accused her of <u>knowing</u> and doing nothing about.) *Does she know, or doesn't she know? It's really hard to keep up. All he really knows is <u>it's beyond a reasonable doubt</u>. You bet.*

Mr. Cotter then goes through doctors' testimony that indicates the rib injuries, the leg injuries, and the massive brain injury---- all which were weeks old---- were said to be intentional, not accidental. "And the last one, the <u>multiple hematomas</u> that is bleeding, and the giant retinal tear, the bleeding in the eyes, the acute bleeding of the brain. Again, what do they <u>all</u> say? That is from child abuse, because doctors are <u>real clear</u> that somebody did that <u>intentionally</u>." (Let's deal with this point by point: (1) It is unclear what Mr. Cotter is referring to by "multiple hematomas." A hematoma is generally a blood clot. If the clots are bleeding, they were rebleeding from three to four week old injuries; (2) The retinal hemorrhages and retinal tear are "<u>consistent with</u>," but not <u>determinative of</u> abuse; (3) He uses the term "bleeding" (in the present tense), to indicate that these are new injuries. But the ophthalmologist, the eye expert, <u>does not label these</u> retinal hemorrhages as <u>new</u>, or <u>bleeding</u>. What we could more logically assume is that these retinal hemorrhages were caused at the same time as the first major brain injury that caused the severe damage; (4) The <u>acute bleeding</u> in the brain. Remember that Dr. Cockerill saw a few drops of new blood in Natalia's brain. He was very tentative about how they got there, how much force would have been required, did not say if the person in charge of Natalia at that time would have been the same person in charge for the earlier massive brain injury, and "<u>could not say</u>" if this possible more recent injury was <u>intentional</u> or <u>accidental</u> when Mr. Cotter asked him that; and (5) Mr. Cotter claims the "<u>doctors are real clear</u> that <u>somebody did that intentionally</u>." Dr. Cockerill said "I can't say." Dr. Okanlami said "it could be intentional. It could be accidental." Neither Dr. Cory nor Dr. Emenim ever spoke concerning retinal hemorrhages.) *This is the <u>most egregious</u> of the several totally untrue statements in this sequence. I've run out of superlatives for just how untrue these statements are. How can "<u>I can't say</u> if it's intentional or accidental,"* *turn into <u>all of the doctors are "real clear</u> that somebody did that intentionally?"   This type of total distortion is altogether too prevalent in both police and prosecutorial statements.*

"Why Barbara Schrock? Why her? Well, let's go through again what we have and <u>who could have done it</u>, and <u>who couldn't have done it</u>. We have the acute blood from July 26 or July 25, within 24-48 hours before (ER). <u>You can rule out July 26</u>." (The prosecutor tries again to eliminate everybody but Barb. He takes the <u>most questionable injury</u> and begins there. But how can he rule out July 26? <u>The doctors couldn't</u>.) "Well, if you remember, <u>even the defendant by July 26 she is concerned</u>. She (Barb) is concerned enough she calls her mom and her mom is coming over anyway, and she has her mom bring the thermometer, and her mom brings the book. And you (jury) are going to have this, you are going to be able to read through it."   (So Mr. Cotter rules out Tuesday, July 26 because Barb <u>was concerned</u> by then. You will recall that Barb and Brant had concerns ever since the July 2 party. The symptoms were increasing in intensity, but would also subside at times. Elaine and Barb talked by phone between July 18 and July 25 about whether to call the doctor or not. Elaine was coming over to Barb's house on Tuesday, July 26, to babysit for both girls, and was planning to bring a thermometer and the medical book when she came. Char saw Natalia on Sunday, July 24. Monday evening, July 25, she called Brant and expressed her concern that Natalia didn't look right. Barb said she would call the doctor the next day after Elaine had a chance to see Natalia. And now, Mr. Cotter is ruling out Tuesday, <u>July 26</u> as a possible injury date because <u>Barb was concerned about Natalia by then</u>. Remember that Dr. Emenim had said to police: "Something could have happened <u>an hour before</u> [the early Wednesday morning 911 call]. I don't know. There's no way to tell.") *Only Mr. Cotter is able to tell.*   "So who are the two people who could have? Brant or Barb." *Strange logic.*

"Second injury. <u>Two to three weeks.</u> These are the tibias and the femur fractures (legs)." (Mr. Cotter considers this a "second" injury. <u>My timing chart</u> shows that these leg injuries could have occurred at the <u>same time as the ribs and major brain injury</u>. Dr. Cory also agreed that it was <u>possible all bone injuries (ribs, knees, and wrist) could have occurred at once</u>. In fact, <u>Mr. Cotter's logic essentially allows the same</u> in his closing argument for <u>Trial One</u> which follows:

> "Dr. Cory tells us <u>three</u> to six weeks for the <u>ribs</u>. Dr. Cockerill says <u>three</u> weeks for the <u>brain</u>. <u>Three and three</u>---that matches. <u>Isn't that consistent</u> that those <u>two things happened at the same time</u>?" *Yeah, it is.* (What he left out was Dr. Cory also timed the <u>leg injuries</u> at two

322

to _three_ weeks. So _three and three and three_---that matches, too.)
They all could have occurred at once.

But he continues on, unaware that his own logic would include the legs in
this early July period. "Who was around her then? Brant and the defendant.
Is Brant around her for any appreciable time alone? No. And then the last
one (massive brain injury, ribs)." _He really means the first one, but he is_
working backwards on his chart here. "Now Char could have done these,
Gary could have done these." (So Mr. Cotter conveniently separates the leg
injuries from the ribs and brain injuries, neglecting the fact that "early July"
is a time given by both of his timing experts for all of these injuries. And
therefore, all of these injuries could have happened at once, suggesting that
Brant's family, the people at the party, Brant, and Barb should all be suspects.
Everyone but Elaine and Dan, who weren't near Natalia at that time.)

Continuing his closing. "She (Michelle) says yeah, I went over and
looked at the child (at the party). Yeah, I work with children. I'm a
psychiatrist." _She's actually a social worker. Whatever. Why bother the jury_
with details. "She looks at the eyes, yeah, the child Natalia she is making
noises normal. She looks at her, everything is fine, she is tracking. So we
know at the party Natalia is okay." (Actually, Michelle said "she just kind of
laid there," and "she looked fine." From those simple comments Mr. Cotter
has deduced that Natalia is "making noises normal," "she is tracking" [no
mention of a flashlight anywhere to check tracking], and "we know at the
party Natalia is okay.") _He's a remarkable man._

"Remember Char and Gary kept her overnight Saturday. So I guess
it could have happened Saturday night, could have happened Sunday. Could
have happened then. But again, what does Barbara tell us? Barbara says
that's when I started suffering from postpartum blues. That's when I am
detached from the child." (A rather questionable way to eliminate Char and
Gary.) "That's when Brant is gone all the time. Brant is working a lot." _He_
was never at home. Except every day.

"Ladies and gentlemen, who would want to batter this child? Why
Barbara Schrock? Ladies and gentlemen, Barbara Schrock didn't attach to
Natalia like she did to Isabella." (For a brief period of time, this was true.
But now the prosecutor launches into a lengthy story concoction that has no
basis in testimony or fact or reality. This is the reason the prosecutor did not
want to have a bench trial. He wanted a jury. He can play with their
emotions.) "Natalia was a problem for her. Natalia didn't interact the way
she expected a child to interact. Natalia was small. She didn't have all these
medical problems when she came home. She was a tiny thing. She couldn't

323

get away. Because if you remember almost immediately after Isabella was born, what happens every weekend literally with Isabella? Isabella is really loved by everybody. Isabella is going to grandma all the time. She is going to the cousins all the time. She (Barb) has weekends away. She can kind of relax because <u>Brant is not there</u>." (This time with Isabella <u>before Natalia was born</u> is the period of time the prosecutor alleges that <u>Brant didn't work as much</u>. So why is he not there?) *It makes no sense.*

"She (Isabella) is there (away) and now we have a weekend. I can go do things. I can be me and not a mom." (Of course this is total speculation on the part of the prosecutor. In Trial One, the prosecutor said this in his closing argument: "<u>Maybe Barbara got upset</u> because, hey, Isabella had all these facial expressions and was reacting, and Natalia was not. <u>I don't know</u>. You know, <u>it really doesn't matter</u>." *He certainly acts as if <u>he knows now</u>, and that it <u>does matter</u>.*) For this trial, he has joined the ranks of Char, Gary, and Brant in both <u>ratcheting up, and adding to</u>, their previous statements.

One <u>could</u> also get the idea from Char and Gary <u>that they had Isabella every weekend</u>. But what did Char testify?

Question: Would you see Isabella?
Char: "Just about every weekend."
Question: What would you do with Isabella?
Char: "Take her <u>shopping</u>, take her to <u>Chuck E. Cheese</u>, just take her to the <u>movies</u>, take her <u>bowling</u>.

This is not a <u>two month old</u> Isabella that is doing all these things with Char and Gary. Isabella was with Barb and Brant for much of the first few months of her life, just like Natalia. But the prosecutor needs this image to make this phony comparison between the two girls. He goes on. *And on.* "She is stuck with her child who is not growing the way Isabella did, and Barb is doing all kinds of things with her (Isabella) now because she is two years old and she is fun. Now clearly Barbara, according to everything we know, treated Isabella extremely well. But Natalia is a different type of child, and <u>she doesn't know how to deal with it</u>. And it got to the point where she couldn't deal with it." *I thought these cases were supposed to be <u>based on facts</u>. This isn't even circumstantial evidence. He made it up.*

"Ladies and gentlemen, it's not an easy thing to find a person guilty. It's certainly not an easy thing to find a mother guilty of hurting her child. <u>But facts are facts.</u> And <u>the facts are</u> that she hurt that child severely to the point where that child will never ever, ever function the way a person ought to function." *This all sounds more <u>emotional</u> than factual. <u>I guess I just don't understand "facts."</u>*

324

"And Barbara Schrock by July 25 and 26 knew---uh-oh---, and she gets this <u>book</u>. <u>Look in the book</u>, look in the back. Look under <u>lethargy</u>. It's on page eight. Look in the back of the glossary. <u>You know exactly where it is</u>." *How in the world does the <u>jury</u> know exactly where it is? <u>He</u> has the book.* "I'm sorry, it's on page six. <u>Severe</u> lethargy." (Notice the <u>deft move</u> from lethargy, to <u>severe</u> lethargy.) "She reads those. She tells you. <u>And listen to the tape</u>." (This is a <u>technique</u> I first noticed in the police interviews. If you have a weak point, but want to emphasize it strongly, tell them to look it up [if they don't believe you], or listen to the tape [again, if they don't believe you]. It sounds like you are certain and have strong documentation of what you are saying. And usually this technique comes across so convincingly that the person doesn't do what you suggest they do.) "She is frantically reading this thing. She doesn't call the doctor. <u>She doesn't call the next day</u>." (Barb got this book on <u>Tuesday</u>, July 26, and didn't start looking through it until later that evening for a few hours. The call to 911 was made several hours later. The doctor's office is not open at midnight. And she had just gotten off the phone with the doctor after 6:00 pm that evening, with the doctor telling her to call the next day for an appointment. Actually, though, the prosecutor is partially right. She <u>didn't</u> call the next day. There <u>is</u> no next day for calling. Natalia was in the ER early the next morning. The prosecutor once again has his days mixed up, and is confusing everybody.) *Is there any possibility that the jury can sort the <u>truth</u> out from all of this misinformation?*

"What about the low temperature? Look at the temperature in the back (of the book.) Look at fever. Fever---you just have to turn the page. All of the preceding symptoms----talking about fever---- <u>all of the preceding symptoms are stronger indicators of serious illness than is the level of fever</u>." (I underlined this sentence because it highlights <u>exactly what Elaine was saying. And Dr. Simpson</u>. Temperature is well down the line in terms of importance for serious illness. <u>What are the other symptoms</u>? <u>How were the other vital signs</u>? Yet, the prosecutor in reading this sentence <u>doesn't even notice it's importance to this case</u>. He simply plows on to <u>temperature</u>.) "In infants, a rectal temperature of less than 97.5 degrees can also be serious." (There was no rectal temperature taken. But the prosecutor simply points to anything in the book and says Barb should have known this. <u>She read it</u>.)

"<u>She read this book and she did nothing</u>." (I would challenge anybody to read that thick medical book in a few hours. She thumbed through a few pages, not knowing for certain what she was looking for.) "<u>She waited until the next day to call</u>." (Again, this is not true. The prosecutor is once again <u>confused and confusing</u>. If he's after facts, the call to Dr. Simpson was a <u>few hours before</u> she paged through the medical book.

The 911 call was a <u>few hours after</u> she paged through the book.) "Why? Because by then everybody knows that really something is wrong. Everybody knows and the <u>cat's out</u>. Ladies and gentlemen, find her guilty of <u>neglect</u> and <u>battery</u>." *Wow!*

Now **Jeff Sanford** begins his closing argument. He says that as he began looking at this case and reading the police reports he found many disturbing questions. "What is it that the state has? What can they show me, or what can they show the jury that would indicate my client is responsible for those terrible, terrible injuries. What thing can they point to?"

He starts by stating his <u>major concern about how the investigation was handled</u>. "Sgt. Kaps had already made up his mind on July 29, I think, a day and a half after he was called." (Actually, Sgt. Kaps testified that he was "very confident" he had his person on the <u>first</u> day, Wednesday, July 27. It was Friday, in Char and Gary's interview, that he told them he and his partner felt comfortable ruling Brant out as a suspect. Essentially, this meant that both Sgt. Kaps and Lt. Richmond felt it would be easier to build a case against Barb than Brant. <u>They weren't aware at that point that they needed to be looking back three or four weeks for suspects</u>.) Jeff works through the various "red flags" that Sgt. Kaps outlined in his testimony that caused him to go after Barb.

I have dealt with these earlier, but will include comments by Jeff on each. First, Sgt. Kaps said <u>he found out it wasn't true that Barb talked to Dr. Simpson about PPD</u>. I think it has been established that this remains a question, probably tilted in Barb's favor. Dr. Simpson <u>forgot</u> some fairly major things in her testimony. But Jeff asks <u>what if</u> she (Barb) forgot who all she mentioned it to? She volunteered to the police and doctors that she had felt detached from Natalia for a period of time. And she had talked with Brant and Elaine about this. <u>She had no reason </u>to lie about talking to Dr. Simpson about it. So what is the concern? But <u>this</u> was a reason Sgt. Kaps chose Barb as his suspect.

Jeff reminds the jury of the context in which Barb gave her police statement. "She had gone to the hospital about 5:30 am in the morning. She had been in the hospital for seven or eight hours. She had been told that her children were being taken away from her." (He left out that she had <u>one to two hours sleep</u> the prior night, and most importantly of all, that <u>Natalia was near death</u>.)

At this point Jeff reminds the jury of the many <u>inconsistent statements</u> of the state's three witnesses; <u>Brant, Char, and Gary</u>. And the fact

326

that Sgt. Kaps, knowing that Barb was his suspect from day one, didn't really question anyone else, other than to gain information against Barb. He then runs through at length the various inflammatory comments that these family members alleged that Barb had said regarding Natalia, and the fact that these statements should have been made to the police immediately if they were true, not three years later. How could anyone overlook such statements when talking to the police? "So we look at the inconsistent statements that the state and their three witnesses have come forward, and inconsistency by omission, because it would seem to me that those things would be significant things."

Next Jeff deals with what Sgt. Kaps called excuses. "I find that kind of galling, and I will tell you why. None of the doctors described it as that (excuses.) As a matter of fact, I think Dr. Okanlami came and testified, and said in response to questions by the state, 'well, was she rationalizing what happened and what she was saying?' And her response was 'She was asking me questions, or she was responding to my questions.' That's what the doctor said. And what I find particularly interesting is, I asked Sgt. Kaps, you asked her, you know, 'Hey, did Natalia fall?' he asked her that. You heard it on the tape. And he testified, 'Yeah, I asked her that.' Giving her an excuse. What did Barb say? 'No, she didn't fall.' He is giving her an opportunity to come up with an excuse to justify what happened to this child, and she is not coming up with an excuse. There might be a couple other things he asked her. All excuses. And he said it was a technique he used. And I asked him, 'Did she bite on that? Did she make any excuse to him on that tape? No.'"

He moves on to red flag number three. "This is a good one. Primary care giver. How do we know Barb did it? Mr. Cotter said in his closing, well, gee, she is the primary care giver. She was the primary care giver, and who else could have done it?" Jeff goes over the doctors estimates of how long it would take to injure Natalia in this way. The range was from " matter of seconds" to an outside limit of "forty seconds." "So when you talk about well, you know, poor Brant was working all the time. Well, he wasn't. Unless from the time of May until July he was only in the house for less than forty seconds, then that excuse rings hollow as well. Because he did have access to the child. And the state concedes that. It doesn't take twenty minutes, or thirty minutes, or an hour and a half to inflict those sort of injuries. Their own witnesses have said that. It takes a matter of seconds. I guess since Barb chose to take care of her kids, the state referred to her 'not working,' then she must be the prime suspect. Now the other thing I find interesting is Sgt. Kaps said in an interview with Char and Gary, hey, you know, 80 percent of the time it's the father or the boyfriend, and then we go to the care giver (daycare.) And usually the <u>mother is on the bottom</u>. That's what he said. So the argument she was the primary care giver, and that's the reason (for her guilt), that's one of the factors that rings hollow with me, too."

"But the fourth one he talks about is, and I put this <u>demeanor</u>. Demeanor evidence. She didn't cry. The testimony is Brant is upset and crying. I think Char testified she cried, and Gary testified he cried. The only person who didn't cry was Barb." (Actually she did cry, but not much in public.) "But is that a reason to convict her of a crime----she didn't cry? She is trying to find an explanation as to what happened." But if she is really as cold and heartless as Brant suggested in this Second Trial, and she was abusing Natalia, "why not at least act like you're upset? Why bring suspicion to yourself? Why not act upset? And she didn't. Did that help her out? No. If she was engaged in a systematic beating of her child, why would she run the risk of taking her to the doctor? Why would she risk that? Risk getting exposed as a child beater? Why would she do that? It's not consistent. Ask yourself, does this make sense?"

Jeff brings up some of the disagreements and differences between doctors. "Dr. Cory said, yes, it was <u>possible those injuries all could have been caused at the same time</u>. And you heard some of the doctors talk about how this (timing) <u>isn't an exact thing</u>. This is a range of time. It could be more. It could be less."

"Circumstantial evidence is based on an inference. A conviction may be based solely on circumstantial evidence. Where proof of guilt is by circumstantial evidence only----<u>it must be so conclusive and point so convincingly to the guilt</u> of the accused that the <u>evidence excludes every reasonable theory of innocence</u>. Every reasonable theory of innocence. Now she starts out with the presumption of innocence. I don't think the state has met its burden in regard to who inflicted these injuries. They based their decision because Sgt. Kaps didn't like the way she reacted to the news of the injury to her child, claims she was making excuses, claims she gave inconsistent statements. And she was the primary care giver, ignoring his own experience and his statement to Char and Gary Mullins."

"Now if you take that timeline out further (three or four weeks), there is a lot more people who could have been responsible for this event----this crime. Could have been Gary, could have been Char, could have been Brant, could have been Dan Schrock, could have been Elaine Schrock. Five people could be responsible for those injuries. Five of them. Did we ever investigate them? No. No, we never did. Never looked into that. He made a decision. He made a decision 36 hours later that she is the guilty one. I got

328

my man based on those factors that he testified to, factors that I think I have blown a lot of holes into. And one other thing----she had postpartum depression. You heard her therapist talk about her reactions to what happened. But you never heard him diagnose her with postpartum depression."

Jeff ends with a story about a boy who ate a whole blueberry pie and then got worried what would happen when his dad found out. So he let the dog lick the pie pan and get blueberry stuff all over his face, circumstantial evidence that the dog is guilty of eating the pie. "That's really what we have here. And if you go back there (in the jury room) and you spend some time looking at the evidence and looking at the factors that determine whether she was guilty----their determination she was the perpetrator. Those four factors you are going to find ring pretty hollow. When you see that rings pretty hollow, you are going to be convinced that the state didn't prove its case to you. I am asking you now to find her not guilty, because the state hasn't met its burden." (Jeff finished and came back to the table. Then he whispered to Barb and me---they weren't with me. I hoped he was wrong.)

Now **Mr. Cotter** gives his rebuttal argument. (I don't like this part because he can say whatever he wishes and there is no comeback for the defense. He has the last word.) Mr. Cotter begins again by saying that it doesn't matter what anybody other than the jury thinks about this case. "It matters what you think. And frankly, what matters is what are the facts. Not my opinion. Not gee, this is how I look at it, this is how he looks at it, this is how the judge looks at it. The facts are what you look at. You don't make this on emotion." (Whenever he says this, I have an uneasy feeling that he means just the opposite. That's why he wanted a jury trial.) " No, ladies and gentlemen, she is charged because she committed this crime. She is charged because she severely injured this child." *Now that's the kind of strong factual evidence we need.* The prosecutor refers to all the other people that could have hurt Natalia. "But let's first talk about the people themselves. Did anybody else say they had postpartum depression? Don't characterize him (Dr. Rutt, the psychiatrist) as a therapist, because he wasn't her therapist. He was a hired gun." *We must be near the end. He's getting really nasty now.*

"And what do we have here? We have a woman who is used to having her weekends, and we have a woman who is used to being able to go out if she wanted to. We have a woman who is now instead stuck with this tiny child, and she doesn't know how to deal with it. She is isolated. We have a woman who has unrealistic expectations because Natalia is not Isabella in her eyes." *Facts?* "The fact of the matter is, ladies and gentlemen, did she commit the crime of neglect, and did she commit the crime of battery?" Could "all five of these other people could have committed some of these batteries? Maybe so. Char could have done the ribs. She could have done the chronic (brain injury). But she's <u>nowhere near</u> Natalia 24-48 hours before she presents." *Well, she did have Natalia 60 hours before. That's pretty near for the "inexact" science of injury timing. But more importantly, we aren't even certain there <u>was</u> an injury 24-48 hours before. That's the very questionable one. There is no absolute confirmation of a second brain injury. There is some possible conjecture.* "<u>She is nowhere near the leg injuries.</u>" (The jury needs to see the timing chart <u>we</u> have prepared. Dr. Cory dates the leg injuries as happening somewhere around <u>early to mid-July</u>. Char and Gary kept Natalia for the weekend in <u>early July</u>.) *The prosecutor rules people, other than Barb, out of the picture with ridiculous ease.* "So <u>Char couldn't have done those batteries.</u>"

"Mr. Sanford does point out that Dr. Cockerill does say, you know, I can't tell whether that is acute or chronic (the possible second brain injury). <u>Whether that is a rebleed of the original.</u>" (Unfortunately, neither Dr. Cockerill nor Mr. Sanford said this. I certainly <u>wish</u> Dr. Cockerill would have said it. I believe it would have been <u>more accurate</u> of him to say <u>he doesn't know</u>, rather than to say it's <u>possibly another event</u>. He admits he doesn't know how the few drops of new blood got there. He believes probably that the blood from the original massive brain injury <u>should have resolved</u> by then. But he <u>stonewalls the idea that an old injury could continue to bleed, or even rebleed later on</u>. Remember that the out-of-state neurosurgeon said brain injuries on this massive scale are open to to oozing and rebleeding at any time with little force, or even spontaneously. Dr. Cockerill apparently knows he has made a controversial statement by suggesting a possible second injury, so then pleads ignorance when asked about the amount of force [perhaps a sneeze] required to produce this "injury," or whether it would have been intentional, or anything else related to it. He has done his work for the prosecutor. He has at least created the <u>illusion of a second injury</u>, even if not a solid one. But now the prosecutor, once again <u>confused and confusing</u>, doesn't like Dr. Cockerill, his brain expert, anymore, both because of what <u>he thinks he has said</u>, and because Dr. C <u>isn't definite enough</u> about how the few drops of fresh blood got into Natalia's brain. And he needs <u>solid verification</u> of a second, new injury of some kind---any kind. So the prosecutor decides that Dr. Emenim and Dr. Okanlami, the pediatricians, are his <u>new best experts</u>. <u>They know.</u>)

"Dr. Emenim and Dr. Okanlami <u>all</u> said, <u>yes, that is acute</u> (the possible secondary brain injury)." *He begins to stretch the truth beyond the breaking point.* "They both (Dr. E and Dr. O) say, yeah, it's <u>one to two days prior</u>." [Actually, Dr. Emenim gives the following testimony: "You <u>won't</u>

330

find 24-48 hours anywhere in my notes" (not a new injury).] "And why do they say that? Because the eyes have fresh blood and fresh blood had to have occurred soon because bleeding in the eyes, they also told us, that bleeding in the eyes isn't going to continue over and over and over. It's not going to be like the chronic in the brain." (If you had trouble following that, don't feel bad.) *Where to begin?* Let's look first at Dr. Emenim's testimony. He mentions the word "eyes" twice. Each time he is referring to his own eyes. He never once mentions Natalia's eyes, bleeding in her eyes, her eyes having fresh blood, or that eyes don't bleed over and over. Not once. The prosecutor made this up. Nor does the ophthalmologist, Dr. Gerber, in his written medical report refer to fresh blood, or that eyes do not rebleed like the brain. Nor does Dr. Cockerill, the brain specialist, refer to any new blood in Natalia's eyes. Dr. Cockerill, who had read the ophthalmologist's report, was asked specifically if the few drops of new blood in the brain were the result of an intentional trauma. And he wasn't able to say that. One must assume that if he thought there was new blood in the eyes----and eyes hemorrhages are thought by some, including Dr. Cockerill, to be indicators of possible shaken baby syndrome----wouldn't he have associated any new blood in the eyes with a few drops of new blood in the brain and have said these injuries were both (eye and brain) intentional, and happened at the same time. But Dr. Cockerill didn't say that. So why is the prosecutor making the above statement? Dr. Gerber (ophthalmologist) and Dr. Cockerill, neurosurgeon, don't mention it. And Dr. Emenim, pediatrician, who is not an expert in this arena, never even mentions Natalia's eyes. Is the prosecutor assuming that no one will ever check on what was said?

Now Dr. Okanlami, the pediatrician, does think there was a recent brain injury. Why? (1) She believes the shaken baby theory (symptoms are immediate); (2) She originally believed the skull fracture was recent (the prosecution's own experts and the prosecutor, himself, agree that the skull fracture most likely happened weeks before, at the original injury time; and (3) She believed the ophthalmologist's report had said the retinal hemorrhages were acute, which she only learned during this trial was not the case. She has not had time yet to rethink her position. But Dr. Okanlami does leave herself an out. She says that the timing of injuries is the province of the radiologists, not pediatricians. And she adds that "the examination of the retina is the jurisdiction of the ophthalmologist.") *So what doctors is the prosecutor talking about? Imaginary doctors?*

(I recognize that all of the above, with retinal hemorrhages and new blood in the brain, might be rather difficult to follow. But I have included it here in some depth because I believe it is the most significant factor in this case. Was there a second "injury," or not? If there was... and it's a huge IF...

the most likely persons to have injured Natalia were Elaine, Barb, and Brant, with Char and Gary as lesser possibilities if you count 60 hours within the "inexactness" or 24-48 hours. If there was no second injury, anybody could have harmed Natalia. And there remain serious questions if Natalia was indeed injured at all, or if something else was responsible for her condition.)

"So we know there is an injury here (24-48 hours on the chart he is pointing to), and we know because the force that was required for the eyes to bleed, and the retina to detach, that that happened and that was severe enough that somebody had to have done that." (None of the doctors could say how much force was needed to cause the few drops of blood in the brain. The prosecutor's own idea that a severe force had to happen to cause the retinal hemorrhages only solidifies the likelihood that the retinal hemorrhages happened at the time of the first major brain injury weeks earlier. That's when the severe force supposedly happened.)

"We know the leg injuries were there (pointing to his timetable). We know the rib injuries were there. We know when the chronic (massive brain injury) one was. But the only constant between all of those is her (Barb). She knew she suffered from postpartum depression. She is detached, she is isolated, she is frustrated. And so is she guilty of neglect? You bet. You bet." Then the prosecutor refers to Mr. Sanford's talking about the discrepancies, inconsistencies, and omissions of Char, Gary, and Brant. "Well, what about Ms. Schrock? I will point out one that you got to see, and you got to hear her other sworn statement about throwing her in the air, right? And show me. And the person (Sgt. Kaps) asked 'how much is that? Is that about a foot?' 'Oh, I'm not good with distances.' Well, ladies and gentlemen, if she doesn't leave her hands, then she's not going to be talking about 'I'm not good at distances. She going to say, 'she never left my hands'." (Actually, that is essentially what Barb did say to Sgt. Kaps in the police interview: "It's not like I'm throwing her up in the air. I'm just kinda doing this." What Barb said at trial three years later: "She didn't really leave my hands.") *Not that different. He doesn't seem to grasp that Natalia could slide up in Barb's hands quite a few inches without ever leaving her hands. But these are all part of his "facts." Whatever this has to do with anything except "gotcha."*

"We're not here for a show for me. We're not here for a show for him (Mr. Sanford). We're not here for you guys to hear how upset we are. Put it on. Put her back on." (He is now forcefully and loudly telling his aide to put the gut wrenching picture of Natalia back on the screen.) *This is why he wants a jury... to see this show he has prepared.* "We're here because that little girl was hurt by the person who should have been protecting her the most, by the person who should have been making sure that nothing is going

332

to happen to that girl. Does that make me angry? Sure. Does that make her guilty because I'm angry? No. <u>What makes her guilty are the facts</u>. <u>Facts don't lie. Your doctors have no reason to tell you anything else but the truth, and that girl was hurt severely by that woman</u>, and find her guilty." *Facts. Facts. Facts. When you don't have facts, you must <u>emphasize that you do</u>.* (Reread that last sentence by Mr. Cotter. His final sentence to the jury. What is the prosecutor saying? <u>The doctors are telling you the truth, and that girl was hurt by that woman</u>. Yet not one doctor in either trial ever said Barb was the one who hurt Natalia.) *But that didn't stop Mr. Cotter from definitely making it sound like they did. Perception, not truth.*

So Trial Two is now over. How will the jury decide? What is the truth? Since there was no significant medical opposition in this trial, will they therefore decide that this is a case of <u>shaken baby syndrome</u>? If so, how did Natalia survive an accident comparable to a drop from a five-story building? Why is there a lucid interval of three to four weeks? Why was no MRI done to determine the causation in this type of case? Why do different doctors apply the tenets of shaken baby syndrome so differently? Why are there no baseline birth scans to compare with? Why would family witnesses for the prosecution say they saw seizures ever since Natalia came home from the NICU? Why does the prosecutor need to use false statements to impact the jury? Is the shaken baby theory as black and white as it is made out to be? Is any <u>lay</u> jury on the planet capable of sorting out this medical dilemma?

And if the jury decides, in spite of all these questions, that <u>beyond a reasonable doubt</u> this is a case of shaken baby syndrome, what conclusion will they reach regarding <u>who</u> caused these injuries? Why did so many doctors disagree so extremely on the timing of the injuries, while all looking at the same CD of the brain/bone scans? Why did doctors even disagree on which bones were broken? Why did doctors share confidential medical information with everyone nearby? Why would police purposely distort the truth, plant untruths, and give confidential injury information to potential suspects and witnesses, all the while attempting to split the family apart? Why would the police settle on a suspect in the first day? Why would the police dismiss other suspects so easily and quickly? Why would the prosecutor deny the defendant a bench trial? Why would the prosecutor appeal to emotion, while trumpeting "fact?" Why would the prosecutor distort testimony to the jury?

CHAPTER TWENTY

The trial had ended and the jurors headed into the deliberation room. Our group headed across the street to a Christian coffee house. There were about 15 to 20 of us. The Ugly Mug was planning to be closed during this time, but thankfully decided to stay open for us. They were setting up for a Christian music concert later that evening. So we ordered sandwiches and drinks, sat on the variety of chairs and sofas, and pulled up tables as necessary. People were less somber than at this same point in Trial One. We laughed quietly and even joked occasionally. But we still understood the seriousness of the moment. The place was essentially ours since they had planned to be closed. The persons who ran the coffee house were happy for our business, and genuinely seemed to care about our situation. We had necessarily gathered into small groupings for table space and conversation. Barb moved from group to group in her usual garrulous way, and thanked each of them for being there for her. We only had to wait about two hours this time. Barb got a call on her cell phone from Jeff that the jury had reached a decision. It seemed very quick, (too quick?) and we were uncertain how to read that. But Barb said "let's go," and we all followed her out the door, across the street, and back into the courtroom. As we gathered in our respective places, the bailiff said "all rise," and the judge entered. We continued to stand as the jurors started to enter the room. Looking intently at the first jurors, I felt their eyes meet ours and quickly glance away. The judge asked them if they had reached a verdict, and they said they had. The verdict was read. On the charge of neglect------guilty. On the charge of battery------guilty. The breath went out my lungs, and I looked at Barb. She was standing beside me, rather pale and numb. After the judge thanked the jury, he dismissed them.

Brant's family left the courtroom rather hurriedly. For them, this was a victory. This was "justice." The rest of us just sat where we were for a while. In front of me on the table was the injury timing chart, showing how all of the injuries most likely happened at one time. Would it have helped? I put my arm around Barb as we continued to sit beside each other. This had to be sucking the life out of her. The people most important to her very being were now further away then ever, and any life goals she had were now shattered in the wake of a felony conviction. The possibility of a prison sentence was now in her future. Jeff sat down with us, looked directly into Barb's eyes, and said "In the eyes of the law you have been declared guilty. But in every other way, you are no more guilty now than you ever have been." That was true, but the verdict and the law have overwhelming power to change your life direction. Life would never return anywhere close to "normal" for Barb, or for any of us. What do we do now? Can Barb go home with us? Jeff said that sentencing would be in December and that Barb was free until then. Gradually our friends left the courtroom and waited for us in the atrium. When Barb, Elaine, and I finally left the courtroom, one of our friends said, "What do we do now? We've never been <u>here</u> before." That kind of summed things up for all of us. We decided that we all needed to try to get some sleep. Barb said "Let's get out of here." I could see she was moving from shock to anger. I grabbed the overhead projector and we headed out the front doors of the courthouse.

As Elaine, Barb, our niece Val, and I started the one hour trip back to Goshen, things inside the minivan were dark and quiet. No one knew quite what to say. Finally Barb broke the silence. She expressed her anger at the police, the prosecutor, at Brant's family, the jury, and at God. We let her vent. Val was quiet but, as she would tell us later, no less upset. By the time we were nearing home, Barb had worked through some of her feelings during the hour of travel time. She was less angry at God, and even let go of some of the anger towards the others involved in this tragedy. I was amazed at how quickly she had let up on the anger, and moved to what might be ahead. Of course, that didn't mean the feelings were gone forever. We arrived at home and were able to have a somewhat "normal" conversation. Most of our sentences, however, were questions. Val left to talk for a while with some of her relatives that lived in the Goshen area. And later on we all eventually headed to bed.

Saturday morning, my sister Nancy and her husband Ron, came by for breakfast. The six of us were in somewhat of a fog, still trying to figure out what had happened, how it could have happened based on the questionable evidence presented, and at the same time trying to ask questions and seek answers about the future. After eating and visiting for a while, my sister and her family left for their home in Michigan. Sunday was back to church. Klaudia, one of our ministers, had been with us Friday during the trial and verdict, so knew the situation quite well. Others from our Sunday School Class had also been present. There was much interaction, hugging, commiseration, and support for us. We are blessed to have people who know us and care about us. Church members and friends brought flowers, apple dumplings, pie, and love. But we were still hurting.

Monday Barb headed back to her work in housekeeping at Goshen General Hospital. She had been there three years now and was in the middle of taking an EMT class. Jeff called the next day and said that he felt Barb was the perfect candidate for community corrections (a closely supervised assignment requiring the guilty party to work for the community to pay back the debt owed society), and would be recommending that to the judge. He also said it would be helpful if people would write to the probation department with letters of recommendation for Barb. Many people did that. We also were pleased that her supervisors at Goshen Hospital would be able to write recommendations of her character and work there. The fact that she had a good job could be a large factor in the judge sentencing her in this way. And the ministers at our church sent a letter indicating they were willing to be responsible for monitoring Barb if the court so desired. Those factors, along with the fact that Barb had no previous record, and was a danger to no one, seemed to be strongly in her favor for getting a non-prison sentence.

On Wednesday, Barb received a call from the Personnel Department at Goshen Hospital, asking her to come in at 4:00 pm. She did, and they fired her. That was another large disappointment. Not only would that lessen her chances for a community corrections assignment, but it meant she just had to sit and wait for a few months until the sentencing date came. And she loved her work. (A guilty verdict in court may not change who you are, or what you did or did not do, but it certainly changes how people respond to you. After three years of exemplary work, all of which happened <u>after</u> the alleged crime, twelve people said guilty, and Barb was fired. She can no longer be trusted.) I understood why the hospital felt a need to do what they did. They don't want to be sued for being negligent if anything were ever to happen. And that's to protect them from a society that has become ultra-litigious. For anything negative that happens in life, someone must be blamed.

With Barb having been declared "guilty," another serious issue became a very real possibility. Would the prosecutor decide to go after Elaine, too? When all of these accusations were being thrown around over three years earlier, everyone who knew Elaine, and all of our attorneys agreed that the charges against Elaine were simply to build pressure. The theory was that the police and prosecutor thought Elaine knew something and she was covering up. If Barb had done something to Natalia, this would pressure either Barb or Elaine into being honest. (Remember, the police at first thought that Brant was covering up, too, because nothing was fitting the "theory." And no wonder. You have two doctors, both devotees of the shaken baby theory, one who says Natalia was <u>unconscious for three to four weeks,</u> and the other who says she <u>wouldn't be eating for that same period of time.</u> It's one thing for the prosecutor to deal with Barb, a young mother, who says that Natalia was eating and somewhat active. But is was altogether another source of concern for him to have a school nurse with over 30 years of impeccable experience--- who knows <u>conscious from unconscious,</u> and who had the credentials needed to tell if an infant is <u>taking its bottle or not</u>---challenging these two pediatricians, notwithstanding their knowledge of "the theory.") *And who weren't present to see Natalia.*

Elaine and Dan

So would the prosecutor drop Elaine's charges now that he had an "answer" for those who elected him. That was the general consensus. But those people didn't know this prosecutor. Apparently he was feeling rather heady after the conviction of Barb, and decided that he could probably get another one, too. (And the scary part was that since he got a conviction with the kind and amount of "evidence" he had in Barb's case, he probably had good reason to feel confident in convicting Elaine, also.) So the trial of Elaine was on. Elaine's trial, originally scheduled for December, was "continued" into January. At the same time we were preparing for Barb's sentencing, we were also connecting more with Elaine's attorney, Chuck Lahey. Since the issue concerned whether Elaine was <u>lying</u> or not, <u>character witnesses</u> were the only defense possible. Consequently, we had established a strong core of people who knew Elaine very well, including a seminary professor, her principal, the president of Goshen College, her spiritual director, nursing faculty professors, the Superintendent of Schools, the Lead School Nurse at Westview Schools, with other people waiting in the wings. These people all held strong feelings about how Elaine was being falsely accused, and were very ready to let the court know what kind of person Elaine really is.

As we headed into December, we were getting close to the Record Date when everyone must agree if they were ready to go to trial. According to attorneys, December is a <u>slow month</u> in terms of getting anything done in the court system. *We had thought perhaps we were in a slow decade.* (Barb's sentencing date had now been moved to January.) It became clear to Chuck that for the prosecutor to prove neglect, he would need to prove that Elaine, by having Barb call the <u>pediatrician</u> instead of taking Natalia to the <u>ER</u>, somehow had caused Natalia physically to have a more negative outcome. He wondered if I remembered anything from the Trial One transcripts that would show that Natalia <u>could not have been helped</u> at the point Elaine babysat her. (We did not yet have the transcripts from Trial Two.) I responded that there was testimony in both trials to that effect. So after that meeting with him, I went home and checked out some of the testimony. I sent Chuck 18 different references from Trial One where doctors indicated the massive brain injury was <u>three to four weeks old</u>, that from then onward Natalia's <u>brain was dying</u>, and that there is "not a lot you can do to treat that." So Natalia had become "untreatable" weeks before Elaine came over to babysit on Tuesday, July 26.

Chuck showed this testimony to the prosecutor fairly early in December. The December Record Date was December 18. At that court appearance Chuck raised the question to the judge of whether the prosecution could prove what they needed to prove. (Elaine had hoped they might dismiss the case at that time.) But the prosecutor wanted to check with the doctors again. Consequently, the judge said we will plan to have a trial beginning January 5 unless I hear differently. Everyone was planning to take time off during the following week. I believe, but cannot prove, that the prosecutor was totally aware by that time that he couldn't prove anything against Elaine. Having been through two trials in which the things I had pointed out to Chuck were mentioned numerous times, the prosecutor was likely no less aware of these statements than I was. But he wouldn't give up the chase easily. Finally, on Christmas eve, we got a call from Chuck that the charges against Elaine had been dropped. *Great! What a Christmas gift.* Elaine, Barb, and I were jubilant upon hearing the news. But it was a short, bittersweet celebration. Barb was living with us, awaiting sentencing for her "crimes." How do you celebrate in the midst of anguish and disgust? Shortly after hearing the news about Elaine, we headed off to CMC for the Christmas Eve service. We met one of our ministers on the way into the sanctuary and told him briefly of the dismissal of Elaine's charge. He happened to be the minister leading the service that evening. During his prayer thanking God for the many gifts of the Christmas season, he very inconspicuously slipped "thankfulness for Elaine's freedom" into that listing of gifts. Some in the congregation caught what that meant, and others, particularly visitors, likely didn't understand. But following the service we were asked many questions, and given many hugs, in a wonderful celebration of thanksgiving and support.

We learned a few days later that the charge against Elaine had been dismissed <u>without prejudice</u>. That sounded even better. There had been so much prejudging going through all of this that it was comforting to know she would no longer be prejudged. Because she had been charged, Elaine could no longer get her teaching license renewed. (She had both a <u>teaching</u> and <u>nursing</u> license in her school nurse position.) Not because she was <u>convicted</u>--- just because she was <u>charged</u>. The attorney who told us "In this country you are <u>innocent until charged</u>" must have been speaking from experiences like ours. We decided to have the charge against Elaine <u>expunged</u> (removed from her record). Then she could work again if she wanted to. It was at that point we learned that her charge being dismissed <u>without prejudice</u>, in legal language actually meant "<u>with</u> prejudice" towards Elaine. She could not have the charges expunged. The prosecutor, in dropping the charge, left himself the possibility of reopening the case against Elaine at any time in the future that he finds additional evidence. We were not worried in that respect, because <u>there is no evidence</u>. And never was any. But why does a prosecutor have the power to totally stop your career in its tracks for the rest of your life simply by <u>charging</u> you? That's a <u>huge weapon</u> with great potential for being used abusively. *And we believe it was used abusively with Elaine.* One gets the feeling that a prosecutor never really believes <u>anybody</u> is actually "innocent." He/she just doesn't have enough evidence <u>at this time</u> to prove the person's "guilt."

Elaine and I have often recognized how people's view of the world may become distorted. She would sometimes come home from a full day of work as a school nurse and feel that <u>everybody is sick.</u> I would come home after a hard day of work as a counselor and feel <u>everybody has serious problems</u>. We would talk about that and laugh. As professionals we knew what the world looked like to us on those days was not an accurate view. And we adjusted our psyches accordingly for the next day. But I fear that people who work day after day in the justice system sometimes get hardened and cynical about human behavior. <u>Everybody is guilty</u>. <u>Everybody lies</u>. The only question is----can we prove it or not? Can we "win?" And the <u>threshold for proof</u> gets set lower and lower by laws supported by a society desperate to get "unsavory" people off the streets. In fact, all you may need to do is to charge the person. And for Elaine that meant the "C" ("charged") brand is embedded on her forehead for life.

So Elaine's trial was canceled. But Barb's sentencing on January 13 was approaching. We waited. This is heavy. Will she get community service, will she get probation, or will she get prison time? The church has agreed to be cooperative in any way they can, but she no longer has a job at the hospital. Tuesday, January 13 comes, and a snow storm has hit. We had often wondered what would happen at any one of these court dates if we couldn't get to South Bend. The snow is deep in Goshen, but even deeper in South Bend and beyond because of the lake effect from Lake Michigan. We have no choice but to head out for South Bend. So we allow ourselves plenty of extra time. The roads are not good, but by driving cautiously we are able to reach the courthouse in time. Several friends have also made the trek. We park, walk up the front steps of the courthouse, and through security. Across the way in the large atrium are Brant and members of his family. And nearby is the foster mother----with NATALIA. The shock for Elaine and me was enormous. We had not seen our granddaughter for three and a half years. And here she was. We wanted to run and hug her, but knew we would each probably end up in prison ourselves if we did that. So we just sat there 30-40 feet across the atrium, aching to touch her. Barb, who had seen her once in the last three and a half years was somewhat less shocked, but more disgusted at the foster mother for bringing her over 60 miles through this snow storm. What were her plans if Natalia had a seizure, or vomiting, or her vehicle got stuck along the road? This is the woman who felt it was physically too dangerous for Natalia to go nine miles to a social service agency on sunny days for Barb to visit her. So she asked the judge to stop visitation. And he did. Now what? Why is she here? Will they make a spectacle of Natalia in the courtroom?

We all file into the courtroom. Barb and Jeff sit at one table. The prosecutor at the other. The rest of us file into the few benches for family and friends. We stand, and the judge enters. "Have a seat, folks." The judge has at his discretion the possibility of sentencing Barb to an alternative to prison time, or from 6-20 years in prison. Brant is the first witness for the state. He states the losses that Natalia has, and what she will never be able to do. He asks the judge to punish Barb to the <u>full extent</u> of Indiana law. Then Cynthia Lorentzen, the foster mother, was next, and said she brought Natalia so the judge could see what her life had been reduced to. "She was viciously and repeatedly attacked by Barb Schrock. <u>What makes the abuse more horrible is that Barb won't admit responsibility or show remorse</u>. Please give her the <u>maximum sentence</u>." Then Mr. Cotter mentions the age of the child, and that the child could not defend herself. He also mentions "<u>shaken baby syndrome</u>. That's actually enumerated in the statute itself. <u>I don't think I have to say anything more</u>." Additionally he stresses "the multiple injuries and multiple acts you heard the testimony from the doctors that <u>absolutely</u> more than one incident occurred. We know we have the brain injury that happened three to six weeks before, we know the broken bones happened after that, and we know a secondary brain injury occurred." And finally was the severity of the injuries. "The state believes that <u>eighteen years is appropriate</u>, and all of that should be executed (in prison)."

Jeff then states that "Ms. Schrock is entitled to maintain she is innocent," and the judge agrees. "It does not show a lack of remorse on her part." He adds that there are mitigating factors, such that she has been going to school, has been working, and has strong family support. He asks for a six year suspended sentence, probation, and community corrections. "I think the mitigators in this case outweigh the aggravators. I think Barb can contribute to society. Sitting in prison, while it may make some people in this courtroom feel good about things, I don't think really solves anything or does anything other than to be vindictive. I think she would benefit from a term of probation with conditions put on by you, judge. I don't think you are going to see Barb in a courtroom again. She has been dealing with this case for three years. She has been to every court hearing that she was required to be at, she has followed the order and rules of the court, and I think that speaks of her ability to be able to respond under the rules of probation."

Barb then was permitted to speak. "For three and a half years I have been accused of a crime that is unspeakable, because the police decided that I was the one who did it. I am just asking everybody for a minute to think a

342

little bit about what if I didn't do this, and I have gone through this----not me but my children. I remain innocent in this. And from here I leave this up to you and to God, and I just hope that some day the truth will come out."

The judge leaves and returns after a recess of several minutes. He begins, "First and foremost, I guess, Ms. Schrock, you're not here today because the police decided that you injured your daughter. You're here because a jury of twelve persons who heard evidence over the course of four or five days made that determination." (The judge is technically correct. But it was the police who steered everyone to Barb on the very first day. And the judge must know this.) Two words crossed the judge's mind. "Inexplicable---why you are here, looking at your prior criminal record, your character and condition as evidenced by the pre-sentence report. And "unspeakable----what happened to your daughter and to Mr. Benson's daughter is unspeakable." He then goes over the mitigating and aggravating circumstances one by one. "I don't think there is any question that this lady would respond affirmatively to probation or short term imprisonment that exists. Somewhere in the statute it talks about the character and condition of the defendant, and I guess that goes to the explicable part." (I'm not certain, but I believe he meant the "inexplicable" part.) "I accept the verdict of the jury. I trust the verdict of the jury." *I think he clearly recognizes that there are many who do not. He's not in a position, however, to say he doesn't trust the verdict of the jury.* "I don't think anybody in the courtroom can figure out why. I am going to sentence you to the department of corrections. I'm going to make a sentence of eighteen years in the department of corrections. The amount I will suspend will be five years. You are actually going to be sentenced to a thirteen year imprisonment in the department of corrections. And the amount of that term being greater than the advisory sentence (this is a longer sentence than typical) is I think an acknowledgment of the amount of damage that was done and the circumstances that are outlined. In lieu of the suspended sentence, you will be on probation for the period of five years."

"Lastly, because this conviction is a result of a finding of a jury, you have the right to appeal your conviction to a higher court. Do you wish to appeal? Barb: "Yes." Judge: "Do you anticipate that you are in need of appointed counsel, or do you intend to hire an attorney to represent you? Barb: "I won't be able to afford to hire one on my own." Judge: "I assume that's because at this point you have no savings and ultimately being in custody will not be able to work to hire an attorney. I will appoint the public defender of St. Joseph County to appoint one of his deputies to handle the appeal for you and they will undertake that on your behalf. That's the judgment of the court."

And as the judge left the courtroom, deputies came for Barb, put her hands behind her back, handcuffed her, and walked her out of the courtroom. She turned back and looked at Elaine and me, mouthed the words "I love you," and was gone. The storm outside was nothing compared to our storm inside. We all were devastated. Elaine and I headed home. A friend rode with us and sat in Barb's spot. When we got home we realized that for the first night in three and a half years, Barb would not be sleeping downstairs.

The next day we called Jeff's office to see what information we could find out. Wendy, who takes incoming calls and runs the office, told us that she had talked with someone at the St. Joseph County Jail and they said that Barb was on <u>suicide watch</u>. Somehow that didn't lower our anxiety about the situation. We were given a visiting time of 6:15 pm Saturday evening that we could see Barb. There would be no contact with her until then. This was Wednesday. So we muddled through the rest of the week until Saturday finally arrived. Although the snow had made roads difficult to navigate once again, we headed out for the St. Joseph County Jail, not knowing what we might find. It was dark when we arrived. Elaine and I walked tentatively up to the front desk, the same desk where three and a half years earlier I had waited to issue bond money for both Barb and Elaine, while they were being fingerprinted, mugshot, etc.

This time we said we were there to visit Barbara Schrock. The person at the front desk looked through her sheets of inmates and finally found Barb's name. Then she said, "Your visitation time has been changed to 6:30 am on Saturday mornings." And since we had missed our changed visitation time, we would need to wait until next Saturday. Another officer was in the vicinity of the desk. He started to ask some questions. *Perhaps because Elaine and I had just disintegrated into a pile of ashes on the floor.* After a telephone call to somewhere, they said we could see Barb now, but not for the full hour normally allotted. At that point, a full hour was not high on our priority list. We thanked them and put our valuables and non-valuables in a locker. After waiting for a while, a guard came into the large room where we were and buzzed us through several locked, sliding doors. Then we were assigned a numbered cubicle. There we found a phone and a plexiglass window. The uncertainty of what condition Barb would be in kept running through our minds. A few minutes later we saw her coming down the hall in an orange jumpsuit, with a chain around her waist and arms. When she saw us her face lit up with a big smile like the Barb we have always known. Before we even said a word to each other, our own worst fears had somewhat abated. Barb sat down on the other side of the plexiglass and picked up the phone. Since we had only one phone on our side, too, Elaine grabbed that one. I could hear Elaine talk, but had to read Barb's lips.

It didn't take long to share concerns both directions. We explained to her what we had heard. She sort of laughed and said she wasn't thinking of killing herself----she was just totally scared of the new situation. Barb had asked to be put in solitary confinement because she didn't trust anybody. They did put her there, and also gave her an orange jumpsuit to indicate that status. She laughed as she said the other inmates kind of move to the side when the ones with orange jumpsuits come by. That apparently lessened her fears. Elaine finally let me have the phone, and we had a good visit. None of us really cared when we were stopped short of the full hour. As Elaine and I grabbed our belongings out of the locker and headed outside to the parking lot, we were relieved beyond measure. Not that Barb's situation was a good one, but that she was beginning to cope. And we headed cautiously back to Goshen through snow and darkness----- but feeling a bit more settled inside.

Back in March 2008, months before Barb's second trial, DCS wanted Barb and Brant to voluntarily give up their parental rights for Natalia--- Barb because of her charges, and Brant because he couldn't take care of Natalia. Barb went to the hearing in South Bend and refused to voluntarily relinquish her rights to Natalia. Her parental status with Natalia was delayed until after the second trial. Brant never showed up for that March hearing. According to the CASA report, "Mr. Benson's parental rights were subsequently terminated by default." Now, during Barb's time in the St. Joseph County Jail a hearing was held again to remove her parental rights to Natalia, either voluntarily or involuntarily. Our attorney advised Barb that if she didn't relinquish her rights to Natalia voluntarily, it would likely negatively impact her future status with Isabella. Given that alternative, Barb reluctantly signed the papers. The emotional impact of giving up parental rights to your child "voluntarily" is devastating. When Elaine called DCS several months later to see if we would ever again be informed about anything related to Natalia, she was told Natalia was up for adoption and we could not be given any further information. That was an overwhelming realization for us, too.

Barb asked, somewhat in desperation I think, if I would email Dr. Barnes, the Stanford Medical School doctor, once more--- directly this time. Previously all correspondence had been done through the other Stanford Doctor. So I did email him and got an immediate response. "We are, and have been, very willing to assist the attorney with this case. Please have the new attorney contact us by email asap." This was gratifying to hear, but I knew it was too late. The window of helpfulness had passed. The trial was over. Barb had been sentenced. The appeals process did not allow for the testimony that the Stanford doctors could have provided.

Our visits with Barb at the jail were indeed rescheduled to 6:30 am Saturday mornings. We had to get up at 4:30 am, but weren't complaining. Anyone who knows us closely, however, knows that is the middle of the night for us. After Barb had stayed in the St. Joseph County Jail for about four weeks, she told us during one visit that she would likely be moved to the Rockville Correctional Facility. Rockville is a small town about an hour west of Indianapolis near the Illinois line, and about four hours away from Goshen. Barb said nobody would be told ahead of time when she was to be moved, and that it would take place in the middle of the night. One day near the end of February, we received a call from the St. Joseph County Jail asking us to come and pick up Barb's belongings. At that point we knew she had been transferred.

Communication from Barb at Rockville was fairly easy. She could call (collect), e-mail, or write. There was a cost attached to each form of communication, but we could communicate. Since Barb is not much of a writer, emailing seemed to work best. Barb, however, did not want us, or anyone else to visit her the first year she was at Rockville. Her rationale was that while she would enjoy the visits, she didn't think she could handle our walking out the front door of the prison while she stayed behind. We could understand her having those feelings, but that didn't make it any easier. One week in August Elaine and I decided to attend the Indianapolis Colts training camp in Terre Haute, Indiana. On our way we passed through Rockville (on purpose) and stopped at the prison parking lot. We at least got a view of the complex of buildings, grass, sidewalks and fences before being told to "move on" by some friendly guards. That's about as physically close as we ever got to Barb during the first year. She formed some friendships there, although friendships can only go so deep in those circumstances.

CHAPTER TWENTY-ONE

Once Barb had been moved to Rockville, Elaine and I decided to request grandparent visitation with Isabella. A hearing was held in which Brant showed up with an attorney and made it clear that he and his family vehemently opposed such visitations. The magistrate apparently wasn't anticipating this heavy resistance, so assigned us all to a mediation process as an alternative to going through a lengthy, contentious court process. Elaine and I felt this might really be more appropriate than a court process which arrives at a final decision, but typically leaves severely damaged relationships in its wake. Isabella did not need more heightened emotions in her life to try to comprehend. So a mediation date was set for April 30, 2009.

In preparation for the mediation session, the mediator asked us each to complete a list of the things we appreciated about the other person (in our case, Brant), and in his case (us). Also we were asked to write about our memories of Isabella, and the losses we felt by not being able to see her. (I assumed this would not be given to Isabella, but was intended for Brant and us.) We each were to meet separately with the mediator several days before the mediation session to become acquainted, and for us to give him our written lists. Then we would all gather with our attorneys and the mediator on April 30. Elaine and I met with the mediator before the scheduled mediation date, and then arrived in South Bend around 10:00 am the morning of April 30. We were told by the mediator that Brant had not shown up for the earlier individual session with him, and had not submitted his list of things he appreciated about us. (Not a good sign.) He also reported that Brant and his attorney might be late for our session. So we sat there alone with our attorney for about an hour and a half. Finally Brant came, and later his attorney. The strategy was to have all of us except Brant meet in one room to go over our needs and concerns. And following that, in another room, everyone except Elaine and me would meet for the same purpose. Then all of us would meet <u>together</u> to try to blend a compromise. *That was the plan.*

Elaine and I met with the mediator and the two attorneys, and then Brant did likewise. But when the time came for all of us to meet together, Brant did not join with the rest of us. Apparently he felt we were "evil," and did not want to meet in the same room with us. All of us were quite disappointed. We had lunch brought in to each of us in separate rooms. Then, after lunch, the group minus Brant, talked with us again. They said they would make another attempt to convince Brant of the value of meeting with us face-to-face. So they went back to his room for another attempt to get him to come into a room with us. Failure again. The group came back to us once more and said they weren't certain Brant would budge. His anger seemed aimed at Barb, and he didn't want Isabella to grow up knowing her mother (or her family). He likely feared that we would take Isabella to visit her mother in prison. Anyway, another attempt to get Brant into a room with us also failed, and the day was over. He had successfully stonewalled the whole process. It seemed like a day of shuttle diplomacy, with no movement. The group (minus Brant) apologized to us that they were unable to make any progress. We weren't totally surprised, having known of Brant's strong will over the years. But we <u>were</u> disappointed, hoping that he might have seen the value for Isabella in such visits. Unfortunately, it turned out to be a significant waste of money and time. Our bill for the mediator and our attorney was $2,100 for that day. *And nothing changed.*

A criminal appeal was filed regarding Barb's guilty verdict. The "evidence" seemed both to our attorney and to us insufficient to lead to a conviction. We had hoped that the appeals court might take a fresh look at this evidence. That didn't happen. The following statement from the appeals court makes clear their standard of review: "It is not the role of the appellate courts to assess <u>witness credibility</u> and weigh the evidence to determine whether it is sufficient to support a conviction. When appellate courts are confronted with <u>conflicting evidence</u>, they must <u>consider it most favorably to the trial court's ruling</u>." Consequently our concerns for a fresh look at the evidence were not a part of what they did. If Barb said she had PPD---- she had PPD. It Brant said Barb asked why they didn't just put Natalia up for adoption---- that's what Barb said. When the doctors disagreed----the most helpful doctor to the "guilty" outcome was assumed to be correct. These judges even made a few assertions that the doctors didn't make. Because Dr. Simpson didn't notice any significant problems at the June 27 check-up, and another doctor said somewhere that it would be painful to have these "fractures," the appeals court made a "reasonable inference" that all injuries occurred after June 27. (This seems like a somewhat spurious conclusion to me. The same doctor they quote said later at trial that one would not necessarily know if Natalia's bones were broken until x-rays were done. But the fact they deduced that "all injuries occurred after June 27" only lends more credence to my assertion of the likelihood that all injuries occurred at one time----the <u>first week of July</u>.) And they took all injury timings as <u>absolute and exact.</u> So the appeal went nowhere.

Back in family court it took until October to finally get a hearing with the magistrate that had assigned us at first to mediation. In the courtroom, no indication of <u>why the mediation had failed</u> was allowed. This hearing was to determine if the magistrate would permit us to visit Isabella. We felt that visitation would be helpful to Isabella, and to us. Several years earlier the magistrate had appointed a guardian ad litem to represent Isabella's best interests. That attorney was now called upon once again to collect information in relation to this grandparent visitation request. She personally interviewed nine different witnesses, and read letters submitted by nine others. We were given a court date of October 29, and rounded up witnesses to be present at that time. Witnesses made the trip to South Bend on that date and waited several hours, before being told the magistrate would not be able to see us. Everyone had to head back home. Another "continuance." This time in the family court. The next court date was set for November 19.

The guardian ad litem reported her findings, both orally and in writing at that court date. Her conclusion follows: "After talking with Dan and Elaine Schrock, their references, and reviewing letters written by their friends, and the police and trial transcripts, I do not have any concerns regarding Isabella's well being if she visits with them. It was obvious during my interviews that Dan and Elaine love Isabella and want to have a relationship with her. Not one person who has known the Schrocks for years had one negative thing to say about them. In fact, after speaking with their references and reviewing letters from their friends, I believe Isabella would benefit from developing a relationship with her grandparents. I also believe that Brant and his family have a lot of anger due to what happened to Natalia, and believe that they are letting that anger taint their attitudes about Isabella developing a relationship with the Schrocks. In the transcripts from Brant's police interviews he stated on more than one occasion the Schrocks are 'laid back, caring and loving people.' Additionally, Charlene also spoke highly of the Schrocks during the police interview. In sum, Isabella would greatly benefit from developing a relationship with her maternal grandparents which would be beneficial in her development of her personal identity."

Brant took the stand and gave an estimate to the magistrate that we had kept Isabella fewer than five times at our house in Goshen (in an attempt to show that we didn't really like Isabella). Char then came in to the courtroom and took the stand, saying we had Isabella only three times at our house. Just like in the criminal courtroom, they pulled numbers out of the sky that fit their needs. (No documentation, no nothing. Just whatever numbers they thought might advance their case with the magistrate.) When we produced calendars for the years in question showing that we had Isabella 18 different days at our house, their attorney just made some snide remark about "who keeps calendars that long?" Brant's other comments to the guardian ad litem were that "Isabella does not want to see them," "they (Dan and Elaine) do not like young kids," and "they want visitation so they can keep Barb informed." On the stand again Brant said that "Dan and Elaine don't believe Barb is guilty" (that one is true) and "they must really have a lot of people fooled." Char said "there are lots of secrets on the Schrock side of the family" and "they would mess up Isabella's mind."

Their attorney said we are in "denial," were "egocentric" for wanting to visit Isabella, and would cause "'cognitive dissonance' in Isabella if they were to tell her that her mother loves her." *It would only cause "cognitive dissonance" if Brant and his family were telling her something else.* And to top off their presentation, the prosecutor (Mr. Cotter) came over from the criminal court to the family court and made negative comments about Elaine. He had also made statements to the guardian ad litem. Mr. Cotter believes that "Elaine allowed Natalia to <u>wallow in injury</u>, and that <u>her unconcern allowed Natalia's injury to worsen</u> (the very thing doctor's said was not the case, and why he dismissed her charge.) Additionally the prosecutor stated that Elaine had said "Natalia was 'eating,' when the doctors said she could not have been." And finally, "Elaine had been providing care for Natalia, and Natalia had a broken arm, leg, and ribs in various stages of healing, and Elaine <u>did not address</u> those injuries." (You will recall that doctors said there was no way anyone could have known Natalia had "fractures" without taking x-rays and bone scans.) One has to wonder what this <u>prosecutor's relationship was to Brant's family</u> that caused him to come to the family court to make these kinds of statements.

Brant and his attorney played the tape of Elaine's police interview in court. Somehow they felt that would show the magistrate that Elaine was someone not to be trusted. Of course, it didn't show that. Brant had never heard that tape directly before, only through the statements by police who were trying hard to turn him against Elaine and our family. Brant and his attorney had also decided to put Lt. Richmond on the stand to talk about Elaine's police interview. That added very little. We had decided earlier to have the tape of Brant's second police interview played in court. When Lt. Richmond was done testifying, the magistrate suggested that Lt. Richmond bring the tape of Brant's second interview to our next hearing, which was scheduled for December 3 and 4.

Lt. Richmond showed up at the December hearing with one 90-minute audio tape of the interview in question. He indicated that there was <u>only one tape</u>. (Remember the police "lost" the CD of Natalia's brain/bone scan for over a year in the criminal trial.) So now we were all to believe Lt. Richmond that one 90-minute tape was all there was. When I indicated to the magistrate that the interview was over four hours long, he was faced with

with the dilemma of believing Lt. Richmond, or me. Actually, it wasn't all that much of a dilemma. It was clear who he believed----until I pulled out copies of all three 90-minute tapes that I had along with me. Then things got interesting. Lt. Richmond began to mumble a bit more, and finally said he would have to check the files again. And wonder of wonders, he came back to the next hearing with all three tapes. These were the tapes on which Lt. Richmond was cussing and swearing, and telling Brant all kinds of untrue things that Elaine and others had said to him, in a successful attempt to brainwash Brant and garner him as a witness for the prosecution. We thought it might be helpful for Brant to hear what Elaine actually said along side what Lt. Richmond attributed to her. Unfortunately, we were not able to finish the tapes until January 7, 2010. By that time Brant had likely forgotten what was said in early December, or at least failed to connect the dots. Whatever happened, the facts didn't change his mind about anything.

In the end, the magistrate ruled according to how the law is written, and though painful, we accepted that. The overall ruling had to be in Isabella's best interests. We agreed with that. The law reads that "special weight must be given to a fit parent's decision to <u>deny or limit visitation</u>," when such visitation is sought by grandparents. Comments by the magistrate indicated the following: "Neither the Father, the Maternal Grandfather, or Maternal Grandmother have acted in any way detrimental to the best interests of Isabella. The Maternal Grandfather and Maternal Grandmother <u>have established</u> that it is <u>not</u> in Isabella's best interests for her to be totally separated from knowledge of them and their love and concern for her. It <u>is</u> in Isabella's best interests for her maternal Grandparents to be allowed to be a part of her life, if they choose to, by providing her with birthday gifts, Christmas gifts, and other gifts on other special occasions, and congratulations for her achievements. In his care for Isabella, it is not in her best interests for the Father to act as if her maternal Grandparents are non-existent as well as to refuse to provide [Isabella] with the gifts and congratulations that might typically be provided to a child by grandparents. <u>It is not in the best interests of Isabella at this time for the court to enter an order of grandparent visitation</u>."

When we honestly looked at this situation, we had to agree that given Brant's dogged stance against our visiting Isabella, she would likely have been caught in the middle if it were so ordered. And that's not a good thing. We had hoped that Brant might be able to see the value for Isabella in knowing up close and personal that her grandparents love her. But that didn't happen. And we are deeply saddened by that. We will send gifts on her special occasions, trusting that Brant will see that she gets them. That has not always been the case in the past, and we have little faith that this order will change things. There is no enforcement provision. We have received no pictures, and have no knowledge of her occasions which deserve congratulations. We do continue to send birthday and Christmas gifts and cards, but are uncertain if Isabella ever sees them, or knows who sent them if they are given to her. We do send everything registered mail so that some day we will be able to show Isabella that we tried. But we are sad about this arrangement.

During the time that we were trying for grandparent visitation, Barb was moved from Rockville Correctional Facility to the Indiana Womens' Prison (IWP) near Indianapolis. Overall, this appears to be a better situation for Barb. There seem to be more opportunities for her in terms of work options and courses. She completed a horticulture class from Purdue, assisted the teacher of the horticulture class when the next group of horticulture students came in, also assisted in the recreational/fitness building, completed parenting classes, post traumatic stress syndrome certification, anger management, and culinary arts. She also volunteers for making mosquito netting for African countries where malaria is a concern. It took well over a year before Barb could really focus on anything other than getting out of prison and seeing her kids again. She still has those needs. Gradually, however, she came to the recognition that doing the best she could within her circumstances would be the best way to spend her time. She is largely back to her old social self, and seems to know every inmate, guard, and administrator in the facility of over 600 persons. As with most of us, however, some days go better than others. But overall, she is being constructive with her time.

Elaine and I visit approximately once a month for a few hours. It is a seven hour round trip, so takes the better part of a day by the time we return home. Visiting is reasonable most of the time. After going through metal detectors and being patted down, we are buzzed through locked doors into a room about 60 feet by 40 feet. There are roughly 20 round tables with four chairs around each table. Barb also is searched thoroughly when coming into, and going out of, this room. We sit around one of the tables, and can hug and touch each other. There are vending machines with popcorn, sandwiches, and drinks. A microwave is also available. Barb talks about prison life and what she hopes for the future most of the two hours we are there. She longs for her girls. Recognition of the difficulties that lie ahead have been part of her thinking more recently. Because of the felony conviction, her options are cut way down from the nursing and EMT hopes she had earlier. But her overall outlook on life and faith remains positive.

Our visits have normally been hassle free. But one time we arrived and parked in the parking lot outside the front doors of the prison. Walking up to the doors we passed four men who were just leaving, dressed in suits and carrying clipboards. Neither Elaine nor I gave much thought about these men. We entered and went through our normal routine of handing in our ID's, getting a locker, putting belts, watches, jewelry, billfolds, and coats in the locker. Elaine was dressed in a sleeveless top covered by a long sleeved shirt, and jeans. (It gets very cool sometimes in the visitation room.) The female officer at the front desk said she could not go in to visit that way, because the outer clothing article was a jacket. Elaine would need to take the "jacket" off and put it in the locker. When she took it off, however, the sleeveless top didn't pass muster either. The officer said I'm sorry, but you'll have to buy a tee shirt, and pointed in a direction to somewhere on the outskirts of Indianapolis. Apparently tee shirts are okay. Well, we didn't want to get back in our minivan and start hunting for a tee shirt somewhere in Indianapolis, so I said to Elaine, "Why don't you just take my shirt, go into the restroom and remove your sleeveless top, and put my shirt on. The officer said that would be okay, and I had a tee shirt underneath my shirt anyway. Problem solved. *Not.* As soon as I removed my shirt, the female officer immediately said, "You can't wear that shirt inside." I said, "Why? You just said we should go out and buy one." Well, I was wearing a vee-necked shirt. Vee-necks are no good. I asked what was wrong with a vee-neck, and a nearby male officer responded visually with his hand that I needed a high necked one. *I think that's what his gesture meant. Either that, or maybe it was a motion indicating that he was going to cut my throat if I didn't shape up. The hand signs look surprisingly similar.* Now I don't typically get riled very easily, but I could feel myself bristling a bit at this ridiculousness. I regained my inner calm and remembered that since it was October weather, I had worn a pile lined shirt into the prison from the car and had put it in the locker. So I opened the locker and put on the shirt and appeared again at the front desk. "Nope. That's a jacket." *Grrrr.* I fought to keep control of myself, and reluctantly put it back in the locker.

By that time Elaine had moved through the metal detector with my shirt, and was ready to go into the visitation room. She went through a final pat down and the officer found money in her shirt pocket. I had put it there because you're allowed to take $20 into the visitation room for use in the vending machines. So Elaine had to go back through the metal detector and be patted down again. This time the officer found quarters in Elaine's pants pocket. "Put those in the tray. Haven't you ever been here before?" barked the officer's voice. Well, actually, we had been there quite a few times before and had taken our money in the same way each time. Next, a voice from the hidden, door-buzzing room came crackling through the speaker. It was garbled much like a train conductor's announcement. Elaine answered, "What?" The voice came through the speaker once again, this time more clearly. "Do you have any weapons on you?" *Unbelievable!* After going through this rigorous searching routine, Elaine had to squelch her impulse to say something smart. Fortunately, "no," was the answer that came out of her mouth. Once again, no one had ever asked that question before, nor have they since. But finally Elaine was ready to go visit Barb. "What are you going to do?" she asked me across the front desk counter. My face was likely getting redder by now. I said "I think I'll just sit here for two hours." (It really wasn't a very good idea since we had just driven three and a half hours to see Barb, but that's what I heard myself saying.)

Elaine went inside to visit Barb (with my shirt.) It took me about a 60 seconds to decide I was not going to run around Indianapolis looking for a high necked tee shirt. But I do carry all sorts of clothing and seats in the back of my minivan for when I attend various MYF youth group outdoor games and events. So I went out in the parking lot to take a look. There, amidst the overcoats and raincoats, was a blue sweatshirt. I grabbed it, knowing the odds were slim that it would be accepted. But it was all I had. When I got through the front doors of the prison, I held it up and said sweatSHIRT, and the officer said, "Yep, that's okay." What? I couldn't believe it. Did I hear her right? I quickly pulled it over my vee-neck undershirt before she changed her mind. I raced through the metal detector, and into the pat down. Then, to my total surprise, the officer said, "I apologize." She must have recognized my frustration. (And here I thought I had disguised it so well.) I said, "That's okay. I really wasn't trying to cause any trouble. I guess I just don't know what a shirt is." And I was buzzed through the door. When Barb heard this story she was somewhat pleased. "Now you know what I go through on a daily basis." But I must say that type of crazy scrutiny only happened once. The officers normally have been very kind and polite, almost without exception. (Perhaps those four men in suits and clipboards were inspectors who had just emphasized the need for stiff rule enforcement.)

In April 2010, our church (CMC) asked Elaine and me if we would update the congregation on where things were in our lives these days. We agreed to speak to the congregation, but also said we would like to express our thankfulness for their support through this whole tragedy. It seemed appropriate to schedule our part of the service after the sermon, during the time set aside for "The Church At Work." So when that time of the service came, we shared the following:

Sunday, April 18, 2010
"Church At Work"

(ELAINE)
Some in the congregation have asked if we would share where things are currently in our family legal situation. And we also wanted a chance to thank the church for walking with us through this time. So we appreciate this opportunity today.

First an update:
Our granddaughter Natalia is now nearly 5. As far as we know she remains in foster care in NW Indiana. Undoubtedly, she is still very low functioning. Natalia is no longer legally a part of our family.

Granddaughter Isabella, 7, lives in Michigan with her father. We believe she is in 2nd grade. In January, after numerous court hearings over several months, Dan and I were denied grandparent visitation with Isabella. We may send a card and gift for birthday and Christmas. It is uncertain if she actually gets to see what we send her.

Barb, our daughter, is in prison in Indianapolis. At this point, after the huge disappointment of losing the appeal of her conviction, she is now trying to make the most of these prison years, recognizing that she and we cannot change this. (We have certainly tried.) Barb probably has 4 - 5 more years in prison.

Dan and I are finally permitted to visit Barb and have now 3 times. That has helped us finally to see her face to face, hug, talk, and to know that she has not lost her spunk. (It helped relieve some of my wildest mother-imaginations.) We can also write to Barb; she is allowed to write and phone us. She wants you to know she is very appreciative of the mail she has received from many of you, though she doesn't write back to each of you --- or us.

My felony charges were dismissed over a year ago. That means I am free, for which I am very grateful. The prosecutor, however, could re-file charges whenever he wishes. We're fairly certain that will never happen, but those charges cannot be cleared from my record.

For Dan and me, the feelings of pain and loss and sadness remain. However, the battles(legal battles) are over (we think). There is some relief in that, even though we are stuck with the bad outcomes. We no longer have that daily, disturbing feeling of a nearly five year fight with the powers-that-be. Fighting is not our natural way. There were times when we were concerned that our inability to get ANY GOOD news (for which we and you had earnestly prayed) was too much/too heavy to bear--- for us and also for you who were helping carry the load.

I have been wearing this bracelet every day for months. It is engraved with Reinhold Niebuhr's prayer, sometimes known as the Serenity Prayer. On many levels/ways, it is a constant help for me. It is my prayer:

God, Grant me the Serenity to accept those things I cannot change,
The Courage to change those things I can,
And the wisdom to know the difference.
Living one day at a time;
Enjoying one moment at a time;
Accepting hardship as the pathway to peace.
Taking, as He did, this sinful world as it is, not as I would have it.
Trusting that He will make all things right if I surrender to His Will;
That I may be reasonably happy in this life,
and supremely happy with Him forever in the next. Amen.

(DAN)
During these last few years of legal struggles, our family was being torn down in a very calculated --- and very methodical way. Whenever I was in St. Joe County I felt like I had a sign around my neck that said "unclean." And Elaine and Barb experienced much, much worse than I did. At the same time, however, we were being held high by our church, our families, and our friends. The prayers, the caring, the support, and the uplifting were amazing. But these two totally opposite forces, the tearing us down ---- and the holding us up, were part of our life for almost five years. And at times it felt like "emotional whiplash."

I want to share a few of the ways you people lifted us up:

People would come up to us in the grocery store ... or many other places and with tears in their eyes would ask, "How are you?"

Many people were symbolically 'walking the journey with us' around this sanctuary, or somewhere else .... For years ....

Many of you sent us notes, cards, and e-mails, called or visited. Some on a weekly basis. Again, for years!

There was food and flowers and theater tickets.

Financial gifts from the church, or from individuals, personal words of encouragement, and hours of helpful listening.

It was just unbelievable how often someone shared with us how they were praying for us on their way to work, or while exercising, or in so many different ways and times.

356

We had two different trials in South Bend, each a week long. And each day a CMC minister was present. So were many of the rest of you.

Worship services during this time were particularly meaningful to us.

A group of professionals from church, representing a range of disciplines, gave us much helpful counsel and support.

And finally, there were many who were just present with us. Just being there.

For example:

One Sunday morning, early in our journey, during a particularly meaningful child dedication service here at CMC, our wounds were still very fresh. At a certain point in the service Elaine told me she needed to leave, and left during the next hymn. Within ten seconds of her leaving, Kent Beck came from some part of the congregation, (I don't know where), slid into the bench beside me, and asked, "May I sing with you?" He stayed there for the rest of the service. And I knew he cared.

We had hoped through all of this time to remain faithful and maintain our integrity. Some days that seemed easier than others. But we were particularly heartened one Sunday morning when Ron Kennel put his arms around both of us after we'd received a particularly difficult court decision, and said, "Dan and Elaine, your house is built on a rock." That was a very welcome affirmation for us, and felt really good, but we knew, too, that sand kept blowing in around the foundation and the rains kept coming down. During those years we probably made 400-500 difficult decisions, each of which had the potential for either 'keeping our family together', or 'allowing it to be ripped apart.' That was very stressful. Fortunately for us, ... God ..... and many of you ..... and the MYF ... helped us sweep most of the sand away from the foundation. And our house stood firm.

As we dealt with our stress, Elaine tended to choose 'solitude' most of the time. I, on the other hand, found that the MYF was important in my dealing with the stress. There were more than a few days that I would get home around 6:00 pm from a really hard day in court, or after receiving a particularly traumatic decision, and almost immediately head off to a concert, a soccer match, or some other event that an MYFer was involved in. I did that partly to let the MYF know of my commitment to them. But just as importantly, I needed to be there for myself. There was something very healing and very perspective-giving in being with the MYF at those times, whether singly or in a group.

The MYF spent an evening about half way through this five year ordeal allowing me to share our story with them. Then they asked me how I'd like them to pray. After thinking a bit, I responded "<u>Pray that I don't become a bitter person</u>." They left the MYF room, went upstairs, and prayed for our family while walking around the outside of the sanctuary for the rest of the evening meeting. Then they wrote some very loving, and very caring notes to our family.

There were times during the past five years when we questioned whether any of the various prayers offered on our behalf were being heard. Things certainly turned out differently than we were hoping. But God clearly was walking with us. And I thank God ..... and the MYF ..... <u>that I am not a bitter person today</u>.

We suggested to Klaudia that our sharing this morning come under the "Church at Work" part of the service. What CMC has done for us has been huge .... and nothing describes that better than "the church at work." THANK YOU ALL SO VERY MUCH. You've been God's faithful servants to us.

It's almost fashionable in some circles these days to say, "I'm a Christian," or "I'm a Jesus follower," or "I love God " .... and then rather quickly follow-up with "<u>but I don't need the church</u>." .... If anyone listening today is ever tempted to think that way..... come and talk with us.

The rest of 2010 seemed somewhat uneventful. By the time 2011 rolled around, Elaine and I were achieving some semblance of normalcy in our lives once again. And Barb was doing more long range thinking and planning. She said recently, "I still want out of here. But I know I can do this if I have to."

Thursday, March 31, 2011, our phone rang. I checked the caller ID and saw it was the South Bend Tribune. We already get two daily newspapers, and I didn't feel much like taking a call for a third one. So I graciously handed the ringing phone to Elaine. It was a reporter from the South Bend Tribune. She asked Elaine if she had any comment on <u>Natalia's death</u>. *Wham!* Since we had no idea that Natalia had died, it was totally shocking news. Elaine was kind, found a seat, and asked as many questions as she could. The reporter acted very much like she wanted to do a story that would represent the perspective from our family, as well as the perspective from Brant's family. Elaine talked quite a while with this reporter, and was encouraged with the reporter's attitude. She had remembered that Barb at sentencing had maintained her innocence. When the reporter hung up, we didn't know whether to be outraged that we had to find out about Natalia's death from a reporter, or to be thankful that we found out at all.

Going online and checking the South Bend newspaper the next day, we found Natalia's obituary. She had died March 25, and a memorial service had been held in Michigan just minutes before the reporter had called. In reading through the obituary, we noticed Natalia's father (Brant), grandparents (Char and Gary), uncles, sister, stepbrother, stepsister, Brant's father, three great grandmothers, and a great grandfather were all mentioned. Also receiving special recognition were the foster mother's family, and the CASA worker (Paula). But apparently Natalia had no mother or maternal grandparents.

Since we could not call Barb (she can only call us), we sent an email letting her know of Natalia's death, and suggesting she call us immediately to talk about it. She called us the next day, but we soon became aware that she had not yet received our email. So we had to break the news to her on the phone. That was a tough call. The rest of the conversation was through tears. Barb just kept repeating, "What can I do? I can't do anything." We had decided before the call that we would not indicate to Barb that the prosecutor (as we had also found out in the newspaper) was now weighing the possibility of homicide charges against her. One tragedy at a time was enough. And there would have been nothing she could have done but sit and stew over possible new charges. We visited Barb shortly after the phone call. (But it would be several months before we told her of the possible murder charges.) While Barb was continuing to work through Natalia's death, she did seem somewhat consoled that Natalia was done with all of her bodily woes, and in a better place now. A mother never gets over her child's death, however, let alone being unable to be there because she is in prison.

On Saturday, April 2, the front page headline on the South Bend Tribune, with a picture, was "Girl Abused As Baby Dies At Five." While there were a few quotes from Elaine, the larger story was about the horrific injuries that Barb had inflicted on Natalia. Brant was quoted extensively. It noted that the prosecutor in Barb's trial had attended the memorial service. This story also raised the question of whether more charges would be brought against Barb. And the foster mother was quoted as saying "I want people to know what happened to her. The gruesome details. The reality of it is that her mom took away Natalia's life and left a shell of a child." (The foster mother only saw Barb in case conferences, the final one following Barb's first visit with Natalia when she requested that Barb no longer be able to see Natalia. But she apparently felt she knew everything she needed to know about Barb.)

On that same day we got a call from Gary, Brant's step-dad. Elaine answered. He asked if Elaine knew that Natalia had died. She responded that she had found out from a reporter on Thursday, and apologized for not being at the memorial service. (Elaine has always felt that Gary might be the one person in Brant's family who could bring some reason to the situation.) She thanked him for calling. Gary then said, "I just wanted to let you know that I will do everything I can, even if it means losing my house, to see that your daughter spends as much time in prison as possible." Elaine simply said, "I'm sorry." And he hung up.

On Friday, April 8, another front page story, picture, and headline by the same reporter blared out "Should Baby's Mother Be Charged With Murder?" The first sentences of the story read, "Barbara Schrock ended her daughter's life in July 2005. But Natalia Benson didn't die until March 25, nearly six years after she was violently abused as a 3-month-old." The consensus of those legal persons interviewed by this reporter seemed to be that such a charge would be possible in a case like this. Mr. Cotter, however, noted that he would have to prove "intent to kill." According to him, "evidence of that was <u>not abundant</u> in Schrock's battery trial." *What a huge understatement!*

Sunday afternoon, April 17, we had a memorial service for Natalia at CMC. The pastoral team felt this would be a good idea. We did, too, but weren't certain many would show up for it. Only one or two people had ever even seen Natalia. But after listening to the ministers, it became apparent that this could be very helpful to us, to the congregation, and to Barb. So Elaine and I planned a service with the team. We suggested that we use the small chapel which would hold about ninety or a hundred people. They convinced us we needed to use the sanctuary.

We were able to use Natalia's picture from the obituary on the internet for the worship folder. It was a very meaningful service with music, scripture, prayer, and a children's choir. During the remembrance time, pictures of Natalia and the rest of our family were shown on the large screens up front while <u>Children of the Heavenly Father</u> was being sung. On the back of the program were listed Natalia's father <u>and</u> mother, and <u>both</u> sets of grandparents. Elaine and I were totally surprised that nearly 300 people came to this service, since we had not announced it anywhere other than the church bulletin. As I looked around the sanctuary, my heart was warmed by the presence of so many who cared. And although most young people don't normally get to memorial services, it was pleasing to see a full row of current and former youth group members there. They actually sang one of the songs as a group. We were also surprised by the carload of relatives from Ohio that attended. DVD's of the service were made to keep as a record for Barb, and perhaps Isabella at a later time. Following the service we had a receiving time in the Fellowship Hall. Animal crackers, salty fish crackers, popcorn, and punch were served. Most of the 300 people waited in line for an hour or more to share their condolences and love. It was an uplifting time, and removed any feelings of hesitancy we might initially have had about holding such a service.

It was a good feeling to know that those who had walked with us without ever knowing Natalia took time to be part of her memorial service. Elaine decided to send a condolence card and a copy of the memorial service to Brant, in case they were keeping a scrapbook. Evidently that wasn't well received. We got it back several days later with markings of "murderer" and "psycho" and "accomplice" all over it. It makes us feel sad to know how much hatred Brant and his family have towards us. Do they not understand what all of that hatred is doing to themselves?

CHAPTER TWENTY-TWO

REFLECTIONS

Innocence:

The criminal justice system in the U.S. is set up to deal with <u>guilty persons</u>. The worst of all possibilities is if you happen to be innocent. When you are <u>guilty</u> of the charges against you, you can <u>plea bargain</u> with the prosecution and often get a lesser penalty. At <u>sentencing</u>, you can accept responsibility for your actions, ask forgiveness, and normally get a more reasonable sentence. And when you are before a <u>parole board</u>, the first thing they want to know before deciding to release you or not, is whether you accept responsibility for your actions. If you are <u>innocent</u> of the charges, there is <u>no opportunity</u> for a plea bargain. You are considered to be arrogant, unrepentant, and <u>lacking remorse</u> at sentencing. And you will be an <u>unlikely candidate</u> for parole. In all of these venues, the presumption is that you are guilty, but just won't admit it. After all, twelve people said you were. And nothing provokes the wrath of the judicial system more than refusing to accept responsibility for your actions.

Juries:

The jury is central to the U.S. justice system. But in the trial of a case like the one written about in this book, it is next to impossible for a jury to understand the meaning of the medical terminology, to evaluate the quality of the research behind the shaken baby theory, to have an adequate knowledge of the relative precision/imprecision of injury timing, or to adequately comprehend the variations in doctors' readings of brain and bone scans based upon their acceptance of "the theory." And the speed and quantity of this technical medical information, presented throughout the week, is simply fatiguing. All of which can lead a weary jury to the temptation of assuming not only that the doctors must know what they are doing by diagnosing what happened as a crime, but also that the police must have good reasons for pointing out this particular suspect. Why else would this person be charged? And when attorneys and prosecutors intentionally or unintentionally mangle the medical terminology and facts, or switch an acute injury for a chronic one, how can we expect lay juries to follow any logic? (In England I understand that in some cases with technical information like this one, they have paid "expert" jurors to render such decisions.) As you read this book you may have found some parts that were difficult to follow. That was after seeing it on the written page, put there by a writer who was consciously trying to make it understandable, and offering you the ability to go back over it as often as you like. The jury simply doesn't have that luxury. They may get some pieces of information, but need to move on when the next witness takes the stand. And there is precious little time to put together the larger picture. There is simply too much information. They are reliant on the trustworthiness of the "authorities."

Shaken Baby Syndrome:

I could try to provide a rationale for why this theory needs stronger research underpinning than it currently has. But that is better done by the medical doctors and other scientists who are challenging this theory today. My own small contribution to this questioning is to show how the application of this theory begets "tortured logic" when possible abuse cases that don't fit are forced into the shaken baby mold. You have seen much of that in this book. But why would a prosecutor try to force a case into this shaken baby mold? As the popular bumper sticker says, "If your only tool is a hammer, everything looks like a nail." So too, with shaken baby theory. This is not their only tool, but with the conviction rate for these cases among the highest in any criminal trial, it's their best tool. It's a perfect setup for the prosecutor. Why not force any otherwise unsolvable case into this theory? It creates the "appearance" of specificity. And juries are easily wowed by that. But as I wrote earlier, forcing inappropriate cases into this theory also causes some fairly intelligent medical people to utter some patently absurd statements in their attempts to make a non-fitting case "fit." Comments like she's "not going to be awake (unconscious)" or "after an injury of sufficient force to crack their skull, they won't eat," both referring to the three-four weeks since the first massive brain injury, are examples of such statements, when everyone who has seen the child knows otherwise. When a theory does this to an otherwise rational mind, perhaps the theory needs retooling.

The attempts, highlighted in this book, of doctors trying to divine black and white answers from gray material not only causes one to have serious questions, but also creates far too much "collateral damage in people and families." The more people that are "convicted" of shaken baby syndrome (which is nearly everyone charged with it), the higher the statistical numbers that are attributed to this particular abuse crime. The higher the numbers, the more it becomes a concern to society. The more it becomes a concern to society, the more people feel the need for new laws requiring even less evidence for conviction. With less evidence needed, there are more convictions and higher statistics. Needless to say, the concern just snowballs. And there is no defense against this particular charge. What could you possibly say in your own defense? So why even bother with a trial, other than to make society feel better about its fairness in dealing with these cases?

Evidence:

Perhaps the most flagrant of all of the abuses by the police and prosecutor (other than totally misrepresenting the truth in numerous statements throughout this book) were the things they considered "evidence." The total list is far too large to cite here, but the following are representative: (1) "She was calm;" (2) "She went back to get her shoes;" (3) "Her demeanor was not accurate;" (4) "She called it postpartum depression, even though Dr. Rutt said she didn't have that;" (5) "She was looking at the medical book to get excuses;" (6) "Who else had 'appreciable time' with Natalia?" (7) "She was the primary caregiver;" (8) "Barb does nothing (to help Natalia);" (9) "She crossed her arms;" (10) "Barb had Brant call 911;" (11) "Barb had no pictures up of Natalia;" (12) "Barb told 'stories';" (13) "Brant cried;" (14) "Brant worked a lot;" (15) "Brant was totally stunned." Apparently the prosecutor felt if he could just gather enough of this "evidence," and add to it the multiple manufactured statements by himself and police that were attributed to Barb, but mysteriously never showed up in her police interview, he could get a conviction. And with the additional help from Brant and his family, he did.

Reasonable Doubt:

What does "beyond a reasonable doubt" mean? Maimonides, an eleventh century Rabbi and medical doctor, is credited with saying that it was better to let 1000 guilty go free than to wrongly convict a single innocent. Many centuries later, it is reported that Ben Franklin gave his ratio as 100 to one. William Blackstone, an English juror who wrote the code for British Common Law, is quoted as having said, "It is better that ten guilty persons escape than that one innocent suffer." Benjamin Cardozo, nineteenth century U.S. Supreme Court Justice, lowered his ratio to five to one. All of these ratios express a diminishing concern for safeguarding against the conviction of innocent parties. "Beyond a reasonable doubt. You bet," as Mr. Cotter would say. In our current climate of getting the "perps" off the streets, locking them up, and throwing away the keys, is it any wonder that we have five percent of the world's total population, but 25 percent of the world's incarcerated inmates? Our need for black and white answers is taking its toll. Are our people really that much worse than the other people of the world? How much cost are we willing to bear in our attempt to remove all ambiguity from life? How much "collateral damage" can we as a society tolerate? And how long will it be until the above ratio for "reasonable doubt" is popularly understood as one to one? When it gets to that point, we may as well forget about the need for a trial. Just flip a coin.

Who Really Wins?

In our own particular case I continue to ask myself, "Who is better off because 'justice has been served'?" Well, <u>Mr .Cotter</u> continues in his role, undoubtedly having received accolades for his skillfulness in the conviction he was able to get in this case. And <u>Lt. Richmond</u> has been promoted to Captain. But is <u>Natalia</u> better off? Clearly, nothing the justice system could have done would have helped her. She never had a chance. Is <u>Isabella</u>? She no longer has the loving relationship she had with her mother (or grandparents). And she most likely feels deserted. Will the kids at school treat her differently because of where her mother is? Is <u>Barb</u>? She sits in prison in Indianapolis trying both to understand what has happened, and to make the most out of her unfortunate circumstances. Neither of her children are available to her, and the father of her children and his family have turned against her. Where does she go from here with more years in prison and a felony conviction on her record? Is <u>Brant</u>? He has suffered losses, too. And the anger within him could potentially destroy him. Is <u>Elaine</u>? She no longer has access to either grandchild, and may no longer work as a teaching-certified school nurse. Not because she was <u>convicted</u> of anything. Only because she was <u>charged</u>. And what about <u>me</u>? I probably came out of this with the fewest scars. But I have been wounded, and have been separated from two complete generations of our small family.

During the time of the Viet Nam war, the following quote was attributed to one of the U.S. officers concerning an attack on a peasant village: "We had to destroy the village to save it." I have thought about that quote many times over the past few years. That same attitude, or "tortured logic," seems to prevail too often in our justice system: "We had to destroy this family to save it."

Our Family:

"Is this the best we can do as a society?" I offer that question as a challenge to all of us. Was <u>our</u> family's experience <u>typical</u> of the judicial system, or was it <u>unique</u>? We don't know. This was our only exposure to that system. What we <u>do</u> know is that our family <u>will</u> survive. We will continue to be strong in our faith. And we will gather together again. Our goal for now, as in the past, is to be able to reflect the apostle Paul's words in his letter to the Galatian church: "...the fruit of the Spirit is love, joy, peace, patience, kindness, goodness, faithfulness, gentleness, and self-control. Against such things <u>there is no law</u>."

We have strong support. And we have much for which to be thankful. But we are also sad.

CPSIA information can be obtained at www.ICGtesting.com
Printed in the USA
LVOW111211220512

282766LV00002B/2/P